PARENTING
An Ecological Perspective

Edited by

Tom Luster
Michigan State University

Lynn Okagaki
Purdue University

LEA   LAWRENCE ERLBAUM ASSOCIATES, PUBLISHERS
1993   Hillsdale, New Jersey   Hove and London

HQ
759.8
.P37
1993

Cover design by Rosalind Orland

Lawrence Erlbaum Associates, Inc., Publishers
365 Broadway
Hillsdale, New Jersey 07642

Library of Congress Cataloging-in-Publication Data

Parenting : an ecological perspective / edited by Tom Luster, Lynn
   Okagaki.
        p.   cm.
     Includes bibliographical references and index.
     ISBN 0-8058-0792-6 (hbk. : alk. paper). − ISBN 0-8058-0857-4
     1. Parenting.   2. Social ecology.   I. Luster, Tom.   II. Okagaki,
Lynn.
     [DNLM: 1. Child Rearing−psychology.   2. Parenting−psychology.
WS 105.5.C3 P2282]
HQ759.8.P371993
649′.1−dc20
DNLM/DLC
for Library of Congress   92-48667
                                                                CIP

Books published by Lawrence Erlbaum Associates are printed on acid-free
paper, and their bindings are chosen for strength and durability.

Printed in the United States of America
10 9 8 7 6 5 4 3 2 1

Contents

Foreword

Urie Bronfenbrenner
Cornell University

This well-conceived and well-timed volume is the first to bring together in one place the results of research on parents and children conducted from the perspective of an ecological paradigm. Although, as reflected in the pages that follow, some instances of the *de facto* application of the paradigm preceded its formal exposition (Bronfenbrenner, 1977, 1979), the number and scope of investigations explicitly or implicitly employing an ecological model has increased substantially over the past two decades, with most of the attention focused on the family system as the primary context of childrearing, and its dynamic linkages with other key contexts that affect development, both immediate (e.g., child care, school, parents' workplace, neighborhood), and more remote (e.g., class and culture). To date, however, the research reports dealing with these phenomena, as well as topical reviews, have been widely scattered across journals and edited volumes directed at particular disciplines. As a result, it has been difficult for teachers, students, and researchers themselves to obtain an integrated picture of the enterprise as a whole.

In their creative design and editing of this volume, Tom Luster and Lynn Okagaki have done more than enable readers to view the full range of this domain within the same two covers. In their thoughtful selection of chapter authors (happily including themselves), they have been successful in attracting scholars who are leading researchers in the area about which they are writing. The special benefits of such background are reflected in the judicious selection of relevant studies, richness and rigor in the interpretation and integration of research findings, and in the special ability of the authors to discern promising directions and concrete hypotheses for further research.

By way of example, and further enticement, I offer a foretaste from the diverse yet balanced array of entrees that Luster and Okagaki provide for the reader.

In the opening chapter, Joan Vondra and Jay Belsky set out to explore the "Developmental Origins of Parenting," and thereby confront, in one of its many Protean forms, the classical "chicken or egg" problem of developmental science. Their question: What is the role of personality versus environmental factors in shaping parental behavior? Scrupulously resisting a foregone conclusion, the authors review an extensive and diversified body of research to arrive at an impressively substantiated and balanced assessment.

> The effects of a troubled and/or problematic childhood for parenting difficulty and dysfunction appear to depend very much on opportunities to rework poor relationship experiences. When children have alternative relationship models available to them and/or can participate in a supportive relationship amidst the stressors of their childhoods, when young adults can rework relationship issues by their long-term involvement (whether personal or professional) with a caring and supportive individual, the relationships they create with their own children need not mirror the hardships of their upbringing.

The same note is sounded within a broader scale in Jacqueline Lerner's (chapter 4) review of research bearing on "The Influence of Child Temperamental Characteristics on Parent Behaviors." Her examination of studies of temperament across age, class, and culture lend support to her general thesis that parents' reactions to particular temperamental qualities of the child depend in appreciable degree on the prevailing belief systems in the parents' world regarding the significance, or nonsignificance, of the behavior in question. In her terms, it's a matter of goodness of fit.

Perhaps the most compelling evidence to date for the power of belief systems in shaping parental processes and children's development appears in Lynn Okagaki and Diana Johnson Divecha's chapter on "Development of Parental Beliefs" (chapter 2). Among other researchers pointing in the same direction, they summarize and integrate the results of several studies conducted by Harold Stevenson and his colleagues on the role of family and school in the development of children in Japan, Taiwan, the People's Republic of China, and the United States. A major aim of the investigation was to identify the sources for the relatively poor performance of U.S. school children, compared to those from other modern societies, on measures of school performance. In their chapter, Okagaki and Divecha highlight four answers emerging from Stevenson's cross-cultural research: (a) the belief, widespread in U.S. culture, and thereby among U.S. parents as well, that differences in performance are mainly biological in origin; (b) the conviction among U.S. parents that their own children are "above average"; (c) the hollow pursuit of high self-esteem as an end in itself; and (d) the abandonment of parents' share of responsibility for fostering their children's development both in competence and in character.

Tom Luster and Mary Mittelstaedt's (chapter 3) comprehensive review of research on teen-age motherhood concludes with a challenging reinterpretation of the new substantial evidence of disarray in the lives both of the mothers themselves and of their children. They suggest that the heart of the problem lies not in the age at which a young mother bears a child, but in the ecology in which she lives. In the authors' words: "The critical factors that put teens at risk for becoming adolescent parents would also put them at risk for performing poorly in the parenting role."

An equally provocative reinterpretation emerges in chapter 5 by Robert Emery and Michelle Tuer. Expanding the parenting model from a dyad to a triad, they reexamine existing evidence on the reciprocal relationships between the parent–child dyad and that of husband and wife. Taking cognizance of the now well-replicated finding that the transition to parenthood leads to decreased emotional intimacy and equalitarianism in marital roles, the authors argue that this shift is in fact adaptive in meeting the needs of the child. Indeed, their own conclusion may risk violating the unwritten rules of contemporary political correctness in this domain: "Views about what men's and women's family roles ought to be should not cloud interpretation of evidence about what they are."

As further evidence of parental role specialization, Emery and Tuer call attention to several studies indicating that each parent behaves differently when alone with the child than when the spouse is also present. In general, they conclude, triadic interaction tends "to exaggerate parental role differentiation."

Ann Crouter and Susan McHale (chapter 7) take the family triad beyond the home into the world of work. Taking as a point of departure Melvin Kohn's classic finding that parents' work experience influences the values they want for their children, the authors marshall evidence from subsequent studies demonstrating that the work-derived parental values are also translated into day-to-day parental behavior. Especially impressive in this regard are the findings from Crouter's own study of the spillover effects into the home of policies of worker participation introduced in the workplace (in this instance a large manufacturing plant). The results of Crouter's systematic analysis of interview data are epitomized in the following quotation from one of her subjects:

> I say things to my daughter that I know are the result of the way things are at work. I ask her, "what do you think about that?" or "How would you handle this problem?" I tend to deal with her the way we deal with people at work.

Crouter and McHale's chapter also provides cross validation for the conclusion, reached independently by Emery and Tuer from a different set of studies, that the behavior of a parent toward the child varies systematically depending on whether the spouse is present (and also on the gender of the child). It is clear that such differences should be taken into account in future research, particularly in assessing the developmental consequences of differences in the parent's behavior toward the same child. As the authors of both chapters note, this is an area of both theoretical and practical significance that still remains largely unexplored.

Moncrieff Cochran (chapter 6), "Parenting and Personal Social Networks," embarks on a cross-cultural course from the very outset. Having gathered comparable data in four societies (West Germany, Wales, Sweden, and the United States), Cochran and his colleagues documented both continuities and contrasts. For example, in the former domain, in all four countries, mothers in white-collar, two-parent families reported larger networks than did women in blue-collar households, with the class differences being about the same in every country except the United States, where the contrast by socioeconomic status was even larger. These class differences were overshadowed, however, by even greater variations between cultures. Specifically, mothers' social networks in Sweden, and especially the United States, were not only larger but specialized far more in the domain of social and emotional relationships outside the family. Cochran offers, and provides persuasive demographic data in support for, the hypothesis that this difference is the product of "the roles women are permitted or encouraged to adopt (mother vs. worker, for instance), and the extent to which they can develop identities beyond those roles."

In their chapter, James Garbarino and Kathleen Kostelny (chapter 8) were faced with the paradoxical task of surveying what remains the most uncharted and, at the same time, probably the most critical context of family life in the United States today—neighborhood and community. It is regrettable that Garbarino's own pioneering studies, conducted over more than a decade ago, have not been followed up, for they remain among the few that, both in conception and research design, have treated the neighborhood as a concrete system located in space and time that can, and does, produce synergistic effects on families and children over and above those attributable to socioeconomic status, ethnicity, and other demographic features. As a result, the authors' chapter is far richer in the research questions and hypotheses that are generated by the information it presents than in documenting well-designed investigations that have indeed demonstrated the operation of "Neighborhood and Community Influences on Parenting." In summary, in this dual domain, there are many windows of opportunity left open in every direction.

In a final, integrative chapter, Tom Luster and Lynn Okagaki not only point out particularly promising avenues for future research, but also take stock of progress achieved through the application of an ecological paradigm in the study of the influences shaping parental behavior and its outcomes. At the broadest level, they view the work accomplished as validating, in a particular research domain, a more general ecological principle. As applied to this more restricted context, they translate the principle as follows: "Characteristics of the parent, of the child, and of the context in which the parent–child relationship is evolving contribute to differences among parents in their approaches to childrearing.'' In their view, this principle also has an important, and demanding, operational corollary: ''Consequently, it stands to reason that our understanding of parenting behavior will be enhanced if we consider the combined influence of several factors rather than thinking about each factor singly.'' To be sure, this is a complex task. But perhaps the most important contribution of this volume is the demonstration that the task can be accomplished, and, when this is done, not only brings new knowledge but also opens new vistas for the realization of human potential.

REFERENCES

Bronfenbrenner, U. (1977) Toward an experimental ecology of human development. *American Psychologist, 32*, 515–531.
Bronfenbrenner, U. (1979). *The ecology of human development: Experiments by nature and design.* Cambridge, MA: Harvard University Press.

Preface

For several decades, researchers have studied the relation between parenting practices and developmental outcomes in children, and have documented the importance of what transpires in the home for the developing child. Given the importance of parenting behavior for children, there has been growing interest in influences on parenting behavior. In particular, what factors contribute to differences among parents in how they interact with, teach, guide, and nurture their children?

Over the past 10 years, a great deal has been learned about influences on parental behavior. Because relevant studies are found in journals serving psychologists, sociologists, health-care professionals, educators, and others, keeping abreast of advances in this burgeoning area of research is difficult. We were motivated to edit this volume because we were unable to find a source that summarized research from multiple disciplines and was written at an appropriate level for upper level undergraduate and graduate students.

The organization of the book was influenced by Bronfenbrenner's (1979, 1989) ecological framework and Belsky's (1984) influential work on the determinants of parenting. Belsky proposed that parental behavior is determined by characteristics of the parent, characteristics of the child, and the context in which the parent–child relationship is evolving. The first four chapters of the book describe the ways in which characteristics of the parent and the child affect the parent–child relationship. The next four chapters examine contextual factors that influence parenting, and are concerned with both the immediate context and the larger context in which families function.

Each of the first eight chapters focuses on a particular factor that contributes to individual differences in parenting behavior. In the last chapter, we review illustrative studies that have considered the combined influence of several factors on parenting behavior. The studies demonstrate various ways in which the simultaneous examination of multiple influences on parenting behavior have enriched our understanding of why parents do what they do.

As editors, we were very pleased to have leading scholars in their respective areas contribute chapters for this book. Not only have they described research that includes a broad range of theoretical perspectives and utilizes diverse methodological techniques, but they have also added their insightful synthesis and critiques of the work done in their fields. We believe that professionals from many disciplines as well as students who are interested in parenting will be well served by the combined efforts of these scholars.

Finally, we would also like to acknowledge the contributions of our friend and mentor, Urie Bronfenbrenner, whose writings on the ecology of human development provided the impetus and the framework for many of the studies that are reviewed in this volume. His insights into the ways in which human development is influenced by the interaction between person and context over time have led researchers who are interested in child development to broaden their focus. In particular, he recognized that proximal and distal forces that influence family processes, including parental behavior, must be understood by those who study children and those who work on behalf of children and families.

Tom Luster
Lynn Okagaki

REFERENCES

Belsky, J. (1984). The determinants of parenting: A process model. *Child Development, 55,* 83–96.
Bronfenbrenner, U. (1979). *The ecology of human development.* Cambridge, MA: Harvard University Press.
Bronfenbrenner, U. (1989). Ecological systems theory. In R. Vasta (Ed.), *Annals of child development* (Vol. 6, pp. 187–249). Greenwich, CT: JAI Press.

Chapter 1

Developmental Origins of Parenting: Personality and Relationship Factors

Joan Vondra
University of Pittsburgh

Jay Belsky
The Pennsylvania State University

We begin this chapter with a premise: Understanding individual differences in parenting requires understanding of a parent not only as an individual psychological agent, but also as a partner in close relationships. Consider the fact that individual psychological functioning—as well as previous experiences in close relationships—affect both the choice of an adult relationship partner and the quality of the relationship that is established and maintained over time. The relationship, in turn, has important influences on the psychological well-being and functioning of each partner. Of greatest importance for this discussion, both individual functioning and relationship functioning affect the very nature of the pregnancy and birth experience. From then on, they shape the quality of relationship and interaction that evolves between each parent and the developing child. In this chapter we map out these various pathways of influence, giving careful consideration to the hypothesized processes and to data consistent with them.

In seeking to understand how and why individual differences in parenting arise, we adopt a developmental perspective. On the one hand, we consider how patterns of individual and relationship functioning relevant to parenting demonstrate both consistency and, at times, predictable inconsistency across the life course. At the same time, we note that both individual and relationship functioning have developmental origins in experience within the family system across childhood, an assumption long held within clinical theory and practice. We view individuals as carrying forward from their prior relationship experiences, attitudes, expectations, emotions, and behavioral patterns that shape the way they function—as parents and as spouses—in the families they establish.

The arguments we raise here and mechanisms we advance to support them are by no means new ones. On the contrary, they harken back to psychoanalytic theorizing about the genesis of adult pathology and dysfunction, including dysfunctions of parenting (see Framo, 1970; Meissner, 1978). However, we present them in the context of a growing research base that offers empirical support for some of the hypothesized processes, but also in an intellectual climate that places increasing emphasis on plasticity in development. This is not to deny the critical impact of contemporaneous individual and family circumstances that range from economic impoverishment to physical disability and handicap. Rather, it is an effort to address two notable observations. First is the sometimes surprising degree of interrelation between various parenting risk (or support) factors. More often than not, bad things (or good things) go together when it comes to influences on parenting. A second observation involves either unanticipated continuity or predictable discontinuity in relevant individual and relationship behavior patterns over time. Under certain circumstances, early patterns possess unexpected predictive power for subsequent behavior. At other times, it is the lack of continuity itself that is predictable. In both cases, early behavior and experiences offer substantial insights into the genesis of parenting behavior.

We begin our analysis with a summary of evidence indicating that personality and relationship attributes contribute to individual differences in parenting. Particular constellations of factors and/or aggregated characteristics have proven useful in distinguishing qualitative differences in parental care or in the parent–child relationships. This summary is accompanied by discussion on hypothesized processes of influence linking personality and relationships with parental functioning. Researchers have proposed a number of potential mechanisms by which personality and relationship factors shape parenting behavior. Several are described here. Following this discussion, we proceed with an examination of theoretical and research models of the impact of developmental history on individual and dyadic psychological functioning in adulthood. By and large, these have been interpreted along simple input–output lines. However, recent reexamination of these models has highlighted increasingly sophisticated "conditions of continuity" that underlie the operation of each. We therefore devote attention to work that begins to elaborate both conditions of continuity and of discontinuity across development and across generations.

In doing so, we seek to redress some historical criticism of developmental models that have been, to some extent, misrepresented by research efforts that failed to capture their conceptual sophistication. A case in point is attachment theory, research, and criticism (Lamb, Thompson, Gardner, Charnov, & Estes, 1984; Skolnick, 1986). Bowlby's (1969, 1973, 1980) theoretical work and recent attachment research (Egeland & Farber, 1984; Erickson, Sroufe, & Egeland, 1985) described early development trajectories as modifiable in response to environmental conditions. In contrast, the first wave of studies investigating early attachment security and developmental status did not—understandably—show appreciation of this complexity. With evidence for attachment–development links, however, researchers began to explore developmental process issues outlined—but previously ignored—in Bowlby's conceptualization.

As is increasingly apparent throughout this chapter, developmental research has made important strides toward representing and testing the complexity of hypothesized mechanisms of continuity, change, and developmental influence. As a result, early models of both normal and abnormal development have acquired a new usefulness and relevance in current theorizing. Discussion in each of the following sections illustrates this.

PERSONALITY AND PARENTING

In earlier publications, we proposed a model of the determinants of parenting that assigns a central role in filtering a variety of sociocontextual influences on parenting to personality (Belsky, 1984; Belsky & Vondra, 1985). In essence, we argued that the impact of marriage, work, social support, and developmental history on parenting were, in part, mediated through their effects on individual psychological functioning. For example, a conflicted marital relationship may alter parental functioning directly, as when disagreement about childrearing practices interferes with effective child guidance, but much of the impact may be expressed through changes in parental psychological functioning. Increased parental distress, irritability, and depression resulting from marital conflict may lead to impatience, inconsistency, and/or emotional unavailability as a parent. Certainly, research supports the notion that differences in psychological functioning and adjustment are associated with qualitative differences in parental care.

Data linking psychological factors with parenting encompass both the normal and clinical range. There is a lack of consistency across studies, however, about specific aspects of personality or even specific psychological disorders associated with individual differences in parenting. It is at the broader level of psychological maturity, integration, and adjustment, which begin to resemble such clinical concepts as the *self* (Kohut, 1971, 1977) and *self-differentiation* (Bower, 1978), that results converge in finding predictable individual differences. These results may be summarized according to three general patterns: (a) greater psychological maturity and differentiation predicts more competent parenting, whereas (b) higher negative affectivity—expressed as anxiety or depression—and/or (c) greater severity of mental health impairment is associated with less competent parenting. A select set of research examples effectively illustrates these patterns.

Psychological Differentiation

Psychological maturity, complexity, and integration are reflected on a variety of "personality" measures, each of which has greater or less relevance for particular populations. A measure that proves useful in distinguishing higher quality caregiving among White, middle-class mothers, may demonstrate poor discriminative power among a sample of high-risk, low-income teen-age mothers. Measure considerations, including the population for which it was designed, the sample(s) on which it was normed, and the intent and language of the items, can account for this discrepancy. This circumstance helps to explain inconsistencies across studies regarding specific measured characteristics that correlate with measures of parenting. Also relevant is the measure of parenting employed, which typically ranges from self-reported attitudes or perceptions of competence, to detailed behavioral observations or ratings. Given construct and measurement variation, the fact that convergence of findings can be discerned across studies is probably testament to the strength of the relation. The trend across many studies examining personality factors is to find childrearing differences relating to overall psychological maturity and differentiation.

Among mothers who are at risk for parenting difficulties due to extreme youth, lack of education, poverty, and/or the absence of a stable intimate relationship, measures of ego development (Levine, Coll, & Oh, 1984), locus of control (Stevens, 1988), and hostility–defensiveness (Egeland & Farber, 1984) have distinguished those who provide nurturant, responsive, and nonpunitive care to their infants and toddlers. In their extensive work with high-risk mothers, Brunnquell, Crichton, and Egeland (1981) found their greatest predictive power in an aggregate factor they termed *psychological integration*. This factor included scores on intelligence, locus of control, anxiety, dependence, succorance, and encouragement of reciprocity between parent and child. It discriminated between those mothers providing care rated as "excellent" by observers, those providing adequate care, and those considered to maltreat their 3-month-old infants.

Among low-risk, middle-class mothers, another composite personality factor, also termed *psychological integration*, but this time including measures of ease and comfort versus anxiety with parenting, ability to empathize with one's infant, conflicted feelings about work and family, and security in one's self-image, has been effective in distinguishing mothers rated as more sensitive in the care of their infants (Benn, 1985, 1986). In the researcher's own words, this factor represents the extent to which women are "warm and secure in their sense of self. . .emotionally balanced and satisfied with themselves. . .and enjoy intimacy with those important to them" (Benn, 1985, p. 12). By 12 months of age, the infants of these mothers were significantly more likely to be securely attached. In fact, when the measure of psychological integration was statistically controlled, the association between sensitive care and attachment security was substantially attenuated. These results, consistent with the line of reasoning being developed here, led Benn (1985) to conclude that "the characteristics of acceptance and sensitivity are overt manifestations of maternal integration which become associated with child development outcomes because of their connection to this more underlying property in mothers" (p. 12).

Cox and her colleagues (Cox, Owen, Lewis, & Henderson, 1989) found that two empirically derived summary factors based on measures of anxiety, depression, adjustment, locus of control, and ego development were effective in predicting both attitudes toward the infant and the parenting role, as well as observed warmth and sensitive responding among married, middle-class mothers and fathers. Other broad personality factors that have distinguished quality of care among middle-class mothers with infants include ego flexibility (Heinicke, 1984; Heinicke, Diskin, Ramsey-Klee, & Given, 1983), interpersonal trust, an active coping style (Mondell & Tyler, 1981), and self-efficacy (Donovan & Leavitt, 1985).

Among fathers, personality integration, emotional stability, and the absence of anxiety or depression characterize those individuals who are more likely to demonstrate physical and emotional involvement in child care (Heath, 1976). Archival data, furthermore, indicate that irritability/explosiveness and hostility are associated with inconsistent, arbitrary discipline of children by fathers (Elder, Liker, & Cross, 1984).

As we have argued elsewhere (Belsky & Vondra, 1985), it is unlikely that an individual who is caught up with his or her own psychological concerns will have the ability to decenter and take the perspective of a dependent infant. Without the psychological resources to understand, and consequently tolerate, the daily demands and frustrations of an infant or young child (let alone a teen-ager), a parent will be hard pressed to demonstrate the patience, sensitivity, and responsiveness that effective parenting requires. This is even more apparent among parents who suffer from a variety of mental health problems.

Negative Affectivity

In considering the continuum of mental health, from psychological integration to mental illness, it seems especially useful to draw upon a two-factor model describing core dimensions of personality and psychological functioning. Recent research demonstrates that such a model accounts for much of the individual variation chronicled across a wide variety of studies using a range of measurement tools. McCrae and Costa (1980, 1984; McCrae, 1982), following Eysenck and Eysenck (1969), used the terms *neuroticism* and *extraversion* to refer to these higher order constructs, whereas Watson and his colleagues

(Watson & Clark, 1984; Watson & Tellegan, 1985) prefer the labels *negative affectivity* and *positive affectivity*.

Extraversion/positive affectivity reflects interpersonal warmth, attachment, and sociability, as well as activity and excitement seeking. Persons displaying high levels of extraversion tend to be friendly and compassionate, to have an intimately involved style of personal interaction, and to be busy, active, energetic, and experience positive emotions frequently.

Neuroticism/negative affectivity reflects the inclination of an individual to be anxious, depressed, hostile, self-conscious, emotionally unstable, impulsive, and low in ego strength; that is, to be psychologically maladjusted. McCrae and Costa (1984) found that persons displaying high levels of neuroticism "are prone to violent and negative emotions that interfere with their ability to deal with their problems and to get along with others" (p. 43).

Across a number of different studies examining personality factors and parenting, this hypothesized negative affectivity factor seems able to account for notable variation in parenting attitudes and behavior. Even prior to birth, maternal anxiety and negative responses to the pregnancy experience are predictive of labor complications, prematurity, and poorer relations between mother and infant (Egeland & Farber, 1984; McDonald, 1968). Postpartum depression is associated with less sensitive care of infants, decreased feelings of efficacy as a parent, and insecure attachment relations with the baby by the end of the first year (Cutrona & Troutman, 1986; Donovan & Leavitt, 1989; Field, 1984; Field et al., 1985). In epidemiological work by Rutter (1979; Rutter et al., 1975), negative affectivity among mothers was one of six family risk factors predictive of psychopathology among latency-aged children. Given the data on parental care among depressed adult populations, it is not unreasonable to attribute such child outcomes, in part, to substandard and/or inadequate care.

Both depressive symptoms and the clinical disorder of depression have received a great deal of attention in parenting literature due to their association with disturbances in parental care. Research on face-to-face interactions between depressed mothers and their young infants (Bettes, 1988; Cohn, Matias, Tronick, Connell, & Lyons-Ruth, 1986), and on quality of child care among depressed parents (Colletta, 1983; Crnic & Greenberg, 1985; Tronick & Field, 1986) are persuasive in demonstrating that the emotional unavailability and self-preoccupation symptomatic of depression interfere with a parent's ability to nurture and respond sensitively to the needs of children. Fathers (Zaslow, Pedersen, Cain, Suwalsky, & Kramer, 1985) and mothers (Field et al., 1985) who report experiencing frequent negative affective states tend to be less attentive and responsive to their infants, and more power assertive and inconsistent in discipline with their school-age children (Conger, McCarty, Yang, Lahey, & Kropp, 1984; Forehand, Lautenschlager, Faust, & Graziano, 1985).

The psychological distress and unavailability occasioned by negative affective states are critical features of many different forms of mental illness. Regardless of the specific defining characteristics of such disorders as schizophrenia, borderline personality, generalized anxiety, and depression, the presence of mental illness suggests that psychological resources for parenting may be compromised or absent altogether. It stands to reason, then, that severity of mental illness plays an important role in determining the extent to which parents are able to provide sensitive or even adequate care to their children. Comparative data using clinical populations indicate that this is, in fact, the case.

Severity of Psychological Impairment

Prospective studies of parental care and child development outcomes among adults with a psychiatric disorder have noted that current psychological impairment—particularly negative affectivity and emotional withdrawal—can be as predictive of parental functioning and child developmental status as type of disorder (Kokes, Harder, Fisher, & Strauss, 1980; Sameroff, Seifer, & Zax, 1982). Indeed, parental psychiatric diagnosis appears to be most discriminating in terms of child outcome when it provides information about the degree of affective disturbance and unavailability in the parent–child relationship. Radke-Yarrow and her colleagues (DeMulder & Radke-Yarrow, 1991; Radke-Yarrow, Cummings, Kuczynski, & Chapman, 1985; Zahn-Waxler, Cummings, Ianotti, & Radke-Yarrow, 1984) observed consistently worse child functioning among families with a parent suffering from bipolar versus unipolar depression. At the same time, they noted that, in contrast to the relatively functional behavior of parents with unipolar depression, those with bipolar depression showed a more consistent pattern of difficulties across many areas of individual and interpersonal functioning.

Similar results emerged in a series of studies by Baldwin, Cole, and Baldwin (1982) on parental, familial, and child functioning in a sample of some 100 families with a psychiatrically diagnosed parent (e.g., schizophrenia, affective disorder, personality disorder) and a son between the ages of 4 and 10 years. Both a poorer level of general (i.e., nonacute phase) psychological functioning and the presence of any disorder other than one involving depression were associated with a lack of parental warmth and involvement. Behavioral measures of parental emotional unavailability, in turn, predicted poorer child outcomes. In Baldwin et al.'s (1982) words:

> It appears that the most competent children were from families where the parents had affective types of diagnoses and maintained an emotional reactivity, albeit sometimes overly strong, to their environment and therefore to their children. These parents seemed to provide their children the opportunity to react and grow. They at least acknowledged the existence and ongoing behavior of their children. . . . The less competent children appeared to come from families in which

the parents were chronically impaired. These parents often failed to respond to any type of behavior performed by their children. (p. 33)

Two conclusions are evident from these studies. First, some forms of mental illness are more disruptive of parental functioning than others, depending on the degree to which they interfere with a parent's attentional and emotional responsiveness. Second, across the wide spectrum of mental illness, chronicity and severity of psychological disturbance are critical in determining the extent to which an individual's capacity to parent is impaired. In both instances, psychological functioning at the broad level of adjustment and well-being determine, to a large degree, the amount of psychological resources available for childrearing.

Across the continuum from psychological differentiation and maturity to psychological disturbance and mental illness, then, the story line is similar: As personal psychological resources increase, so does a parent's ability to provide sensitive and responsive care to infants and children. Parental personality and adjustment are, in some sense, the most proximal determinants of parenting. As we argue in the next section, they are also the cornerstone in a network of contextual factors that impinge on parenting, in large part through the mechanism of parental psychological functioning.

QUALITY OF CLOSE RELATIONSHIPS

In the context of discussion about the role of personality factors and processes in parenting, it is noteworthy that an important prognostic indicator of psychological functioning is the quality of close relationships an individual is able to establish. Among normal populations, this is apparent in the consistent finding that links marital (or close relationship) satisfaction and adjustment with individual psychological adjustment. Distressed or dissatisfying marriages tend to involve relatively more distressed or less well-adjusted individuals (Elder, Caspi, & Downey, 1986; Eysenck, 1980; Zaleski & Galkowska, 1978). As early as the 1930s, research on the self-descriptions of spouses in happy and unhappy marriages indicated this (Terman, 1938). It was observed that happily married women possessed "kindly attitudes toward others," "expected kindly attitudes in return," were "cooperative," self-assured, and optimistic, whereas unhappily married women were emotionally tense, moody, aggressive, irritable, and egocentric (Terman, 1938, pp. 145–146).

Among clinical populations, the same principle is reflected in strategies of clinical diagnosis. In this case, a variety of relationship problems often serve, in part, as criteria for determination of the presence of specific disorders. Thus, criteria for diagnosis of borderline personality include "a pattern of unstable and intense interpersonal relationships characterized by alternating between extremes of overidealization and devaluation'' and ''frantic efforts to avoid real or imagined abandonment.'' Diagnostic criteria for schizoid personality disorder include ''neither desires nor enjoys close relationships, including being part of a family'' and ''has no close friends or confidants other than first-degree relatives.'' Finally, a typical identifying symptom for many disorders involves ''impairment in occupational functioning or in usual social activities or relationships with others'' (American Psychiatric Association, 1987).

If the quality of marital or other close relations predicts psychological functioning, and psychological functioning predicts quality of parental care, it should come as no surprise that marital satisfaction is also associated with individual differences in parenting. At least two different processes of influence may account for this association. On the one hand, a satisfying intimate relationship tends to be one providing emotional support and instrumental assistance to both partners, as each functions in a variety of roles.

Using this line of reasoning, it can be argued that one becomes more effective in dealing with emotionally demanding situations (like parenting) when personal and situational needs are met through a supportive close relationship. This appears to be the ''buffering'' effect Rutter and his colleagues found in their longitudinal study of women who had or had not been institutionalized during childhood as a result of parenting breakdown (Quinton, Rutter, & Liddle, 1984; Rutter, Quinton, & Liddle, 1983). Regardless of parenting breakdown experience and/or previous behavioral deviance, women who were able to develop a supportive relationship with a spouse or partner were less likely to show parenting problems themselves. Development of a supportive intimate relationship itself appeared to be less a direct result of prior adjustment than an outcome associated with positive school experiences (including peer relations) and with opportunities to cultivate expanded social networks. Similar relationship buffering effects have been documented among young concentration camp victims who were able to establish supportive relationships after the experience (Moskovitz, 1985), and buffering effects have also been observed repeatedly for teen-aged mothers who experience interpersonal support (Colletta, 1981; Crockenberg, 1987). For example, Unger and Wandersman (1988) reported that among a sample of poor, Black, adolescent mothers, most of them living with their own mothers, maternal responsivity to an 8-month-old infant was associated with concurrent perceptions of support from a male partner and perceptions, prenatally, that her family of origin was supportive. It should be pointed out that both sources of support predicted maternal reports of general life satisfaction, suggesting the role of intimate support as a source of emotional enhancement.

Facilitative effects of a supportive intimate relationship have been implicated for middle-class samples as well (Crockenberg & McCluskey, 1986). Cox et al. (1989) reported a positive effect on parental behavior or attitudes for middle-class mothers and fathers who, regardless of psychological adjustment, described and demonstrated a close and confiding marital relationship prenatally. Perceived prenatal support from husband and friends predicted feelings of self-efficacy versus postpartum depression at 3 months in a study of married, middle-class mothers by Cutrona and Troutman (1986). Finally, the middle-class mothers in a study by Donovan and Leavitt (1989) who reported the least help from their husbands in caring for their 5-month-old infants and the most depressive symptoms felt the greatest conflict about work and family relations and showed the poorest habituation and greatest aversive conditioning to infant crying in an experimentally manipulated situation. In a previous study, the authors linked these same responses to infant crying with behavioral insensitivity as a parent (Donovan & Leavitt, 1985).

There is, however, another likely process of influence that accounts for the relations between psychological functioning, relationship satisfaction, and quality of parenting. This alternative process highlights the role of personality characteristics and personal adjustment in the creation and maintenance of all close relationships, whether between parent and spouse, parent and friends, or parent and child. According to this line of reasoning, the individual who possesses psychological resources that can be used to enhance relationship functioning—for example, a basic sense of security and self-worth, the ability to be nurturant and to regulate one's emotions, feelings of efficacy, and enjoyment of intimacy—is likely to establish close and supportive relations with others (Bowen, 1978; Kobak & Sceery, 1988).

The two pathways of influence—marriage to personality to parenting and personality to marriage and parenting—are surely not mutually exclusive. Psychological functioning no doubt facilitates the development of positive and supportive relationships that, in turn, enhance psychological functioning within and beyond those relationships. Viewed another way, the individual with a positive sense of self, an openness to new ideas and experiences, and a belief in his or her own ability to make changes may be more likely to leave unsatisfactory relationships, to help create positive relationships, and to express greater satisfaction with good relationships. With a supportive partner and satisfying relationship(s), this individual gains in emotional resources and in reinforcement of selfhood. In other words, "those who have . . . get." With such internal and external resources, the challenges and demands of parenting (and, typically, working outside the home as well) are more manageable.

What sort of evidence exists to support the role of psychological functioning as a "third variable" that shapes both the quality of the marital relationship and individual differences in parental care? All research documenting zero-order correlations between personality factors, marital relations, and quality of care is obviously consistent with either interpretation of effects. Analyses that control statistically for one factor (e.g., personality measures) and continue to find unique variance accounted for by the second factor (measures of marital quality) begin to address the issue of *statistical* priority (e.g., Cox et al., 1989; Cutrona & Troutman, 1986). However, only longitudinal research measuring relevant factors over time and assessing temporal precedence can indicate with any authority the likely operation of either pathway of influence. Fortunately, a small body of such research, along with a large number of supportive investigations, does exist. This research considers the significance of developmental history for the functioning of individuals during adulthood.

THE ROLE OF DEVELOPMENTAL HISTORY

The question of where individual differences in adult psychological and relationship functioning originate has been the basis of a long research tradition linking experiences in the family of origin with adult and/or parental characteristics and behavior. Much of this tradition involves relatively naive empirical efforts to demonstrate developmental history effects through simple input–output models, linking retrospective events to current functioning. Increasingly, however, the research involves sophisticated methodological efforts to examine the nature and influence of intervening experience to explain both continuity and discontinuity in development (Rutter, 1989).

This is not to say that early theoretical models lacked in conceptualization of process. On the contrary, work by John Bowlby on the development of attachment working models, by Anna Freud on the acquisition of defense mechanisms during adolescence, and by Harry Stack Sullivan and others on the influence of interpersonal processes on personality and adjustment explicitly incorporate the notion of developmental dyssynchrony resulting from individual experiences of and reactions to environmental circumstances and events. The issue has been to translate these more complex pathways in developmental research, attempting to model "lawful discontinuity" in development (Belsky & Pensky, 1988). The data summarized hereafter reflect these changing efforts to capture the complexities of developmental theory, both past and present. We begin with evidence linking early experiences to subsequent adult depression and to close relationships (parent–partner, parent–child) among both normal and clinical samples. This is followed by consideration of studies focused on developmental process and mechanisms of intergenerational transmission of patterns of adult and parental functioning. We conclude by qualifying and integrating the findings relating to developmental history, personality, close relationships, and parental care.

Development History and Adult Depression

Beginning in the 1940s with studies by Spitz (1945, 1946; see also Skodak & Skeels, 1949), who documented features of a depressive syndrome (termed *hospitalism*) in infants who had been separated from their mothers and institutionalized, there have been numerous efforts to link experiences of interpersonal loss in childhood and adolescence with later depression and other dysfunction in adulthood (Bifulco, Brown, & Harris, 1987; Frommer & O'Shea, 1973; Harris, Brown, & Bifulco, 1990). According to psychoanalytic—and, later, attachment—principles, such loss can produce intense and unresolved anxiety, guilt, and anger, making an individual emotionally vulnerable to such feelings during subsequent development in the face of perceived loss or lack of caring (Bibring, 1953; Bowlby, 1980). Increased vulnerability to depressive symptoms and a tendency to experience strong negative emotions, it should be recalled, represent core features of negative affectivity. Thus, evidence to suggest that early experiences contribute to adult negative affectivity is pertinent to an understanding of the developmental origins of parenting behavior.

The psychoanalytic perspective reflected in Spitz's work was initially translated into research as a simple, main effects model: Experience of early loss increases later emotional vulnerability (i.e., depression). As noted earlier, several research studies reported just this finding, based on the incidence of recalled parental loss among populations of depressed adults. Psychoanalytic models of development are, of course, much broader in scope regarding the impact of early experience on subsequent development than these studies suggest. Indeed, psychological loss of a parent occurs with considerably more frequency than physical loss through death or family breakdown. Thus, a number of investigations have been successful in documenting connections between presumed psychological unavailability or mistreatment by parents and psychological difficulties in adulthood. These studies consider the origins of depression, depressive affect, loneliness, and other expressions of negative affectivity in adulthood. Negative affectivity, it should be recalled, represents a significant personality factor associated with the quality of parental care.

Retrospective investigations documenting poorer parenting experiences in childhood among depressed versus nondepressed adults represent one body of evidence for long-term effects of developmental history (Abraham & Whittock, 1969; Jacobson, Fasman, & DiMascio, 1975; Raskin, Boothe, Reatig, & Schulterbrandt, 1971). Findings in common across these studies include: (a) more negative and rejecting parental attitudes and behavior recalled by depressed adults, (b) less parental warmth and involvement recalled, and (c) the poorest experiences recalled by the most severely depressed. Needless to say, the relative accuracy of recall from childhood among adults suffering from a major affective disorder remains in serious doubt.

Similar data from research employing nonclinical populations provide some measure of validity. Among college students, ratings of parents as positive figures correlate with less loneliness, fewer depressive symptoms, less self-criticism, and higher self-esteem (Blatt, Wein, Chevron, & Quinlan, 1979; Lobdell & Perlman, 1986). In contrast, lonely adults typically depict their parents as lacking in warmth and nurturance (Rubenstein, Shaver, & Peplau, 1979).

Mothers of young children from disadvantaged backgrounds are more likely to describe themselves as depressed if they recall punishment and lack of warmth during childhood (Lyons-Ruth, Connell, Grunebaum, Botein, & Zoll, 1984).

Again, however, it is critical to consider the effect of current mood state on retrospective recall (Acklin, Sauer, Alexander, & Dugoni, 1989; Bower, 1981). Clinical populations and/or adults who experience frequent negative mood states may be inclined to dwell on the more negative aspects of their experience, past and present (Jacobson, Waldron, & Moore, 1980). Research by Wolkind and Zajicek (1983) provides evidence that this may be the case. In their investigation, relations between memories of exposure to marital conflict during childhood and depression in adulthood emerged only when retrospective data were collected at the time women were depressed. On the other hand, adult depressive mood may serve to improve recall of experiences in similar mood states during childhood (Bower, 1981). There is, in fact, substantial (about 70%) sibling agreement for factual information on family history interviews, and agreement is not affected by the presence of depression or alcoholism in one sibling (Robins et al., 1985). However, agreement was lower when questions involved inference, value judgments, or estimates of frequency. Thus, the value of family history data as an objective account of parenting experiences in childhood remains equivocal. Regardless of their accuracy, it is clear that retrospective studies such as those just summarized are notably limited in providing evidence of causal processes.

Developmental History and Adult Attachment Patterns

A second set of retrospective data provides comparable empirical evidence, although perhaps somewhat stronger theoretical underpinnings, for the role of early family experiences in the quality of subsequent parent–child and adult close relationships. Many of the studies furnishing these data are based on the theoretical work of Bowlby (1969, 1973) regarding "working models" of relationships. The premise underlying this body of research is that an infant, child, and later adult acquires internal representation(s) about primary attachment figure(s) that serve as blueprints for other close relationships (Bretherton, 1985; Sroufe & Fleeson, 1986). What was experienced in the family of origin shapes what an individual expects from other close relationships including, presumably, both one's partners and one's child(ren). Empirical efforts, however, focus less on the developmental process than on establishing direct links between presumed adult working models and patterns of current relationships. Nevertheless, when linked with data about the significance of infant attachment (i.e., working models) for subsequent psychological and social development, these research efforts have clear process implications regarding the contribution of developmental history (in this case, attachment working models) to parenting (Lewis, Feiring, McGuffog, & Jaskir, 1984; Sroufe, 1983; Sroufe & Fleeson,

1988). The studies, summarized hereafter, encompass both clinical and normal populations, and consider adult attachments to other adults as well as to their own children.

Dysfunctional Families

Child Maltreatment.   Much of the emphasis on linking early experiences with adult parent–child relationships originated in the field of child maltreatment. In their efforts to understand the etiology of child abuse and neglect, researchers examined the incidence of maltreatment and other instances of parenting breakdown in the abusive parent's family of origin. The results concur with psychoanalytic theory and clinical case studies in finding that abusive and neglectful mothers are unable to mobilize resources in support of their infants' development until their own history of attachment disturbances are acknowledged and addressed (Fraiberg, 1980; Fraiberg, Adelson, & Shapiro, 1975; Greenspan et al., 1987). Although the associations are by no means perfect (Kaufman & Zigler, 1989), there is ample evidence that a high proportion of parents who maltreat and/or who have a child removed from their care have experienced disturbances and disruptions in relations with their own parents, without necessarily having suffered the identical form of maltreatment they themselves perpetrate (Altemeier, O'Connor, Vietze, Sandler, & Sherrod, 1982; Engfer & Schneewind, 1982; Herrenkohl, Herrenkohl, & Toedter, 1983; Kotelchuck, 1982; Lyons-Ruth, Zoll, Connell, & Grunebaum, 1989; Polansky, Chalmers, Williams, & Buttenwieser, 1981).

The fact that these studies are retrospective in nature and document troubled relationships in the family of origin only after the fact of maltreatment in an identified population argues for the role of early experiences of attachment dysfunction as a risk factor, rather than a necessary and sufficient cause, in the etiology of maltreatment (DeLozier, 1982; Vondra, 1990). Poor relationships with parents in childhood and adolescence, in and of itself, may not lead to dysfunctional parenting. However, when combined with other risk factors, such as poverty, lack of education, teen pregnancy, absence of a stable partner, and life event stress, the probability of child maltreatment appears to increase substantially (Egeland, Breitenbucher, & Rosenberg, 1980; Egeland, Jacobvitz, & Papatola, 1987; Quinton et al., 1984).

Spouse Abuse.   Although not as extensively documented as child maltreatment, data from both small sample research and large sample survey studies indicate that spouse abuse is also intergenerationally repetitive (Pagelow, 1981; Roscoe & Benaske, 1985; Straus, Gelles, & Steinmetz, 1980). Of special interest is the finding that individuals who report having witnessed spouse abuse and/or child maltreatment in their family of origin are more likely to describe both their dating relationships (Gwartney-Gibbs, Stockard, & Bohmer, 1987) and their marriages as being violent (Gelles, 1976; Kalmuss, 1984). Results suggest that intergenerational transmission of violence is particularly strong for violence within congruent relationships (i.e., marital to marital, parent–child to parent–child). Once again, without empirical consideration of process, the evidence suggests that relationships witnessed or experienced in the family of origin are often recreated in adulthood with one's spouse and children.

Normal Families

Critical to broader discussion of individual differences in parenting, however, is the ability to demonstrate similar developmental history "effects" among normal populations of parents. With the development of the Adult Attachment Interview (Main & Goldwyn, in press), a clinical self-report instrument designed to capture differences in the quality, quantity, and style of adult recall of childhood experiences, an increasing number of studies are documenting predictable patterns of covariation between adult memories of and reactions to early care and the quality of adult close relationships.

Infant–Parent Attachment.   Several of the studies just alluded to relate self-reported adult attachment patterns with observed security of infant–parent attachment, without attention to the presumed intervening variable of parental care. There is growing evidence from this research alone that parents who experience unresolved anger and distress over troubled childhood relations with their own parents tend to have insecure relationships with their infants and young children (Main, Kaplan, & Cassidy, 1985; Ricks, 1985). Morris (1982), for example, reported that mothers of securely attached children were more likely than mothers of insecurely attached children to identify positively with their mothers and to perceive them as strong, nurturant, and emotionally available.

Other studies have been able to document that these predictive differences in adult attachment models are also associated with decreased sensitivity and attunement to infants, the proposed mechanism of attachment transmission. In a sample of White, middle-class mothers and their preschoolers, security based on the adult attachment interview was associated with greater support and assistance for the preschooler during difficult structured tasks, a less controlling style of interaction, and a decreased likelihood that the preschooler had been recruited from a psychological clinic (Crowell & Feldman, 1988). Similarly, among two samples of German mothers with young children from a range of socioeconomic backgrounds, responses to the adult attachment interview corresponded not only to infant attachment security measured 4 to 5 years previously, but also to the quality of maternal interactions during late infancy and maternal descriptions of her toddler and his or her needs (Grossmann, Fremmer-Bombik, Rudolph, & Grossmann, 1988). In the researchers' words:

It appears that a mother who remembers well how she felt when something bad had happened to her and how her parents responded or *should* have responded to comfort her, will listen empathically to her own infant's distress signals. . . . A mother who cannot remember much of her childhood distress, or remembers only in a distorted form, seems less able to listen openly and feel sympathetic with her infant. She may push aside memories of her own former distress by ignoring her infant's distress. (pp. 255–256)

These findings and interpretations clearly begin to delineate some of the processes that link developmental history and parental functioning. Nevertheless, because they continue to rely on retrospective data without information about the developmental interim, there is much in the way of process and mechanism that remains obscure.

Adult Relationships.   Continuity of relations among normal populations from family of origin to family of procreation is not limited to data on parent–child relationships. Both marital satisfaction and marital stability show some correspondence across generations. As early as the 1930s, research (Terman, 1938) indicated that "marital happiness appears to be a condition that tends to run in families" (p. 35), based on retrospective and self-report data. The relation has been replicated numerous times since then (Eysenck & Wakefield, 1981; Goodrich, Ryder, & Rausch, 1968; Snyder, 1979). Spouses who recall amicable relations between their parents are more likely to report satisfaction with their own marriage.

On the other hand, growing up in a home with a conflicted marriage, as indicated by the occurrence of divorce, appears to place an individual at greater risk of having his or her own marriage end in divorce. In his analysis of survey data compiled over a decade (1973–1986), Glenn found that the risk of divorce is more than 25% greater for men from broken homes and more than 50% greater for women from such families of origin (Glenn & Kramer, 1986; Glenn & Shelton, 1983). Increased risk of unstable marital relations under such circumstances is a relatively well-established finding (Korbin & Waite, 1984; Kulka & Weingarten, 1979; Mott & Moore, 1979; Mueller & Cooper, 1986).

SPECIFYING DEVELOPMENTAL PROCESS

Together, the data regarding relations between patterns of functioning in the family of origin and patterns of functioning in adulthood indicate continuity of experience from childhood to adulthood. Risk factors and stressors in childhood are associated with psychological health and quality of relationships in maturity, a simple input–output model. However, both the fact that the data are retrospective and the studies fail to include process factors in their research design limit the conceptual utility for those interested in specifying develop-

mental pathways. In fact, such studies do not capture effectively the sophistication of the developmental and clinical models on which they were based.
For example, although the studies concerned with adult attachment models
that were described earlier implicitly take into account any changes over time
in how individuals process their early experience, there are no direct attempts
to establish links between childhood experiences, conditions of continuity or
discontinuity, adult psychological and social functioning, and quality of parental
care. These connections are all implicit in the correlation between recall of developmental history and, for instance, the security of the parent–infant relationship. Furthermore, it is entirely unclear from these data under what
conditions one would expect to find continuity over time and when, instead,
discontinuity would be predicted. Developmental and clinical theory, to some
extent, argue that adversity in childhood will be expressed in adulthood only
so long as the vulnerability it creates is further challenged later in development or the conditions underlying vulnerability remain stable over time (Bowlby, 1980; Rutter, 1984). Although all the studies cited earlier demonstrate less
than perfect prediction from developmental history to current functioning, few
attempt to explain and/or investigate those cases where continuity is not apparent.

In the remainder of the chapter we elaborate and extend the empirical and
conceptual ideas raised about the developmental origins of parenting, with an
emphasis on understanding: (a) the processes by which developmental history
shapes both personality and patterns of relationship, and thereby parenting
and (b) the conditions under which continuity is predicted and documented.
In order to do this, we consider two important bodies of research: First, evidence about the development of psychological and interpersonal functioning
in childhood, and second, evidence about continuity and discontinuity of functioning in adulthood.

Developmental Process in Childhood

Mechanisms for the transmission of family experiences into patterns of adjustment and dysfunction in the individual are most apparent in selected research
on attachment and on psychological resiliency and vulnerability. Illustrative
examples of this research are used here to flesh out models of developmental
process within the causal framework for parenting already outlined. In each
case, process-oriented empirical work provides a more solid basis of support
for the causal inferences about the origins of individual differences in parenting that have been drawn from cross-sectional and retrospective studies.

Attachment in Childhood.   As described earlier, attachment theory advances
the concept of internal working models, affect-laden mental representations
of the self, others, and relationships. Bowlby (1980) proposed that internal work-

ing models are derived from early interactional experiences and function (outside of conscious awareness) to direct attention and organize memory in a way that shapes attributions about oneself, that guides interpersonal behavior, and that alters the interpretation of social experience. Recent research derived from this theory has become increasingly effective in articulating how and when early internal working models demonstrate continuity over time and appear to influence broader patterns of psychological and interpersonal functioning.

With respect to psychological functioning, a series of investigations on attachment and behavior problems and behavioral disregulation indicate that attachment insecurity in infancy increases the probability of difficulties in early childhood when early insecurity is combined with poorer parenting and/or greater environmental stress in childhood (Lewis et al., 1984). Erickson et al. (1985) studied some 60 preschoolers from disadvantaged backgrounds who had shown stable patterns of security or insecurity in the second year of life. Although the anxiously attached infants were, on the average, later performing more poorly on a variety of teacher and observer measures of persistence, frustration tolerance, compliance, dependency, and peer relations in preschool, the likelihood of subsequent behavior problems among both securely and anxiously attached youngsters was substantially greater when parental care after infancy was less supportive. Among children who had been anxiously attached, behavior problems were fewer or absent when mothers reported more social support and a stable intimate relationship with a spouse or partner.

These data support the argument that problematic parent–child relations represent one origin of later negative affectivity and/or maladjustment. They further suggest that it is only when troubled relations are maintained over time in the context of family stress (unstable marital relations, low social support, poor parenting), that subsequent psychological well-being is compromised (see also Weisner, Bernstein, Garnier, Rosenthal, & Hamilton, 1990). Developmental trajectories, even among socially and economically disadvantaged populations, demonstrate malleability in the context of environmental support. Nevertheless, continuity over time is clearly apparent both in studies of early behavior problems, as just noted, and of problem relationships, as illustrated by the research described later.

Recent childhood attachment studies have moved beyond assessments of individual child functioning or parent–child interaction to provide insights about the origin of troubled interpersonal relations. In particular, a subset of 40 preschoolers from the disadvantaged sample just described were studied in two experimental nursery school classes (Sroufe & Fleeson, 1988). Across many 15-minute play sessions, intriguing patterns of peer relations evolved on the basis of previous attachment history. When paired with a peer who had been insecurely attached in infancy, children who had shown a stable pattern of avoidance (one form of attachment insecurity) during infancy were more likely to develop a victimizing relationship, in which one of the children would physically exploit, deride, be sarcastic of, or otherwise reject the other. Children with a stable pattern of security in infancy neither victimized nor were victims in any peer pairs, whereas those with a stable pattern of resistance (a second form of attachment insecurity) varied depending on their peer partner. When paired with a child having a resistant attachment history, the latter tended to develop relationships characterized by immaturity and social incompetence, when paired with a peer having an avoidant history, they tended to be victimized, and when paired with a peer from the secure group, they tended to elicit leadership and nurturance.

Comparable findings resulted when relations with preschool teachers were compared across attachment groups. Teachers had higher expectations of compliance for children with secure attachment histories and provided both less control and less nurturance than they did to children with insecure attachment histories. Expectations of compliance were lower for children from the resistant attachment group, who elicited more control, tolerance, and nurturance from their teachers. Children with avoidant histories also elicited more control and lower expectations of compliance from their teachers, but also, the only instances of anger observed during data collection.

These findings are reminiscent of data reported by George and Main (1979, 1980) indicating that young maltreated children tend both to avoid and aggress against peers and teachers in preschool. Particularly unusual was their tendency to respond to distress in peers with aggression, a form of victimization. Given the fact that maltreated children show an extreme preponderance of insecure attachments in infancy (Carlson, Cicchetti, Barnett, & Braunwald, 1989; Crittenden, 1988), the data dovetail neatly with Sroufe and Fleeson's (1988) preschool attachment findings in supporting a developmental history model from infant–parent attachment to relations with peers and other caregivers, and potentially, to adult close relationships as well. The mechanism for this proposed developmental trajectory is attachment working models. When children's working models are derived from and maintained over time on the basis of insecure attachment relations, it can be expected that relationships with significant others will tend to reflect patterns of insecurity the child carries with him or her into relationships with others, in terms of social cognition, perceptual biases, affective reactions, and interpersonal behavior. As is seen when we discuss process-oriented adult research, these working models probably influence partner and network selection itself, as well as the patterns of relations established within each dyad.

Psychological Resiliency in Childhood. The critical importance for developmental adaptation of experiencing, early on, a positive, nurturant relationship with a caregiver—whether within or outside the family—is especially apparent in research on children at biological and ecological risk for psychopathology. Radke-Yarrow and Sherman (in press), using a case-study approach with children of clinically depressed parents, noted that "goodness of fit'' between parental needs and child characteristics appeared to explain the surprising resiliency of a small subset of school-age children who did not exhibit the social, emotional, and cognitive deficits typical of the larger group. These children appeared to possess qualities that attracted whatever resources the parents and family were able to marshal. With the special attention and care they derived (relative to other children and other family members), these children appeared, at least temporarily, buffered against the difficulties in behavior and adjustment that their peers exhibited.

Birtchnell (1980) noted from case report data that adults who experienced the early loss of a mother showed better adjustment in adulthood when there was a supportive relationship with a mother replacement during childhood (see also Harris, Brown, & Bifulco, 1986). Similarly, children who remain in the custody of a divorcing parent with whom a positive relationship has already been established show fewer adjustment problems following the divorce (Hetherington, Cox, & Cox, 1982; Tschann, Johnston, Kline, & Wallerstein, 1989). Finally, in their longitudinal investigation of a birth cohort on Kauai, Hawaii, Werner and Smith (1982) reported that positive childhood and adolescent adjustment outcomes among children with four or more risk factors (including birth prematurity, family poverty and/or instability, parental mental illness, and/or lack of education) were associated with high levels of parental attention in infancy, fewer prolonged separations from their mothers, more positive interactions with mothers during childhood, and the ability to elicit more positive reactions from adults. Comparable data on the significance for current and later adjustment of experiencing and eliciting supportive relationships during early childhood with parents and other adults has been reported for nonrisk samples as well (Murphy & Moriarty, 1976; White & Watts, 1973).

Psychological Vulnerability in Childhood.   Another set of process data relevant to the issue of transmission of psychological functioning within the family is emerging from studies of young children's responses to controlled displays of affect in laboratory settings. These data indicate that repeated exposure to particular affective displays in the home provokes, or perhaps exaggerates, unique patterns of affective regulation in children. Consistent with the kind of dynamic theorizing embedded in attachment working models, these regulatory or coping patterns are not mere imitations of adult behaviors, but involve broader reactions at the level of emotional arousal and affective response that can be expected to carry over into other interpersonal relationships.

Even among very young infants, predictable patterns of response or lack of response to a maternal *still-face* procedure (sustained unresponsive, blank expression during face-to-face interaction) differentiate infants with depressed or nondepressed mothers (Field, 1986). Infants of depressed mothers tend to show less positive affect and more avoidance during normal face-to-face interaction, and little change in behavior during the still-face procedure, unlike infants of nondepressed mothers who shift from positive engagement to distress and/or protest behavior. The former infants appear to have developed defensive strategies for dealing with protracted maternal affective unavailability, strategies that they carry over into interactions with other, nondepressed adults, and that appear to elicit less responsive and stimulating care (Field, 1992; Field et al., 1988).

In toddlerhood, young children of depressed parents demonstrate more preoccupation with distress behaviors exhibited by others, both adults and children, and less ability to reengage in activities following an episode of simulated distress (Zahn-Waxler et al., 1984). Together with the infant data, these results suggest that affective disorders within the family alter young children's responses to expressions of affect by others, with likely ramifications for the affective components of subsequent relationships (see Swann, 1983). It has been noted at least anecdotally that depressed individuals, for example, are likely to develop social ties with other depressed persons, and may marry a partner who also shows signs of maladjustment (Zahn-Waxler et al., 1984).

Assortative mating/marriage on the basis of level of adjustment, an explicit element in some clinical theory (e.g., Bowen, 1978), is obviously a critical conceptual link between experience in the family of origin and later adult functioning. Although no studies exist at present to substantiate, at one time, all the links proposed here, there is certainly evidence to support a causal pathway from parental maladjustment to reactive child coping strategies, to altered interpersonal relationships that may ultimately feed back to affect adult functioning and parental care.

Additional process-oriented data are provided by Cummings and his colleagues (Cummings, Ianotti, & Zahn-Waxler, 1985; Cummings, Zahn-Waxler, & Radke-Yarrow, 1981; J. S. Cummings, Pellegrini, Notarius, & Cummings, 1989) in a series of investigations exploring the effect of background adult conflict and anger on young children's affect and behavior. These investigators reported that children experience a contagion of affect in terms of distress and aggression in play following exposure to simulated anger and conflict. Even more importantly, there is evidence of a sensitization effect, whereby young children who are exposed to repeated adult–adult anger/conflict episodes—either simulated in the lab or reported in the home—show more extreme and/or sustained disruptions in affect and behavior. Furthermore, relatively coherent patterns of coping responses, ranging from avoidance and denial to solicitous caretaking and role reversal have been documented (Cummings, 1987).

Evidence, such as the research described previously, that children may be sensitized to and may devise self-regulatory patterns around particular expressions of affect in the home offers, along with childhood attachment data, further empirical footing for correlational research on the recreation of family roles and relationships in adulthood (Kalmuss, 1984; Sroufe, Jacobvitz, Mangelsdorf, DeAngelo, & Ward, 1985). They also support the hypothesized links between childhood experiences in the family and subsequent adult functioning explored in retrospective studies.

In summary, recent data from different domains of developmental research converge in finding early relationship experiences crucial to the immediate and longer term adjustment of children, considered both in terms of individual and interpersonal functioning. The significance of early relationships appears to rest in dynamic cognitive and affective patterns, internalized by the child, that develop in response to and are organized around repeated affective experiences within the family and, particularly, within the relationship between child and primary caregiver. These patterns—whether considered in terms of attachment working models, self-regulation, or coping strategies—do, nevertheless, demonstrate malleability over time. As indicated by research on developmental continuity, both stability and change in adaptational patterns can be anticipated on the basis of family and parenting circumstances that improve, degrade, or remain unchanged over time. These conditions of continuity (Belsky & Pensky, 1988) are also apparent in research on relations between early experiences, current circumstances, and parental functioning in adulthood. It is to the issue of continuity for adult and parental functioning that we now turn our attention.

Continuity in Adulthood

We have seen that the very characteristics found to be predictive of individual differences in parenting, namely psychological adjustment and quality of close relationships, have their origins in experiences within the family during childhood. We have also seen that under changed circumstances or, in the case of childhood resiliency, under exceptional circumstances, developmental *discon*tinuity can be predicted. We also summarized data suggesting that direct associations could, nevertheless, be discerned between reported childhood experiences and later parenting. The fact that these associations are far from perfect argues that, as with childhood prediction, prediction of adult functioning—in this case parenting—must take contextual, as well as developmental history, factors into account. The final set of data described here offer evidence of the role that contextual factors play in altering developmental trajectories and thereby changing parenting outcomes. These data, once again, derive from both normative and clinical samples, and are discussed according to this distinction.

Normative Samples.   Even across relatively short periods of time—6 months to 3 years—contextual factors appear to alter the quality of care provided by parents. Factors of greatest significance seem to be those representing emotional support available to parents through their close relationships. Thus, among a disadvantaged population, loss of or conflict with one's partner predicts poorer than expected maternal sensitivity, whereas a sense of being emotionally supported predicts greater than expected maternal sensitivity from 6 to 42 months after the birth of a child (Pianta, Sroufe, & Egeland, 1989). Among middle-class mothers, feeling supported by partner, family, and friends 3 months after an infant's birth predicts increased sensitivity toward the infant at 12 months, particularly when the infant is rated by observers as more irritable at birth (Crockenberg & McCluskey, 1986).

Notable discrepancies in parenting outcomes are also apparent in studies examining prediction on the basis of developmental history and intervening circumstances. In these studies, as well, partner support during adulthood takes on special significance for differences in observed care. Crockenberg (1987) observed that teen-aged mothers who reported lower maternal acceptance during childhood were more likely to behave in an angry, power-assertive manner with their toddlers during structured tasks only when they also felt their current partners did not help them out much. In another study, middle-class mothers who reported parental rejection during childhood who also described their current marriages as relatively low in support were the most negative in affect toward their preschool-age children in a lab setting (Belsky, Youngblade, & Pensky, 1989). In both cases, poorer prediction of parental behavior from negative childhood experiences was found among mothers who reported relatively greater support from an intimate relationship in adulthood.

Clinical Samples. Developmental discontinuity is often even more striking among parents from atypical or dysfunctional populations. Recent studies of parents who were maltreated during childhood are a case in point. Although, as reported earlier, robust associations exist between maltreatment in one's family of origin and maltreatment of one's own child(ren), inquiry into those cases representing an exception to the trend—parents who provide adequate or good care to children despite an apparent background of maltreatment—has provided important insights about mechanisms underlying both continuity and discontinuity across development.

Based on parental reports of childhood maltreatment and observer ratings of parental care in the lab and at home across a period of 2 years following the birth of an infant, Egeland, Jacobvitz, and Sroufe (1988; see also Hunter & Kilstrom, 1979) successfully distinguished between mothers who carried their own experiences into the parental role, and those who overcame early maltreatment to provide adequate care for their infants. The critical factors consistently involved the quality of relationships established and maintained in the interim. These included having a supportive relationship with someone other than the abusive parent during childhood, having undergone extensive psychotherapy, reporting a stable and/or satisfying relationship with a nonabusive partner, and engaging in fewer fights with family members and friends. Personality factors were also implicated, in that mothers who carried forward their own experiences of maltreatment repeatedly scored higher on measures of negative affectivity, in this case, anxiety and depression (and less consistently, aggression).

Relationship factors again emerged as likely buffers in a similar investigation by Lyons-Ruth and her colleagues (Lyons-Ruth et al., 1989). Hostile interactions with their 12- and 18-month-old infants were notably less frequent among mothers with the most deviant childhood experiences (placement in foster care, maternal psychopathology, or repeated severe physical punishment) who nevertheless reported a warm relationship with one parent and/or close, satisfying peer relations. Supportive peer, but not adult, relationships were significantly correlated with parental behavior among mothers without such deviant experiences in childhood.

In a study described earlier, Quinton et al. (1984) linked a developmental history of parenting breakdown and child institutionalization with "persisting handicaps in interpersonal relationships" (p. 113) beginning in adolescence, with teen pregnancy, with the absence of a stable intimate heterosexual relationship or marriage to a partner with psychosocial problems, and with serious parenting dysfunction. However, of those high-risk women who entered into a supportive marital relationship, parenting outcomes were notably more positive (see also Hodges & Tizard, 1989, for a similar study on adoption of institutionalized children). Indeed, the authors concluded that there was little direct effect of developmental history on parenting, but considerable indirect effect via poorer interpersonal relationships and living conditions established in adulthood and greater susceptibility to stressful circumstances such as these.

The mediating role of supportive close relationships for developmental history effects on parenting may take place only indirectly. For example, data indicate that the relation between loss of a mother in childhood and depression in adulthood is stronger when a woman's current relationship has failed (Bifulco et al., 1987; Brown, Harris, & Bifulco, 1986). But because negative affectivity and psychological adjustment are clearly significant for caregiving outcomes, relationship issues again qualify the relation between developmental history and parenting.

In summary, the effects of a troubled and/or problematic childhood for parenting difficulty and dysfunction appear to depend very much on opportunities to rework poor relationship experiences. When children have alternative relationship models available to them and/or can participate in a supportive relationship amidst the stressors of their childhoods, when young adults can rework relationship issues by their long-term involvement (whether personal or professional) with a caring and supportive individual, the relationships they create with their own children need not mirror the hardships of their upbringing.

It becomes moot, at this stage, to argue how much psychological adjustment versus supportive relationships contribute to parental outcomes; the two are inextricably linked and even, as we pointed out earlier, to some extent redundant issues. As Bowlby (1973) argued in his attachment work, and as Sullivan (1953) argued in his clinical work, individuals define themselves very much in terms of their interpersonal relationships. Relationships—attachment working models—that are conflicted, insecure, and/or troubled not only undermine individual well-being, but also undermine positive conceptions about oneself (or reinforce negative ones). Individuals with adjustment problems usually experience greater than average difficulties developing and maintaining supportive relationships. The two combined are clearly critical determinants of caregiving and the quality of care. To the extent that both are set in motion on developmental trajectories that begin in childhood, they represent important process variables for understanding how developmental history is played out in later parenting. To the extent that both demonstrate some malleability on the basis of later experiences, they represent important process variables for understanding how contextual factors shape parenting as well. If we are to gain a full understanding of the determinants of parenting, it is obvious that both pathways must be taken into account.

CONCLUSION

We have summarized data in this chapter attesting to the significance of early experiences for subsequent development, including individual differences in parenting. By no means, however, have we argued for simple linkages from childhood to adulthood. Early experiences within the family help to select and shape experiences in school, with peers and, ultimately, in adult relationships. They do so through the medium of psychological and interpersonal resources and behavior patterns. In no case, however, can one assume a simple main effects model. Whether the childhood legacy is documented maltreatment, institutionalization, or unconditional love, intervening experiences hold the power to deflect early developmental trajectories.

Consistent with both attachment theory and clinical models, research to date suggests that the most potent intervention involves interpersonal relationships experienced across development. Nevertheless, the interdependency between close relationships and psychological functioning, and the significance of each for parenting, makes it clear that both deserve special attention in research on the determinants of parenting. Increasingly, both are receiving attention in studies that consider the *ecology* of parenting, the interplay of individual and environmental factors that together shape parental behavior. More sophisticated, process-oriented empirical work of this sort has made considerable strides toward understanding the mechanisms underlying both developmental continuity and discontinuity. By assuming an ecological perspective, by investigating the *outliers*—cases that do not conform to prediction—and by adopting a longitudinal design, research has begun to provide a more adequate test of developmental and clinical theory on the origins of parenting.

We conclude this discussion with recognition of the rapprochement that has been gradually emerging between clinical and empirical efforts to understand adult functioning and, in particular, individual differences in caregiving. Indeed, the analysis we have undertaken in this chapter is predicated on advances that have been made in applying clinical theory to research settings. These include greater specification of developmental process within clinical theory, the creation of clinical instruments for use in research, and increasing sophistication of research designs for capturing developmental process. As a result, empirical support for clinical constructs and mechanisms has grown, but at the same time, research has gained a notable measure of depth and relevance. The consequence of both has been better understanding of both the factors and the processes involved in the evolution of individual differences in parenting.

REFERENCES

Abraham, M., & Whittock, F. (1969). Childhood experience and depression. *British Journal of Psychiatry, 115*, 883–888.

Acklin, M. W., Sauer, A., Alexander, G., & Dugoni, B. (1989). Predicting depression using earliest childhood memories. *Journal of Personality Assessment, 53*, 51–59.

Altemeier, W. A., O'Connor, S., Vietze, P. M., Sandler, H. M., & Sherrod, K. B. (1982). Antecedents of child abuse. *Journal of Pediatrics, 100*, 823–829.

American Psychiatric Association (1987). *Diagnostic and statistical manual of mental disorders* (3rd ed. rev.). Washington, DC: Author.

Baldwin, A. L., Cole, R. E., & Baldwin, C. T. (1982). Parent pathology, family interaction, and the competence of the child in school. *Monographs of the Society for Research in Child Development, 47*, (5, Serial No. 197).

Belsky, J. (1984). The determinants of parenting: A process model. *Child Development, 55*, 83–96.

Belsky, J., & Pensky, E. (1988). Developmental history, personality, and family relationships: Toward an emergent family system, In R. Hinde & J. Stevenson-Hinde (Eds.), *Relationships within families: Mutual influences* (pp. 193–217). Oxford: Oxford University Press.

Belsky, J., & Vondra, J. (1985). Characteristics, consequences, and determinants of parenting. In L. L'Abate (Ed.), *Handbook of family psychology and therapy* (pp. 523–536). Homewood, IL: The Dorsey Press.

Belsky, J., Youngblade, L., & Pensky, E. (1989). Childrearing history, marital quality, and maternal affect: Intergenerational transmission in a low-risk sample. *Development and Psychopathology, 1*, 291–304.

Benn, R. K. (1985, April). *Factors associated with security of attachment in dual career families.* Paper presented at the biennial meeting of the Society for Research in Child Development, Toronto.

Benn, R. K. (1986). Factors promoting secure attachment relationships between employed mothers and their sons. *Child Development, 57*, 1224–1231.

Bettes, B. A. (1988). Maternal depression and motherese: Temporal and intonational features. *Child Development, 59*, 1089–1096.

Bibring, E. (1953). The mechanism of depression. In P. Greenacre (Ed.), *Affective disorders* (pp. 13–48). New York: International Universities Press.

Bifulco, A. T., Brown, G. W., & Harris, T. O. (1987). Childhood loss of parent, lack of adequate parental care, and adult depression: A replication study. *Journal of Affective Disorders, 12*, 115–128.

Birtchnell, J. (1980). Women whose mothers died in childhood: An outcome study. *Psychological Medicine, 10*, 699–713.

Blatt, S. J., Wein, S. J., Chevron, E., & Quinlan, D. M. (1979). Parental representation in normal young adults. *Journal of Abnormal Psychology, 88*, 388–397.

Bowen, M. (1978). *Family therapy in clinical practice.* New York: Jason Aronson.

Bowen, G. H. (1981). Mood and memory. *American Psychologist, 36*, 129–148.

Bowlby, J. (1969). *Attachment and loss: Vol. 1. Attachment.* New York: Basic Books.

Bowlby, J. (1973). *Attachment and loss: Vol. 2. Separation.* New York: Basic Books.

Bowlby, J. (1980). *Attachment and loss: Vol. 3. Loss, sadness, and depression.* New York: Basic Books.

Bretherton, I. (1985). Attachment theory: Retrospect and prospect. In I. Bretherton & E. Waters (Eds.), Growing points in attachment theory and research. *Monographs of the Society for Research in Child Development, 50*, (1-2, Serial No. 209), 3–38.

Brown, G. W., Harris, T. O., & Bifulco, A. (1986). Long-term effects of early loss of parent. In M. Rutter, C. E. Izard, & P. B. Read (Eds.), *Depression in young people: Developmental and clinical perspectives* (pp. 251–296). New York: Guilford Press.

Brunnquell, D., Crichton, L., & Egeland, B. (1981). Maternal personality and attitude in disturbances of child rearing. *American Journal of Orthopsychiatry, 51*, 680–691.

Carlson, V., Cicchetti, D., Barnett, D., & Braunwald, K. (1989). Disorganized/disoriented attachment relationships in maltreated infants. *Developmental Psychology, 25*, 525–531.

Cohn, J. F., Matias, R., Tronick, E. Z., Connell, D., & Lyons-Ruth, K. (1986). Face-to-face interactions of depressed mothers and their infants. In E. Z. Tromck & T. Field (Eds.), *New directions for child development: Maternal depression and infant disturbance* (Vol. 34, pp. 31–45). San Francisco: Jossey-Bass.

Colletta, N. D. (1981). Social support and the risk of maternal rejection by adolescent mothers. *Journal of Psychology, 109*, 191–197.

Colletta, N. D. (1983). At risk for depression: A study of young mothers. *Journal of Genetic Psychology, 142*, 301–310.

Conger, R., McCarthy, J., Yang, R., Lahey, B., & Kropp, J. (1984). Perception of child, child-rearing values, and emotional distress as mediating links between environmental stressors and observed maternal behavior. *Child Development, 55*, 2234–2247.

Cox, M. J., Owen, M. T., Lewis, J. M., & Henderson, V. K. (1989). Marriage, adult adjustment, and early parenting. *Child Development, 60*, 1015–1024.

Crittenden, P. M. (1988). Relationships at risk. In J. Belsky & T. Nezworski (Eds.), *Clinical implications of attachment* (pp. 136–174). Hillsdale, NJ: Lawrence Erlbaum Associates.

Crnic, K. A., & Greenberg, M. T. (1985, April). *Parenting daily hassles: Relationships among minor stresses, family functioning, and child development.* Paper presented at the biennial meeting of the Society for Research in Child Development, Toronto.

Crockenberg, S. (1987). Predictors and correlates of anger toward and punitive control of toddlers by adolescent mothers. *Child Development, 58*, 964–975.

Crockenberg, S., & McCluskey, K. (1986). Change in maternal behavior during the baby's first year of life. *Child Development, 57*, 746–753.

Crowell, J. A., & Feldman, S. S. (1988). Mothers' internal models of relationships and children's behavioral and developmental status: A study of mother–child interaction. *Child Development, 59*, 1273–1285.

Cummings, E. M. (1987). Coping with background anger in early childhood. *Child Development, 58*, 976–984.

Cummings, E. M., Iannotti, R. J., & Zahn-Waxler, C. (1985). Influence of conflict between adults on the emotions and aggression of young children. *Developmental Psychology, 21*, 495–500.

Cummings, E. M., Zahn-Waxler, C., & Radke-Yarrow, M. (1981). Young children's responses to expressions of anger and affection by others in the family. *Child Development, 52*, 1274–1282.

Cummings, J. S., Pellegrini, D. S., Notarius, C. I., & Cummings, E. M. (1989). Children's responses to angry adult behavior as a function of marital distress and history of interparent hostility. *Child Development, 60*, 1035–1043.

Cutrona, C. E., & Troatman, B. R. (1986). Social support, infant temperament, and parenting self-efficacy: A mediational model of postpartum depression. *Child Development, 57*, 1507-1518.

DeLozier, P. O. (1982). Attachment theory and child abuse. In C. M. Parkes & J. Stevenson-Hinde (Eds.), *The place of attachment in human behavior* (pp. 95-117). New York: Basic Books.

DeMulder, E. K., & Radke-Yarrow, M. (1991). Attachment with affectively ill and well mothers: Concurrent behavioral correlates. *Development and Psychopathology, 3*, 227-242.

Donovan, W. L., & Leavitt, L. A. (1985). Simulating conditions of learned helplessness: The effects of interventions and attributions. *Child Development, 56*, 594-603.

Donovan, W. L., & Leavitt, L. A. (1989). Maternal self-efficacy and infant attachment: Integrating physiology, perceptions, and behavior. *Child Development, 60*, 460-472.

Egeland, B., Breitenbucher, M., & Rosenberg, D. (1980). Prospective study of the significance of life-stress in the etiology of child abuse. *Journal of Consulting and Clinical Psychology, 48*, 195-205.

Egeland, B., & Farber, E. A. (1984). Infant-mother attachment: Factors related to its development and changes over time. *Child Development, 55*, 753-771.

Egeland, B., Jacobvitz, D., & Papatola, K. (1987). Intergenerational continuity of parental abuse. In J. Lancaster & R. Gelles (Eds.), *Biosocial aspects of child abuse* (pp. 255-276). New York: Jossey-Bass.

Egeland, B., Jacobvitz, D., & Sroufe, L. A. (1988). Breaking the cycle of abuse. *Child Development, 59*, 1080-1088.

Elder, G. H., Jr., Caspi, A., & Downey, G. (1986). Problem behavior and family relationships: Life course and intergenerational themes. In A. Sorensen, F. Weinert, & L. Sherrod (Eds.), *Human development and the life course* (pp. 293-340). Hillsdale, NJ: Lawrence Erlbaum Associates.

Elder, G. H., Jr., Liker, J. K., & Cross, C. E. (1984). Parent-child behavior in the Great Depression: Life course and intergenerational influences. In P. B. Baltes & O. G. Brim, Jr. (Eds.), *Life-span development and behavior* (Vol. 6, pp. 109-158). New York: Academic Press.

Engfer, A., & Schneewind, K. A. (1982). Causes and consequences of harsh parental punishment. *Child Abuse and Neglect, 6*, 129-139.

Erickson, M. F., Sroufe, L. A., & Egeland, B. (1985). The relationship between quality of attachment and behavior problems in preschool in a high-risk sample. In I. Bretherton & E. Waters (Eds.), Growing points in attachment theory and research. *Monographs of the Society for Research in Child Development, 50*, (1-2, Serial No. 209), 147-166.

Eysenck, H. (1980). Personality, marital satisfaction, and divorce. *Psychological Report, 47*, 1235-1238.

Eysenck, H., & Eysenck, S. (1969). *Personality structure and measurement.* San Diego: Robert R. Knopp.

Eysenck, H., & Wakefield, J. (1981). Psychological factors as predictors of marital satisfaction. *Advances in Behavioral Research and Therapy, 3*, 151-192.

Field, T. (1984). Early interactions between infants and their postpartum depressed mothers. *Infant Behavior and Development, 7*, 527-532.

Field, T. (1986). Models for reactive and chronic depression in infancy. In E. Z. Tronick & T. Field (Eds.), *New directions for child development: Maternal depression and infant disturbance* (Vol. 34, pp. 47-60). San Francisco: Jossey-Bass.

Field, T. (1992). Infants of depressed mothers. *Development and Psychopathology, 4*, 49-66.

Field, T., Healy, B., Goldstein, S., Perry, S., Bendell, D., Schanbergh, S., Zimmerman, E. A., & Kuhn, C. (1988). Infants of depressed mothers show "depressed" behavior even with nondepressed adults. *Child Development, 59*, 1569-1579.

Field, T., Sandberg, D., Garcia, R., Vega-Lahr, N., Goldstein, S., & Guy, L. (1985). Prenatal problems, postpartum depression, and early mother-infant interactions. *Developmental Psychology, 12*, 1152-1156.

Forehand, R., Lautenschlager, G., Faust, J., & Graziano, W. (1985). Parent perceptions and parent-child interactions in clinic-referred children: A preliminary investigation of the effects of maternal depressive mood. *Behavior Research and Therapy, 14*, 1-3.

Fraiberg, S. (1980). *Clinical studies in infant mental health: The first year.* New York: Basic Books.

Fraiberg, S., Adelson, E., & Shapiro, V. (1975). Ghosts in the nursery: A psychoanalytic approach to the problems of impaired infant–mother relationships. *Journal of the American Academy of Child Psychiatry, 14,* 387–421.

Framo, J. (1970). Symptoms from a family transactional viewpoint. In N. Ackerman (Ed.), *Family therapy in transition* (pp. 125–171). Boston: Little, Brown.

Frommer, E., & O'Shea, G. (1973). The importance of childhood experiences in relation to problems of marriage and family building. *British Journal of Psychiatry, 123,* 157–160.

Gelles, R. (1976). Demythologizing child abuse. *The Family Coordinator, 25,* 135–141.

George, C., & Main, M. (1979). Social interactions of young abused children: Approach, avoidance, and aggression. *Child Development, 50,* 306–318.

George, C., & Main, M. (1980). Abused children: Their rejection of peers and caregivers. In T. Field (Ed.), *High-risk infants and children: Adult and peer interactions* (pp. 293–308). New York: Academic Press.

Glenn, N., & Kramer, K. (1986). *The marriages and divorces of the children of divorce.* Unpublished manuscript, Department of Sociology, University of Texas, Austin.

Glenn, N., & Shelton, R. A. (1983). Pre-adult background variables and divorce. A note of caution about overreliance on explained variance. *Journal of Marriage and the Family, 45,* 405–410.

Goodrich, W., Ryder, R., & Rausch, H. (1968). Patterns of newlywed marriage. *Journal of Marriage and the Family, 30,* 383–389.

Greenspan, S. I., Weider, S., Nover, R., Lieberman, A., Lourie, R., & Robinson, M. G. (Eds.). (1987). *Infants in multirisk families.* Madison, WI: International Universities Press.

Grossmann, K., Fremmer-Bombik, E., Rudolph, J., & Grossmann, K. E. (1988). Maternal attachment representations as related to patterns of infant–mother attachment and maternal care during the first year. In R. A. Hinde & J. Stevenson-Hinde (Eds.), *Relationships within families: Mutual influences* (pp. 241–260). Oxford: Oxford University Press.

Gwartney-Gibbs, P. A., Stockard, J., & Bohmer, S. (1987). Learning courtship aggression: The influence of parents, peers, and personal experiences. *Family Relations, 36,* 276–282.

Harris, T., Brown, G. W., Bifulco, A. (1986). Loss of parent in childhood and adult psychiatric disorder: The role of lack of adequate parental care. *Psychological Medicine, 16,* 641–659.

Harris, T., Brown, G. W., & Bifulco, A. (1990). Loss of parent in childhood and adult psychiatric disorder: A tentative overall model. *Development and Psychopathology, 2,* 311–328.

Heath, D. H. (1976). Competent fathers: Their personality and marriages. *Human Development, 19,* 26–39.

Heinicke, C. (1984). Impact of pre-birth personality and marital functioning on family development: A framework and suggestions for further study. *Developmental Psychology, 20,* 1044–1053.

Heinicke, C., Diskin, S., Ramsey-Klee, D., & Given, K. (1983). Pre-birth characteristics and family development in the first year of life. *Child Development, 54,* 194–208.

Herrenkohl, E. C., Herrenkohl, R. C., & Toedter, L. J. (1983). Perspectives on the intergenerational transmission of abuse. In D. Finkelhor, R. J. Gelles, G. T. Hotaling, & M. A. Straus (Eds.), *The dark side of families: Current family violence research* (pp. 305–316). Beverly Hills, CA: Sage.

Hetherington, E. M., Cox, M., & Cox, R. (1982). Effects of divorce on parents and children. In M. E. Lamb (Ed.), *Nontraditional families* (pp. 233–272). Hillsdale, NJ: Lawrence Erlbaum Associates.

Hodges, J., & Tizard, B. (1989). I.Q. and behavioral adjustment of ex-institutional adolescents. *Journal of Child Psychology and Psychiatry, 30,* 53–75.

Hunter, R., & Kilstrom, N. (1979). Breaking the cycle in abusive families. *American Journal of Psychiatry, 136,* 1320–1322.

Jacobson, N. S., Waldron, H., & Moore, D. (1980). Toward a behavioral profile of marital distress. *Journal of Consulting and Clinical Psychology, 48,* 696–703.

Jacobson, S., Fasman, J., & DiMascio, A. (1975). Deprivation in the childhood of depressed women. *Journal of Nervous and Mental Diseases, 160,* 5–13.

Kalmuss, D. (1984). The intergenerational transmission of marital aggression. *Journal of Marriage and the Family*, *46*, 11–19.

Kaufman, J., & Zigler, E. (1989). The intergenerational transmission of child abuse and the prospect of predicting future abusers. In D. Cicchetti & V. Carlson (Eds.), *Child maltreatment: Research and theory on the consequences of child abuse and neglect* (pp. 129–150). Cambridge, MA: Harvard University Press.

Kobak, R. R., & Sceery, A. (1988). Attachment in later adolescence: Working models, affect regulation, and representations of self and others. *Child Development*, *59*, 135–146.

Kohut, H. (1971). *The analysis of the self*. New York: International Universities Press.

Kohut, H. (1977). *The restoration of the self*. New York: International Universities Press.

Kokes, R. F., Harder, D. W., Fisher, L., & Strauss, J. S. (1980). Child competence and psychiatric risk. Vol. 5: Sex of patient parent and dimensions of psychopathology. *Journal of Nervous and Mental Disease*, *168*, 348–352.

Korbin, F., & Waite, L. (1984). Effects of childhood family structure on the transition to marriage. *Journal of Marriage and the Family*, *46*, 807–816.

Kotelchuck, M. (1982). Child abuse and neglect: Prediction and misclassification. In R. G. Starr (Ed.), *Child abuse prediction* (pp. 66–93). Cambridge, MA: Ballinger.

Kulka, R., & Weingarten, N. (1979). The longer-term effects of parental divorce in childhood on adult adjustment. *Journal of Social Issues*, *32*, 193–207.

Lamb, M. E., Thompson, R. A., Gardner, W., Charnov, E. L., & Estes, D., (1984). Security of infantile attachment as assessed in the "Strange Situation": Its study and biological interpretation. *Behavioral and Brain Science*, *7*, 127–144.

Levine, L., Coll, C., & Oh, W. (1984, April). *Determinants of mother–infant interaction in adolescent mothers*. Paper presented at the International Conference on Infant Studies, New York.

Lewis, M., Feiring, C., McGuffog, C., & Jaskir, J. (1984). Predicting psychopathology in six-year-olds from early social relations. *Child Development*, *55*, 123–136.

Lobdell, J., & Perlman, D. (1986). The intergenerational transmission of loneliness: A study of college females and their parents. *Journal of Marriage and the Family*, *48*, 589–595.

Lyons-Ruth, K., Connell, D., Grunebaum, M., Botein, M., & Zoll, D. (1984). Maternal family history, maternal caretaking, and infant attachment in multiproblem families. *Journal of Preventative Psychiatry*, *2*, 403–425.

Lyons-Ruth, K., Zoll, D., Connell, D., & Grunebaum, H. U. (1989). Family deviance and family disruption in childhood. Associations with maternal behavior and infant maltreatment during the first two years of life. *Development and Psychopathology*, *1*, 219–236.

Main, M., & Goldwyn, R. (1984). Predicting rejection of her infant from mother's representation of her own experience: Implications for the abused-abusing intergenerational cycle. *Child Abuse and Neglect*, *8*, 203–217.

Main, M., & Goldwyn, R. (in press). Interview-based adult attachment classifications: Related to infant–mother and infant–father attachment. *Developmental Psychology*.

Main, M., Kaplan, N., & Cassidy, J. (1985). Security in infancy, childhood, and adulthood: A move to the level of representation. In I. Bretherton & E. Waters (Eds.), Growing points of attachment theory and research. *Monographs of the Society for Research in Child Development*, *50* (1-2, Serial No. 209), 66–104.

McCrae, R. (1982). Consensual validation of personality traits: Evidence from self reports and ratings. *Journal of Personality and Social Psychology*, *43*, 293–303.

McCrae, R., & Costa, P. (1980). Openness to experience and ego level in Loevinger's sentence completion test: Dispositional contributions to developmental models of personality. *Journal of Personality and Social Psychology*, *39*, 1179–1190.

McCrae, R., & Costa, P. (1984). *Emerging lives, enduring disposition: Personality in adulthood*. Boston: Little, Brown.

McDonald, R. L. (1968). The role of emotional factors in obstetric complications: A review. *Psychosomatic Medicine*, *30*, 222–237.

Meissner, W. W. (1978). The conceptualization of marital and family dynamics from a psychoanalytic perspective. In T. Paloino & B. McCrady (Eds.), *Marriage and marital therapy* (pp. 25–64). New York: Brunner/Mazel.

Mondell, S., & Tyler, F. (1981). Parental competence and styles of problem solving/play behavior with children. *Developmental Psychology, 17,* 73–78.

Morris, D. (1982). Attachment and intimacy. In G. Stricker (Ed.), *Intimacy* (pp. 305–323). New York: Plenum Press.

Moskovitz, S. (1985). Longitudinal follow-up of child survivors of the Holocaust. *Journal of the American Academy of Child Psychiatry, 24,* 401–407.

Mott, F., & Moore, S. (1979). The causes of marital disruption among young American women. *Journal of Marriage and the Family, 41,* 355–365.

Mueller, D., & Cooper, P. (1986). Children of single parent families: How they fare as young adults. *Family Relations, 35,* 169–176.

Murphy, L., & Moriarty, A. (1976). *Vulnerability, coping, and growth.* New Haven: Yale University Press.

Pagelow, M. (1981). *Children in violent families: Direct and indirect victims.* Paper presented at the Research Conference on Young Children and Their Families, Anaheim, CA.

Pianta, R. C., Sroufe, L. A., & Egeland, B. (1989). Continuity and discontinuity in maternal sensitivity at 6, 24, and 42 months in a high-risk sample. *Child Development, 60,* 481–487.

Polansky, N. A., Chalmers, M. A., Williams, D. P., & Buttenweiser, E. W., (1981). *Damaged parents: An anatomy of child neglect.* Chicago: University of Chicago Press.

Quinton, D. Rutter, M., & Liddle, C. (1984). Institutional rearing, parenting difficulties, and marital support. *Psychological Medicine, 14,* 107–124.

Radke-Yarrow, M., Cummings, E. M., Kuczynski, L., & Chapman, M. (1985). Patterns of attachment in two- and three-year-olds in normal families with parental depression. *Child Development, 56,* 884–893.

Radke-Yarrow, M., & Sherman, T. (in press). Hard growing: Children who survive. In J. Rolf, A. Masten, D. Cicchetti, K. Nuechterlein, & S. Weintraub (Eds.), *Risk and protective factors in the development of psychopathology.* Cambridge, England: Cambridge University Press.

Raskin, A., Boothe, H., Reitig, N., & Schulterbrandt, J. (1971). Factor analysis of normal and depressed patients' memories of parental behavior. *Psychological Reports, 29,* 871–879.

Ricks, M. (1985). The social transmission of parental behavior: Attachment across generations. In I. Bretherton & E. Waters (Eds.), Growing points of attachment theory and research. *Monographs of the Society for Research in Child Development, 50,* (1-2 Serial No. 209), 211–227.

Robins, L. N., Schoenberg, S., Holmes, S., Ratcliff, K., Benham, A., & Works, J. (1985). Early home environment and retrospective recall: A test for concordance between siblings with or without psychiatric disorders. *American Journal of Orthopsychiatry, 55,* 27–41.

Roscoe, B., & Benaske, N. (1985). Courtship violence experienced by abused wives: Similarities in patterns of abuse. *Family Relations, 34,* 419–424.

Rubenstein, C., Shaver, P., & Peplau, A. (1979). Loneliness. *Human Nature, 2,* 59–65.

Rutter, M. (1979). Protective factors in children's responses to stress and disadvantage. In M. W. Kent & T. W. Rolf (Eds.), *Social competence in children* (pp. 49–73). Hanover, NH: University Press of New England.

Rutter, M. (1984). Continuities and discontinuities in socioemotional development. In R. Harmon & R. Emde (Eds.), *Continuities and discontinuities in development* (pp. 41–68). New York: Plenum Press.

Rutter, M. (1989). Pathways from childhood to adult life. *Journal of Child Psychology and Psychiatry, 30,* 23–51.

Rutter, M., Quinton, D., & Liddle, C. (1983). Parenting in two generations: Looking backwards and looking forwards. In N. Madge (Ed.), *Families at risk* (pp. 60–98). London: Heinemann.

Rutter, M., Yule, B., Quinton, D., Rowlands, O., Yule, W., & Berger, M. (l975). Attainment and adjustment in two geographical areas, III: Some factors accounting for area differences. *British Journal of Psychiatry, 126,* 520–533.

Sameroff, A. J., Seifer, R., & Zax, M. (1982). Early development of children at risk for emotional disorder. *Monographs of the Society for Research in Child Development, 47* (7, Serial No. 199).

Skodak, M., & Skeels, H. M. (1949). A final follow-up study of one hundred adopted children. *Journal of Genetic Psychology, 75,* 85-125.

Skolnick, A. (1986). Early attachment and personal relationships. In P. Baltes, D. Featherman, & R. Lerner (Eds.), *Lifespan development and behavior* (Vol. 7, pp. 173-206). Hillsdale, NJ: Lawrence Erlbaum Associates.

Snyder, D. (1979). Multidimensional assessment of marital satisfaction. *Journal of Marriage and the Family, 41,* 813-823.

Spitz, R. A. (1945). Hospitalism: An inquiry into the genesis of psychiatric conditions in early childhood. *Psychoanalytic Study of the Child, 1,* 53-74.

Spitz, R. A. (1946). Anaclitic depression: An inquiry into the genesis of psychiatric conditions in early childhood, II. *Psychoanalytic Study of the Child, 2,* 313-324.

Sroufe, L. A. (1983). Infant–caregiver attachment and patterns of adaptation in preschool: The roots of maladaptation and competence. In M. Perlmutter (Ed.), *Minnesota symposia on child psychology,* Vol. 16: Development and policy concerning children with special needs (pp. 41-81). Hillsdale, NJ: Lawrence Erlbaum Associates.

Sroufe, L. A., & Fleeson, J. (1986). Attachment and the construction of relationships. In W. Hartup & Z. Rubin (Eds.), *Relationships and development* (pp. 51-71). Hillsdale, NJ: Lawrence Erlbaum Associates.

Sroufe, L. A., & Fleeson, J. (1988). The coherence of family relationships. In R. A. Hinde & J. Stevenson-Hinde (Eds.), *Relationships within families: Mutual influences* (pp. 27-47). Oxford: Clarendon Press.

Sroufe, L. A., Jacobvitz, D., Mangelsdorf, S., DeAngelo, E., & Ward, M. J. (1985). Generational boundary dissolution between mothers and their preschool children: A relationship systems approach. *Child Development, 56,* 317-325.

Stevens, J. H. (1988). Social support, locus of control, and parenting in three low-income groups of mothers: Black teenagers, Black adults, and White adults. *Child Development, 59,* 635-642.

Straus, M. A., Gelles, R. J., & Steinmetz, S. K. (1980). *Behind closed doors: Violence in the American family.* New York: Anchor Press.

Sullivan, H. S. (1953). *The interpersonal theory of psychiatry.* New York: Norton.

Swann, W. B., Jr. (1983). Self-verification: Bringing social reality into harmony with the self. In J. Suls & A. G. Greenwald (Eds.), *Psychological perspectives on the self* (Vol. 2, pp. 33-66). Hillsdale, NJ: Lawrence Erlbaum Associates.

Terman, L. (1938). *Psychological factors in marital happiness.* New York: McGraw-Hill.

Tronick, E. Z., & Field, T. (Eds.). (1986). *New Directions for Child Development: Maternal Depression and Infant Disturbance* (No. 34). San Francisco: Jossey-Bass.

Tschann, J. M., Johnston, J. R., Kline, M., & Wallerstein, J. S. (1989). Family process and children's functioning during divorce. *Journal of Marriage and the Family, 51,* 431-444.

Unger, D. G., & Wandersman, L. P. (1988). The relation of family and partner support to the adjustment of adolescent mothers. *Child Development, 59,* 1056-1060.

Vondra, J. I. (1990). Sociological and ecological factors. In R. T. Ammerman & M. Hersen (Eds.), *Children at risk: An evaluation of factors contributing to child abuse and neglect* (pp. 149-170). New York: Plenum Press.

Watson, D., & Clark, L. (1984). Negative affectivity: The disposition to experience aversive emotional states. *Psychological Bulletin, 96,* 465-490.

Watson, D., & Tellegan, A. (1985). Toward a consensual structure of mood. *Psychological Bulletin, 98,* 219-235.

Weisner, T. S., Bernstein, M., Garnier, H., Rosenthal, J., & Hamilton, C. E. (1990, April). *Children in conventional and nonconventional lifestyles classified as C in attachment at 12 months: A 12-year longitudinal study.* Paper presented at the biennial meeting of the Society for Research in Child Development, Montreal.

Werner, E. E., & Smith, R. S. (1982). *Vulnerable but invincible: A longitudinal study of resilient children and youth.* New York: McGraw-Hill.

White, B. L., & Watts, J. C. (1973). *Experience and environment: Major influences on the development of the young child.* Englewood Cliffs, NJ: Prentice-Hall.

Wolkind, I., & Zajicek, E. (1983). Adult psychiatric disorder and childhood experience: The validity of retrospective recall. *British Journal of Psychiatry, 143,* 188–191.

Zahn-Waxler, C., Cummings, E. M., Ianotti, R. J.,& Radke-Yarrow, M. (1984). Young offspring of depressed parents: A population at risk for affective problems. In D. Cicchetti & K. Schneider-Rosen (Eds.), *New directions for child development: Childhood depression* (Vol. 26, pp. 81–105). San Francisco: Jossey-Bass.

Zaleski, Z., & Galkowska, M. (1978). Neuroticism and marital satisfaction. *Behavior Research and Therapy, 16,* 285–286.

Zaslow, M. J., Pedersen, F. A., Cain, R. L., Suwalsky, J. T. D., & Kramer, E. L. (1985). Depressed mood in new fathers: Associations with parent–infant interaction. *Genetic, Social, and General Psychology Monographs, 111,* 133–150.

Chapter 2

Development of Parental Beliefs

Lynn Okagaki
Purdue University

Diana Johnson Divecha
Sonoma State University

Since the early 1980s, there have been several comprehensive reviews of the parental beliefs literature (e.g., see Goodnow, 1984, 1988; Goodnow & Collins, 1990; Miller, 1988; Seginer, 1983). Rather than duplicate these efforts, we focus only on two basic issues. First we consider several factors that influence the development of parental beliefs. In particular, we look at research that provides insight into the processes that mediate between factors, such as culture and socioeconomic status, and parental beliefs. Second, we examine the relation between parental beliefs and parenting behavior.

As is much of the work represented in this volume, our theoretical framework is based on an ecological or contextual perspective of human development (e.g., Belsky, 1984; Bronfenbrenner, 1979, 1986; Laboratory of Comparative Human Cognition, 1982, 1986; Ogbu, 1981; Rogoff, 1982; Slaughter-Defoe, Nakagawa, Takanishi, & Johnson, 1990). Simply put, we believe that human development is, in part, a function of the environmental context of the individual. Drawing from Bronfenbrenner's (1979) ecology of human development theory and from Belsky's (1984) model of the multiple determinants of parenting behavior, we begin with the hypothesis that the development of parental beliefs is influenced by multiple factors within the individual's context. These factors include influences that are external to the home environment (e.g., parents' social networks and work environments) and influences within the home (e.g., characteristics of the parent, the marital relationship, and characteristics of the children). In the first section, we discuss research that illustrates the relations between several of these factors and parental beliefs. We want to show that environmental context affects development of beliefs by: (a) providing access to information, (b) shaping parents' values and ideas about how the world works and what the individual needs to do to live in that world, and (c) affecting the perceptions parents have of their own children.

DEVELOPMENT OF PARENTAL BELIEFS

Many different sources and influences on parental beliefs have been identified (see, e.g., Goodnow, 1984, 1988; Goodnow & Collins, 1990). We selected a few studies that are representative of both the variety of factors influencing parental beliefs and the different methodologies researchers have utilized in their study of sources of beliefs. In addition, we tried to focus on studies that primarily examined influences on parental beliefs and not primarily on behaviors. To organize this section, we begin with factors outside the home and work inward to characteristics of the parent and of the child.

Factors Outside the Home

Cross-Cultural Studies.   A natural starting point is to look at cultural differences in parenting beliefs and to consider how cultural context might influence the development of parental beliefs. LeVine (1974, 1988) proposed that across cultural groups, there are common, general goals that parents have for their children. These basic goals are: (a) ensuring the child's health and survival, (b) teaching the child skills that will later provide economic security for the child, and (c) developing within the child traits that are consistent with "locally defined virtue." LeVine posited a hierarchical structure to these goals, such that parents want to be assured of the child's physical survival prior to working on the skills the child will eventually need to obtain economic security, and parents give both physical and economic survival priority over cultural virtue. According to LeVine, the specific parenting strategies for obtaining these global objectives will vary across cultural groups and will be a function of the environmental context of the family. For example, in agricultural communities in which each household relies on children to help labor in the fields, fertility rates tend to be high. When unskilled child labor is highly valued and infant mortality rates are high, then mothers adopt strategies (e.g., prolonged breast-feeding and co-sleeping) to maximize the infant's chances for survival (Page & Lesthaeghe, 1981, as cited by LeVine, 1988). In contrast, in urban-industrialized settings in which infant and child mortality rates are low and the skills needed for economic security are complex, fertility rates drop. Families have fewer children, and parents focus on developing each child's cognitive and social abilities, rather than on protection from environmental hazards.

Hoffman (1988) offered an alternative theory for explaining the processes by which cultural context influences parenting. She suggested that children satisfy different needs for their parents, that cultures differ in which needs children are seen as satisfying, and that parental goals and attitudes are a function of the needs children satisfy. Using data from a cross-national study that included parents from Indonesia, Korea, the Philippines, Singapore, Taiwan, Thailand, Turkey, and the United States, she found that the two most commonly cited needs that children meet for their parents are economic utility and the need for love and affection. In countries in which children tend to be valued for their economic utility (e.g., Turkey), parents are more likely to want their children to be obedient and less likely to want them to be independent. In countries in which children are valued primarily because of the love and affection they give to the parent (e.g., the United States), parents desired their children to have personable qualities, such as being warm, outgoing, cheerful, and good natured.

Hoffman's theory suggests that general cultural values (i.e., the way a cultural group views children) will influence parents' attitudes toward and goals for their children. A series of studies by Hess and his colleagues (Hess, Kashiwagi, Azuma, Price, & Dickson, 1980) considered differences in parental beliefs between Japanese and U.S. mothers. The researchers anticipated differences between the groups based on differences in general cultural values. In Japan, there is a stronger emphasis on community and conformity to the group identity. According to Kojima (1991), the Japanese conception of ''self'' is embedded within interpersonal and social contexts, and there is a strong, pervasive cultural value to ''know one's role, to accept one's place in society, and to work hard in order to perform faithfully one's assigned task'' (p. 16). In contrast, in the United States, individuality and independence are highly valued. Hess and his colleagues hypothesized that these differences in general cultural values would be reflected in parental beliefs and in children's behaviors.

Prior to their first-born child's fourth birthday, mothers in both countries were given a set of items related to academic skills, verbal assertiveness, obedience or compliance, social courtesy, emotional maturity, instrumental independence (practical skills), and social skills, and were asked to indicate whether they thought a child should master the skill before age 4, sometime between ages 4 and 6, or after age 6. Consistent with the differences in broader cultural values, the researchers found that Japanese mothers expected their children to be emotionally mature, obedient, and courteous at an earlier age than did U.S. mothers. In contrast, U.S. mothers expected their children to be verbally assertive and to have social skills with peers at an earlier age.

Within the United States, ethnic minority families represent many different cultural heritages. One cultural value that is commonly held among many minority groups is a strong emphasis on familism and group identity (see Harrison, Wilson, Pine, Chan, & Buriel, 1990; Laosa, 1980, 1982; Murillo, 1971;

Tharp, 1989). Consider the following descriptions of one Hispanic and one Asian group:

> For the Chicano, the family is likely to be the single most important social unit in life. It is usually at the core of his thinking and behavior and is the center from which his view of the rest of the world extends. Even with respect to identification the Chicano *self* is likely to take second place after the family. (Murillo, 1971, p. 102)

Similarly, Asian Americans emphasize interdependence and maintaining social relationships (Harrison et al., 1990; Spence, 1985). Writing about Khmer refugees, one of the most recent immigrant groups to the United States, Welaratna (1988) observed:

> Village social values emphasized cooperation rather than competition. Cooperation was essential for a rural subsistence economy that did not have modern mechanized agricultural methods. If people did not work together, irrigated rice could not be grown. . . . Family members generally helped one another by providing both emotional support and goods and services. (p. 21)

In contrast to these cultural values, Anglo-American culture emphasizes the individual and individual achievement (e.g., Kessen, 1979; Triandis et al., 1986; Triandis, Bontempo, Villareal, Asai, & Lucca, 1988). Spence (1985) wrote:

> individualism . . . the belief that each of us is an entity separate from every other and from the group and as such is endowed with natural rights. These beliefs in individuals and individual rights are part of our [American] heritage and are incorporated into our basic sense of self. (p. 1288)

In our own research on parental beliefs (Okagaki, Sternberg, & Divecha, 1990), we expected that variation in cultural heritages would lead to different childrearing goals and different conceptions of intelligence. We asked parents how important they believe it is for parents to develop specific traits and skills in their children. For example, how important is it that "parents should help their first graders set goals and work toward those goals"? These beliefs were divided into four categories: three scales focused on autonomous behaviors (i.e., problem-solving skills, creativity, and practical skills) and one scale considered developing conformity to external standards. The parents in our study consisted of four groups of immigrants—Cambodians, Filipinos, Mexicans, and Vietnamese—and two groups of parents who had been born and raised in the United States—Anglo Americans and Mexican Americans.

For U.S.-born parents, developing independent behaviors, as defined by the items in our scales, was more important than developing conforming behaviors. In contrast, for all four immigrant groups, developing conformity to external standards was rated as the most important behavior to cultivate in their children.

Besides cultural differences, one explanation for this finding could be that immigrant parents view conformity as part of learning how to adapt to a new culture. This explanation seems particularly plausible when we recall that the Mexican-American parents, who were all born and educated in the states, share common cultural backgrounds with the Mexican immigrant parents, but were very much like the Anglo-American parents on these childrearing goals. However, not all differences could be explained by a native-born versus foreign-born distinction. As described hereafter, when we examined parents' conceptions of intelligence, we found that the Mexican-American parents were more similar to the Mexican parents than to the Anglo-American parents in their conception of intelligence.

We asked parents to rate how important specific traits were to their conception of an intelligent first-grade child. Our central question was whether parents' beliefs primarily emphasized cognitive skills, a traditionally Western view of intelligence (e.g., Binet & Simon, 1916; Horn & Cattell, 1966; Thurstone, 1938), or if noncognitive aspects were equally central to their views of intelligence (e.g., social skills, motivation, and practical school-related skills). Several non-Western studies of laypeople's implicit theories of intelligence have found, for example, a social dimension to be important to people's conceptions of intelligence (e.g., Azuma & Kashiwagi, 1987; Dasen, 1984; Serpell, 1984; Wober, 1974). In our study, we found that only Anglo-American parents rated the cognitive skills as being more important to their conception of intelligence than the noncognitive traits were. For all of the minority parents, noncognitive aspects were as important, if not more important than cognitive abilities to parents' views of intelligence. Of particular interest were the Mexican immigrant and Mexican-American parents, for whom the importance of social skills was especially salient. Among the three noncognitive aspects, the average ratings for social skills (e.g., "plays well with other children") were equal to the average ratings for motivation and practical school-related skills. That is, the overall importance of noncognitive traits was not simply because the two more academically related scales (i.e., motivation and practical school skills) were rated highly, but rather social skills were relatively central to Hispanic parents' conceptions of intelligence. This finding seems to fit well with the Mexican cultural emphasis on cooperation and group identity.

The research on cultural values and parental beliefs indicate that cultural context does influence the way parents think about children, their parenting goals and values. What we would like to see is more research that explicitly attempts to link parental beliefs to general cultural values or to examine the ways in which cultural context might influence parenting, rather than simply comparing parents from two cultural groups and finding that their beliefs differ.

Goodnow and Collins (1990) suggested that developmental psychologists could push parental research forward by exploiting, for example, concepts and methodologies used by anthropologists in studies of *cultural models*. Cultural models are sets of beliefs held by a group of people about the way the world works. The social nature of these beliefs means that holding these beliefs is not merely a matter of logical reasoning, but rather, there is a social demand to adhere to them. Using a cultural model framework, one might look for multiple ideas addressing a specific issue (e.g., "too many cooks spoil the broth" and "many hands make work light"). The existence of multiple perspectives or even contradictory views within a group might suggest situations in which parents are more apt to flexibly change their positions or be prepared to adopt new information. Designing research that describes parents' multiple beliefs about an issue as opposed to categorizing parents along single dimensions could lead to finding better links between beliefs and behaviors, to models of change in individual beliefs, and to explanations of change in parenting among segments of a population. Our point is that there are theoretical frameworks and methodologies that could help developmental psychologists get beyond simple comparisons of beliefs held by parents in one group versus another.

Socioeconomic Status.   Besides culture, the major macrolevel influence on human development that has received the attention of behavioral scientists is socioeconomic status (SES). More than simply indicating how much money or education someone has, SES is an index of the types of experiences and opportunities to which the individual has access. How does SES affect development? Seminal research in this area has been done by Kohn (1963, 1969), who posited that: (a) parents from different social classes differ in their parenting practices because they hold different values for their children, and (b) these values resulted from social class differences in the conditions of life experienced by the parents. In particular, Kohn focused on conditions in the father's work setting and demonstrated that the degree to which the father's work setting allowed self-direction (e.g., autonomy, imagination, curiosity, self-control) was related to the degree of importance that fathers placed on self-direction versus conformity (e.g., being neat, obedient, getting along with others) in their children. Kohn argued that all parents want their children to succeed in life, but that parents differ in what traits or behaviors they think their children need to succeed. In particular, if the father's work setting required him to be autonomous and self-directed, then the father tended to value such traits in his children. On the other hand, if the father's work setting emphasized following explicit instructions and orderliness, then the father encouraged similar behaviors in his children. Kohn's research illustrates our contention that environmental context shapes the ideas parents have about how the world works and what skills and abilities one needs to survive in the world.

Later work has shown that social class is also related to other types of parental beliefs (e.g., Luster & Kain, 1987; Schaefer & Edgerton, 1985; Segal, 1985). Schaefer and Edgerton found that conformity and authoritarian beliefs are negatively associated with SES, and in turn, that these beliefs are negatively related to children's cognitive performance. Using data from a national sample of 3,000 parents, Luster and Kain (1987) reported that perceptions of parental efficacy (i.e., beliefs about the degree to which parents can influence their children's development) were negatively related to SES indices of education and income. In addition, perceptions of parental efficacy were related to beliefs about parenting behaviors. High efficacy parents were more likely than low efficacy parents to indicate that the amount of love and affection they give their children and the example they set have an important influence on how the child develops. In contrast, low efficacy parents were more likely to choose discipline as one of two parenting behaviors that has the most influence on the child.

Both Kohn's research and the research it has motivated (e.g., Burns, Homel, & Goodnow, 1984; Luster & Rhoades, 1989; Luster, Rhoades, & Haas, 1989) illustrate that broad macrolevel factors like SES can be thoughtfully examined to expose the processes through which macrolevel variables might influence parenting. As Bronfenbrenner and Crouter (1982) argued, explanations of developmental outcomes that are based solely on differences in SES factors, such as parent income or education, have limited use because they do not provide insight into the processes that lead to group differences.

Work.   Following Kohn's research, interest in the effects of work on family roles has increased in conjunction with the increase in dual-worker families in the United States. Work does more than impinge on one's time and provide financial resources for one's family. Work also affects the experiences and the ideas to which one is exposed. Crouter (1984) conducted an extensive field study that examined the effects of participative work on the employee's family and community roles. In contrast to typical blue-collar work situations, under participative management, the employees are involved in decision making and problem solving at all levels. Crouter interviewed workers in a manufacturing plant in which workers were divided into small work teams. Each team functioned as a decision-making unit monitoring their own work performance and handling all sorts of problems—including hiring and firing of personnel on the team. Team meetings were held to discuss issues, and all team members were expected to participate in the meetings by expressing their opinions, observations, and ideas. In addition, workers were given special training to help develop their communication and group problem-solving skills. According to Crouter, workers—both men and women—reported using the "team meeting" concept at home and using communication skills that had been learned during work training sessions. For example, when asked how the job had affected his personal life, one father responded: "The thing that comes to mind is kids. I have a 16-year-old son and I use some of the things we do at work with him instead of yelling. We listen better here, we let people tell their side'' (p. 81). Crouter suggested participative work may help parents develop more effective parenting strategies and skills.

In short, work settings can affect the goals or values that parents have for their children (e.g., Kohn, 1969) and can increase the skills and strategies that adults bring to their parenting roles (e.g., Crouter, 1984). Work can also influence parents' perceptions of their children, and that influence can be positive, as well as negative. Reviewing the research on maternal employment, Bronfenbrenner and Crouter (1982) observed that although maternal employment appeared to have positive effects on daughters (e.g., daughters had more positive beliefs about women's roles), the effects on sons seemed to be less beneficial, and in some cases, perhaps negative (e.g., maternal employment was associated with lower academic achievement among boys from middle-income families). Bronfenbrenner and his colleagues (Bronfenbrenner, Alvarez, & Henderson, 1984) proposed that maternal perceptions of the child could be the mediating factor between maternal employment and child outcomes. They hypothesized that ''a mother would, from early on, view her children differently as a joint function of her employment status and the sex of the child'' (p. 1363). They looked at three levels of maternal employment (i.e., full time, part time, or not employed) and mothers' perceptions of their 3-year-old children, based on data collected during an open-ended interview in which mothers were asked to describe their children. Using maternal education as an index of SES, they found a significant three-way interaction between work status, gender of child, and maternal education. Specifically, for daughters, if the mothers had a high school education or less, then mothers who were not employed presented the most favorable descriptions of their daughters; whereas mothers who were employed full time were the least positive. However, if the mothers had more than a high school education, then there was a positive relation between the amount of time mothers worked outside the home and positive statements mothers made about the child. The mothers who described their daughters most positively were those who were employed full time.

In contrast, regardless of the mothers' education level, mothers who worked full time were the least positive about their sons. For these mothers, ''praise for self-reliance was replaced with complaints about noncompliance and aggressiveness'' (p. 1366). Interestingly, the most positive picture of preschool boys were given by mothers who worked part time. The researchers suggested an explanation based on the costs and benefits of working. Working part time may benefit the mother in terms of her self-esteem and social development; but the cost in terms of time and energy is not so great that it takes away from her parenting role. For example, ''I want control over how my kids are raised so I feel it's important to be here most of the time now. The time I spend working is time for myself. It saves my sanity. It gives balance to life'' (p. 1374).

Alvarez (1985) took the project a step further by specifically asking whether the effects of work on parental perceptions are a function of factors such as: (a) *role strain* or the conflict mothers feel between home and work responsibilities, (b) the degree of satisfaction the mother expresses about her work, (c) whether or not the mother expresses gains in her self-esteem or personal autonomy because of her work situation, and (d) mothers' reasons for working (i.e., purely by personal choice, partly for financial reasons, or purely for financial reasons). Focusing on mothers who work either part time or full time, he found that motivation for working, role strain, and gains in self-worth all contribute to working mothers' perceptions of their children. For example, as might be expected, mothers who expressed feelings of role conflict between home and work responsibilities had less positive perceptions of their children. In contrast, working mothers who find that outside employment enhances their self-esteem, have more positive perceptions of their children.

Building on the earlier finding by Bronfenbrenner et al. (1984) that maternal employment may differentially impact maternal perceptions of daughters versus sons, Alvarez found a complex relation among gender of child, education, and motivation for working. Generally speaking, mothers of girls and better educated mothers expressed more positive comments about their children than their counterparts did. However, when mothers were working purely from personal choice, perceptions of sons were more positive than perceptions of daughters. In contrast, if mothers worked because of financial reasons, perceptions of daughters were more positive than perceptions of sons. Education attenuated the negative effects of motivation on mothers' positive perceptions of their children, but more for daughters than for sons. That is, for mothers who worked partly or completely for financial reasons, having some college education significantly increased mothers' positive perceptions of their daughters and marginally increased positive perceptions of sons. An important caveat to these findings is the necessity of considering the family's economic situation, and Alvarez acknowledged that maternal employment and the psychological implications of work for the mothers have to be considered within the context of the family's economic situation. Nonetheless, his research demonstrates that the psychological "costs and benefits" of employment to the mother are associated with the way mothers think about their children, and that the effect of maternal employment on mothers' beliefs is not the same for all women.

Greenberger and Goldberg (1989, p. 26) were also interested in identifying the processes that mediate the relation between work and parental perceptions of children. They explored the relations among parents' commitments to work and to parenting and parents' perceptions of their children using questionnaire data from about 300 men and women. Two aspects of commitment to work were measured: (a) the amount of time devoted to work and (b) the importance or salience of work in their lives (e.g., "When I meet people, one of the first things I tell them about myself is the sort of work I do;" "I want to advance to the top of my career, even if it involves some costs in other areas of my life''). Commitment to parenting was also assessed in two ways: (a) importance or salience of parenting in one's life (e.g., ''Being a parent is important to me, but isn't central in how I define myself'' [reverse-scored]; ''I give up personal pleasures, such as extra sleep or socializing with friends, to be with my child'') and (b) the degree to which one believes in one's special abilities to meet the needs of one's child (e.g., ''More than any other adult, I can meet my child's needs best;'' ''I am naturally better at keeping my child safe than any other person''). In addition, they included two measures of parents' perceptions of the child: (a) one focusing on positive behaviors (e.g., ''Is helpful and cooperative; tries to comfort other children when they are upset; likes to explore by himself or herself in new surroundings'') and (b) one assessing behavioral problems (e.g., ''Tends to fight, hit, take toys when playing with other children; is rather high-strung, tense, or anxious; . . . is unhappy, sad, or depressed'').

The data from the questionnaires indicated that work differentially affects mothers and fathers. The first level of analysis consisted of zero-order correlations among the major variables in the study. They found, for example, that neither commitment to work nor total hours worked was related to fathers' commitment to parenting. However, although total hours worked was unrelated to mothers' commitment to parenting, there was a small, negative relation between mothers' commitment to work and their commitment to parenting ($r = -.22, p < .001$). Similarly, fathers' commitment to work was unrelated to their perceptions of their children. In contrast, for mothers, commitment to work was positively related to their positive perceptions of their children and negatively related to their perceptions of their children's behavioral problems (in both cases, the relations were small, but significant). For both mothers and fathers, commitment to parenting was positively related to positive perceptions of their children and negatively related to perceptions of behavioral problems.

The zero-order correlations provided some indication that work and parenting roles may be more closely linked for mothers than for fathers. Recognizing, however, that commitment to work and commitment to parenting do not occur in isolation in working parents, Greenberger and Goldberg (1989) did a second level of analysis in which they looked at patterns of parents' commitments by crossing two levels of work commitment with two levels of parental commitment using a median split on both scales (i.e., low/high work commitment vs. low/high parental commitment). They found that fathers' patterns of commitment to work and parenting were unrelated to their perceptions of their children. Moreover, neither the gender of the child nor the interaction between commitment pattern and the gender of the child were related to fathers' perceptions. For women, commitment type was related to mothers' perceptions of their children, but the gender of the child and the interaction between the gender of the child and commitment pattern were not. More specifically, mothers who were highly committed to both work and parenting had more positive perceptions of their children than women of the other three pattern types.

When the two measures of work commitment and the two measures of parental commitment, along with the gender of the child, were used to predict perceptions of the child, parental commitment was much more important than commitment to work for both men and women. With all five variables in the model, only the parental commitment was significant for fathers. For mothers, exclusive care beliefs, parental commitment, and work commitment were significantly related to positive perceptions of the child, and only the parental commitment scale was significantly related to negative perceptions of the child. Because the gender of the child was not significant, Greenberger and Goldberg (1989) suggested that high parental commitment may override any potential negative impact that working full time may have on the relationships between mothers and sons (Alvarez, 1985; Bronfenbrenner et al., 1984). For this reason, they cautioned that the small, negative relation between mothers' commitment to work and their commitment to parenting should not be overlooked. That is, if high commitment to parenting may attenuate any negative effects of high work involvement, then finding a negative relation between work commitment and parenting commitment is important.

The data from the last two studies are particularly useful in that they take us beyond a simplistic view of categorizing parents as working versus nonworking. Working outside the home is related to parents' perceptions of their children and parents' commitment to parenting. But how does this happen? In the Alvarez study and in the Greenberger and Goldberg study, the researchers looked at the psychological function of work in parents' lives. Like the Crouter study, which shows the transfer of specific skills from work to home, these studies illustrate how an aspect of work—namely, the psychological importance of one's work role—relates to parenting. In addition, they indicate that the relations between work and parenting are very complex and need further research. Two potentially emerging themes can be drawn from this research. First, work may influence parents' perceptions of their children by affecting parents' general well-being. In some cases, working outside the home builds up the parent's emotional reserves and makes the parent better able to meet the demands of parenting. Parents who are psychologically supported are more likely to have positive perceptions of their child. In other cases, work drains parents' psychological and physical reserves. Parents are left with less resources for parenting and are more likely to express negative evaluations of their children. Second, work may affect maternal perceptions of children by giving parents different images of potential adult roles for their children (just as Kohn, 1963, 1969, found that fathers' occupational roles were related to fathers' childrearing goals). Women who have found satisfying and fulfilling

occupational roles may have more positive perceptions of their daughters because they can imagine more positive ways in which their daughters can achieve
and can utilize their characteristics. Thus, the strong-willed daughter can be
viewed as having the confidence and assertiveness to handle challenging career
roles, and not simply as someone who might have difficulties and frustrations
meeting the demands of a traditional at-home role. Besides exploring these
issues in more depth, future research might address the ways in which parents' commitments and perceptions change over time and factors that might
explain the differential impact of work on fathers and mothers. Similarly, there
is a need for more research on factors that might explain the differential impact of parental work on sons versus daughters.

Influence of Friends and Neighbors.   Parents also get exposed to new ideas
about parenting and child development through their informal social networks.
Cohen (1981) did a fascinating ethnographic study of a middle-class housing
estate in Great Britain that examines ways in which mothers' beliefs and attitudes are influenced through participation in informal neighborhood discussions. Cohen described the transition that working-class parents made into what
is called the new middle class in Great Britain. Access into this new middle
class was obtained through career advancement by the fathers into management and professional positions. For most of these men, their new positions
required a great deal of travel, both in long daily commutes and in extended
travel to other parts of the country. This new dimension to their work life required reorganization of the home life and meant that their families began to
develop a lifestyle that was very different from the one in which the parents
had been raised. With fathers away for extended periods of time, daily care
of home and children rested with the mothers. Women's lives and attitudes
changed as they conformed to the neighborhood standards of what constitutes
being a good wife and mother. Cohen (1981) found that:

> Entire morning coffee or afternoon teas would revolve around the question of
> when a small child would be ready to learn to read. Mothers would volunteer
> information and theories based on their own experience, which might later be
> put into practice by others, who would report on their own success. Many other
> childrearing skills were acquired in this way . . . (p. 277)

Cohen reported that mothers' beliefs about discipline, education, children's
chores, and general family life were modified and, in some cases, radically
changed as mothers casually exchanged ideas with each other at teas, coffees,
and Tupperware parties. Cohen provided a unique look at the way informal
social networks are used by parents to obtain information about childrearing.
     In their critique of research on sources of parents' ideas, Goodnow and Col-
lins (1990) called for researchers not only to identify the source of new ideas

but to examine when new information is incorporated into parental belief systems. This encouragement for deeper analyses into the acquisition, modification, and development of parental beliefs also applies to the research in the next section where we discuss the influence of formal psychological theories on parents' beliefs.

Advice From Experts.   Medical practitioners, behavioral scientists, social workers, clergy, and parents themselves do extensive research, theorizing, and writing about child development and parenting. Does this information influence parental beliefs? In the late 1950s, Bronfenbrenner (1958) presented an insightful analysis of changes in parenting practices in the United States in his meta-analysis of studies comparing parenting in working-class and middle-class families from 1930 to 1955. Although his analysis did not directly address the link between parenting and experts' advice, he suggested among his conclusions that, ''Shifts in the pattern of infant care—especially on the part of middle-class mothers—show a striking correspondence to the changes in practices advocated in successive editions of U.S. Children's Bureau bulletins and similar sources of expert opinion'' (p. 424).

Twenty years later, Clarke-Stewart (1978) conducted a series of studies that examined parental exposure to ''expert'' advice on childrearing. Beginning with a survey of Chicago parents, she found that 94% of the parents reported having read at least one child-care article from a popular magazine or one child-care book. The parents in the survey who were most likely to read a book when they encountered a childrearing problem were parents who had little contact with their own parents or relatives. These parents were also most likely to use a babysitter for supplementary child care, rather than relying on a relative. According to the survey results, the parents who read the most about parenting and claimed to be the most influenced by what they read, were younger, more highly educated, and more worried about whether or not they were doing the best things for their children. About half of the parents who participated in the survey were under 40 years of age and half were over 40. Clarke-Stewart divided the sample according to the decade (e.g., 1940s, 1950s, etc.) during which the parents had children who were under 10 years of age. Her analyses indicated that parents in the 1970s were reading more about child care than previous parents had. This finding was further substantiated by examining publication data on child-care books. Whereas 32 new child-care books had been published between 1960 and 1964, 148 new child-care books had been published between 1970 and 1974.

Clarke-Stewart also reported that as part of a study on child-care arrangements, 104 Chicago mothers of preschoolers were asked how much popular literature on child care they read. All of these mothers had read at least one article or book on parenting, and 44% had read more than five books.

Following the initial survey, Clarke-Stewart (1978) conducted a survey of people checking out child-care books from branches of the Chicago Public Library. Questionnaires were distributed when the books were checked out, and the parents were directed to answer the questions about why they were reading the book before reading the book and the questions about their reactions to the book after reading the book. The most commonly cited reason for reading the book was "to get ideas and information about child development" (p. 366). Nearly all of the readers thought the books were useful and that they had learned something from the books. Although Clarke-Stewart's data did not give us specific information about changes in parental beliefs, the data certainly indicate that parents—particularly those who have less contact with their own families—are turning to popular books and articles on parenting for advice.

Another interesting study of the impact of experts on parental beliefs was conducted by Ninio (1979) with low and high SES mothers in Israel. The mothers who participated in this study had either a 1-year-old or a 3-year-old child. They were asked questions about child development and parenting, and they were asked where they obtained information about child development. With respect to mothers' developmental timetables, the two groups of mothers had similar beliefs about physical development, but high SES mothers believed that cognitive skills were acquired earlier than did low SES mothers. Ninio suggested that this difference could be, in part, due to the information parents receive about child development. The majority of mothers in both groups indicated that one should seek advice from medical professionals, and well-baby clinics are a universal health-care service in Israel. Ninio suggested that advice from health-care professionals tended to address only physical development and equalized the mothers' expectations about physical development, but not cognitive development. More high SES mothers than low SES mothers indicated that one should seek advice from books on child development, which generally address issues related to both physical and cognitive development.

These studies provide some evidence that one source of parental beliefs is experts' opinions on childrearing. What they do not indicate, however, is what specific information parents may be incorporating into their belief systems and if and how this information actually affects parenting practice. More attention needs to be given to multiple ideas about particular issues and to the consistency and rigidity of parents' beliefs. Goodnow and Collins (1990) cited an experimental study by Triana and Rodrigo (1989) in which parents were first identified as having a more environmental-centered or more child-centered view of development. Although parents were familiar with both views, they found it easier to read and comprehend information that agreed with their point of view. Creative efforts along these lines could provide greater insight into the acquisition and modification of parental beliefs.

Within-Home Influences

To this point, we have considered several factors outside the home that can influence parents' beliefs, values, and attitudes toward parenting. Now we want to look at how within-home influences can affect parental beliefs.

Characteristics of the Parent. Various characteristics of the parent have been related to parenting beliefs—for example, developmental history of parent (see Vondra & Belsky, this volume), maternal depression (e.g., Cutrona & Troutman, 1986; Donovan & Leavitt, 1989), and gender of parent (e.g., Russell & Russell, 1982; see also Goodnow, 1984). We focus on age and discuss research by Reis (1988) and Rossi (1980).

Reis considered the relation between maternal age and parenting beliefs. Her focus was on the adolescent mother. In one of the few studies of maternal beliefs that used a relatively large sample (696 mothers), Reis compared young adolescent (16 years or younger), older adolescent (17 to 19 years), and adult (20 years and older) mothers' attitudes toward childrearing and their knowledge of developmental milestones. She found that young adolescent mothers had more undesirable attitudes toward childrearing than did older mothers, and that although none of the groups was very knowledgeable about when infants should be able to perform certain skills (e.g., eat with fork and spoon, say first real words, obey the word "no"), younger adolescents were typically less accurate than older mothers were.

Rossi considered the relation between parental perceptions and the physiological and psychological meanings of age. Rossi's study is particularly provocative for two reasons: (a) she asked the question: What is it about "age" that makes a difference in maternal parenting? and (b) she took a life-span approach and considered cohort effects.

The participants in the study were mothers who had at least one early adolescent child between 12 and 16 years of age. The mothers were 36 to 51 years old. Rossi's interest in the relationships between early adolescents and older mothers is captured in her descriptions of the "winding up" adolescent embarking on "a great deal of physical growth and change, erratic levels of endocrine secretion, and major transitions in [their] social ecology" (p. 142) and the "winding down" parent, "particularly older parents in their forties who are experiencing their own endocrine irregularity and change, a whole range of new manifestations of aging in their bodies—skin, hair, teeth, vision, body shape, muscle tone, daily rhythm, sleep needs" (p. 142). Parental perceptions of children's adolescence as being a difficult period for parent–child relations are usually interpreted in light of the changes occurring within the child and the child's social world. Rossi suggested that the parents' own development may bring about additional stress that contributes to the tension between the emerging adolescent and the aging adult.

For the most part, mothers' perceptions of how difficult it is to parent a child increases as the child grows older. The only exception was that 5- to 8-year-olds were seen as being easier to parent than 2- to 4-year-olds were. There was a general trend indicating that the older the mother is at first birth, the more difficult she perceives parenting to be at all stages of the child's life. However, independent of chronological age, psychological aspects of age also affected perceptions of parenting. For instance, women who wanted to be younger felt it was more difficult to raise a teen-ager than did women who were more satisfied with their current age.

Beyond the biological and psychological aspects of age contributing to differences between older and younger mothers in the problems they have with their teen-agers, Rossi suggested that some of the differences may reflect cohort differences between the mothers in her sample. That is, she was distinctly placing the parenting within its historical context. The majority of the younger mothers were in their 20s during the 1960s and may have participated in more experimentation with drugs and sex than the older mothers did. In fact, the younger mothers rated themselves as having been more unconventional during their own adolescence than did the older mothers. In contrast, many of the older mothers already had teen-agers during the mid-to-late 1960s. Consequently, it was their children, and not themselves, who participated in that historical transition in which there was a loosening of behavioral standards. Rossi found that the older the mother, the more criticism she received from her early adolescent (e.g., for being old-fashioned, for not dressing right, for talking about what things were like when she was a teen-ager), the less *limit testing* the child engaged in (e.g., smoking cigarettes, experimenting with drugs, sex, and alcohol), but the more disapproval the mother expressed for limit-testing behavior. Rossi suggested that differences between older and younger mothers in their responses to limit-testing behaviors may, in part, reflect cohort differences in what teen-age life was like for the mothers themselves. Although speculative, Rossi's research is a reminder that parenting beliefs can be influenced by the sociohistorical context in which the parenting occurs and by the sociohistorical context in which the parents themselves were raised.

Marital Relationship.   Within the family context, the marital relationship can influence parental attitudes toward parenting and toward the child. For example, research on child abuse has indicated that parents who had been abused or neglected during their childhoods were more likely to provide poor parenting for their own children. However, adults who had been abused as children, but had subsequently established supportive marital relationships, were less likely to repeat the poor parenting behaviors (e.g., Hunter & Kilstrom, 1979; Quinton & Rutter, 1988).

The importance of the marital relationship on parental attitudes has also been examined within nonabusing families. For instance, Cox, Owen, Lewis, and Henderson (1989) demonstrated that the marital relationship affects parental attitudes toward the infant while controlling for the psychological well-being of the parent. They measured the quality of the marital relationship (i.e., the closeness of the relationship and the intimacy of the communication between partners) prior to the birth of the first child, the psychological well-being of the parents prior to the birth, and attitudes and behaviors toward the infant when the infant was 3 months old. In a hierarchical regression, entering psychological well-being first, they found a significant interaction between quality of the marital relationship and gender of the child for mothers. Specifically, for mothers with daughters, the quality of the marital relationship was positively related both to mothers' attitudes toward the infant and the parenting role and to the warmth and sensitivity the mothers' demonstrated toward their daughters. Quality of the marital relationship had less of an effect on mothers' attitudes and behaviors toward their infant sons. For fathers, the quality of the marital relationship was positively related to fathers' attitudes toward their infants and toward their parenting role, regardless of the child's gender. However, the marital relationship did not significantly contribute to explaining the variance in fathers' behaviors toward their infants after psychological well-being had been accounted for. In general, parents who have supportive marital relationships have more positive attitudes toward their infants and display more warmth and sensitivity toward their infants than do parents who have marriages that are less close and less intimate.

What is not explained in the Cox et al. (1989) study is why supportive marital relationships are associated with more positive attitudes toward infants. It is plausible that people who have the skills to develop stronger relationships are also better equipped to develop a relationship with their children. Alternatively, as the researchers suggest, the emotional support gained from the marital relationship can leave the parent in a stronger position to provide warm, nurturing care for the child because the mother's emotional needs are being met by her spouse. Although in this study, after psychological well-being had been controlled for, the quality of the marital relationship did not predict fathers' behaviors toward the infant, other studies indicated ways in which the marital relationship is linked to fathers' parenting (e.g., Dickstein & Parke, 1988).

Elsewhere in this volume, Robert Emery and Michelle Tuer extensively review the research on the effects of the marital relationship on parenting. Before we leave marital relationships and turn to ways in which the child affects parental beliefs, we want to bridge these two areas by suggesting that consideration of the influence of marital relationships on parental beliefs and of the child on parental beliefs should only be the beginning of research on the ways in which family interactions affect both parent and child outcomes. Just as a husband–wife relationship may directly or indirectly alter the nature of a parent–child relationship, a parent–child relationship may impact the husband–wife relationship. Similarly, sibling relationships and extended family members need to enter into the equation. As we expand the relationships that are examined vis-à-vis parental beliefs, we should also broaden the scope of beliefs that are considered to go beyond the current emphasis on beliefs about individual children, childrearing, and child development to include, for example, ideas about family life, family goals, and balancing of individual goals among family members.

Characteristics of the Child. In Bell's (1979) classic paper on the reciprocal influences of parents and children, he argued that scientists must consider the ways in which children affect the behavior of their parents. In this section, we consider several studies that demonstrate the effects that children have on their parents' beliefs. We examine the effects of children's gender, age, and achievement on parental beliefs.

Undoubtedly, one of the first characteristics that most people notice about a child is whether the child is a boy or a girl. The gender of the child can affect the way in which the child's behavior is interpreted and the expectations the parent has for the child. For example, when parents describe their newborn infants, boys are more likely to be perceived as being strong, firm, and alert. Newborn girls are described as being small, soft, and inattentive (Rubin, Provenzano, & Luria, 1974). Condry and Condry (1976) asked college students to rate the emotional response of an infant to four different stimuli. The infant was identified as a "boy" for some subjects and as a "girl" to other subjects. The researchers found that the identified gender affected ratings of the infant's emotional responses. For example, when the infant is shown a jack-in-the-box, the infant first shows a slight startled reaction and then upon successive presentations, the infant becomes more agitated and finally cries. A female infant is perceived as showing fear, whereas a male infant is thought to be showing anger.

In general, parents' goals for their children depend on the child's gender. For example, parents believe that achievement is more important for sons than it is for daughters (Block, 1973). Similarly, in a survey of 1,259 mothers and 356 fathers, Hoffman (1977) found that parents are more likely to want their sons, rather than their daughters, to be ambitious, intelligent, independent, and hardworking. Parental aspirations for daughters were more likely to include being kind and loving, being attractive, having a good marriage, and being a good parent.

A second basic characteristic of the child is the child's age. One might certainly expect that parental beliefs might change as their children get older. Knight (1981) interviewed 47 couples about their parenting goals, beliefs about child development, and perceptions of parental efficacy (i.e., how much influence do they think they have over their children's development). Parents were divided into two groups based on whether or not at least one of their children was already in school. Parents with older children were much more likely than were parents of younger children to say that genetic factors are most important in determining whether or not a child is bright (70% vs. 36%, respectively). Conversely, parents of younger children were more likely to say that contribution parents make towards their children's intellectual development is primarily environmental, rather than hereditary (81% parents of younger children vs. 39% parents of older children). Along the same lines, parents of younger children were more likely to believe that they have a lot of influence over their children's development than were parents of older children (62% vs. 37%, respectively). Finally, parents of older children were more likely to believe that effort is very important in determining how well their child is doing than were parents of younger children (60% vs. 35%). Although Knight (1981) acknowledged that differences between the two groups of parents could be due to factors such as the age of the parent (parents of older children were slightly older than parents of younger children) or the amount of experience parents have in parenting, she argued that as children grow older and are exposed to more influences outside the home, the parents' level of influence decreases. Parents also have more opportunities (e.g., through children's report cards) to compare their child's abilities against other children's abilities. Parents may come to see their child's performance as being more a function of factors within the child (e.g., heredity and effort) than of factors external to the child (e.g., parenting).

Finally, parents' beliefs are also affected by the child's achievements, that is, what the child does and how well the child does it. For example, parents have different expectations about how well their children will do in school. Entwisle and Hayduk (1978, 1981) wondered if children's actual school performance would affect parents' expectations over time. Prior to the first marking period in first grade, parents were asked to rate their child's general ability to do school work and to indicate what grades they thought their child would receive. Middle-class parents were fairly accurate in their predictions of what grades their children would receive. However, Entwisle and Hayduk concluded that parents' grade expectations were based more on parents' knowledge of grade distributions than of specific knowledge about their child's ability. For working-class parents, the grade expectations were overly optimistic and reflected neither knowledge about their child's ability nor general knowledge about grade distributions. Parents' expectations of grades for subsequent marking periods during first and second grade indicated that their expectations had been modified by the children's previous report card markings. This observation led Entwisle and Hayduk to conclude that it is not that children are living up to their parents' expectations of their school performance, but that parents' expectations are shaped by children's actual school performance.

In short, several different aspects of the individual child can affect, change, or modify parents' beliefs. Other research shows that the number of children can also affect parents' beliefs. For example, Knight (1983, as cited by Goodnow, 1984) found that parents with one or two children put more emphasis on hereditary influences on development than do parents who have three or more children. What we see in all of this research are the reciprocal effects of parents and children on each other. Just as parents influence children's development, the children themselves affect the development of their parents' beliefs.

Summary

The research presented in this section indicates that multiple factors influence the development of parents' beliefs. Many of these studies also give us insight into how these factors affect beliefs. We suggested three processes that mediate between these factors and parental beliefs. First, parents' beliefs are modified when they receive new ideas about parenting. The studies by Crouter, Cohen, and Clarke-Stewart provide evidence that parents gain ideas and information about childrearing from their work settings, network members, and books by experts. Although progress has been made on identifying sources of ideas for parents, very little is known about the conditions under which parents are most likely to modify old beliefs or add new beliefs and the types of information parents are most likely to accept. Second, parents' attitudes toward the parenting role and toward their children are affected by whether they are psychologically built-up or drained in their nonparenting roles. The studies by Alvarez and by Greenberger and Goldberg show that work can both build up parents' self-esteem and their psychological reserves and can drain those reserves. Cox et al. provided evidence that supportive marital relationships can positively influence mothers' perceptions of their infants. Third, parents' beliefs and values are shaped by the functional roles they play. For example, Kohn's data indicate that parents tend to value the skills and characteristics that they have found to be useful in their occupational roles and, in turn, to believe that these attributes are important for their children. Similarly, the effects of child gender on parents' beliefs (e.g., Hoffman's finding that parents want sons to be hardworking and ambitious and girls to be kind and loving) may result, in part, from parents' social experiences in which men have been rewarded for being hardworking and women have been rewarded for being nurturing. One plausible explanation for the differential impact of work on mothers' perceptions of sons versus daughters is that as women go outside the home for employment and they are rewarded for increasingly varied skills and attributes, they may come to value more instrumental characteristics in their daughters.

To date, most research has concentrated on identification of sources of parents' beliefs and comparisons of beliefs between different groups of parents. We suggested that parental research could benefit from examination of the processes through which factors influence the development of parental beliefs and the variables that affect acquisition and modification of parental beliefs over time.

PARENTAL BELIEFS AND PARENTING BEHAVIOR

To this point, we considered different factors that influence what parents believe about parenting and child development. Now we examine the research that links parental beliefs to parenting behavior. In what ways do parental beliefs affect how parents behave toward their children? This question is particularly important when we consider that most parent intervention programs assume that changing parents' beliefs will bring about related changes in their behaviors. In this section, we discuss parental beliefs about child development, specific cognitive processes, gender development, and school achievement.

General Beliefs About Child Development and Parenting Behavior

We begin by considering the relation between general beliefs about child development and childrearing and parenting behavior. In the first two sets of studies, the instruments used to measure parental beliefs vary, but all of the studies use Caldwell and Bradley's (1979) Home Observation for Measurement of the Environment (HOME) as their measure of parenting behavior. Mothers are interviewed in their homes with the target child present. The HOME is a semistructured interview consisting of several subscales that tap, for example, emotional and verbal responsivity of the parent, maternal involvement with the child, and avoidance of restriction and punishment. Importantly, the HOME scale has been shown to be positively correlated with various measures of children's cognitive development (e.g., school achievement scores, ability test scores, and language development) (see Bradley, 1982).

Using the HOME scale as an indicator of parenting skill, Stevens (1984) examined the relation between knowledge about child development and parenting skill. His sample consisted primarily of low-income families with infants between 15 and 30 months of age. Approximately one third of the mothers were Black adolescents; one third were Black adults; and one third were White adults. Two instruments were used to assess parents' knowledge. The first scale, a modified version of the Knowledge of Environmental Influences on Development (KEID) scale includes items related to normative development of infants and to what parents can do to promote development both directly through interaction with their child and indirectly through structuring the environment. The second measure was a short version of the High Scope Knowledge of Early Infant Development (H/SED) scale, which focuses on normative development. Stevens found that both parental beliefs scales were significantly and positively correlated with HOME scores. Moreover, in a hierarchical regression with income and maternal education entered first, 14% of the variance in HOME scores was explained by parental beliefs, with KEID scores contributing more than H/SED scores did. Although the relation between the measured beliefs and behavior was small, this study demonstrates a relation between what parents believe and what parents do.

Also using the HOME scale to measure parenting behavior, Luster and his colleagues (Luster & Rhoades, 1989; Luster et al., 1989) examined the relation between various parental beliefs and parenting behavior. With a sample of 65 mothers and their infants, Luster et al. (1989) looked at mothers' beliefs about conformity, spoiling the child, floor freedom (i.e., the amount of freedom the infant has to explore the home environment), discipline, and talking and reading to the infant. Simple correlations indicated that beliefs about floor freedom and talking/reading were each positively and significantly correlated with total HOME scores (r's = .39 and .58, respectively). In contrast, beliefs about conformity, spoiling the child, and discipline were each negatively and significantly correlated with total HOME scores (r's ranging from $-.31$ to $-.56$). Thus, for example, the more importance mothers placed on talking and reading to the infant, the higher HOME scores were. In contrast, the more emphasis mothers placed on conforming behaviors (e.g., to be polite to adults, to keep his or her clothes clean), the lower the HOME scores were.

In a subsequent study, Luster and Rhoades (1989) compared adolescent and adult mothers' beliefs and parenting behaviors. In general, the relations between adolescent mothers' and their parenting behaviors were similar to the relations that were obtained in the previously mentioned adult sample. However, adolescents' HOME scores were lower than were the older mothers' HOME scores. In addition to considering beliefs about what parents should do, in this study they included beliefs about the mothers' perceptions of how much influence they have over their children's development. The researchers found that adolescent and adult mothers who believe that parenting practices do affect developmental outcomes in children provide more supportive environments than do mothers who believe that parenting practices are less effective in influencing children's development. Interestingly, mothers who viewed themselves as being relatively less competent as parents had higher HOME scores than did mothers who saw themselves as being relatively more competent in their parenting. Luster and Rhoades (1989) hypothesized that:

> parents who have greater reservations about their parenting competencies may have a greater appreciation of the subtleties and complexities involved in providing supportive environments for children...those mothers who perceive themselves as being relatively competent tend to have a more authoritarian outlook on how children should be cared for. (p. 320)

In general, mothers who provided the most supportive care for their infants believed that: (a) parenting does influence their child's development, (b) infants need freedom to explore their environments, (c) parents should be responsive to and attend to infants' cues, and (d) even young children need adequate verbal stimulation. In addition, these mothers place relatively less importance on discipline.

Besides the HOME scale, other measures of parent behavior have included observations of parent–child interaction on various tasks. For example, from the previously mentioned study by Hess and his colleagues (Dickson, Hess, Miyake, & Azuma, 1979; Hess et al., 1980; Price, 1977, as cited by Miller, 1986), recall that mothers in Japan and in the United States were asked to indicate the age at which they expected a child to be able to do various tasks. In addition, the mother's interaction with her 4-year-old child was observed on two tasks. The mother–child dyads did a referential communication task in which they took turns describing one item from a pictorial array in such a way that the listener, who viewed an identical array, could accurately identify the item. The mother and child were able to see each other, to ask and answer questions, and to use gestures. Their behavior was scored for the accuracy of the message. The researchers found that the accuracy of the mother–child communication was positively correlated with mothers' expectation of early verbal assertiveness in the United States, but not in Japan (r's = .125 and .07, respectively).

In addition, mothers were asked to do a block-sorting task in which the mothers taught their child how to sort a group of blocks along two dimensions. In this task, the researchers looked at the degree to which the mother's communication required her child to make verbal responses. Once again, they found that expectation for early verbal assertiveness was positively associated with mothers' communicative behavior for U.S. mothers, but not for Japanese mothers. Hess et al. did not offer an explanation for why the belief-behavior relation only obtained in the U.S. sample. Elsewhere (see Dickson et al., 1979), however, they observed that the Japanese style of communication places more emphasis on nonverbal communication than U.S. communication does, and that Japanese is less explicit than English with respect to pronouns, number, and subject. It is possible that beliefs about verbal assertiveness do not adequately capture Japanese mothers' beliefs about the development of communication skills, thus limiting the relation in the referential communication task. Similarly, the behavioral coding schemes might not have completely represented Japanese mothers' efforts to encourage their children to communicate, thereby limiting the relation in the block-sorting task.

Beliefs About Specific Cognitive Processes and Parenting Behavior

The previous studies focused on general beliefs about parenting and child development. Another approach was to examine parents' beliefs about cognitive development, particularly with respect to different cognitive theories. For ex-

ample, Sigel and his colleagues at the Educational Testing Service (ETS) examined the extent to which constructivist beliefs are held by parents and the
relation between parents' beliefs and behaviors (e.g., McGillicuddy-DeLisi,
1985; Sigel, 1982; Sigel, Stinson, & Flaugher, 1991). To measure parental beliefs, short vignettes about a parent and a 4-year-old child were presented to
the parent, and parents answered a series of open-ended questions about each
story. For example, after reading the story about a child playing with toys in
the bathtub, parents were asked: "Does a 4-year-old know which things float
and which don't?"; "How does a 4-year-old (eventually) come to know which
things float and which don't?"; and "How does a 4-year-old eventually come
to know why some things float and others don't float?" (McGillicuddy-DeLisi,
1985, p. 12). Parents' responses were coded into various categories. For example, responses that were consistent with constructivist beliefs included: (a)
experimentation (e.g., children learn by trying out different things in the water);
(b) *cognitive reorganization* (e.g., after children have had a lot of experience with
different objects, everything clicks into place and they figure out what the
characteristics of floating things are); and (c) *stages* (e.g., children have to understand about weight before they can understand what things float). Responses
that were inconsistent with constructivist beliefs included: (a) *direct instruction*
(e.g., children learn about floating when they are taught it in school) and (b)
observation (e.g., children just see that some things float and others don't).

After the parent interview, parents and their 4-year-old children were videotaped doing one storytelling task and one paper-folding task (i.e., to make a
boat or a plane). The researchers were particularly interested in the degree
to which parents used *distancing strategies* with their children. Distancing strategies are behaviors that require the child to separate from the task in a cognitive sense. For instance, behaviors that require the child to imagine what would
happen if he or she did something, to recall what something used to look like,
or to think about what the next step could be are termed *distancing strategies*.

Interestingly, fathers' constructivist beliefs were related to the extent to which
they used distancing strategies in their interaction with their children. Mothers'
constructivist beliefs were not related to their use of distancing strategies. In
their sample of 120 two-parent families, the majority of mothers stayed at home
with the children. McGillicuddy-DeLisi suggested that mothers' behaviors
toward their own child might be directed by their beliefs about what works
with their specific child rather than by general beliefs about child development.
In contrast, she suggested that the fathers, who had much less daily interaction with the child, might be directed more by their general knowledge than
by specific beliefs about their own child.

Also working with the ETS sample, Skinner (1985) examined the relation
between the sensitivity of mothers' childrearing beliefs and mothers' behavior
toward the child during the paper-folding task. Beliefs indicating the sensitivity of the mother to the child were defined by Skinner (1985) as beliefs that:

"(1) show that primary concern is for the child; (2) take into consideration the needs or stated desires of the child; and (3) give the child active agent status with respect to his or her own development and learning" (p. 65). Sensitivity was assessed with respect to maternal beliefs about situations describing a conflict between parent and child and with respect to maternal beliefs about the ways in which children learn.

Maternal behavior during the paper-folding task was coded for: (a) the mother's directiveness or the degree to which the mother controlled the child's behavioral options; (b) the degree to which the mother's focus during the task was on managing the child's behavior, completing the task, or on the child's involvement in the task; and (c) her responsiveness or the degree to which the mother considered the child's feelings and desires.

In general, Skinner found that mothers who indicated more sensitive beliefs during conflict situations and who viewed the child as an active agent in learning gave the child more freedom to choose what to do (i.e., low directiveness) when the child was actively engaged in the task and when the child's attention was directed toward something off-task. However, more sensitive mothers were highly directive when they were explaining the task to the child. Skinner suggested that being highly directive when explaining how to, for example, make the paper boat may have helped the child be more effective or more competent. To make the paper boat required the child to follow a precise sequence of steps, and the high directiveness of the mothers may have been a function of the task demands. Finally, there was a curvilinear relation between sensitivity of beliefs and responsiveness of behaviors.

Both of these studies indicate that parents' beliefs about the way children learn is related to parents' behaviors, particularly in teaching situations. Parents who believe that children learn by experimenting and exploring their environment are more likely to give their children more leeway during a teaching situation and to use more distancing strategies to help the child think about the situation.

Beliefs About Gender and Parental Behavior

Do parents' beliefs about gender development affect the way they interact with their children? Brooks-Gunn (1985) considered this question by first looking at the degree to which mothers' beliefs about children's characteristics and behaviors were gender-typed. That is, was a particular behavior (e.g., "likes to do dangerous things") more likely to occur in boys or in girls, or was it equally likely to be characteristic of boys and girls? On the basis of their responses, the mothers were divided into three groups: low gender typing (0%–35% of the items were marked as gender-linked), moderate gender typing (41%–66% of the items were gender-linked), and high gender typing (67%–100% of the items were gender-linked). Mothers were then observed interacting with their

24-month-old children in a free-play situation. Mothers who were classified as low in gender-typed beliefs did more active toy play with their daughters than did mothers who were high in gender-typed beliefs. In contrast, the high gender-typed beliefs mothers of boys did more active toy play with their sons than did the low gender-typed group.

Beliefs About School Achievement and Parenting Behavior

Many researchers have considered parents' beliefs about education. One of the most extensive research programs in this area was conducted by Stevenson and his colleagues (e.g., Stevenson, Chen, & Uttal, 1990; Stevenson & Lee, 1990; Stevenson, Lee, & Stigler, 1986; Stevenson et al., 1990). Their studies have included both multinational research and comparisons of different ethnic groups within the United States. One of their major questions is: What factors contribute to national differences in children's mathematics and science achievement? Stevenson et al. (1986) reported that as early as the first grade, U.S. children do not do as well in math as their counterparts in Taiwan or in Japan. On basic cognitive ability tasks (e.g., spatial reasoning, perceptual speed, coding, vocabulary, verbal memory, and general information), however, there were basically no overall differences among the three groups. Moreover, U.S. students are only somewhat outperformed by Chinese students in reading, and they do better than Japanese students do. Besides providing evidence that the amount and type of school instruction in math and reading contribute to these differences, they argued that parents' beliefs play a role in these performance differences. First, their data indicated that U.S. mothers were satisfied with the education their children were receiving. When asked what improvements could be made, less than 6% of the suggestions were to improve instruction in math or science. Stevenson and his colleagues argued that unless parents were concerned or dissatisfied with achievement in a particular area, it was unlikely that schools would make changes in their curriculum and that children's performance in that area would improve.

Second, across the three cultures, parents differed in their beliefs about what factors contribute to children's academic success. Mothers were asked to indicate how much they thought effort, natural ability, difficulty of the schoolwork, and luck contributed to academic success. United States mothers rated effort and ability almost equally. In contrast, both Japanese and Chinese mothers placed much greater emphasis on effort than on ability. All mothers gave relatively little weight to task difficulty and to luck. The researchers hypothesized that in cultures in which performance is primarily considered to be a function of effort, parents may perceive themselves as having a greater effect on influencing children's development and achievement, and thereby do more to encourage their children's achievement.

In a recent study comparing first- and fifth-grade students in Beijing and

Chicago, Stevenson et al. (1990) found similar results. Chinese children in Beijing outperformed U.S. children in math. However, U.S. parents were more satisfied with their children's math performance than were Chinese parents. Similarly, U.S. children are more likely than Chinese students to believe that they are "above average" or "among the best" in math. Stevenson et al. (1990) suggested that U.S. parents have lower standards for math performance than their Chinese counterparts. When asked to predict their child's score on a test in which the maximum score was 100 points and the average score was 70 points, U.S. and Chinese parents did not differ much. However, when asked what was the minimum score with which they would be satisfied, Chinese parents indicated much higher expectations. United States parents would be satisfied with scores a few points above 70. In contrast, for Chinese parents, the minimum acceptable scores were in the high 80s and 90s. The researchers hypothesized that unless parents are dissatisfied with their children's performance, they will not encourage their children to work harder to improve in an area.

Summary

In this section we discussed research that links parental beliefs to parenting behavior. As Miller (1988) observed, the evidence relating beliefs to observed behaviors is limited. Considering the efforts of parent intervention programs to improve parenting practices by changing parental beliefs, more research in this area would be profitable. For example, because most researchers measured beliefs and behaviors at the same time, it is not clear whether beliefs lead to behaviors or whether beliefs are the result of practicing specific behaviors. Assuming the directionality of a link between beliefs and behaviors is not unidirectional, then under what conditions are beliefs and behaviors likely to be linked, what kinds of behaviors typically follow beliefs, and what kinds of behaviors lead to the addition or modification of beliefs? Along the same lines, longitudinal studies that look at parents' childrearing and child development beliefs both prior to the birth of the first child and at various times after the birth of the child and at parenting behaviors would provide useful information on the relation between changing belief systems and changing behaviors.

CONCLUSION

In this chapter we considered three questions: What factors influence the development of parental beliefs? How do these factors operate? and What is the relation between parental beliefs and parenting behavior? The research we presented links several contextual factors in the parent's life to parental beliefs. Probably the most recognizable process by which contextual factors impact parent's beliefs is by providing access to new information and new ideas about parenting and child development. The research on the impact of experts on childrearing by Bronfenbrenner and by Clarke-Stewart illustrate this point. What is not clear from these studies is whether the ideas the parents were exposed to actually changed parenting behaviors. Qualitative evidence of both the process and the effects on parenting behavior can be found in Crouter's research on the effects of work on adult lives and in Cohen's in-depth study of community life and social networking. Particularly in Crouter's research, parents had the opportunity to learn new ideas about how to facilitate communication and how to do problem solving within a group and to put these new ideas into practice at work—trying them out, watching others use the strategies, getting feedback on their own performance, and getting to see the utility of the strategies in multiple situations—before spontaneously transferring them to the home. We found this research to be most intriguing and would hope that others might use their descriptions and findings to motivate larger studies on the ways in which new ideas are introduced and incorporated into parental belief systems. Such research could have important implications for parent intervention programs.

A second way in which contextual factors operate is to shape parents' ideas about what skills and characteristics will best help their children to survive in this world. By showing how conditions in the father's work setting influence father's values, Kohn's research is a classic illustration of this process. The more recent research on maternal employment and, in particular, the relation between maternal employment and mothers' perceptions of daughters also exemplifies this process. In addition, multicultural research that identifies specific cultural values and ideas about children, parents, and families and then links these larger cultural values to specific parental beliefs exemplifies this notion that context shapes the kinds of goals parents have for their children.

Third, parental attitudes and perceptions of children are influenced by situations that build (or drain) the parent's physical and psychological resources so that the parent is in a stronger (or weaker) position to handle the demands of parenting. The studies by Alvarez and by Cox et al. are illustrative of this process. Although the relations among the various contextual, demographic, and personal factors (e.g., work, SES, and gender of child) were complex and need further research to clearly establish the links, these studies direct attention to processes that may link the external factor to parental beliefs (e.g., work—>role strain induced by conflicting home and work demands—>parental perceptions of the child) and suggest areas in which parents may need particular support.

With respect to parental beliefs and parenting behavior, researchers have just begun to establish and define the relation between the two. More research that examines both the relation between parental beliefs and parenting behavior and the relation between parental beliefs/behaviors and child outcomes is necessary if, for example, one of our goals is to adequately inform developers of parent education and intervention programs. In addition, well-designed evaluations of parent education programs could provide information about whether or not beliefs are causally related to behavior. That is, if an intervention program can change parents' beliefs, one could then look for a corresponding change in behavior. We also believe that more precise examinations of the ways in which specific beliefs are translated into actual parenting practices needs to be done.

Finally, although this chapter was not meant to be a comprehensive review and there were many aspects of parental beliefs that we simply chose not to address, there were also issues that seem to have been neglected by researchers. For example, very little has been done on the role of extended families as a source of parental beliefs (the notable exception being research on parents who were abused as children and their subsequent parenting) or on religion as a contextual factor influencing parental beliefs. Another major limitation in the field is that most studies tend to look at parental beliefs at one moment in time and in doing so are unable to inform us as to the development and changes that occur in belief systems. Longitudinal studies that look at families before and after critical life events (e.g., birth of first or subsequent child, mothers and fathers entering, leaving, or reentering the work force) could enrich our understanding of both the development of beliefs and the relations between beliefs and behaviors.

ACKNOWLEDGMENT

Preparation of this chapter was supported in part by a grant to Robert J. Sternberg and Lynn Okagaki from the Spencer Foundation.

REFERENCES

Alvarez, W. F. (1985). The meaning of maternal employment for mothers and their perceptions of their three-year-old children. *Child Development, 56,* 350–360.

Azuma, H., & Kashiwagi, K. (1987). Descriptors for an intelligent person: A Japanese study. *Japanese Psychological Research, 29,* 17–26.

Bell, R. Q. (1979). Parent, child, and reciprocal influences. *American Psychologist, 34,* 821–826.

Belsky, J. (1984). The determinants of parenting: A process model. *Child Development, 55,* 83–96.

Binet, A., & Simon, T. (1916). *The development of intelligence in children.* (E. S. Kite, Trans.). Baltimore: Williams & Wilkins.

Block, J. H. (1973). Conceptions of sex role: Some cross-cultural and longitudinal perspectives. *American Psychologist, 28,* 512–526.

Bradley, R. (1982). The HOME inventory: A review of the first fifteen years. In N. J. Anastasiow, W. Frankenburg, & A. Fandall (Eds.), *Identifying the developmentally delayed child* (pp. 87–100). Baltimore, MD: University Park Press.

Bronfenbrenner, U. (1958). Socialization and social class through time and space. In E. Macco-by, T. M. Newcomb, & E. L. Hartley (Eds.), *Reading in social psychology* (pp. 400–425). New York: Holt, Rinehart & Winston.

Bronfenbrenner, U. (1979). *The ecology of human development: Experiments by nature and design.* Cambridge, MA: Harvard University Press.

Bronfenbrenner, U. (1986). Ecology of the family as a context for human development: Research perspectives. *Developmental Psychology, 22*, 723–742.

Bronfenbrenner, U., Alvarez, W. F., & Henderson, C. R., Jr. (1984). Working and watching: Maternal employment status and parents' perceptions of their three-year-old children. *Child Development, 55*, 1362–1378.

Bronfenbrenner, U., & Crouter, A. C. (1982). Work and family through time and space. In S. Kamerman & C. D. Hayes (Eds.), *Families that work: Children in a changing world* (pp. 39–83). Washington, DC: National Academy Press.

Brooks-Gunn, J. (1985). Maternal beliefs about children's sex-typed characteristics as they relate to maternal behavior. In I. E. Sigel (Ed.), *Parental belief systems: The psychological consequences for children* (pp. 319–344). Hillsdale, NJ: Lawrence Erlbaum Associates.

Burns, A., Homel, R., & Goodnow, J. (1984). Conditions of life and parental values. *Australian Journal of Psychology, 36*(2), 219–237.

Caldwell, B. M. & Bradley, R. H. (1979). *Home observation for measurement of the environment.* Little Rock, AR: University of Arkansas at Little Rock.

Clarke-Stewart, K. A. (1978). Popular primers for parents. *American Psychologist, 33*, 359–369.

Cohen, G. (1981). Culture and educational achievement. *Harvard Educational Review, 51*(2), 270–285.

Condry, J., & Condry, S. (1976). Sex differences: A study of the eye of the beholder. *Child Development, 47*, 812–819.

Cox, M. J., Owen, M. T., Lewis, J. M. & Henderson, V. K. (1989). Marriage, adult adjustment, and early parenting. *Child Development, 60*, 1015–1024.

Crouter, A. C. (1984). Participative work as an influence on human development. *Human Development, 5*, 71–90.

Cutrona, C. E., & Troutman, B. R. (1986). Social support, infant temperament, and parenting self-efficacy: A mediational model of postpartum depression. *Child Development, 56*, 1507–1518.

Dasen, P. R. (1984). The cross-cultural study of intelligence: Piaget and the Baoulé. *The International Journal of Psychology, 19*, 407–434.

Dickson, W. P., Hess, R. D., Miyake, N., & Azuma, H. (1979). Referential communication accuracy between mother and child as a predictor of cognitive development in the United States and Japan. *Child Development, 50*, 53–59.

Dickstein, S., & Parke, R. D. (1988). Social referencing in infancy: A glance at fathers and marriage. *Child Development, 59*, 506–511.

Donovan, W. L., & Leavitt, L. A. (1989). Maternal self-efficacy and infant attachment: Integrating physiology, perceptions, and behavior. *Child Development, 60*, 460–472.

Entwisle, D. R., & Hayduk, L. A. (1978). *Too great expectations: The academic outlook of young children.* Baltimore, MD: John Hopkins University Press.

Entwisle, D. R., & Hayduk, L. A. (1981). Academic expectations and the school attainment of young children. *Sociology of Education, 54*, 34–50.

Goodnow, J. J. (1984). Parents' ideas about parenting and development: A review of issues and recent work. In M. E. Lamb, A. L. Brown, & B. Rogoff (Eds.), *Advances in developmental psychology* (Vol. 3, pp. 193–242). Hillsdale, NJ: Lawrence Erlbaum Associates.

Goodnow, J. J. (1988). Parents' ideas, actions, and feelings: Models and methods from developmental and social psychology. *Child Development, 59*, 286–320.

Goodnow, J. J., & Collins, W. A. (1990). *Development according to parents: The nature, sources, and consequences of parents' ideas.* Hillsdale, NJ: Lawrence Erlbaum Associates.

Greenberger, E., & Goldberg, W. A. (1989). Work, parenting, and the socialization of children. *Developmental Psychology, 25*(1), 22–35.

Harrison, A. O., Wilson, M. N., Pine, C. J., Chan, S. Q., & Buriel, R. (1990). Family ecologies of ethnic minority children. *Child Development, 61*, 347–362.

Hess, R. D., Kashiwagi, K., Azuma, H., Price, G. G., & Dickson, W. P. (1980). Maternal expectations for mastery of developmental tasks in Japan and the United States. *International Journal of Psychology, 15*, 259–271.

Hoffman, L. W. (1977). Changes in family roles, socialization, and sex differences. *American Psychologist, 32*(8), 644–657.

Hoffman, L. W. (1988). Cross-cultural differences in childrearing goals. In W. Damon (Series Ed.) & R. A. LeVine, P. M. Miller, & M. M. West (Vol. Eds.), *New directions for child development: Parental behavior in diverse societies* (Vol. 40, pp. 99–122). San Francisco, CA: Jossey-Bass.

Horn, J. L., & Cattell, R. B. (1966). Refinement and test of the theory of fluid and crystallized general intelligences. *Journal of Educational Psychology, 51*, 253–270.

Hunter, R. S., & Kilstrom, N. (1979). Breaking the cycle in abusive families. *American Journal of Psychiatry, 136*(10), 1320–1322.

Kessen, W. (1979). The American child and other cultural inventions. *American Psychologist, 34*(10), 815–820.

Knight, R. (1981). Parents' beliefs about cognitive development: The role of experience. In A. R. Nesdale, C. Pratt, R. Grieve, J. Field, D. Illingworth, & J. Hogben (Eds.), *Advances in child development and research: Theory and research* (pp. 226–229). Perth: University of Western Australia Press.

Knight, R. (1983). *Parents' ideas about childhood and parenting: A constructivist approach.* Unpublished doctoral thesis, Macquarie University, North Ryde, Australia.

Kohn, M. L. (1963). Social class and parent–child relationships: An interpretation. *American Journal of Sociology, XVIII*, 471–480.

Kohn, M. L. (1969). *Class and conformity: A study in values.* Homewood, IL: The Dorsey Press.

Kojima, H. (1991, July). *Japanese conceptions of interpersonal relationships, self, and human development in a historical perspective.* Paper presented at the International Society for the Study of Behavioural Development Workshop on Asian Perspectives of Psychology. Ann Arbor, MI.

Laboratory of Comparative Human Cognition. (1982). Culture and intelligence. In R. J. Sternberg (Ed.), *Handbook of human intelligence* (pp. 642–722). New York: Cambridge University Press.

Laboratory of Comparative Human Cognition. (1986). Contribution of cross-cultural research to educational practice. *American Psychologist, 41*, 1049–1058.

Laosa, L. M. (1980). Maternal teaching strategies in Chicano and Anglo-American families: The influence of culture and education on maternal behavior. *Child Development, 51*, 759–765.

Laosa, L. M. (1982). School, occupation, culture, and family: The impact of parental schooling on the parent–child relationship. *Journal of Educational Psychology, 74*(6), 791–827.

LeVine, R. A. (1974). Parental goals: A cross-cultural view. *Teachers College Record, 76*(2), 226–239.

LeVine, R. A. (1988). Human parental care: Universal goals, cultural strategies, individual behavior. In W. Damon (Series Ed.) & R. A. LeVine, P. M. Miller, & M. M. West (Vol. Eds.), *New directions for child development: Parental behavior in diverse societies* (Vol. 40, pp. 3–11). San Francisco, CA: Jossey-Bass.

Luster, T., & Kain, E. L. (1987). The relation between family context and perceptions of parental efficacy. *Early Child Development and Care, 29*, 301–311.

Luster, T., & Rhoades, K. (1989). The relation between child-rearing beliefs and the home environment in a sample of adolescent mothers. *Family Relations, 38*, 317–322.

Luster, T., Rhoades, K., & Haas, B. (1989). The relation between parental values and parenting behavior: A test of the Kohn hypothesis. *Journal of Marriage and the Family, 51*, 139–147.

McGillicuddy-DeLisi, A. V. (1985). The relationship between parental beliefs and children's cognitive level. In I. E. Sigel (Ed.), *Parental belief systems: The psychological consequences for children* (pp. 7–24). Hillsdale, NJ: Lawrence Erlbaum Associates.

Miller, S. A. (1986). Parents' beliefs about their children's cognitive abilities. *Developmental Psychology, 22*, 276–284.

Miller, S. A. (1988). Parents' beliefs about children's cognitive development. *Child Development, 59*, 259–285.

Murillo, N. (1971). The Mexican American family. In N. N. Wagner & M. J. Haug (Eds.), *Chicanos: Social and psychological perspectives* (pp. 97–108). St. Louis, MO: C. V. Mosby.

Ninio, A. (1979). The naive theory of the infant and other maternal attitudes in two subgroups in Israel. *Child Development, 50*, 976–980.

Ogbu, J. U. (1981). Origins of human competence: A cultural-ecological perspective. *Child Development, 52*, 413–429.

Okagaki, L., Sternberg, R. J., & Divecha, D. J. (1990, April). *Parental beliefs and children's early school performance*. Paper presented at the annual meeting of the American Educational Research Association, Boston, MA.

Page, H., & Lesthaeghe, R. (Eds.). (1981). *Child spacing in tropical Africa*. New York: Academic Press.

Price, G. G. (1977). How cognitive abilities of preschool children are influenced by maternal teaching behavior: A causal model analysis., *Dissertation Abstracts International, 37*, 6377A.

Quinton, D., & Rutter, M. (1988). *Parenting breakdown: The making and breaking of intergenerational bonds*. Aldershot, UK: Avebury.

Reis, J. (1988). Child-rearing expectations and developmental knowledge according to maternal age and parity. *Infant Mental Health Journal, 9*(4), 287–304.

Rogoff, B. (1982). Integrating context and cognitive development. In M. E. Lamb & A. L. Brown (Eds.), *Advances in developmental psychology* (Vol. 2, pp. 125–170). Hillsdale, NJ: Lawrence Erlbaum Associates.

Rossi, A. S. (1980). Aging and parenthood in the middle years. In P. Baltes & O. G. Brim, Jr. (Eds.), *Life-span development and behavior* (Vol. 3, 137–205). New York: Academic Press.

Rubin, J. S., Provenzano, F. J., & Luria, Z. (1974).l The eye of the beholder: Parents' views on sex of newborns. *American Journal of Orthopsychiatry, 5*, 353–363.

Russell, A., & Russell, G. (1982). Mother, father, and child beliefs about child development. *Journal of Psychology, 110*, 297–306.

Schaefer, E. S., & Edgerton, M. (1985). Parent and child correlates of parental modernity. In I. E. Sigel (Ed.), *Parental belief systems: The psychological consequences for children* (pp. 287–318). Hillsdale, NJ: Lawrence Erlbaum Associates.

Segal, M. (1985). A study of maternal beliefs and values within the context of an intervention program. In I. E. Sigel (Ed.), *Parental belief systems: The psychological consequences for children* (pp. 271–286). Hillsdale, NJ: Lawrence Erlbaum Associates.

Seginer, R. (1983). Parents' educational expectations and children's academic achievements: A literature review. *Merrill-Palmer Quarterly, 29*(1), 1–23.

Serpell, R. (1984). Research on cognitive development in Sub-Saharan Africa. *International Journal of Behavioral Development, 7*, 111–127.

Sigel, I. E. (1982). The relationship between parental distancing strategies and the child's cognitive behavior. In L. M. Laosa & I. E. Sigel (Eds.), *Families as learning environments for children* (pp. 47–86). New York: Plenum.

Sigel, I. E., Stinson, E. T., & Flaugher, J. (1991). Socialization of representational competence in the family: The distancing paradigm. In L. Okagaki & R. J. Sternberg (Eds.), *Directors of development: Influences on the development of children's thinking* (pp. 121–196). Hillsdale, NJ: Lawrence Erlbaum Associates.

Skinner, E. A. (1985). Determinants of mother sensitive and contingent-responsive behavior. The role of childrearing beliefs and socioeconomic status. In I. E. Sigel (Ed.), *Parental belief systems: The psychological consequences for children* (pp. 51–82). Hillsdale, NJ: Lawrence Erlbaum Associates.

Slaughter-Defoe, D. T., Nakagawa, K., Takanishi, T., & Johnson, D. J. (1990). Toward cultural/ecological perspectives on schooling and achievement in African- and Asian-American children. *Child Development, 61*, 363–383.

Spence, J. T. (1985). Achievement American style: The rewards and costs of individualism. *American Psychologist, 40*(12), 1285–1295.

Stevens, J. H., Jr. (1984). Child development knowledge and parenting skills. *Family Relations, 33*, 237–244.

Stevenson, H. W., Chen, C., & Uttal, D. H. (1990). Beliefs and achievement: A study of Black, White, and Hispanic children. *Child Development, 61*, 508–523.

Stevenson, H. W., & Lee, S. (1990). Contexts of achievement. *Monographs of the Society for Research in Child Development, 55*(1-2), (Serial No. 221).

Stevenson, H. W., Lee, S., Chen, C., Lummis, M., Stigler, J., Fan, L., & Ge, F. (1990). Mathematics achievement of children in China and the United States. *Child Development, 61*, 1053–1066.

Stevenson, H. W., Lee, S. Y., & Stigler, J. W. (1986). Mathematics achievement of Chinese, Japanese, and American children. *Science, 231*, 693–699.

Tharp, R. G. (1989). Psychocultural variables and constants: Effects on teaching and learning in schools. *American Psychologist, 44*(2), 349–359.

Thurstone, L. L. (1938). *Primary mental abilities.* Chicago: University of Chicago Press.

Triana, E., & Rodrigo, M. J. (1989, July). *The role played by parental ideas about child development in the elaborations of mental scenarios in text comprehension.* Paper presented at meetings of the International Society for Study of Behavioral Development, Jyväskylä, Finland.

Triandis, H. C., Bontempo, R., Betancourt, H., Bond, M., Leung, K., Brenes, A., Georgas, J., Hui, C. H., Marin, G., Setiadi, B., Sinha, J. B. P., Verma, J., Spangenberg, J., Touzard, H., & deMontmollin, G. (1986). The measurement of the etic aspects of individualism and collectivism across cultures. *Australian Journal of Psychology, 38*(3), 257–267.

Triandis, H. C., Bontempo, R., Villareal, M. J., Asai, M., & Lucca, N. (1988). Individualism and collectivism: Cross-cultural perspectives on self-ingroup relationships. *Journal of Personality and Social Psychology, 54*(2), 323–338.

Welaratna, U. (1988, November). Cambodian refugees: Factors affecting their assimilation and English language acquisition. *The CATSESOL Journal*, pp. 17–27.

Wober, M. (1974). Towards an understanding of the Kiganda concept of intelligence. In J. W. Berry & P. R. Dasen (Eds.), *Culture and cognition: Readings in cross-cultural psychology* (pp. 261–280). London: Methuen.

Chapter 3

Adolescent Mothers

Tom Luster
Mary Mittelstaedt
Michigan State University

The fertility rate for teen-agers has generally declined since the early 1960s. For example, there were over 90 births for every 1,000 females age 15–19 in 1955, 68 births for every 1,000 in 1970, and 51 births for every 1,000 female teen-agers in 1986 (National Center for Health Statistics, 1990). Factors contributing to the decline in the birth rate among teens include an increased use of abortion by teens following the 1973 Roe vs. Wade Supreme Court decision, and increased contraceptive use. In 1985, 42% of teen pregnancies were terminated by abortion compared to 29% of the pregnancies in 1974 (Moore, 1989).

Although the fertility rate has generally declined for 15- to 19-year-olds during the last several decades, there has been an increase in the birth rate for teens since 1986. The rate for 1989 was 58.1 per 1,000 (compared to 50.6 per 1,000 in 1986). The increase in the birth rate for teens was most marked for young teens, those age 15–17; the rate for this group increased from 30.6 per 1,000 in 1986 to 36.5 per 1,000 in 1989. Moreover, the absolute number of children born to teen-agers remains high. In 1989 there were 517,989 children born to teen-agers (Moore, 1992). Most of these mothers kept their children rather than releasing them for adoption. No national adoption figures are available, but it is estimated that more than 95% of teen-agers who give birth choose to parent the child (Hayes, 1987).

During the decade of the 1980s, much was learned about the consequences of teen-age parenthood for the mother, for her children, and for society at large. In addition, research on the parenting practices of adolescent mothers has

69

burgeoned since the early 1980s. Our review, summarizing this research, is divided into four sections. We begin our chapter with a summary of what is known about the consequences of early childbearing. In the second section, research that compares the parenting behavior of adolescent mothers and older mothers (i.e., between-group studies) is reviewed. Next we focus on factors related to the quality of care teen-agers provide for their children (within-group studies). In other words, which teen-age mothers are providing relatively high quality care for their children and which are providing less supportive care? Finally, we conclude with a brief discussion of some options for reducing the rates of adolescent pregnancy and for providing assistance to teens who are parents.

We should point out that this review is limited to studies that have focused on the behavior of teen-age mothers. Systematic studies on the parenting behavior of adolescent fathers are limited in number. That which is known about adolescent fathers has been summarized well by others (Elster & Lamb, 1986). Studies comparing younger and older mothers in terms of childrearing knowledge and beliefs have also been reviewed elsewhere and are not summarized here (Reis, 1988).

THE CONSEQUENCES
OF ADOLESCENT PARENTHOOD

In this section we provide a brief overview of the research that is concerned with the consequences of adolescent parenthood. The outcomes associated with early childbearing are summarized for the adolescent mothers and for their children. The cost of early childbearing for society at large is also discussed.

Consequences of Adolescent Parenthood for the Mothers

There is great diversity in the ways in which teen-agers cope with an early pregnancy and subsequently considerable diversity in the long-term effects of adolescent parenthood on the mother (Furstenberg, Brooks-Gunn, & Morgan, 1987). However, on average, teen-age mothers differ from their peers who delay childbearing on a number of outcomes, and these differences favor those who delay childbearing. For example, adolescent mothers are less likely than their peers to complete high school and go on for postsecondary education. Given their relatively low educational attainment, they tend to have poorer employment prospects than their peers (Hayes, 1987).

Teen-age mothers are more likely than their peers to raise their children as single parents. Since the early 1960s there has been a steady increase in the percentage of births to teens that occur out of wedlock. The proportion of teen births that occurred outside of marriage doubled between 1960 and

1970 from 15% to 30%, and doubled again since that time to 64% in 1987 (Adams, Adams-Taylor, & Pittman, 1989; Moore, 1989). For those who do marry as teens, rates of marital discord and divorce are high. Poor employment prospects, coupled with the fact that many fathers provide little or no financial support, means that a disproportionate number of teen-age mothers will raise their children in poverty.

Teen-age mothers also tend to have larger families (by about one child) than their peers, thus putting a strain on the financial resources that are available to the family. Teen-age childbearing is also associated with closer spacing of births (Hayes, 1987). Teen-age mothers who have several children early in their childbearing years are at risk for not completing high school and for not being economically self-sufficient (Furstenberg et al., 1987).

Outcomes for the Children of Adolescent Mothers

The consequences that have been observed for teen-age mothers indicate that their children are often exposed to a number of risk factors. Thus, it is not surprising that the children of teen-age parents tend to fare less well than their peers on a variety of measures. The differences are apparent from birth because infants born to teen-age mothers are more likely than their peers to experience low birth weights and other medical risk factors. Related to this are higher rates of infant mortality among children born to teen-age mothers; infants born to women under the age of 18 are almost twice as likely to die before their first birthday as infants born to mothers over the age of 20 (Armstrong & Waszak, 1990).

Children born to teen-age mothers tend to perform less well than peers on measures of cognitive competence as well. By the early elementary grades, children born to teen-age mothers tend to score lower than peers born to older mothers on IQ tests and achievement tests. They are also at risk for having to repeat a grade (Baldwin & Cain, 1980; Brooks-Gunn & Furstenberg, 1986; Furstenberg et al., 1987).

Information on the socioemotional adjustment of children born to teen-age mothers is limited in comparison to the data on neonatal status and cognitive outcomes. However, the data that are available indicate that children of early childbearers show more signs of maladjustment than children born to later childbearers. A study of a birth cohort in Great Britain showed that children born to teen-age mothers had higher scores on a behavior problem checklist than their peers at age 5 (Wadsworth, Taylor, Osborn, & Butler, 1984). The relation between age of mother and behavior problems was statistically significant when confounding factors (e.g., socioeconomic status [SES]) were controlled. However, SES and a measure of maternal adjustment were stronger predictors of behavior problems than maternal age.

Socioemotional problems are more common in children having difficulties in school. In the longitudinal study of children born to adolescents in Baltimore, Furstenberg and his colleagues reported that adolescents who had repeated a grade were more likely to have school discipline problems, to have been suspended from school, to have been in trouble in school, and to have received counseling in the past 5 years. The children of teen-age mothers who had repeated a grade were also at greater risk for becoming teen-age parents themselves (Furstenberg et al., 1987).

Children of teen-age mothers clearly fare less well than do children born to older mothers. However, we must not lose sight of the fact that there is great diversity within samples of children born to teen-age mothers. An important question is: Under what circumstances is a child born to a teen-age mother likely to do well? Furstenberg and his colleagues concluded that the life course of the child is strongly linked to the life course of the mother. Children who were doing well tended to have mothers who coped successfully with an unplanned and early pregnancy. For example, children who were not held back in school tended to have mothers who finished high school and who limited further childbearing (less than three additional children during the 17-year period of the study). The mothers of those who were on track academically were also less likely to be on welfare and more likely to be married.

Dubow and Luster (1990) reported findings consistent with those of Furstenberg and his colleagues. They found that school-age children born to teenage mothers were most likely to have academic or behavioral problems if they had been exposed to several risk factors simultaneously. The risk factors that proved to be important included living below the poverty line, having a large number of siblings, and low maternal self-esteem. For example, children who lived in poverty, had four or more siblings, and had a mother who had low self-esteem were three times as likely to exhibit antisocial behavior as children of teen-age mothers who were exposed to none of these risk factors. Similar findings were reported for achievement test scores, with low maternal education and living in an urban setting being additional risk factors associated with low academic achievement.

The Cost of Adolescent Parenthood for Society

It is difficult to gauge the cost of adolescent parenthood to society but some costs can be estimated, such as the cost of Aid to Families with Dependent Children (AFDC) and Medicaid. Armstrong and Waszak (1990) calculated that welfare-related expenditures attributable to teen-age childbearing amounted to $21.55 billion in 1989. This figure included $10.43 billion for AFDC, $3.44 billion for food stamps, and $7.68 billion for Medicaid. This single-year cost estimate is based on total outlays for "all families in which the first birth occurred when the mother was a teenager, even though the mother may now be considerably older" (p. 4). Armstrong and Waszak estimated that if every birth to a teen mother had been delayed until the mother was in her 20s, the United States would have saved $8.62 billion in welfare-related expenditures in that year.

Armstrong and Waszak (1990) also estimated how much the public will pay to support all teen families begun in 1989 over the next 20 years. This single cohort cost is expected to be $6.35 billion for the period from 1989 to 2008. Clearly, the dollar cost associated with teen-age childbearing is substantial and a growing awareness of this cost is one reason for increasing concern about teen-age parenthood.

Research on the consequences of early childbearing for the teens and their children has sparked a considerable amount of interest in the parenting behavior of adolescent mothers. How do we characterize the parenting behavior of adolescent mothers? In what ways, if any, do they differ from older mothers in their approaches to childrearing? Can the poorer outcomes for children born to teen-age mothers be explained, at least in part, by the parenting they receive? Research that has compared the parenting behavior of adolescent and older mothers is examined in the next section.

COMPARISONS OF ADOLESCENT AND OLDER MOTHERS

The studies reviewed for this portion of the chapter are grouped according to the primary outcome variable utilized in the study. The four outcomes discussed here are: (a) the quality of the home environment; (b) mother–child interaction; (c) security of mother–infant attachment; and (d) child abuse.

The Quality of the Home Environment

Five studies were located for this review that have used Caldwell and Bradley's (1984) Home Observation for Measurement of the Environment (HOME) inventory, a measure of the overall quality of the home environment, to assess the parental performance of younger and older mothers. Higher scores on the HOME inventory have been linked to favorable developmental outcomes in children, particularly cognitive outcomes. The version of the HOME for parents with infants yields a total score and six subscale scores: (a) emotional and verbal responsivity; (b) acceptance of child's behavior; (c) organization of the environment; (d) provision of play materials; (e) parental involvement with child; and (f) opportunities for variety.

All of the studies that compared adolescent and older mothers on the total HOME inventory found that adolescent mothers provided less supportive home environments overall for their infants (Garcia Coll, Hoffman, & Oh, 1987; King & Fullard, 1982; Luster & Rhoades, 1989; Schilmoeller & Baranowski,

1985). Three of the four studies comparing younger and older mothers on the total HOME inventory used Caucasian samples; the exception is the study by King and Fullard (1982) who had a sample comprised largely of African-American and Caucasian mothers. One study that focused exclusively on ethnic minority mothers, used only three subscales from the HOME and therefore comparisons could not be made between the younger and older mothers on the total HOME (Darabi, Graham, Namerow, Philliber, & Varga, 1984).

An interesting pattern emerges when comparisons are made between younger and older mothers on the various subscales of the HOME. When significant differences were detected, they tended to be found for the subscales that tap how the mother interacts with the child. For example, with the exception of the study by Darabi and her colleagues (1984), all of the studies reviewed reported a significant difference favoring the older mothers on the emotional and verbal responsivity subscale of the HOME. The emotional and verbal responsivity subscale captures the extent to which the mother talks to her infant and displays positive affect when interacting with the infant. Three of the studies also reported that adolescent mothers had less favorable scores on the acceptance subscale (Garcia Coll et al., 1987; King & Fullard, 1982; Schilmoeller & Baranowski, 1985). The acceptance subscale assesses the degree to which the mother is restrictive and punitive when interacting with her infant. In two of the studies, adolescent mothers had less favorable scores on the parental involvement subscale (Garcia Coll et al., 1987; King & Fullard, 1982). The parental involvement subscale is primarily concerned with the degree to which the mother promotes cognitive advances in the infant through the provision of stimulating and developmentally appropriate activities.

Few differences were found on the subscales that focus on how the mother structures the child's environment—organization of the environment, and provision of play materials. The organization of the environment is concerned with the safety of the home environment and the extent to which the infant is exposed to a variety of settings. The provision of play materials assesses the variety of play materials available to the infant in the home. The only subscale concerned with structuring the child's experiences on which consistent differences between the adolescent and older mothers were found is the opportunities for variety subscale. Two of the five items on this subscale tap father involvement with the child; therefore, differences on this subscale may be due to differences in family structure rather than maternal behavior.

As noted earlier, the study by Darabi and her colleagues (1984) was the only study not to find a difference between the younger and older mothers on the emotional and verbal responsivity subscale of the HOME. One possible explanation for this involves the age of the children in this study. Darabi sampled mothers with children who ranged in age from 2 ½ to 4; the infant version of the HOME is typically used with children from birth to 3 years. This raises the possibility that teens may show less emotional and verbal responsivity than older mothers when their infants are very young, but the differences may disappear as the children become more communicative, and thus more effective at eliciting responses from their caregivers. Unfortunately, very few studies have focused on the parenting behavior of teen mothers beyond the infancy period. Additional research is needed to examine this possibility.

In summary, we have seen that adolescent mothers tend to provide less supportive environments for their infants than older mothers, when assessed on the HOME inventory. When subscale scores are considered, the most consistent finding is that adolescent mothers are less emotionally and verbally responsive to their infants than older mothers. In addition, some of the studies found the adolescent mothers to be more restrictive and punitive, and less involved with their infants than the older mothers.

Mother–Child Interaction

The studies of the home environment just reviewed, for the most part, showed teen mothers to have lower scores on the emotional and verbal responsivity subscale of the HOME. Studies that focused on the mother's style of interacting with her child yielded results that are consistent with the findings on the home environment.

In two studies, investigators compared adolescent and older mothers in the hospital setting while the mothers were feeding their newborns, and in both studies older mothers vocalized more to their infants than younger mothers (Culp, Appelbaum, Osofsky, & Levy, 1988; Sandler, Vietze, & O'Connor, 1981). In the study by Sandler and colleagues, however, the two groups of mothers did not differ on several other behaviors that were recorded. Likewise, Culp and his colleagues did not find differences between the mothers on measures of visual regard and attentiveness to the infant, and found a significant difference favoring the adolescent mothers on a measure of tactile stimulation.

Studies of mother–infant interaction in the home also found the teen mothers to provide less verbal stimulation than older mothers (Garcia Coll et al., 1987; Helm, Comfort, Bailey, & Simeonsson, 1990; Roosa, Fitzgerald, & Carlson, 1982a; Stevenson & Roach, 1988). In the study by Roosa and his colleagues, older mothers were also more likely to respond contingently to the infants' distress vocalizations, but the two groups did not differ on several other behaviors, such as physical contact with the infant. Based on a subsequent analysis of the data, Roosa, Fitzgerald, and Carlson (1982b) argued that the observed differences between the younger and older mothers were due more to differences in SES than maternal age.

Other researchers who studied adolescent mothers commented on the nonverbal parenting style of adolescent mothers. Osofsky and Osofsky (1970) observed adolescent mothers before and during a pediatric exam, and rated the mothers positively on levels of warmth and physical interaction, but assigned low scores for verbal interaction. Epstein (1980) observed 98 teen-age mothers in their homes. A factor analysis of the coded behaviors revealed three styles of interaction: (a) sharing—a generally sensitive, responsive, authoritative style; (b) directing—a commanding, intrusive, authoritarian style; and (c) no talking—a nonverbal style of interacting in which only the physical needs of the babies were attended to by the mother. The nonverbal interaction style was the most characteristic style for this sample of mothers followed by the sharing and directing styles respectively. Epstein (1980) reported that adolescent mothers who were nonverbal lacked knowledge of infant development and tended to underestimate the abilities of infants, "expecting too little, too late" (p. 28). The lack of adult control groups is a limitation of the studies by the Osofskys and by Epstein, but their descriptions of adolescent mothers are consistent with those reported in other studies.

Beyond the finding that adolescent mothers are less verbal with their infants than older mothers, few generalizations regarding adolescent parenting can be made with the available literature. However, other differences were noted in individual studies. These include findings that adolescent mothers tend to exhibit more aggressive behaviors with their infants, such as poking and pinching (Lawrence et al., 1981), less positive affect (Helm et al., 1990; Levine, Garcia Coll, & Oh, 1985), and more inappropriate and negative affect (Hann, Osofsky, Barnard, & Leonard, 1990). Teen mothers were also found to engage in game playing less often with their infants (Field, 1980), and to respond contingently to the cues of their infants less often than older mothers (Field, 1980; Helm et al., 1990).

Few studies reported differences between teens and adults in their basic care routines. In one study, teens differed from older mothers in terms of how they nourished their young infants (Mercer, Hackley, & Bostrom, 1984). The adolescent mothers were less likely than older mothers to breast-feed their babies, and they were more likely to introduce their babies to cereal at 1 month of age and various other foods (e.g., vegetables, meat) during the first 4 months of life. Zuckerman, Winsmore, and Alpert (1979), however, found no difference in the percentage of adolescent and adult mothers who breast-fed their infants; adolescent mothers did, however, have less positive attitudes about breast-feeding.

A limitation of the literature comparing adolescent and older mothers is that nearly all studies are confined to the infancy period. A notable exception, however, is an early study by Oppel and Royston (1971). This study focused primarily on differences in the developmental outcomes of 6- to 8-year-olds born to adolescent or older mothers. However, as part of the study, data were also collected on the parenting behavior of younger and older mothers who had been matched in terms of SES and race. Those women who were teen-age mothers were found to be less anxious, more likely to think that their children should be free to act independently, and less involved with their children. Differences on three other aspects of parenting approached significance with the younger mothers being less likely to wish to control the child, to keep the child closely attached to themselves, and to have intellectual interests. On 19 other subscales of the parenting measure (Maternal Behavior Research Instrument), the two groups did not differ.

In summary, when differences are found between adolescent and older mothers they almost invariably favor the older mothers. In particular, older mothers provide their infants with a richer verbal environment. There is also some evidence that older mothers are more responsive to their infants. Some studies also reported differences favoring older mothers on various affective dimensions; mature mothers were found to exhibit more positive affect and less negative affect when interacting with their infants. Given these differences in parenting, are adolescent mothers and their infants at risk for relationship difficulties? The literature on attachment is considered next.

Secure Versus Anxious Attachment

Surprisingly few studies have looked at the relation between maternal age and the quality of the mother–infant relationship, assessed in the strange situation. One study that used attachment classifications as an outcome compared three groups of mothers and their 12-month-old infants: (a) adolescent mothers who received support and feedback on their child-care practices from the investigators (N = 14); (b) older mothers who received the same intervention (N = 12); and (c) a control group of adolescent mothers (N = 10) (Landy, Montgomery, Schubert, Cleland, & Clark, 1983). No difference was found between the older and younger mothers who received the intervention. The adolescent control mothers, however, were more likely to have infants who were rated as being insecure. Of the 10 control infants, 6 were classified as avoidant or resistant. Given the small subsamples, the findings reported by Landy and her associates must be viewed cautiously.

Lamb, Hopps, and Elster (1987) assessed 40, 14-month-old infants born to adolescent mothers in the Ainsworth strange situation. Of the infants, 48% were classified as avoidant (A), 48% were classified as secure (B), one infant was classified as resistant (c), and one infant was rated unclassifiable. They compared their distribution of attachment classifications with the distribution reported by Ainsworth, Blehar, Waters, and Wall (1978) who sampled 106 adult mothers. A chi-square analysis revealed that the two distributions differed significantly. Further analyses indicated that the proportion of insecure babies (A and C collapsed) did not differ in the two samples, but there was a disproportionate number of the avoidant infants in the adolescent sample (48% vs. 22%).

A third study to examine rates of secure attachment among infants born to teen-age mothers was conducted by Frodi et al. (1984). Thirty infants were classified in the strange situation. Of these, 53% were classified as securely attached (b), 30% were anxious-avoidant (a), and 17% were resistant (c). They noted that the percentage of secure babies in this sample was considerably less than that typically found in middle-class samples. However, the authors pointed out that this distribution of attachment classifications was similar to that reported by Vaughn, Egeland, Waters, and Sroufe (1979) for a low SES sample; the Vaughn sample also included a substantial proportion of teen-age mothers with the median age of the mothers being 19.

Hann, Osofsky, Stringer, and Carter (1988) assessed a relatively large sample (N = 98) of adolescent mothers and their 13-month-old infants in the strange situation. Of the infants, 68% were classified as secure, 22% were avoidant, and 10% were resistant. No comparison group was used in this study.

The limited number of studies and diversity of the results preclude us from drawing any conclusions about the relation between age of mother and security of infant–mother attachments. Moreover, it is difficult to determine if the pattern for adolescent mothers deviates from the expected pattern given that there is considerable diversity in the percentage of children classified as secure and insecure in various studies with adult mothers (Spieker & Booth, 1988). Clearly this is an area where more research is needed.

Child Maltreatment and Adolescent Parenthood

Are the children of adolescent mothers at greater risk for child maltreatment than other children? Given what is known about the antecedents of child abuse, one would expect the children of teen-age mothers to be at risk for maltreatment. Characteristics associated with teen-age parenthood that have also been linked to child abuse include poverty, large family size, marital instability, and poor developmental history. Moreover, the children of adolescent mothers are more likely than other children to be born with low birth weights and other medical risk factors.

Although some studies have found no relation between maternal age at the time of the child's birth and child abuse (e.g., Hunter, Kilstrom, Kraybill, & Loda, 1978), the results of several studies suggest that there is an association between adolescent parenthood and child maltreatment (Kinard & Klerman, 1980; Leventhal, 1981; Miller, 1983, cited in Bolton & Belsky, 1986). In a review of the literature, Leventhal (1981) reported that a statistically significant relation between maternal age and the incidence of abuse was found in 9 of 11 studies he reviewed. All of the studies were retrospective studies and many had methodological limitations; however, the studies that were considered most sound from a methodological standpoint supported the hypothesis that there is an association between young maternal age and child abuse.

Although there appears to be an association between adolescent parenthood and child abuse, the association is less striking than many had expected it to be. Bolton and Belsky (1986) noted that the expected "epidemic" of child maltreatment by adolescent parents "simply failed to materialize" (p. 125). However, as Kinard and Klerman (1980) noted, some studies may underestimate the strength of the association between teen-age parenthood and child abuse because the researchers use the age of the parent at the time the abuse occurred rather than the age of the parent at first birth (or when the index child was born).

A second important question that has seldom been addressed is: Which adolescent mothers are likely to abuse their children? One informative, prospective study that addressed this question was conducted by Bolton and his colleagues in Arizona (Bolton & Belsky, 1986; Bolton, Laner, & Kane, 1980). Bolton followed 960 adolescent mothers from the time their children were born until the children were 2 years old. At birth the families were assessed on a number of risk factors that had been linked to child abuse in previous studies. Official records of substantiated cases of child abuse were examined when the children were 2 years old to determine which of the children had been abused.

At the 2-year follow-up, approximately 2% of the teens had maltreated their children. The mothers who had abused their children differed from the nonabusive mothers on a number of dimensions. Abusive mothers were more likely to have experienced violence in their past, were less healthy at the time of delivery, and experienced their pregnancy less positively than nonmaltreating mothers. Mothers who eventually maltreated their infants were found to provide lower quality care for their infants during the postpartum period and during the first year. According to Belsky and Bolton (1986) "the maltreating mothers had less eye contact, did less touching, were less accepting of their children's needs for reciprocal interaction and failed to demonstrate a positive understanding of the children's needs" (p. 134).

The maltreated children were more likely than the other children to have been born with low birth weights and other medical risks. They were also more likely to be delivered by Caesarean section than nonmaltreated infants.

Somewhat surprisingly, maltreating mothers were twice as likely to be married as their nonmaltreating counterparts (44.5% vs. 21.5%). The authors proposed that this finding may be due to the fact that married mothers received less support in the area of child care from the family of origin than unmarried mothers. Thus, characteristics of the mothers, of the children, and of the families distinguished between adolescent mothers who were abusive and those who were not.

To summarize, it appears that children born to teen-age mothers are at greater risk for abuse than other children but the link between teen-age parenthood and child abuse is less marked than some had anticipated it would be. The antecedents of child abuse among teen-age parents are similar to the antecedents reported for samples of abusive parents who are hetergeneous in terms of age. The elevated rates of abuse among teen-age parents probably reflect the fact that teen-age parents possess or are exposed to more of the risk factors associated with abuse than older mothers (e.g., high levels of stress, poor developmental histories).

Limitations of the Studies Comparing Adolescent and Older Mothers

As noted earlier, one of the limitations of the studies discussed so far is that most are confined to the infancy period. Second, most of the infants are first-born infants. We know virtually nothing about the parenting behavior of adolescent mothers with their second or later born children. A third limitation is that, with few exceptions, the number of adolescent mothers sampled in a given study is quite small. Given the small sample sizes, the power to detect differences that may exist between groups is quite limited in most studies. Fourth, comparisons of adolescent and adult mothers are problematic in that the two groups tend to differ on dimensions other than age (e.g., marital status, level of education achieved, financial resources). Differences between adolescent and adult mothers may be largely due to these other factors rather than to age per se.

Studies comparing the parenting behavior of adolescent and adult mothers are more useful for descriptive purposes than for explanation. It is clear that younger mothers with infants, on average, tend to provide less supportive care than older mothers, particularly in terms of verbal stimulation. However, several investigators have concluded or implied that the observed differences are due to age/maturity. Although this is an intuitively appealing explanation and maturity may indeed contribute to observed differences, it is difficult to isolate the effects of age from other confounding variables. The tendency to attach great importance to age/maturity per se in these studies may be due to the fact that research on adolescent parenting has largely been done in isolation from research on the causes or antecedents of adolescent parenthood.

Although teen parents are found throughout the social strata, the adolescents who become parents are not representative of all teen-agers. Those who become teen-age mothers are more likely than their peers to come from low SES homes, from single-parent households, from homes where the mother was a teen-age parent herself, and from homes characterized by discord and disharmony (Harris, Brown, & Bifulco, 1987; Hayes, 1987; Quinton & Rutter, 1988). They are also more likely than their peers to have been victims of abuse (Butler & Burton, 1990). In addition, adolescent parents are more likely than peers to have low intellectual ability, to perform poorly in school, and to have relatively low educational aspirations (Flick, 1986; Hayes, 1987). There is also some evidence indicating that a disproportionate number of teen mothers and their male partners have had encounters with law enforcement officials (Elster et al., 1987; Lamb, 1988). Many of the factors that put teens at risk for becoming adolescent parents would also put them at risk for performing poorly in the parenting role (Small & Luster, 1990).

FACTORS RELATED TO PARENTING COMPETENCE AMONG ADOLESCENT MOTHERS

Comparisons of adolescent and adult mothers tend to mask the fact that there is great variability in the quality of care parents provide within each group. An important question that is receiving increasing attention is: What factors distinguish between adolescent mothers who are providing relatively supportive care for their children and their peers who are providing less supportive care? Utilizing Belsky's (1984) model of the determinants of parenting as a framework, research that has shed light on this question is reviewed in this section. Belsky proposed that there are three primary determinants of parenting behavior: (a) the personal and psychological resources of the parent, (b) characteristics of the child, and (c) the broader context in which the parent–infant relationship is evolving. Studies falling into each of these three categories are summarized.

The Personal and Psychological Resources of the Teen Mother

The characteristics of the teen mothers that have been studied include: (a) personality characteristics/psychological well-being, (b) age, and (c) childrearing attitudes, beliefs, and knowledge.

Personality/Psychological Well-Being. A limited number of studies tested the notion that the psychological well-being of the adolescent mother is related to the quality of care she provides for her child. LeResche, Strobino, Parks, Fischer, and Smeriglio (1983) assessed the mental health status of adolescent mothers with Goldberg's (1982) General Health Questionnaire, and related this measure to maternal behavior. Positive adjustment on the part of the mothers was correlated with the amount of time they spent in physical contact with their infants in a nursery-playroom setting, but was unrelated to the other five maternal behaviors assessed.

Reis and Herz (1987) were also interested in the influence of mental health on parenting behavior. The well-being of 177 adolescent mothers was assessed with the CES-D depression measure. They found the level of depression to be unrelated to HOME total scores. It was, however, related to the maternal involvement subscale of the HOME, with depressed mothers being less involved with their infants.

Utilizing data from the National Longitudinal Survey of Youth (NLSY), Luster and Dubow (1990) assessed the extent to which maternal self-esteem and intelligence predicted the quality of care that adolescent mothers provided for their school-age children. A modest, although statistically significant, positive correlation was obtained between maternal self-esteem and the quality of the home environment, even though the data on self-esteem had been collected 6 years prior to the assessment of the home environment. Maternal intelligence was also positively correlated with the quality of the home environment ($r = .35$), but the relationship was reduced to nonsignificance when other factors (e.g., current financial resources) were controlled, suggesting that the effects of maternal intelligence on quality of the home environment are largely indirect in this population. Spieker (1989) also reported a positive correlation between IQ scores of teen mothers and their scores on the HOME and Barnard's (1978) teaching scale.

Unger and Wandersman (1985) found that adolescent mothers with high self-esteem tended to provide relatively supportive environments for their infants. In addition, *mastery*, a measure of the extent to which the mothers believed their lives were under their own control, was related to parental performance. Mothers who perceived themselves as having considerable control over events that affected their lives provided more supportive environments.

In contrast to Unger and Wandersman's finding for mastery, Stevens (1988) found no relation between locus of control orientation and scores on the HOME inventory in a sample of teen mothers. However, an internal locus of control orientation was associated with more favorable HOME scores for the adult mothers in the study. Likewise, Helm and his colleagues (1990) found an internal locus of control orientation to have a positive effect on the behavior of adult mothers but it was unrelated to the behavior of adolescent mothers.

Although some inconsistencies are noted across studies, taken together, these studies provide support for the notion that the psychological well-being of the teen-age mother is reflected in her parenting style. This is consistent with the finding reported for mothers who are hetergeneous in terms of age (Vondra & Belsky, this volume).

Age.   Younger teens are often thought to be at greater risk for poor parenting than older teens. The extent to which there is empirical support for that viewpoint is considered next.

King and Fullard (1982) reported a modest zero-order correlation ($r = .23$) between maternal age and the scores on the HOME inventory for their sample of adolescent mothers. Reis and Herz (1987) also found a significant relation between maternal age and scores on the HOME in their sample of young mothers ($r = .29$). Luster and Rhoades (1989) reported a correlation between age and HOME scores that was similar in magnitude for their smaller sample of teen-age mothers, but the relation was not statistically significant.

Spieker (1989) also used the HOME inventory to compare 125 teen mothers who were over 18 years of age with 89 younger teens. Significant differences were found between the two groups favoring the older teens. However, when the two items in the HOME that specifically refer to paternal behavior were eliminated, no difference was found between the two groups. Spieker argued that the difference between the groups on the total HOME score could be explained by the fact that fewer young teens had partners who interacted with their infants.

Studies using Barnard's (1978) teaching and feeding scales produced mixed results. Spieker (1989) found no differences between younger and older teens on the teaching measure. Ruff (1987) reported that older teens had more favorable scores on the feeding scale than younger teens, during the neonatal period and at 6 to 12 weeks postpartum. At each assessment, however, the correlation between maternal age and parenting competence was small in magnitude (rs = .15 and .23 respectively).

In a study described earlier, Epstein (1980) found that younger teen mothers tended not to engage in verbal interchanges with their babies as much as older teens. Culp and his associates reported a similar finding (Culp et al., 1988). LeResche and colleagues found that older adolescents looked at and held their babies in the en face position more frequently than younger mothers (LeResche et al., 1983).

McAnarney and her colleagues videotaped 75 teen mothers as they interacted with their infants in a laboratory setting during the postpartum period (McAnarney, Lawrence, Aten, & Iker, 1984). Eight maternal behaviors were coded from the videotapes, including positive vocalizations and negative vocalizations. Maternal age was unrelated to how the teen mothers cared for their newborns. However, the mothers and infants were videotaped again when the infants were approaching their first birthday, and substantial differences were found in the parenting behaviors of younger and older teens (McAnarney, Lawrence, Ricciuti, Polley, & Szilagyi, 1986). Older teens were rated as being more accepting, cooperative, accessible, and sensitive when interacting with their infants. They also provided a more stimulating verbal environment. To account for differences between the initial study and the results at follow-up, the investigators posited that the infants presented more of a challenge for the mothers as they became mobile and hence, more independent; older teens may be better able to cope with these more challenging behaviors.

Although most studies have produced support for the viewpoint that younger teens are particularly at risk for parenting problems, Frodi and colleagues (1984) found that younger teens were more likely than older teens to have infants who were rated as securely attached in the strange situation. However, the investigators noted that age was confounded with level of social support in this sample. The younger teens tended to receive more social support than the older teens.

In summary, the results of several studies suggest that there is a modest relation between maternal age and parenting competence within samples of teen mothers. This finding is congruent with the results of a recent study indicating that school-age children who were born to very young teen-age mothers are at somewhat greater risk for academic and behavioral problems than children who were born to older teens (Dubow & Luster, 1990). However, even within samples of teen-age mothers, age at first birth and other risk factors are likely to be confounded, thus making it difficult to determine causal processes.

Childrearing Attitudes, Beliefs, and Knowledge.   Adolescent mothers, like their older counterparts, have differing levels of knowledge about child development and diverse views on appropriate childrearing practices. A few recent studies have examined the relation between adolescent parents' ideas and knowledge about child care and their parenting practices. Reis and Herz (1987) found that younger teens had more punitive childrearing attitudes than older teens, and mothers with more punitive attitudes tended to provide less supportive environments, as assessed by the HOME. In another study, teen mothers with more responsive attitudes exhibited more smiling and eye contact with their babies, but the attitude measure was not significantly related to the speed with which the mothers responded to their crying infants (Crockenberg, 1987a).

Luster and Rhoades (1989) reported that adolescent mothers who provided relatively supportive home environments for their infants differed from their less supportive peers in terms of their childrearing beliefs. Mothers who provided the most supportive environments emphasized the importance of talking to their infants early and often, and believed that infants should be given considerable leeway in exploring their surroundings. Less supportive care was provided by mothers who believed that babies are likely to become spoiled if the mother is responsive and affectionate, and by mothers who emphasized the importance of being a disciplinarian.

In addition to examining beliefs about appropriate childrearing practices, Luster and Rhoades assessed the mothers' beliefs about the extent to which parents influence the development of their children. The young mothers who provided the most supportive care believed that parents exert considerable influence on the developing child. Similarly, LeResche et al. (1983) found that adolescent mothers' perceptions of their ability to influence their children were positively related to the amount of smiling the mothers exhibited when interacting with their babies; however, perceived influence was not related to other maternal behaviors such as vocalizing to the infant.

Mothers who are more knowledgeable about child development were also found to provide more supportive environments for their infants. Johnson (1990) reported that more knowledgeable teens outperformed less knowledgeable peers on a number of parenting dimensions during a teaching task. Ward and her colleagues found relatively knowledgeable teens to be more sensitive and responsive than other teen mothers when their infants were 4 months of age (Ward et al., 1988). However, knowledge was unrelated to the same parenting measures at 8 months.

Characteristics of the Child

It seems reasonable that parents who lack maturity and who often have several other stressors to contend with would not deal well with a temperamentally difficult infant or a biologically at-risk infant (e.g., premature infant). Unfortunately, studies of teen parents that tested this hypothesis are few in number, and in the case of temperament, the studies that are available provide little support for the hypothesis. Several studies fail to detect any relationship between infant temperament and parenting behavior in samples of teen mothers (Crockenberg, 1987a, 1987b; Luster & Rhoades, 1989; Ward et al., 1988), and in one study, irritability on the part of the infant was associated with more positive mother–infant interaction during a feeding episode (Wise & Grossman, 1980).

One study to find the expected relation between infant temperament and parenting behavior was a relatively rare study of the behavior of adolescent mothers with their later born infants (the mothers were now in their 20s). Luster, Boger, and Hannan (1990) reported that infants who were generally cheerful received more supportive home environments than their less cheerful peers. In contrast, infant irritability was negatively related to the quality of care provided for the infants. An irritable infant may be especially difficult for an early childbearer if she has other children competing for her attention and if she has few resources. Alternatively, caregivers with competing demands may be relatively unresponsive to the cues of the infants, thus contributing to increased irritability on the part of the infant (Bell & Ainsworth, 1972; Crockenberg & Smith, 1982).

Even fewer studies examined the effect of having a biologically at-risk infant on the parenting behavior of teens, but the studies that have been done suggest that teens may have difficulty coping with these conditions, at least during the early infancy period. Field (1980) noted a number of deficiencies in the parenting behavior of low SES teens with preterm infants. The teens with the high-risk infants were less vocal and generally less involved with their infants than other teens, or adult mothers with preterm infants. Wise and Grossman (1980) found that both birth weight and Apgar scores were related to mother–infant reciprocity during a newborn feeding situation. Teen mothers interacted more positively with their babies if the infants were heavier and if they had more favorable Apgar scores at birth. These findings are consistent with those showing that adolescent mothers were more likely to mistreat their infants if the babies were undersized or experienced other medical complications (Bolton & Belsky, 1986).

Contextual Influences

Having looked at the characteristics of the child and the teen mother, an ecological perspective requires that we consider the context in which the parent–child relationship takes place. What characteristics of the environment allow for or hinder successful parenting and optimal child development? We review research on five contextual influences: (a) social support, (b) residential status and division of child-care responsibilities, (c) socioeconomic status, (d) number of children, and (e) sociocultural background.

Social Support.   Of these five factors, the effect of social support on adolescent parenting has been studied most extensively. Several studies found that mothers who are well supported by their family of origin and/or male partner perform more competently in the parenting role than mothers with lower levels of support (Helm et al., 1990). In a study of British adolescents, Crockenberg (1988) reported that mothers with high levels of emotional and instrumental support from their families responded relatively quickly when their babies cried. Likewise, seeking help from extended family members was related to the provision of a supportive home environment in a sample of teens studied by Stevens (1988). Another study to document the importance of support for teen parents focused on security of attachment as the outcome; Frodi et al. (1984) found that a secure attachment between the infant and the mother was more likely to occur if the mother had an extensive support network, and if the grandmother helped with child care. Similarly, Colletta (1981) found that teen mothers with inadequate support systems rejected their infants more often than teens who were well supported.

Some research suggests that the type and source of support that is most valuable for the adolescent mother may change over time (Crockenberg, 1988). Crockenberg (1987a) found that support from the family of origin was positively related to the mothers' sensitivity and accessibility to their 3-month-old infants. In contrast, family support was unrelated to the extent to which the mothers exhibited angry and punitive behavior when the children were 2 years old (Crockenberg, 1987b). Partner support, however, was important at the 2-year follow-up if the mother had a history of nonacceptance by her own mother. The most angry and punitive mothers had experienced rejection in childhood and lacked support from their current partners.

Unger and Wandersman (1985) also found evidence that the source and type of support that was predictive of positive maternal behavior changed over time in two samples of teens. In the first sample, mothers provided more supportive environments for their 1-month-old children when the baby's father helped with child care, and when the mothers had relatives nearby who provided child-care assistance. By 8 months of age, child care by the father was not related to scores on the HOME inventory. Unger and Wandersman suggested that the declining importance of the father's child-care activities may be due to the unstable nature of the relationship between the mothers and the biological fathers in this sample. Family support was not related to HOME scores in this sample at either 1 or 8 months of age.

In the second study with a larger sample, family support, assessed prenatally, was positively related to the quality of the home environment young mothers provided for their 8-month-old infants. Support from a male partner, who often was not the biological father, was also related to positive parenting behaviors at 8 months. Support from the baby's biological father, assessed prenatally, was not related to scores on the HOME inventory.

Although there is substantial evidence indicating that social support is positively related to the quality of care teen mothers provide for their children, several qualifying statements are in order. First, some studies have found little relation between social support and measures of adolescent maternal behavior (Lamb & Elster, 1985; Reis & Herz, 1987). Second, some studies have assessed several aspects of support and related these measures to various indicators of parental behavior. Although this approach is valuable for discerning which aspects of support are most important for adolescent mothers, it also increases the risk of making a Type 1 error. Finally, most studies report zero-order correlations between social support measures and parenting measures. As Crockenberg (1987a) noted, it is possible that in some cases the relation between support and parental behavior is spurious. She offers the example of women whose childhoods were characterized by rejection by their parents. As mothers, these women may continue to lack support from their families of origin and may be relatively unskillful parents themselves. However, the poor parenting may be largely due to the developmental history of the women rather than to the current level of support they receive from their families. Studies that control for possible confounding variables would provide more compelling data on the importance of social support for competent parenting by adolescent mothers.

Residential Status and Division of Child-Care Responsibilities. Some investigators suggested that a young mother is likely to benefit from living in the same household as her mother, if the mother and the grandmother do not have conflicts regarding appropriate child-care practices or role responsibilities (Wilson, 1989). A few studies examined the influence of coresidence with the grandmother on adolescent mothers and their children. At the 5-year follow-up, Furstenberg and Crawford (1978) found that single mothers who were living with their mothers derived some benefits from that arrangement. These mothers were more likely than single mothers living independently to complete high school and to be employed; consequently they were less likely to receive welfare payments. Living with the grandmother also tended to have a positive effect on the cognitive development of the children, but showed no relationship with the mothers' childrearing patterns.

At the 17-year follow-up, the children of adolescent mothers who continued to reside with the grandmother showed poorer attainment and adjustment than their peers (Furstenberg et al., 1987). To explain the difference between the findings at the 5-year and the 17-year follow-ups, Furstenberg suggested that the least capable adolescent mothers may be the ones who maintain a long-term dependent relationship with their mothers.

Results consistent with this interpretation are provided by other studies. King and Fullard (1982) found that adolescent mothers who lived with their parents were less punitive with the infants than other adolescent mothers. In contrast, Luster and Dubow (1990) reported that adolescent mothers who had school-age children provided somewhat less supportive home environments for the children if they resided in the home of the maternal grandmother.

In contrast to those studies just described, some studies examined how childcare responsibilities are divided between the mother and the grandmother when the mother lives with her family of origin. Epstein (1980) found that adolescent mothers who provided the most favorable care for their infants (an authoritative style of rearing) tended to share childrearing responsibilities with the grandmother and/or the baby's father. Mothers who did all of their own child care tended to be directive or authoritarian with their children. Teenage mothers who relinquished responsibility for child care in large part to the grandmother also interacted less favorably with their infants. Epstein argued this is because these mothers have not had the chance to develop a synchronous interactive style with the infant.

Field, Widmayer, Stringer, and Ingatoff (1990) compared teens who were primary caregivers (i.e., spent most of her daytime hours at home) with teens who were secondary caregivers (spent most daytime hours away from home). Secondary mothers received more favorable scores on the HOME inventory overall. As was the case in the Epstein study, teen mothers who shouldered most of the responsibility for child care tended to be more restrictive and punitive when dealing with their infants.

In contrast to the studies by Epstein (1980) and Field et al. (1990), Free (1989) discovered that role sharing may be a better arrangement for the mother than for the infant. Role sharing allowed the teen to continue her education, adolescent friendships, and career planning. However, role-sharing mothers were less responsive to their infants than adolescent mothers who assumed all of the parenting tasks and responsibilities. Clearly more research is needed to determine the optimal level of childrearing involvement on the part of other adults, when the adolescent mother lives with her family of origin.

Socioeconomic Status.   Assessing the SES level of a teen-age mother poses problems for researchers. Having a low paying job has different implications for teen mothers living independently than for mothers who reside with their families. In addition, many adolescent mothers resume their educational careers at varying points after the birth of their first child (Furstenberg et al., 1987); thus, measures of the mothers' education have little meaning when the teen mothers are typically being studied, that is, after the birth of their first children. Therefore, data collected on the mothers' SES in the postinfancy period is likely to be more valuable.

Data from the NLSY showed that early childbearers who were living in poverty provided relatively unsupportive environments for their school-age children (Luster & Dubow, 1990). This finding is consistent with studies showing that the adjustment and achievement of older children born to teen-age mothers are positively related to the financial resources of the family (Dubow & Luster, 1990; Furstenberg et al., 1987).

An alternative to measuring the mother's income or education is to measure the SES level of her family or origin. Two studies have documented a relationship between the educational level of the adolescent's father and the quality of care she provides for her children (King & Fullard, 1982; Luster & Dubow, 1990). Thus, both the SES of the mother's family of origin and her current SES level have been linked to the quality of care the mother provides.

Number of Children.   Little is known about the effect of family size on the child-care practices of adolescent mothers. However, a few studies suggest that early childbearers often do not have the personal or financial resources to attend to the needs of several children. Luster and Dubow (1990) reported an inverse relation between number of children the mother had and the quality of the home environment, after controlling for possible confounding factors. Other studies linked large family size to poor developmental outcomes for the children of adolescent mothers (Dubow & Luster, 1990; Furstenberg et al., 1987). Furstenberg found that the number of births in the first 5 years of the study was more strongly related to child outcomes than number of births in the later part of the study. Rapid repeat pregnancies are likely to limit the life options of the mothers and the time they can devote to a given child (Polit & Kahn, 1986).

Sociocultural Background.   Another possible influence on the adolescent's parenting behavior that has received relatively little attention is sociocultural background. Although studies examining the influence of sociocultural background on adolescent parenting behavior are few in number, there is substantial evidence that adaptive responses to early parenthood vary as a function of ethnicity (Battle, 1987; Franklin, 1988; Salguero, 1984). For example, African-American teens are less likely than Caucasian teens to marry the father to legitimate a birth (Hayes, 1987). African-American families are likely to respond to early childbearing by incorporating the teen and her infant into an extended family household with other adults in the household assisting with child care (Wilson, 1989).

Additional evidence that the experience of adolescent parenthood may differ for women from various sociocultural groups comes from the National Longitudinal Survey of Youth. Luster and Dubow (1990) found ethnic group differences in the circumstances of women who had been teen-age mothers but now were in their 20s. Consistent with other studies, African-American mothers were less likely than Caucasian or Hispanic mothers to be living with a spouse or male partner, and were more likely to be living with the grandmother. The African-American mothers, on average, had achieved a higher educational level than the other two groups, yet were more likely to be living in poverty. To some extent the elevated rate of poverty for African-American families was due to differences in marital status, but even in two-parent families, African-American families were twice as likely as Caucasian families to be living in poverty (26% vs. 13%).

Obviously, sociocultural background is confounded with other factors, thus making it difficult to assess the effects of ethnicity per se on parenting. Nevertheless, sociocultural background may influence parenting after the effects of SES and family structure have been taken into account. Differing beliefs about appropriate child care are likely to evolve in various sociocultural groups over time, and these beliefs may, in turn, contribute to differing approaches to childrearing (Brooks-Gunn & Furstenberg, 1986; Ogbu, 1981). One interesting study that investigated this possibility with a sample of adolescent mothers was conducted by Field and her associates (Field, Widmayer, Adler, & De Cubas, 1990). Field compared Cuban-American and African-American adolescent mothers, who were similar in terms of SES, on a number of parenting dimensions. The Cuban-American subsample received more favorable scores on each of the six subscales of the HOME inventory. The Cuban-American teens were also more likely to read to, touch, look at, talk to, and smile at their infants during a play session. Field attributed differences between the two groups of mothers largely to differing childrearing attitudes and expectations that were associated with their cultures, and noted that the differences between the teens' mothers paralleled those found for adult mothers from these two sociocultural groups (Field & Widmayer, 1981). Cuban-Americans were regarded as having more indulgent views on childrearing; the more restrictive and punitive style of the African-American mothers resulted from their greater fears about spoiling the child and their expectation for earlier autonomy on the part of their offspring.

It is also possible that factors that are important predictors of parenting quality in one sociocultural group may be less important or unrelated to parenting measures in a second group. Luster and Rhoades (1989) found differing relations between childrearing beliefs and HOME scores for African-American and Caucasian teens. Given the small subsample sizes, conclusions about the generalizability of these findings must await replication. Nevertheless, assumptions that the relations among variables are the same across ethnic groups are not warranted (Luster & Dubow, 1990).

Limitations of the Within-Group Studies

The literature just reviewed suggests that adolescent parenting practices are multiply determined, with differences among the teens due to characteristics of the mothers, characteristics of their children and the contexts in which the relationships are evolving. Although much has been learned about factors that contribute to differences in the parenting practices of teens over the past decade, it is also apparent that much research remains to be done in this area.

The available research is limited in that very few longitudinal studies of teen parents have been conducted. Furstenberg et al. (1987) documented the changing nature of the life circumstances of teen parents over a 17-year period; these changing circumstances had implications for the well-being of their children. Studies aimed at understanding the relation between various ecological transitions (e.g., having a second child, returning to school, moving from an extended family household into a single-parent household) and parent–child relations in samples of adolescent mothers could prove to be quite valuable.

A second limitation is that some factors that may influence the parenting behavior of adolescent mothers have not been adequately studied. For example, only one study examining the relation between developmental history and parenting among teens was located for this review (Crockenberg, 1987b). In addition, younger and older teen-age mothers may differ in their cognitive competencies (e.g., formal operational abilities), but to date, no one has examined the relation between these capabilities and parenting performance. Other factors that require further study include family size, sociocultural background, and division of child-care responsibilities in extended family households.

Although it is known that marriages precipitated by early pregnancies are at risk for discord and dissolution, little is known about the effects of marital quality on family dynamics among teen parents. Lamb and Elster (1985) found little relation between marital quality and the way in which adolescent mothers and their partners interacted with their infants. However, Crockenberg (1987b) reported that partner support was particularly important if the mother had experienced poor rearing experiences in her childhood; this finding is consistent with those reported by Quinton and Rutter (1988) for ex-institutional women who were in their 20s. Furstenberg et al. (1987) found the marital status of adolescent mothers to be a better predictor of developmental outcomes when the children had reached adolescence than when they were preschoolers. They proposed that marital support may be particularly important as teens become less dependent on their families of origin. Therefore, it would be important to examine the effects of marital status and marital harmony on parenting behavior over time.

Finally, many of the limitations noted for between-group studies (i.e., studies comparing adolescent and older mothers) are also found in the within-group studies. These include the use of small samples in many studies, the tendency to focus only on mothers with infants, and the failure to control for confounding variables in many analyses.

CONCLUSION: PROGRAM AND POLICY IMPLICATIONS

Concern about teen-age pregnancy and parenthood has increased in the United States since the early 1980s and there is nothing in this review to suggest that this concern is unwarranted. Approximately 11% of females between the ages of 15 and 19 become pregnant each year. By age 20, 18% of the females in the United States will have had an abortion and 20% will have given birth (Moore, 1989). We have seen that the children of teen-age mothers are more likely than other children to perform poorly in school and to exhibit behavioral problems. The children of teen mothers are more likely than their peers to be exposed to a variety of risks including living below the poverty line and, on average, to experience less optimal rearing environments than the children born to older mothers.

Policymakers recognize that steps must be taken to reduce the number of unintended pregnancies among teen-agers, but there are marked differences of opinions among policymakers about the most appropriate method for achieving this goal. The least controversial prevention efforts are those aimed at encouraging teens to abstain from sexual activity, and during the 1980s, teen-agers were admonished to "just say no." Thus far, there is little to indicate that this approach has been effective (Roosa & Christopher, 1990). Recent data indicates that teens were more likely to be sexually active in 1988 than they were in 1982 (Forrest & Singh, 1990). Moore (1989) found that of 19-year-old females, 4 out of 5 have had intercourse.

Most other industrialized countries have lower birth rates for teens than the United States. The U.S. rate is 58.1 births per 1,000 15- to 19-year-old females. For comparison purposes, the rates in Canada and the Netherlands were 26.4 and 9.0 per 1,000 respectively in 1981 (Jones et al., 1986). Why are these other countries having more success? There are several reasons (for an overview see Jones et al., 1985). One major difference is that many other countries have focused on teen-age *pregnancy* as the problem rather than teen-age *sexuality* (Furstenberg et al., 1987). Subsequently, they "provide excellent and comprehensive sex education and contraceptive services and do so enthusiastically'' (Furstenberg et al., 1987, p. 151). In the United States, there is evidence that making contraception more available to teens also leads to a reduction in teen-age pregnancy (Edwards, Steinman, Arnold, & Hakanson, 1980; Schorr, 1988). However, there has been vocal opposition among some groups to making contraceptive services more accessible to teens because of the belief that teens will perceive this as an endorsement of premarital sexual activity. Similar opposition to making contraceptives available to young, unmarried mothers was expressed initially by conservative groups in some European countries (e.g., France, the Netherlands). However, over time consensus emerged that expanding contraceptive services for teens was justifiable given the alternatives of rising abortion rates and high rates of teen-age childbearing (Jones et al., 1985). Increasing awareness of the costs associated with teen-age parenthood combined with the fact that over 400,000 U.S. teens have abortions each year, may also eventually lead to consensus in the United States that expanded contraceptive services for teens are needed.

There is a growing realization in this country, however, that making contraceptives readily available to teens is not all that is required to substantially lower the rate of teen-age pregnancy (Adams et al., 1989; Dash, 1989; Furstenberg et al., 1987; Schorr, 1988). Teens who delay sexual activity and use contraceptive devices when sexually active tend to be successful students with high educational aspirations and are likely to be hopeful about future employment prospects. In contrast, if one is having difficulty completing high school and economic prospects are bleak, there may be insufficient incentives to avoid early childbearing. Indeed, some teens may actually choose parenthood as a relatively attractive option (Dash, 1989). Thus, our view of pregnancy prevention efforts must be broadened. For example, programs aimed at reducing the rate of school failure should be part of our prevention efforts. As Adams and her colleagues (1989) argued: ''Teens need reasons to believe that delaying pregnancy and parenthood is in their best interests. Our task is not merely to persuade them to wait, but to provide every teen (including every poor teen) with other positive and rewarding options so that he/she can personally see the benefits of waiting'' (p. 225).

Program planners and policymakers must also address the needs of teens who are pregnant or parenting. It is clear that adolescent mothers need an array of support services to ensure that parenthood does not severely limit their life options and to promote the optimal development of their children. For example, greater efforts must be made to ensure that teen-agers receive prenatal care in a timely fashion. Only half of all pregnant teen-agers began prenatal care in the first trimester of pregnancy in 1988, compared to 85% of older mothers (Armstrong & Waszak, 1990). School-based clinics have had success recruiting pregnant teens into the health-care system early (Hayes, 1987).

Following the birth of the baby, adolescent mothers need family planning services to avoid subsequent unintended pregnancies. They also need services that will help them return to school and graduate. Title IX legislation that prohibited discrimination in education because of pregnancy, childbearing, or marital status has had a positive effect on the educational attainment of teen mothers. In 1958, only 19% of women in their 20s had completed high school if they had their first child at age 17 or younger; the comparable figure for 1986 was 56% (Moore, 1989). Despite this progress, teen mothers are still much less likely than their peers to complete high school. Alternative school programs that are tailored to the needs of young mothers and include day-care services had some success in improving graduation rates for teen mothers (Hayes, 1987). Other services that are likely to be useful to teens include job training and job placement programs, day-care and respite child-care services. In addition to providing services in the community for teens, it is imperative that teens know how to access these services. Moreover, community efforts to ensure that services for teens are coordinated rather than fragmented are likely to pay dividends in terms of effectiveness.

Some programs are aimed at enhancing the parenting competence of teen mothers and the development of their children. Although only a handful of these family support programs have been carefully evaluated, there is some evidence that these programs can have positive effects on both maternal behavior and child outcomes (see Clewell, Brooks-Gunn, & Benasich, 1989, for a review). For example, David Olds' intervention program in Elmira, New York, was successful in reducing the rates of child abuse among disadvantaged teen-age mothers (Olds, Henderson, Chamberlin, & Tatelbaum, 1986). Clearly, however, there is a pressing need for more research in this area to determine what works and for whom. In particular, we need to know more about the effectiveness of more typical community based parenting programs for teens (i.e., programs that are not model demonstration projects), such as parenting classes taught at alternative high schools and mentoring programs that link teen mothers with mature women from the community.

Based on information gained from successful intervention programs, it seems likely that effective programs targeting the parenting of teens will include several components (Olds & Kitzman, 1990; Schorr, 1988). First, the primary person providing the intervention must establish a close relationship with the young mothers. This may well be the most important element of any successful program for teen mothers (Schorr, 1988). Second, the support program should be ecological in orientation. In other words, it cannot focus exclusively on child development and parenting, nor on linking the mother to needed services, nor on the support system of the mother. In the words of Olds and Kitzman (1990):

> To be optimally effective, programs must address simultaneously the psychological needs of the parents (especially their sense of mastery and competence); the parental behaviors that influence maternal, fetal and infant development; and the situational stresses and social supports that can either interfere with or promote their adaptation to pregnancy, birth, and early care of the child. (p. 114)

A third element is that the program must be of sufficient duration. Short-term intervention programs may not allow the intervenor an opportunity to establish a therapeutic relationship with the client, and may not provide the intervenor with sufficient time to help the mother cope with various stressors that may undermine her parenting performance (Heinicke, Beckwith, & Thompson, 1988; Olds & Kitzman, 1990; Quint & Riccio, 1985). Fourth, as Schorr (1988) suggested, the person providing the intervention must be able to cross traditional service delivery boundaries; a teen is not likely to consult several different service providers to locate the one who has responsibility for the problem that is most salient for her. Finally, to the extent possible, provision of services should begin prenatally. In that way, an invitation to participate in a program cannot be construed by the young mother as a criticism of her parenting practices (Olds, 1983).

The ideal programs envisioned by Olds, Schorr and others are comprehensive and long term. In addition, service providers will need relatively small case loads if they are to develop supportive relationships with the young mothers and if they are to tailor their assistance to the individual needs of each client. Providing such programs will no doubt be costly. However, the research conducted since the early 1980s should convince us that not providing these services is also costly for teen parents, their children, and for us as a society.

REFERENCES

Adams, G., Adams-Taylor, S., & Pittman, K. (1989). Adolescent pregnancy and parenthood: A review of the problem, solutions, and resources. *Family Relations, 38*, 223–229.

Ainsworth, M. Blehar, M., Waters, E., & Wall, S. (1978). *Patterns of attachment.* Hillsdale, NJ: Lawrence Erlbaum Associates.

Armstrong, E., & Waszak, C. (1990). *Teenage pregnancy and too-early childbearing: Public costs, personal consequences* (5th ed.). Washington, DC: Center for Population Options.

Baldwin, W., & Cain, V. (1980). The children of teenage parents. *Family Planning Perspectives, 12*(1), 34–43.

Barnard, K. (1978). *Nursing child assessment training: Instructor's learning resource manual.* Seattle: NCAST Publications.

Battle, S. (1987). *The Black adolescent parent.* New York: Haworth Press.

Bell, S., & Ainsworth, M. D. S. (1972). Infant crying and maternal responsiveness. *Child Development, 43*, 1171–1190.

Belsky, J. (1984). Determinants of parenting: A process model. *Child Development, 55*, 83–96.

Bolton, F. G., & Belsky, J. (1986). The adolescent father and child maltreatment. In A. Elster & M. Lamb (Eds.), *Adolescent fatherhood* (pp. 123–140). Hillsdale, NJ: Lawrence Erlbaum Associates.

Bolton, F. G., Laner, R. H., & Kane, S. P. (1980). Child maltreatment risk among adolescent mothers: A study of reported cases. *American Journal of Orthopsychiatry, 50*(3), 489–504.

Brooks-Gunn, J., & Furstenberg, F. (1986). Antecedents and consequences of parenting: The case of adolescent motherhood. In A. Fogel & G. Melson (Eds.), *Origins of nurturance: Developmental, biological, and cultural perspectives on caregiving* (pp. 233–258). Hillsdale, NJ: Lawrence Erlbaum Associates.

Butler, J. R., & Burton, L. M. (1990). Rethinking teenage childbearing: Is sexual abuse a missing link? *Family Relations, 39,* 73–80.

Caldwell, B., & Bradley, R. (1984). *Home observation for measurement of the environment.* Little Rock: University of Arkansas at Little Rock.

Clewell, B. C., Brooks-Gunn, J., & Benasich, A. A. (1989). Evaluating child-related outcomes in teenage parenting programs. *Family Relations, 38,* 201–209.

Colletta, N. D. (1981). Social support and risk of maternal rejection by adolescent mothers. *The Journal of Psychology, 109,* 191–197.

Crockenberg, S. (1987a). Support for adolescent mothers during the postpartum period: Theory and research. In C. F. Z. Boukydis (Ed.), *Research on support for parents in the postnatal period* (pp. 3–24). Norwood, NJ: Albex.

Crockenberg, S. (1987b). Predictors and correlates of anger toward and punitive control of toddlers by adolescent mothers. *Child Development, 58,* 964–975.

Crockenberg, S. (1988). Social support and parenting. In H. E. Fitzgerald, B. M. Lester, & M. Yogman (Eds.), *Theory and research in behavioral pediatrics* (Vol. 4, pp. 141–174). New York: Plenum.

Crockenberg, S., & Smith, P. (1982). Antecedents of mother–infant interaction and infant irritability in the first three months of life. *Infant Behavior and Development, 5,* 105–119.

Culp, R. E., Appelbaum, M. I., Osofsky, J. D., & Levy, J. A. (1988). Adolescent and older mothers: Comparison between prenatal maternal variables and newborn interaction measures. *Infant Behavior and Development, 11,* 353–362.

Darabi, K. F., Graham, E. H., Namerow, P. B., Philliber, S. G., & Varga, P. (1984). The effect of maternal age on the well-being of children. *Journal of Marriage and the Family, 46,* 933–936.

Dash, L. (1989). *When children want children: The urban crisis of teenage childbearing.* New York: William Morrow.

Dubow, E. F., & Luster, T. (1990). Adjustment of children born to teenage mothers: The contribution of risk and protective factors. *Journal of Marriage and the Family, 52,* 393–404.

Edwards, L. E., Steinman, M. E., Arnold, K. A., & Hakason, E. Y. (1980). Adolescent pregnancy prevention services in high school clinics. *Family Planning Perspectives, 12*(1), 6–14.

Elster, A. B., & Lamb, M. E. (1986). *Adolescent fatherhood.* Hillsdale, NJ: Lawrence Erlbaum Associates.

Elster, A. B., Lamb, M. E., Peters, L., Kahn, J., & Tavare, J. (1987). Judicial involvement and conduct problems of fathers of infants born to adolescent mothers. *Pediatrics, 79*(2), 230–234.

Epstein, A. S. (1980). *Assessing the child development information needed by adolescent parents with very young children* (Final report). Washington, DC: U.S. Dept. of Health, Education and Welfare.

Field, T. M. (1980). Interaction of preterm and term infants with their lower- and middle-class teenage and adult mothers. In T. Field, S. Goldberg, D. Stern, & A. Sostek (Eds.), *High-risk infants and children: Adult and peer interaction* (pp. 113–132). New York: Academic Press.

Field, T., & Widmayer, S. (1981). Mother–infant interaction among lower SES Black, Cuban, Puerto Rican, and South American immigrants. In T. Field, A. Sostek, P. Vietze, & A. H. Leiderman (Eds.), *Culture and early interactions* (pp. 41–62). Hillsdale, NJ: Lawrence Erlbaum Associates.

Field, T., Widmayer, S., Adler, S., & De Cubas, M. (1990). Teenage parenting in different cultures, family constellations, and caregiving environment: Effects on infant development. *Infant Mental Health Journal, 11*(2), 158–174.

Field, T. M., Widmayer, S. M., Stronger, S., & Ingatoff, E. (1980). Teenage, lower-class, Black mothers and their preterm infants: An intervention and developmental follow-up. *Child Development, 51,* 426–436.

Flick, L. H. (1986). Paths to adolescent parenthood: Implications for prevention. *Public Health Reports, 101*(2), 132–147.

Forrest, J. D., & Singh, S. (1990). The sexual and reproductive behavior of American women, 1982-1988. *Family Planning Perspectives, 22*(5), 207–214.

Franklin, D. L. (1988). The impact of early childbearing on developmental outcomes: The case of Black adolescent parenting. *Family Relations, 37*, 268–274.

Free, T. A. (1989). Relationship of family patterns to adolescent mother–infant interactions. *NCAST National News, 5*(4), 1–7.

Frodi, A., Keller, B., Foye, H., Liptak, G., Bridges, L., Grolnick, W., Berko, J., McAnarney, E., & Lawrence, R. (1984). Determinants of attachment and mastery motivation in infants born to adolescent mothers. *Infant Mental Health Journal, 5*(1), 15–23.

Furstenberg, F. F., Brooks-Gunn, J., & Morgan, S. P. (1987). *Adolescent mothers in later life*. Cambridge: Cambridge University Press.

Furstenberg, F. F., & Crawford, A. G. (1978). Family support: Helping teenage mothers to cope. *Family Planning Perspectives, 10*, 322–333.

Garcia Coll, C. T., Hoffman, J., Oh, W. (1987). The social ecology and early parenting of Caucasian adolescent mothers. *Child Development, 58*, 955–963.

Goldberg, D. P. (1982). *The detection of psychiatric illness by questionnaire*. London: Oxford University Press.

Hann, D., Osofsky, J., Barnard, K., & Leonard, G. (1990, April). *Maternal emotional availability in two risk groups*. Paper presented at the International Conference on Infant Studies, Montreal, Canada.

Hann, D. M., Osofsky, J. D., Stringer, S. S., & Carter, S. S. (1988, April). *Affective contribution of adolescent mothers and infants to the quality of attachment*. Paper presented at the International Conference on Infant Studies, Washington, DC.

Harris, T., Brown, G. W., & Bifulco, A. (1987). Loss of parent in childhood and adult psychiatric disorder: The role of social position and premarital pregnancy. *Psychological Medicine, 17*, 163–183.

Hayes, C. (1987). *Risking the future: Adolescent, sexuality, pregnancy and childbearing* (Vol. 1). Washington, DC: National Academy Press.

Heinicke, C. M., Beckwith, L., & Thompson, A. (1988). Early intervention in the family system: A framework and review. *Infant Mental Health Journal, 9*(2), 111–141.

Helm, J. M., Comfort, M., Bailey, D. B., & Simeonsson, R. J. (1990). Adolescent and adult mothers of handicapped children: Maternal involvement in play. *Family Relations, 39*, 432–437.

Hunter, R. S., Kilstrom, N., Kraybill, E. N., & Loda, F. (1978). Antecedents of child abuse and neglect in premature infants: A prospective study in a newborn intensive care unit. *Pediatrics, 61*(4), 629–635.

Johnson, E. (1990, April). *Role of knowledge of child development in adolescent and adult mothers' teaching interaction*. Paper presented at the International Conference on Infant Studies, Montreal, Canada.

Jones, E. F., Forrest, J. D., Goldman, N., Henshaw, S., Lincoln, R., Rosoff, J. I., Westoff, C. F., & Wulf, D. (1985). Teenage pregnancy in developed countries: Determinants and pollicy implications. *Family Planning Perspectives, 17*(2), 53–63.

Jones, E. F., Forrest, J. D., Goldman, N., Henshaw, S., Lincoln, R., Rosoff, J. I., Westoff, C. F., & Wulf, D. (1986). *Teenage pregnancy in industrialized countries*. New Haven: Yale University Press.

Kinard, E. M., & Klerman, L. V. (1980). Teenage parenting and child abuse: Are they related. *American Journal of Orthopsychiatry, 50*(3), 481–488.

King, T., & Fullard, W. (1982). Teenage mothers and their infants: New findings on the home environment. *Journal of Adolescence, 5*, 333–346.

Lamb, M. (1988). The ecology of adolescent pregnancy and parenthood. In A. R. Pence (Ed.), *Ecological research with children and families* (pp. 99–121). New York: Teachers College Press.

Lamb, M. E., & Elster, A. B. (1985). Adolescent mother–infant–father relationships. *Developmental Psychology, 21*(5), 768–773.

Lamb, M. E., Hopps, K., & Elster, A. B. (1987). Strange situation behavior of infants with adolescent mothers. *Infant Behavior and Development, 10*, 39–48.

Landy, S., Montgomery, J. S., Schubert, J., Cleland, J. F., & Clark, C. (1983). Mother–infant interaction of teenage mothers and the effect of experience in the observational sessions on the development of their infants. *Early Child Development and Care, 10*, 165–186.

Lawrence, R. A., McAnarney, E. R., Aten, M. J., Iker, H. P., Baldwin, C. P., & Baldwin, A. L. (1981). Aggressive behaviors in young mothers: Markers of future morbidity? *Pediatric Research, 15*, 443.

LeResche, L., Strobino, D., Parks, P., Fischer, P., & Smeriglio, V. (1983). The relationship of observed maternal behavior to questionnaire measures of parenting knowledge, attitudes, and emotional state in adolescent mothers. *Journal of Youth and Adolescence, 12*(1), 19–31.

Leventhal, J. M. (1981). Risk factors for child abuse: Methodologic standards in case-control studies. *Pediatrics, 68*(5), 684–690.

Levine, L., Garcia Coll, C. T., & Oh, W. (1985). Determinants of mother–infant interaction in adolescent mothers. *Pediatrics, 75*(1), 23–29.

Luster, T., Boger, R., & Hannan, K. (1990, April). *Infant affect and home environment.* Paper presented at the International Conference on Infant Studies, Montreal, Canada.

Luster, T., & Dubow, E. (1990). Predictors of the quality of the home environment adolescent mothers provide for their school-age children. *Journal of Youth and Adolescence, 19*(5), 475–494.

Luster, T., & Rhoades, K. (1989). The relation between child-rearing beliefs and the home environment in a sample of adolescent mothers. *Family Relations, 38*, 317–322.

McAnarney, E. R., Lawrence, R. A., Aten, M. J., & Iker, H. P. (1984). Adolescent mothers and their infants. *Pediatrics, 73*(3), 358–362.

McAnarney, E. R., Lawrence R. A., Ricciuti, H. N., Polley, J., & Szilagyi, M. (1986). Interactions of adolescent mothers and their 1-year-old children. *Pediatrics, 78*(4), 585–590.

Mercer, R. T., Hackley, K. C., & Bostrom, A. (1984). Adolescent motherhood: Comparison of outcome with older mothers. *Journal of Adolescent Health Care, 5*(1), 7–13.

Miller, S. M. (1983). *The influence of adolescent childbearing on the incidence, type, and severity of child maltreatment.* New York: Child Welfare League of America.

Moore, K. (1989). *Facts at a glance.* Washington, DC: Child Trends.

Moore, K. (1992). *Facts at a glance.* Washington, DC: Child Trends.

National Center for Health Statistics (1990). Advance report of final natality statistics, 1988. *Monthly Vital Statistics Report, 39*(4), Supplement.

Ogbu, J. (1981). Origins of human competence: A cultural-ecological perspective. *Child Development, 52*, 413–429.

Olds, D. L. (1983). An intervention program for high-risk families. In R. Hoekelman (Ed.), *Minimizing high-risk parenting* (pp. 249–268). Media, PA: Harwal Publishing.

Olds, D. L., Henderson, C. R., Chamberlin, R., & Tatelbaum, R. (1986). Preventing child abuse and neglect: A randomized trial of nurse home visitation. *Pediatrics, 78*, 65–78.

Olds, D. L., & Kitzman, H. (1990). Can home visitation improve the health of women and children at environmental risk? *Pediatrics, 86*(1), 108–116.

Oppel, W. C., & Royston, A. B. (1971). Teen-age births: Some social, psychological, and physical sequelae. *American Journal of Public Health, 61*(4), 751–756.

Osofsky, H. J., & Osofsky, J. D. (1970). Adolescents as mothers: Results of a program for low-income pregnant teenagers with some emphasis upon infant's development. *American Journal of Orthopsychiatry, 40*(5), 825–834.

Polit, D. F., & Kahn, J. R. (1986). Early subsequent pregnancy among economically disadvantaged teenage mothers. *American Journal of Public Health, 76*(2), 167–171.

Quint, J. C., & Riccio, J. A. (1985). *The challenge of serving pregnant and parenting teens: Lessons from Project Redirection.* New York: Manpower Demonstration Research Corporation.

Quinton, D., & Rutter, M. (1988). *Parenting breakdown: The making and breaking of inter-generational bonds.* Aldershot, UK: Avebury.

Reis, J. (1988). Child-rearing expectations and developmental knowledge according to maternal age and parity. *Infant Mental Health Journal, 9*(4), 287–304.

Reis, J. S., & Herz, E. J. (1987). Correlates of adolescent parenting. *Adolescence, 22*(87), 599–609.

Roosa, M. W., & Christopher, F. S. (1990). Evaluation of an abstinence-only adolescent pregnancy prevention program: A replication. *Family Relations, 39*, 363–367.

Roosa, M. W., Fitzgerald, H. E., & Carlson, N. A. (1982a). Teenage and older mothers and their infants: A descriptive comparison. *Adolescence, 17*(65), 1–17.

Roosa, M. W., Fitzgerald, H. E., & Carlson, N. A. (1982b). A comparison of teenage and older mothers: A systems analysis. *Journal of Marriage and the Family, 44*(1), 367–377.

Ruff, C. C. (1987). How well do adolescents mother? *American Journal of Maternal and Child Nursing, 12*(4), 249–253.

Salguero, C. (1984). The role of ethnic factors in adolescent pregnancy and motherhood. In M. Sugar (Ed.), *Adolescent parenthood* (pp. 75–98). New York: Spectrum.

Sandler, H. M., Vietze, P. M., O'Connor, S. (1981). Obstetric and neonatal outcomes following intervention with pregnant teenagers. In K. G. Scott, T. Field, & E. G. Robertson (Eds.), *Teenage parents and their offspring* (pp. 249–263). New York: Grune & Stratton.

Schilmoeller, G. L., & Baranowski, M. D. (1985). Childrearing of firstborns by adolescent and older mothers. *Adolescence, 20*(80), 805–822.

Schorr, L. (1988). *Within our reach: Breaking the cycle of disadvantage.* Garden City, NJ: Anchor Press/Doubleday.

Small, S., and Luster, T. (1990, November). *Youth at risk for teenage parenthood.* Paper presented at the Creating Caring Communities Conference, East Lansing, MI.

Spieker, S. (1989). Adolescent mothers: Parenting skills measured using the NCATS and HOME. *NCAST National News, 5*(4), 3–8.

Spieker, S. J., & Booth, C. L. (1988). Maternal antecedents of attachment quality. In J. Belsky & T. Nezworski (Eds.), *Clinical implications of attachment* (pp. 95–135). Hillsdale, NJ: Lawrence Erlbaum Associates.

Stevens, J. (1988). Social support, locus of control, and parenting in three low-income groups of mothers: Black teenagers, Black adults, and White adults. *Child Development, 59*, 635–642.

Stevenson, M. B., & Roach, M. A. (1988, April). *Mother–infant communication at 12 months: Adolescent and adult single mothers.* Paper presented at the International Conference on Infant Studies, Washington, DC.

Unger, D. G., & Wandersman, L. P. (1985). Social support and adolescent mothers: Action research contributions to theory and application. *Journal of Social Issues, 41*(1), 29–45.

Vaughn, B. E., Egeland, B., Waters, E., & Sroufe, L. A. (1979). Individual differences in infant–mother attachment at 12 and 18 months: Stability and change in families under stress. *Child Development, 50*, 971–975.

Wadsworth, J., Taylor, B., Osborn, A., & Butler, N. (1984). Teenage mothering: Child development at five years. *Journal of Child Psychology and Psychiatry, 25*(2), 305–313.

Ward, M. J., Plunkett, S. W., Galantowicz, B., DeMuralt, M., Olthoff, D., Weisman, J., & Kessler, D. B. (1988, April). *Adolescent mothers and their infants: Caregiving, infant behavior, and development.* Paper presented at the International Conference on Infant Studies, Washington, DC.

Wilson, M. N. (1989). Child development in the context of the Black extended family. *American Psychologist, 44*(2), 380–385.

Wise, S., & Grossman, F. K. (1980). Adolescent mothers and their infants: Psychological factors in attachment and interaction. *American Journal of Orthopsychiatry, 50*, 454–468.

Zuckerman, B., Winsmore, G., & Alpert, J. (1979). A study of attitudes and support systems of inner city adolescent mothers. *The Journal of Pediatrics, 95*(1), 122–125.

Chapter 4

The Influence of Child Temperamental Characteristics on Parent Behaviors

Jacqueline V. Lerner
Michigan State University

The idea that children influence the behaviors, ideas, and expectations of their caregivers is not a new one. Bell (1968) as well as others has made us aware that child socialization is a mutual process where children affect their parents as their parents are affecting them (Bell & Harper, 1977; Lerner & Spanier, 1978; Lewis & Rosenblum, 1974; Sameroff, 1975).

Preceding Bell's (1968) influential paper on the direction of effects in socialization, Thomas and Chess (e.g., Thomas, Chess, Birch, Hertzig, & Korn, 1963) emphasized that different children may have differential effects on others in their social world as a consequence of their specific characteristics of behavior or temperamental individuality; by affecting those who affect them, children may provide a source of their own development—they may contribute to their further individual trajectory of development. This view about the potential role of the child in parent–child relations was involved in the recognition among social scientists that both parent and child were developing organisms and were active in their social exchanges with each other (e.g., see Lerner & Spanier, 1978; Lewis & Rosenblum, 1974). One example of this view is that the nature of the parent's own development (as a parent or spouse, for instance) places limits on the effects of the child's individuality on him or her but at the same time, the child influences the parent's further individual and social development (Bell, 1974; Lerner, 1978, 1979; Spanier, Lerner, & Aquilino, 1978). Thus, temperamental characteristics have been seen as useful dimensions of individuality with which to study child effects on others, to study transactional relations between children and their social context, and to study the means by which children can promote their own development.

In this chapter, the notion that the temperamental individuality of the child influences parenting is explored through a review of research from the Thomas and Chess (Thomas, Chess, & Birch, 1968; Thomas, Chess, Birch, Hertzig, & Korn, 1963) New York Longitudinal Study (NYLS), from my own research based on the theoretical framework of Thomas and Chess, from the cross-cultural research of Super and Harkness, and from the work of Susan Crockenberg and others, whose research on temperamental characteristics and their influence on caregiving has added considerably to the field.

This chapter is divided into four sections. First, I define temperament and discuss the "goodness of fit" model of temperament-context relations from which my research is derived. Second, I review the research that has come out of the NYLS and my laboratory that demonstrates the influence of a child's temperamental characteristics on the context, paying specific attention to how those characteristics affect parenting behaviors. Next, I discuss the research of Super and Harkness, which lends further support to the notion that child temperament influences parents. The research of Susan Crockenberg and others on temperamental influences on caregiving behaviors are also reviewed in this section. In the concluding section, I make suggestions for future research.

TEMPERAMENT–CONTEXT RELATIONS

The Definition of Temperament

There are several definitions of temperament found in the literature (e.g., Buss & Plomin, 1975; Rothbart & Derryberry, 1981; Strelau, 1972). There is, however, only partial agreement among researchers as to what constitutes temperamental characteristics, whether they are biologically based, and how stable they are. There is some consensus that temperament refers to the "how" or "stylistic" component of behavior. That is, while all children sleep, temperamental differences would refer to the regularity of sleep–wake cycles, and the level of activity during sleep. Most researchers agree that temperament has some biological/constitutional basis and expresses itself at birth, but they differ as to the extent to which these characteristics are genetic in origin and to the extent to which they are modifiable. (See Goldsmith, 1985, for a discussion of these issues.) The Thomas and Chess (1977) definition, as the stylistic components of behavior—not what the person does, but how he or she does whatever is done—is predominant in the field (see Lerner & Lerner, 1983, for a review). Because its use in providing an empirical base for the theoretical view of temperament that I argue is most compelling—the contextual interpretation of temperament—I, too, am attracted to the Thomas and Chess (1977) conception.

Thomas and Chess conceptualized nine categories of behavioral style: rhythmicity, activity level, attention span-persistence, distractibility, adaptability, approach–withdrawal, threshold, intensity of reaction, and mood. To illustrate the meaning and use of their definition of temperament as the stylistic component of behavior, consider that one could describe a large portion of the content of a young infant's behavioral repertoire as eating, sleeping, and excreting. Inasmuch as all infants engage in such behaviors, one could not easily discriminate among infants by use of these descriptors. But if one infant ate at regular intervals and another ate at irregular times, discrimination between the two could be achieved. Because the terms *regularity* and *irregularity* qualify eating and specify the distinction between otherwise identical eating behaviors, the terms are used as designators of the stylistic aspect of behavior.

In my view, it is this stylistic component of behavior that gives a normative behavioral repertoire its distinctiveness, especially at early ages (cf. Dunn & Kendrick, 1980). To presage a later argument, it is this distinctiveness that in turn serves to mark the young organism as a unique individual—to parents (especially experienced ones), to teachers, and to others in the social network of the young person who must discriminate him or her from among many in order to interact most appropriately. It is this distinctiveness that may serve to channel the child along interindividually different trajectories, trajectories that may be associated with interindividual differences in development. I am implying, then, that the significance of the definition of temperament as behavioral style lies in its impact on the social context of the person.

This notion is quite consistent with the position advanced by the authors of recent reviews of the temperament literature. For example, Goldsmith and Campos (1982) noted that, "rather than referring merely to differences in the infant's susceptibility to experiences, temperament is now generally considered to include processes which help to regulate the child's social relationships" (p. 3) and that "the temperament phenomena of prime importance during infancy are those which have socially communicative functions" (p. 21). Similarly, Bates (1980) contended that "temperament has its main impact on socially relevant outcomes through a process of transaction between the child and the social environment" (p. 316). Just such a role for temperament is found in the Lerner and Lerner contextually based goodness of fit model (see Lerner & Lerner, 1983).

A Goodness of Fit Model of Temperament–Context Relations

The conception that the relationships between an organism and its context must involve congruence, must match, or simply must fit in order for adaptive transactions to exist is an idea traceable at least to Darwin (1859). As explained by White (1968), this idea has permeated the thinking of U.S. and to some extent European social science, albeit in formulations as seemingly diverse as those of G. S. Hall (1904), Clark Hull (1952), and George Herbert Mead (1967). A version of this idea that has been attracting increasing attention in the human development literature was introduced by the psychiatrists Thomas and Chess (1977) and has been elaborated by the present author and others (Lerner, 1984; Lerner & Lerner, 1983).

The Thomas and Chess goodness of fit model indicates that adaptive developmental outcomes occur when the physical and behavioral characteristics of the person are consonant with the demands of the physical and social context within which the person is developing. In other words, as a consequence of characteristics of physical distinctiveness (e.g., in regard to gender, body type, or facial attractiveness; Berscheid & Walster, 1974) and/or psychological individuality (e.g., regarding conceptual tempo or temperament; Kagan, 1966; Thomas & Chess, 1977), children promote differential reactions in their socializing others; these reactions may feed back to children, increase the individuality of their developmental milieu, and provide a basis for their further development.

Through the establishment of such "circular functions" in ontogeny (Schneirla, 1957), children may be conceived of as producers of their own development (Lerner & Busch-Rossnagel, 1981), and may indeed influence the parenting they receive. However, in order to understand the specific characteristics of the feedback or parenting (e.g., its positive or negative valence) children receive as a consequence of their individuality, one must recognize that there are also demands placed on children by the social and physical components of the setting. These demands may take the following form:

1. attitudes, values, or stereotypes held by others in the context regarding children's attributes (either their physical or behavioral characteristics);

2. the attributes (usually behavioral) of others in the context with whom children must coordinate, or fit, their attributes (also, in this case, usually behavioral) for adaptive interactions to exist; or

3. the physical characteristics of a setting (e.g., the presence or absence of access ramps for the motorically handicapped) or the *affordances* (Wohlwill, in press) of the stimuli in the child's context, which require the child to possess certain attributes (again, usually behavioral abilities) for the most efficient interaction within the setting to occur.

Children's individuality, in differentially meeting these demands, provides the basis for the feedback they get from the socializing environment. Considering the demand domain of attitudes, values, or stereotypes, for example, nonfamilial caregivers (e.g., those in day-care settings or teachers of preschool or early grade levels) and parents may have relatively individual and distinct expectations about behaviors desired of their students and children, respectively.

Teachers may want students who show little distractibility, because they would not want attention diverted from the lesson by the activity of other children in the classroom. Parents, however, might desire their children to be moderately distractible, for example, when they require their child to move from playing with toys or from watching television to eating dinner or to going to bed. A child whose behavioral characteristics are such that he or she is either generally distractible or generally not distractible would thus differentially meet the demands of these two contexts. Problems of adaptation to school or to home might thus develop as a consequence of a child's lack of match (or goodness of fit) in either or both settings. As is elaborated later, the development of cognitive variables may be influenced in either case; for instance, differences in attention to a teacher or other caregiver may lead to differences in knowledge attained in a setting (Lerner, Lerner, & Zabski, 1985).

Similarly, considering the second type of contextual demands—those that arise as a consequence of the behavioral characteristics of others in the setting—problems of fit might occur when children who are highly irregular in their biological functions (e.g., eating, sleep–wake cycles, and toileting behaviors) interact in a family setting composed of highly regular and behaviorally scheduled parents and siblings, or in a school setting wherein arrhythmicity (e.g., in toileting behaviors) is distracting to a teacher. In addition, children who are fussy—for example, withdrawing from and slow to adapt to new stimuli and/or people, having negative mood and high intensity reactions—might not fit well in a behavioral exchange with a person whose behaviors must be routinized and/or precise in order for an appropriate interaction to occur. Two examples of people involved in such behaviors are a pediatrician conducting an infant physical examination and a psychological examiner conducting an infant psychomotor assessment.

In turn, considering the third type of contextual demands—those that arise as a consequence of the physical characteristics of a setting—a child who has a low threshold for response and who also is highly distractible might find it difficult to perform efficiently in a setting with high noise levels (e.g., a crowded home, a preschool situated near the street in a busy urban area) when tasks necessitating concentration and/or attention are required. That is, the physical–social characteristics of a situation have what Wohlwill (in press) termed *affordances*—distinctive features that permit but also require (for successful use of, or appropriate interaction with, them) specific behaviors on the part of the child.

For example, a problem-solving task, if it is solvable, affords (i.e., permits and requires) approach and attention; if one could not come near to and remain focused on a stimulus array because of that array's characteristics, one could not acquire information about it. However, while requiring such behaviors as approach and attention, a solvable information-containing task or situation also requires such behaviors of the interacting child if the child is to deal with it adaptively. This being the case, a withdrawing, highly distractible child would not fit with the psychosocial demands imposed by such task affordances.

I return again to considering the implications of the types of demands present in a child's context. Here, however, I should note that Thomas and Chess (1977, 1980, 1981) and Lerner and Lerner (1983) believed that adaptive psychological and social functioning do not derive directly from either the nature of the child's characteristics of individuality per se or the nature of the demands of the contexts within which the child functions. Rather, if a child's characteristics of individuality match (or fit) the demands of a particular setting, adaptive outcomes in that setting will ensue. Those children whose characteristics match most of the settings within which they exist should receive supportive or positive feedback from the contexts and should show evidence of the most adaptive behavioral and cognitive development. It is these children who in theory receive the most positive parenting. In turn, of course, mismatched children, whose characteristics are incongruent with one or most settings, may be exposed to more negative incidences of parenting and, therefore, show alternative developmental outcomes.

The major support for these ideas about goodness of fit comes from research in the temperament literature. Thus, before discussing the relevance of the goodness of fit model for understanding the link between temperament and parenting, it is useful to summarize the details of this research. The contributions from the Thomas and Chess NYLS are considered first, followed by the cross-cultural research of Super and Harkness. Third, the research from my own laboratory is discussed. Finally, the research of Susan Crockenberg and others is reviewed.

EMPIRICAL SUPPORT FOR THE GOODNESS OF FIT MODEL

The New York Longitudinal Study (NYLS)

Within the NYLS data set, information relevant to the goodness of fit model exists as a consequence of the multiple samples present in the project. First, the NYLS core sample is composed of 133 White, middle-class children of professional parents. In addition, a sample of 98 New York City Puerto Rican children of working-class parents were followed for about 14 years. Each sample subject was studied from at least the first month of life onward. Although the distribution of temperament attributes in the two samples was not different, the import of the attributes for parenting techniques and for the child's subsequent psychosocial adjustment was quite disparate. Two examples may suffice to illustrate this distinction.

First to be considered is the impact of low regularity or rhythmicity of behavior, particularly in regard to sleep–wake cycles. The Puerto Rican parents studied by Thomas and Chess (1977; Thomas, Chess, Sillen, & Mendez, 1974) were very permissive. No demands in regard to rhythmicity of sleep were placed on the infant or child. Indeed, the parents allowed the child to go to sleep any time the child desired, and permitted the child to awaken any time as well. The parents molded their schedule around the children. Because parents were so accommodating, there were no problems of fit associated with an arrhythmic infant or child. Indeed, neither within the infancy period nor throughout the first 5 years of life did arrhythmicity predict adjustment problems. In this sample arrhythmicity remained continuous and independent of adaptive implications for the child (Korn, 1978; Thomas et al., 1974).

In White, middle-class families, however, strong demands for rhythmic sleep patterns were maintained. Thus, an arrhythmic child did not fit with parental demands, and consistent with the goodness of fit model, arrhythmicity was a major predictor of problem behaviors both within the infancy years and across time through the first 5 years of life (Korn, 1978; Thomas et al., 1974).

It should be emphasized that there are at least two ways of viewing this finding. First, consistent with the idea that children influence their parents, it may be noted that sleep arrhythmicity in their children resulted in problems in the parents (e.g., reports of stress, anxiety, and anger; Chess & Thomas, 1984; Thomas et al., 1974). Such an effect of child temperament on the parent's own level of adaptation has been reported in other data sets wherein, for instance, infants who had high thresholds for responsiveness to social stimulation and thus were not soothed easily by their mothers evoked intense distress reactions in their mothers and a virtual cessation of maternal caregiving behaviors (Brazelton, Koslowski, & Main, 1974). Therefore, it is possible that the presence of such child effects in the NYLS sample could have altered previous parenting styles in a way that constituted feedback to the child that was associated with the development of problem behaviors in him or her.

In turn, a second interpretation of this finding arises from the fact that problem behaviors in the children were identified initially on the basis of parental report. It may be that irrespective of any problem behavior evoked in the parent by the child and/or of any altered parent–child interactions that thereby ensued, one effect of the child on the parent was to increase the probability of the parent labeling the child's temperamental style as problematic and reporting it to the NYLS staff psychiatrist. Unfortunately, the current state of analysis of the NYLS data does not allow us to discriminate between these obviously nonmutually exclusive possibilities.

However, the data in the NYLS do allow us to indicate that the parents in the middle-class sample took steps to change their arrhythmic children's sleep patterns; and as most of these arrhythmic children were also adaptable, low rhythmicity tended to be discontinuous for most children. That the parents behaved to modify their child's arrhythmicity is also an instance of a child effect on its psychosocial context. That is, the child "produced" in his or her parents alterations in parental caregiving behaviors regarding sleep. That these *child effects* on the parental context "fed back" to the child and influenced his or her further development is consistent with the findings above that sleep arrhythmicity was discontinuous among these children.

Thus, in the middle-class sample early infant arrhythmicity tended to be a problem during this time of life but proved to be neither continuous nor predictive of later problems of adjustment. In turn, in the Puerto Rican sample, infant arrhythmicity was not a problem during this time of life but was continuous and—because in this context it was not involved in poor fit—was not associated with adjustment problems in the child in the first 5 years of life. (Of course, this is not to say that the parents in the Puerto Rican families were not affected by their children's sleep arrhythmicity; as was the case with the parents in the middle-class families, it may be that the Puerto Rican parents had problems of fatigue and/or suffered marital or work-related problems due to irregular sleep patterns produced in them as a consequence of their child's sleep arrhythmicity; however, the current nature of data analysis in the NYLS does not allow an investigation of this possible child effect on the Puerto Rican parents.)

However, the data do underscore the importance of considering fit with the demands of the psychosocial context of development by indicating that arrhythmicity did begin to predict adjustment problems for the Puerto Rican children when they entered the school system. Their lack of a regular sleep pattern interfered with their obtaining sufficient sleep to perform well in school and, in addition, often caused them to be late to school (Korn, 1978; Thomas et al., 1974). Thus, before age 5 only one Puerto Rican child presented a clinical problem diagnosed as a sleep disorder. However, almost 50% of the Puerto Rican children who developed clinically identifiable problems between ages 5 and 9 were diagnosed as having sleep problems.

Another example is given illustrating how the differential demands existing between the two family contexts provide different presses for adaptation. This example pertains to differences in the demands of the physical contexts of the families.

As noted by Thomas et al. (1974), as well as by Korn (1978), overall there was a very low incidence of behavior problems in the Puerto Rican sample children in their first 5 years of life, especially when compared to the corresponding incidence among the core sample children. However, if a problem was presented at this time among the Puerto Rican sample it was most likely to be a problem of motor activity. In fact, across the first 9 years of their lives, of those Puerto Rican children who developed clinical problems, 53% were diagnosed as exhibiting problematic motor activity. Parents complained of excessive and uncontrollable motor activity in such cases. However, in the core sample's clinical group only one child (a child with brain damage) was characterized in this way. It may be noted here that the Puerto Rican parents' reports of "excessive and uncontrollable" activity in their children does constitute, in this group, an example of a child effect on the parents. That is, a major value of the Puerto Rican parents in the NYLS was child obedience to authority (Korn, 1978). The type of motor activity shown by the highly active children of these parents evoked considerable distress in them, given their perception that their children's behavior was inconsistent with what would be expected of obedient children (Korn, 1978).

Of course, if the middle-class parents had seen their children's behavior as excessive and uncontrollable, it may be that—irrespective of any major salience placed on the value of child obedience—problems would have been evoked in the middle-class parents, and feedback to the child, derived from such evocation, would have ensued. Thus, an issue remains as to why the same (high) activity level should evoke one set of appraisals among the Puerto Rican parents but another set among the middle-class parents (i.e., in the latter group no interpretation of excessive and uncontrollable behavior was evoked). Similarly, it may be asked why high activity level is highly associated with problem behavior in the Puerto Rican children and not in the middle-class children. The key information needed to address these issues may be related to the physical features of the respective groups' homes.

In the Puerto Rican sample the families usually had several children and lived in small apartments. Even average motor activity tended to impinge on others in the setting. Moreover, it may be noted that even in the case of the children with high activity levels, the Puerto Rican parents were reluctant to let their children out of the apartment because of the actual dangers of playing on the streets of East Harlem. In the core sample, however, the parents had the financial resources to provide large apartments or houses for their families. There were typically suitable play areas for the children both inside and outside the home. As a consequence, the presence of high activity levels in the homes of the core sample did not cause the problems for interaction that they did in the Puerto Rican group. Thus, as Thomas et al. (1968, 1974) emphasized, the mismatch between temperamental attribute and physical environmental demand accounted for the group difference in the import of high activity level for differences in parenting and for the development of behavioral problems in the children.

In summary, data from the NYLS are not fully consonant with the methodology required for a direct and complete test of the goodness of fit model. For example, measures of temperament were not directly related to measures of the context. However, in spite of such limitations, the NYLS data set provides results compatible with the goodness of fit model and show how individual child temperamental characteristics affects parents' caregiving behaviors. Data independent of the NYLS also lend some support.

Cross-Cultural Research by Super and Harkness

Support both for the generalizability of the temperamental attributes studied by Thomas and Chess (1977, 1980, 1981) and for the goodness of fit model is provided in a cross-cultural study by Super and Harkness (1981), who studied infants in a rural farming community in Kenya named Kokwet and infants in suburban families living in the metropolitan Boston area.

Super and Harkness reported that the dimensions studied in the NYLS ''are not, by and large'' (p. 79) artifacts of the U.S. setting. In both samples the dimensions of mood, adaptability, intensity of reaction, and rhythmicity, or regularity, of biological functions (eating, sleeping, and elimination) were identified in interview as well as naturalistic observational data. However, because of cultural differences between the two settings, the imports of these temperamental attributes were quite different; and as Super and Harkness reported, children with the same temperament attribute scores had different fits and different developmental outcomes as a consequence of the different contextual demands. That is, the parents in the two samples had different ideas and expectations regarding their child's behavior and the physical environment of the two cultures imposed different demands.

In many homes in their Boston sample, physical space was altered in anticipation of the arrival of the baby (e.g., a room was decorated for the infant). Typically the mother made arrangements to change her schedule once the baby arrived. However, in none of these families was there more than one person generally at home during most of the day (i.e., typically either the mother or a babysitter was present). This one-to-one ratio of caregiver to infant presents a limitation on the moment-to-moment flexibility of the caregiver; he or she cannot engage in noncaregiving activities when the infant makes unanticipated demands.

The people of Kokwet (Kipsigis) created a much different niche for an infant. In the first months of life the baby is in the exclusive care of the mother and is rarely separated from physical contact with her. Such constant and close physical contact is not at all characteristic of the mother–infant relationship in the Boston sample. Moreover, in Kokwet the mother is rarely alone with the infant. During the day an average of five additional people are in the house.

Some of the impact of these cultural differences may be seen by considering the dimensions of rhythmicity and adaptability. In the Boston sample the infant's activities are often highly temporally scheduled in order to meet the needs of both the mother and infant. In Kokwet, however, the baby spends much of his or her waking day being held or sitting on the lap of the mother while she is pursuing her duties. As noted, if the mother needs a break or has to do a task where the infant cannot be carried, the infant is attended to by another nearby caregiver. Within this situation the infant is free to sleep at will and nurse at the mother's breast virtually at will (at most the mother is only a short walk away).

Thus, an infant who does not show rhythmicity of sleeping and eating would not have a problem of fitting the cultural demands imposed by the Kokwet setting and would not be likely to evoke negative reactions in the mother as a consequence of this feature of its temperament; that is, even mothers who were themselves not particularly adaptable could adjust easily to the infant's behavior of the moment through using the support network (the other caregivers present in the context, in this case) at hand as a consequence of the cultural system. However, an infant in the Boston setting who had the same low level of rhythmicity would not fit well with the demands imposed on him or her. Moreover, if this infant was low in adaptability the problems related to fit— for example, the schedule the mother tried to impose—would be enhanced, and the potential problems for adequate development would be increased. Such problems would likely be enhanced if such an infant were coupled with a mother low in adaptability, given her lack of immediate social support. In turn, an infant in Kokwet who had a low adaptability score would not have a poor fit because there is no schedule imposed on him or her to which adaptation is required, and, as noted, his or her mother's level of adaptability is not the issue it may be within the Boston setting.

Super and Harkness (1981) pointed out that there are several developmental consequences of these cultural differences in the meaning of temperament. For example, although it starts out similarly, by 4 months of age the sleep–wake cycle of Boston and Kokwet infants is quite different, with the average Boston infant sleeping for 8 hours a night and the average Kokwet infant continuing to wake briefly and nurse. In addition, maternal impressions of the infant are different in each setting. The Kokwet mothers are not concerned with characteristics like negative mood, low rhythmicity, and low adaptability, and do not view them as indicative of long-term problems. However, the Boston mothers in the Super and Harkness sample have precisely the opposite evaluation of these temperamental attributes (e.g., they view these temperament characteristics as undesirable and as presenting immediate and potentially long-term problems). Thus, as in the NYLS data set, the same temperamental characteristic has a different impact on others as a consequence of its embeddedness in a different cultural context.

Testing the Goodness of Fit Model

The research from my laboratory is focused on testing the ideas put forth in the "goodness of fit" model described earlier. By assessing the child's characteristics of temperament and the demands of the context we have been able to discern whether children whose characteristics fit have more positive outcomes than children whose characteristics do not fit. Although we have looked at the parent, teacher, and peer contexts, I review only those studies pertinent to the parent or home context, in order to provide support for the idea that temperamental characteristics can and do influence parent behaviors.

Procedures in Testing the Model.   Our research to date, has followed a general methodological strategy. First, in order to measure temperament, one of two instruments is used: the Dimensions of Temperament Survey (DOTS) and the Revised Dimensions of Temperament Survey (DOTS-R). The DOTS measures five temperament attributes (attention span–persistence vs. distractibility; adaptability-approach vs. withdrawal; activity level; rhythmicity; and reactivity). The DOTS-R measures seven temperament attributes: activity level (general), activity level (sleep), rhythmicity, attention span–distractibility, approach–withdrawal, mood, and flexibility–rigidity.

In accordance with the goodness of fit model, the second measurement task is to assess a feature of the child's context relevant to his or her temperament. As explained earlier, there are at least three contextual presses, or demands, that may be relevant to a child's temperament. These are: expectational demands about temperament held by significant others, demands imposed by the temperaments of significant others, and the demands on behavior style imposed by the physical ecology. To date, the focus has been mostly on the expectational type of demands.

In using the DOTS to assess the expectational demands about temperament held by a child's significant others, items have been recast to relate to the preferences held by either parents, teachers, or peers. For example, a DOTS item pertinent to persistence is: "I stay with an activity for a long time." To assess a parent's expectational demands for this item, it is recast to read, "I want my child to stay with an activity for a long time."

With the DOTS-R a somewhat different, more explicitly theory-guided approach to measuring expectational demands has been taken. Thomas and Chess (1977), as part of their NYLS, conducted extensive interviews with parents. If a child had particular scores on a specific set of five of the nine temperament attributes they assessed in the NYLS, it was difficult for the parent to have positive interactions with the child. The five attributes comprising the difficult-to-interact-with child are low rhythmicity, slow adaptability, high intensity, negative mood, and withdrawal. In addition, a short attention span and high level of distractibility also present difficulty in interaction, but primarily in the school for teachers (Lerner et al., 1985).

The point here is that the levels of scores, or the signs of the difficult child, present problems only because they constitute a basis of poor interaction between the child and a significant other in his or her context. The attribute provides a basis for poor interaction because it is not something the significant other wants or expects from the child. In other words, temperamental difficulty resides not in the child per se, not in a particular level of a particular attribute being processed. Rather, difficulty derives from the failure of an attribute to facilitate positive interaction between a child and the significant others comprising his or her context. It is the context, then, that defines what is difficult.

Super and Harkness (1982) made this point quite clear. They stress that people in different contexts may have distinct ideas about how difficult a given temperamental attribute may be. They term the belief system of people of a particular context an *Ethnotheory*, and believe that in different contexts there exists different ethnotheories of temperamental difficulty.

Following the lead of Super and Harkness, we have used the DOTS-R items to formulate a means to assess the Ethnotheory of temperamental difficulty held by the parents, the teachers, and the peers of the children being studied. For instance, the DOTS-R item, "My child gets sleepy at different times every night," is rated by a parent in respect to how difficult it would be for the parent to interact with his or her child if the child always showed the behavior described in the item. It should be reiterated, however, that unlike the NYLS and the Super and Harkness (1981) research, the data being presented does not include information about the reactions evoked in significant others when a child fits or does not fit with the others' demands.

Although such direct measurement needs to be included in future tests of the model, to date the nature of such child effects on the basis of the Ethnotheory score has been inferred, and these inferences have been used to predict outcomes in the child (i.e., to predict the presumed result of feedback to the child). These procedures constitute the third and last piece of the general methodology—putting temperament scores and demands together. In effect, the goodness of fit model is used to formulate the inference that the specific demands of the significant others comprising a child's context (e.g., teachers in school, parents at home) allow one to predict or explain any relation between temperament and psychosocial functioning. Thus, the general hypothesis guiding the integration of child temperament scores and demand scores from significant others is that a given temperament score is positively related to adaptive psychosocial functioning when, on the basis of the demand score, it promotes adaptive child-context interactions; in turn, temperament is negatively related to adaptive psychosocial functioning when it is incongruent with the demands of the context.

In summary, using this three-pronged approach to research, we tested the goodness of fit model of person-context relations. As this research has progressed, increasing evidence in support of the model has been obtained. Some of this support is presented hereafter.

Results From My Laboratory.   In one study, Palermo (1982) used the DOTS to assess fifth graders' ratings of their own temperaments, the fifth graders' mothers' ratings of their children's temperaments, and the demands for behavioral style held by the teachers and mothers of the fifth graders. Outcome measures included teacher ratings of classroom ability and adjustment, classroom peers' sociometric appraisals of each subject's positive and negative peer relations, and mother's reports of problem behaviors shown at home. Again, better fit children had more favorable scores on teacher-, peer-, and mother-derived outcome measures than did less well fit children. Most interestingly, the best predictors were fit scores computed between mother-rated temperament and teacher demands. In other words, Palermo's (1982) data illustrate that the functional significance of temperament is not a within-the-person phenomenon but it is a relational phenomenon; scores for goodness of fit between temperament rated by one source (the mother) and demands derived from another independent source (the teacher) not only were the best predictors of adaptation within the mother- and teacher-rated contexts but also within a third, independent (peer) context.

In other studies using the DOTS-R (Lerner et al., 1986; Windle et al., 1986), temperament and its fit with contextual demands was assessed among early and late adolescents. Among the former group the relations between temperament and dimensions of perceived competence, as measured by Harter's (1982) Perceived Competence Scale, could be accounted for by the goodness of fit model. Harter's scale measures four components of perceived competence—cognitive, social, physical, and general self-worth. Use of this scale was predicted on the view that children who have positive interactions with significant others should come to perceive themselves as competent actors, at least in regard to those features of self-evaluation likely to be influenced by feedback from others. The cognitive, social, and self-worth components are particularly relevant in this regard. No predictions were made regarding the physical component; this factor was included for exploratory purposes.

It was expected that temperament scores that diverged most from the teachers' Ethnotheory scores would be associated with high—that is, positive—scores on these three components of perceived competence. The teachers reported that high general activity level, high sleep activity level, low rhythmicity, low (i.e., negative) mood, low attention span, low flexibility, and low approach (or conversely high withdrawal) would present difficulties for interaction. Thus, positive correlations were expected between cognitive, social, and general perceived competence, on the one hand, and rhythmicity, flexibility, mood, attention span, and approach, on the other. In turn, negative correlations between these competence domains and the two activity attributes were expected. For 14 of the 21 relationships for which predictions were made (i.e., for 67%) significant correlations were found, and all of these were in the expected direction. Moreover, the multiple correlations between temperament and each of the three relevant competence domains are significant.

These results were essentially cross-validated within the late-adolescent sample. Here the ethnotheories of both parents (mostly mothers) and peers (i.e., other college students) were studied. It was found that, for both groups, high general and sleep activity level and low rhythmicity, flexibility, approach, and attention span, and low (i.e., negative) mood constitute temperament levels that are rated to make for difficulty in interaction. As such, it was predicted that high scores on the temperament attributes of rhythmicity, mood, flexibility, attention span, and approach would vary positively with favorable scores on the cognitive, social, and general components of the Perceived Competence Scale and, in addition, would vary negatively with high scores on the Center for Epidemiologic Studies-Depression Scale, the CES-D scale. In turn, low scores on general and sleep activity level were expected to vary negatively with high scores on the three competence components and positively with CES-D scores. It should be noted that the CES-D was used by Windle et al. (1986) because of the findings that failure to meet the demands of one's context (i.e., failure to be interactively competent) may be associated with feelings of depression (Seligman, 1975). For 17 of the 28 relationships for which predictions were made (i.e., for 61%), significant correlations were found. All were in the expected direction. Finally, it was again found that the multiple correlations between temperament and each of the three relevant competence domains were significant.

Thus, as was found with early adolescents, the assessment of late adolescents indicates that knowledge of the fit between a young person's temperament and the expectational demands of his or her context aids substantially in understanding the relationship between temperament and adaptive psychosocial functioning. As mentioned earlier, we can only infer that the reactions by parents to a child who did not meet their expectations would be negative. This inference seems plausible based on the findings within the NYLS and the Super and Harkness research. Obtaining actual measurements of the mother–child and father–child interactions is an important part of testing the goodness of fit model. Data on these variables are now being collected as part of the Replication and Extension of The Pennsylvania Early Adolescent Transition Study (REPEATS). Data from the REPEATS, however, is still in the collection phase and therefore not reportable. Many of our current tests of the goodness of fit concept have occurred within our conducting The Pennsylvania Early Adolescent Transition Study (PEATS), a short-term longitudinal study of approximately 150 northwestern Pennsylvania early adolescents, from the beginning of sixth grade across the transition to junior high school and to the end of the seventh grade.

In a study derived from the PEATS, Talwar, Nitz, and Lerner (1988) found that poor fit with parental demands (especially in regard to the attributes of Mood and Approach-Withdrawal) at the end of sixth grade was associated in seventh grade with low teacher-related academic and social competence and negative peer relations. Corresponding relations were found in regard to fit with peer demands. Moreover, and again underscoring the importance of considering the context within which organismic characteristics are expressed, goodness of fit scores (between temperament and demands) were more often associated with adjustment than were temperament scores alone; this was true in regard to both peer and parent contexts at the end of the sixth grade, and for the peer context after the transition to junior high school (at the beginning of seventh grade). Finally, Talwar et al. (1988) grouped the PEATS subjects into high versus low overall fit groups (by summing fit scores across all temperament dimensions). Adolescents in the low-fit group in regard to peer demands received lower teacher ratings of scholastic competence, and more parent ratings for conduct and school problems, than did the adolescents in the high-fit group in regard to peer demands. Comparable findings were found in regard to low versus high fit in regard to parent demands. Thus, we may venture to conclude that the findings derived from the PEATS lend support to the notion that the child's characteristics of temperament are influencing the people in the child's context in ways that feedback to the child to further influence his or her trajectory of development.

Additional Support.   Research from others outside of our laboratory, although not directly testing the goodness of fit model, lends support to the idea that the temperament of the child indeed influences maternal behaviors. Although much of this research is limited by methodological problems, (i.e., nonindependence of measures) the associations reported are worthy of note (see Crockenberg, 1986, for a fuller discussion of these studies).

First, temperamental difficulty (i.e., high intensity of response, irregularity in biological functions, negative mood, low adaptability, and withdrawal) has been associated with less responsive caregiving or less stimulating contact from mothers (Crockenberg & Acredolo, 1983: Dunn & Kendrick, 1980; Kelly, 1976; Klein, 1984; Linn & Horowitz, 1983; Milliones, 1978; Peters-Martin & Wachs, 1984).

Some studies that do employ relatively independent measures of maternal behavior and infant temperament found that mothers are less engaged with their babies if they are difficult or irritable (Crockenberg & Acredolo, 1983; Linn & Horowitz, 1983.) These studies are countered by findings of studies reporting that mothers of difficult or irritable babies are more engaged with their babies than are mothers of easy, less irritable babies (Bates, Olson, Pettit, & Bayles, 1982; Caron & Miller, 1981; Crockenberg & Smith, 1982; Fish & Crockenberg, 1981; Klein, 1984; Peters-Martin & Wachs, 1984; Pettit & Bates, 1984). Crockenberg (1986) noted that several factors may be responsible for the inconsistent findings; for example, curvilinear effects—mothers increasing their involvement in relation to their infants' needs and withdrawing only if the infants are extremely difficult or irritable; the influence of some third variable such as maternal attitudes or the gender of the infant; or an interaction between temperament and some other characteristic of the caregiver or caregiving environment. Even with these inconsistencies, these findings lend further support to the notion that infant temperament is influencing maternal behaviors. Future research should be aimed at delineating additional factors that may be part of this influence.

CONCLUSIONS

These studies and those from the NYLS, the research of Super and Harkness, and the data from the PEATS all combine to suggest that temperamental characteristics influence parenting behaviors in various ways. For the afore-mentioned reasons, the relationship is not always a straightforward one, and can conceivably change across time. For example, the same child characteristic that may promote negative parent behaviors in infancy and early childhood (i.e., frequent withdrawal behaviors to new stimuli), may not be salient during adolescence, when parents are less involved in caregiving.

In addition to the age of the child interacting with temperament, the gender of the child can also play a role in how parents perceive and react to various temperamental characteristics. Parents who hold gender-based expectations for child behavior may find themselves more restrictive or punishing toward a daughter who exhibits a high activity level. This same activity level, however, may be reinforced and accepted in a son.

Because I argued that temperament can change in relation to the context, parents need to understand that it is their demands, their attitudes, their evaluations, and their interpretation that give much of the functional significance of the child's individuality to the behavioral exchange they have with them. The child brings these temperamental characteristics to the parent–child relationship but parents need to understand their own psychology and how it combines with the child's characteristics to influence the interaction.

In addition, parents need to understand that they impose demands on the child and the physical context imposes demands on the child as well. As a result, a better or lesser fit will emerge. For example, if a child has a low threshold of reactivity and a high intensity of reactions, he or she should not sleep in a bedroom next to a busy street. If a child is not very rhythmic in terms of eating, but parents hold strict demands for when meals are served, a poor fit between the child's characteristics and the parents' demands will result. This poor fit may lead to negative interactions between parent and child. Because temperamental characteristics can be modified, parents can attempt to change the child's rhythmicity to get him or her to eat at regular times. If, however, change appears to be difficult, parents may need to be more flexible in their demands or alter their demands to create a better fit. The important thing is for parents to be perceptive about the fit that their child has with the context, to be able to assess what demands are being imposed on the child, and to be able to assess their child's individuality. If they can make these assessments with the help of professionals, they will be in a position to enhance the fit that their child has with his or her context, thereby promoting more positive interactions with others and thereby enhancing the child's development.

The usefulness of the earlier presentation of the goodness of fit model lies in the interpretation that because of different exchanges between children and their contexts, their temperamental characteristics may place them at risk for negative interactions with parents or caregivers. These interactions may further place the child at risk for negative adjustment. Future research should be aimed at a more thorough evaluation of the parent–child interactions that are influenced by various child characteristics—temperament, gender, physical attractiveness, and the like. In addition, future research should be aimed at a precise delineation of the risks associated with these interactional patterns.

ACKNOWLEDGMENT

The writing of this chapter was supported in part by NICHD Grant HD23229 to Richard M. and Jacqueline V. Lerner.

REFERENCES

Bates, J. E. (1980). The concept of difficult temperament. *Merrill-Palmer Quarterly, 26*, 299–319.
Bates, J., Olson, S., Pettit, G., & Bayles, K. (1982). Dimensions of individuality in the mother–infant relationship at six months of age. *Child Development, 53*, 446–461.
Bell, R. Q. (1968). A reinterpretation of the direction of effects in studies of socialization. *Psychological Review, 75*, 81–95.
Bell, R. Q. (1974). Contributions of human infants to caregiving and social interaction. In M. Lewis & L. A. Rosenblum (Eds.), *The effect of the infant on its caregiver* (pp. 1–20). New York: Wiley.
Bell, R. Q., & Harper, L. V. (1977). *Child effects on adults.* Hillsdale, NJ: Lawrence Erlbaum Associates.
Berscheid, E., & Walster, E. (1974). Physical attractiveness. In L. Berkowitz (Ed.), *Advances in experimental social psychology* (Vol. 7, pp. 157–215). New York: Academic Press.
Brazelton, T. B., Koslowski, B., & Main, M. (1974). The origins of reciprocity in mother–infant interaction. In M. Lewis & L. A. Rosenblum (Eds.), *The effect of the infant on its caregiver* (pp. 49–76). New York: Wiley.
Buss, A., & Plomin, R. A. (1975). *Temperamental theory of personality development.* New York: Wiley-Interscience.
Caron, J., & Miller, P. (1981, March). *Effect of infant characteristics on caretaker responsiveness among the Gusii.* Paper presented at the biennial meeting of the Society for Research in Child Development, Boston.
Chess, S., & Thomas, A. (1984). *The origins and evolution of behavior disorders: From infancy to early adult life.* New York: Brunner/Mazel.
Crockenberg, S. (1986). Are temperamental differences in babies associated with predictable differences in caregiving. In J. V. Lerner & R. M. Lerner (Eds.), *Temperament and child development: New directions for child development* (pp. 53–73). San Francisco: Jossey-Bass.
Crockenberg, S., & Acredolo, C. (1983). Infant temperament ratings: A function of infants, or mothers, or both? *Infant Behavior and Development, 6*, 61–72.

Crockenberg, S., & Smith, P. (1982). Antecedents of mother–infant interaction and infant irritability in the first three months of life. *Infant Behavior and Development*, 5, 105–119.

Darwin, C. (1859). *Origins of species.* London: John Murray.

Dunn, J., & Kendrick, C. (1980). Studying temperament and parent–child interaction: Comparison of interview and direct observation. *Developmental Medicine and Child Neurology*, 22, 484–496.

Fish, M., & Crockenberg, S. (1981). Correlates and antaecedents of nine-month infant behavior and mother–infant interaction. *Infant Behavior and Development*, 4, 69–81.

Goldsmith, H. H. (1985, April). *Handout for theories of temperament.* Prepared for the conversation hour at the meeting of the Society for Research in Child Development, Toronto.

Goldsmith, H. H., & Campos, J. J. (1982). Toward a theory of infant temperament. In R. N. Emde & R. Harmon (Eds.), *Attachment and affiliative systems: Neurobiological and psychobiological aspects* (pp. 161–193). New York: Plenum.

Hall G. S. (1904). *Adolescence.* New York: Appleton.

Harter, S. (1982). The perceived competence scale for children. *Child Development*, 53, 87–97.

Hull, C. L. (1952). *A behavior system.* New Haven, CT: Yale University Press.

Kagan, J. (1966). Reflection-impulsivity: The generality and dynamics of conceptual tempo. *Journal of Abnormal Psychology*, 71, 17–24.

Kelly, P. (1976). The relation of infant's temperament and mother's psychopathology to interactions in early infancy. In K. F. Riegel & J. A. Meacham (Eds.), *The developing individual in a changing world* (pp. 664–675). Chicago: Aldine.

Klein, P. (1984). The relation of Israeli mothers toward infants in relation to infants' perceived temperament. *Child Development*, 55, 1212–1218.

Korn, S. (1978, September). *Temperament, vulnerability, and behavior.* Paper presented at the Louisville Temperament Conference, Louisville, KY.

Lerner, J. V. (1984). The import of temperament for psychosocial functioning: Tests of a "goodness of fit" model. *Merrill-Palmer Quarterly*, 30, 177–188.

Lerner, J. V., & Lerner, R. M. (1983). Temperament and adaptation across life: Theoretical and empirical issues. In P. B. Baltes & O. G. Brim, Jr. (Eds.), *Life-span development and behavior* (Vol. 5, pp. 197–230). New York: Academic Press.

Lerner, J. V., Lerner, R. M., & Zabski, S. (1985). Temperament and elementary school children's actual and rated academic performance: A test of a "goodness of fit" model. *Journal of Child Psychology and Psychiatry*, 26, 125–136.

Lerner, R. M. (1978). Nature, nurture, and dynamic interactionism. *Human Development*, 21, 1–20.

Lerner, R. M. (1979). A dynamic interactional concept of individual and social relationship development. In R. Burgess & T. Huston (Eds.), *Social exchange in developing relationships* (pp. 271–305). New York: Academic Press.

Lerner, R. M., & Busch-Rossnagel, N. (1981). Individuals as producers of their development: Conceptual and empirical bases. In R. M. Lerner & N. A. Busch-Rossnagel (Eds.), *Individuals as producers of their development: A life-span perspective* (pp. 1–36). New York: Academic Press.

Lerner, R. M., Lerner, J. V., Windle, M., Hooker, K., Lernerz, K., & East, P. L. (1986). Children and adolescents in their contexts: Tests of a goodness of fit model. In R. Plomin & J. Dunn (Eds.), *The study of temperament: Changes, continuities, and challenges* (pp. 337–404). Hillsdale, NJ: Lawrence Erlbaum Associates.

Lerner, R. M., & Spanier, G. B. (1978). A dynamic interactional view of child and family development. In R. M. Lerner & G. B. Spanier (Eds.), *Child influences on marital and family interaction: A life-span perspective* (pp. 1–22). New York: Academic Press.

Lewis, M., & Rosenblum, L. A. (Eds.). (1974). *The effect of the infant on its caregiver.* New York: Wiley.

Linn, P., & Horowitz, F. (1983). The relationship between infant individual differences and mother–infant interaction during the neonatal period. *Infant Behavior and Development*, 6, 415–427.

Mead, G. H. (1967). *Mind, self, and society from the standpoint of a social behaviorist.* Chicago: University of Chicago Press.

Milliones, J. (1978). Relationship between perceived child temperament and maternal behaviors. *Child Development, 49,* 1255–1257.

Palermo, M. (1982). *Child temperament and contextual demands: A test of the goodness of fit model.* Unpublished doctoral dissertation, The Pennsylvania State University, University Park.

Peters-Martin, P., & Wachs, T. (1984). A longitudinal study of temperament and its correlates in the first 12 months. *Infant Behavior and Development, 7,* 285–298.

Pettit, G., & Bates, J. (1984). Continuity of individual differences in the mother–infant relationship from 6 to 13 months. *Child Development, 55,* 729–739.

Rothbart, M. K., & Derryberry, D. (1981). Development of individual differences in temperament. In M. Lamb (Ed.), *Advances in developmental psychology* (Vol. 1, pp. 37–86). Hillsdale, NJ: Lawrence Erlbaum Associates.

Sameroff, A. L. (1975). Transactional models in early social relations. *Human Development, 18,* 65–79.

Schneirla, T. C. (1957). The concept of development in comparative psychology. In D. B. Harris (Ed.), *The concept of development* (pp. 78–108). Minneapolis, MN: University of Minnesota Press.

Seligman, M. E. P. (1975). *Helplessness: On depression, development, and death.* San Francisco, CA: Freeman.

Spanier, G. B., Lerner, R. M., & Aquilino, W. (1978). Future perspectives on child–family interactions. In R. M. Lerner & G. B. Spanier (Eds.), *Child influences on marital and family interaction: A life-span perspective* (pp. 327–344). New York: Academic Press.

Strelau, J. A. (1972). A diagnosis of temperament by nonexperimental techniques. *Polish Psychological Bulletin, 4,* 97–105.

Super, C. M., & Harkness, S. (1981). Figure, ground, and gestalt: The cultural context of the active individual. In R. M. Lerner & N. A. Busch-Rossnagel (Eds.), *Individuals as producers of their development: A life-span perspective* (pp. 69–86). New York: Academic Press.

Super, C. M., & Harkness, S. (1982, October). *Constitutional amendments.* Presentation at the 1982 Occasional Temperament Conference, Salem, MA.

Talwar, R., Nitz, K., & Lerner, R. M. (1988). *Relations among early adolescent temperament, parent and peer ethnotheories, and adjustment: A test of the goodness of fit model.* Unpublished manuscript, The Pennsylvania State University, University Park.

Thomas, A., & Chess, S. (1977). *Temperament and development.* New York: Brunner/Mazel.

Thomas, A., & Chess, S. (1980). *The dynamics of psychological development.* New York: Brunner/Mazel.

Thomas, A., & Chess, S. (1981). The role of temperament in the contributions of individuals to their development. In R. M. Lerner & N. A. Busch-Rossnagel (Eds.), *Individuals as producers of their own development: A life-span perspective* (pp. 231–255). New York: Academic Press.

Thomas, A., Chess, S., & Birch, H. (1968). *Temperament and behavioral disorders in childhood.* New York: University Press.

Thomas, A., Chess, S., Birch, H. G., Hertzig, M. E., & Korn, S. (1963). *Behavioral individuality in early childhood.* New York: University Press.

Thomas, A., Chess, S., Sillen, J., & Mendez, O. (1974). Cross-cultural study of behavior in children with special vulnerabilities to stress. In D. F. Ricks, A. Thomas, & M. Roff (Eds.), *Life history research in psychopathology* (pp. 53–67). Minneapolis: University of Minnesota Press.

White, S. H. (1968). The learning-maturation controversy: Hall to Hull. *Merrill-Palmer Quarterly, 14,* 187–196.

Windle, M., Hooker, K., Lenerz, K., East, P. L., Lerner, J. V., & Lerner, R. M. (1986). Temperament, perceived competence, and depression in early- and late-adolescents. *Developmental Psychology, 22,* 384–392.

Wohlwill, J. F. (in press). The concept of development and the developmental research methodology. In P. van Geert & L. P. Mos (Eds.), *Annals of theoretical psychology.* New York: Plenum Press.

Chapter 5

Parenting and the Marital Relationship

Robert E. Emery
Michele Tuer
University of Virginia

Not only do mothers and fathers affect their children independently as parents, but the relationship between the parents can also have a profound influence on children. The effect of the parental relationship is seen most clearly in extreme cases of distress, such as serious marital conflict, separation, and divorce. But marital and parenting roles are inextricably linked in day-to-day interaction as well. Mothers and fathers treat their children differently in the presence or absence of their spouse, and parents can offer (or withhold from) each other feedback and support in everyday parenting.

Just as the marital relationship influences children, so do children affect the marital relationship. The direct influence of children on the marriage has been documented by research on changes in marital satisfaction during the transition to parenthood, studies of the effect of difficult or disturbed children on marital happiness, and evidence concerning the influence of children on the likelihood of divorce. Although empirical evidence is most compelling in documenting children's negative effect on marital satisfaction and their protective influence on divorce, children clearly also affect their parents' day-to-day interactions with each other. The practical demands of parenting, as well as the shared emotional investment in childrearing, have many ordinary but powerful effects on the marriage.

In addition to its sweeping practical importance for the understanding of family life, the study of the relation between marriage and parenting presents exciting theoretical challenges. One of the most important is the necessity of focusing on triadic interaction. Triadic interaction is far more complex to analyze than is dyadic interchange, the traditional focus of parenting studies. One must not only consider the three pairs of dyadic relationships within the triad, but also the influence of the third member on each of the dyads. Although the theoretical model is far from complete, in this chapter several compelling, if sometimes vague, principles from family systems theory are used in an attempt to promote a conceptual understanding of the relation between marriage and children.

This chapter therefore has two goals. First, it summarizes some illustrative research on the reciprocal relation between marriage and parenting. Second, the research findings are integrated using some innovative conceptual perspectives offered by systems theory. The summaries of both the research and the theoretical issues are intentionally selective. The goal is to illuminate basic findings and conceptual views, not to offer an extensive literature review.

THEORETICAL BACKGROUND

Both psychoanalytic and social learning theorists suggested various hypotheses predicting why a relation between the marriage and child development is expected. Of the many positions that have been offered, theorizing about Oedipal conflicts and subsequent identification with the same-gender parent surely is the best known psychoanalytic view on the importance of the mother–child–father triangle. Perhaps the major focus of speculation about the triad from the perspective of social learning theory is the idea that parents model behavior in their own interactions that may be imitated by their children.

Although psychoanalytic and social learning views offer useful concepts about the relation between marriage and parenting (cf. Emery, Joyce, & Fincham, 1987), both of these theoretical positions are reductionistic in their perspectives on family interaction. Psychoanalytic theorists tend to reduce family interaction to the level of the individual, whereas social learning views of the family generally treat the dyad as the unit of analysis (Emery et al., 1987). A third force in theorizing about marriage and parenting, family systems theory, holds an antireductionist perspective. According to systems views, the whole cannot be understood as a sum of its parts (von Bertalanffy, 1968). Thus, the mother–child–father triad can only be understood as a unit, not as a collection of individuals or dyads (e.g., P. Minuchin, 1985; S. Minuchin, 1974). Systems theory has been valuable to the authors' conceptualization of the relation between marriage and parenting, and recent research is consistent with this antireductionist perspective. For these reasons and because the principles of family systems theory are not widely discussed in developmental psychology, a brief overview of some basic concepts is in order.

Some Family Systems Concepts

Many empirically oriented psychologists are distressed by the imprecision and overlap of the various concepts that comprise family systems theory. We count ourselves among this group. Family systems concepts have been discussed primarily in a clinical literature, and support for the theorizing is based largely on case history data. The systems concepts discussed in this clinical literature often are imprecise, making them extremely difficult to operationalize and test. A major challenge to the field is to refine and specify the conceptual base of family systems theory. In this regard, Patricia Minuchin (1985) offered one such straightforward summary, and her presentation is integral to the following discussion.

The central concept of systems theory is that any system must be considered as an irreduceable whole that is comprised of interdependent parts. This is the antireductionist position already mentioned. This most basic systems concept has had a profound effect on many scientific disciplines. Perhaps the most familiar is its influence on biological perspectives of the interdependence of organisms in the natural ecology. In relation to the present topic, the principle refocuses the nurture of child development in the family from its dominant concern with parenting. From the systems perspective, parenting is just one of several categories of family relationships that influence children's development (especially because other family relationships are hypothesized to affect parenting in important ways). Family systems theorists expect the development of children to be affected by multiple family interactions, including those relationships in which the children's direct participation is secondary (e.g., the marriage).

A second principle of systems theory is now well-accepted in the developmental literature on parenting. Causality is not linear, but it is reciprocal. Parents both influence children and are influenced by them (Bell, 1968). Because the family is conceptualized as a whole, systems theory further predicts that children both influence the relationship between their parents and are influenced by that relationship, the central point of this chapter. Systems theorists frequently use the term *circular causality* to refer to this principle of reciprocal influence. This is confusing because, as the term implies, a literal postulation of circular causality is tautological. In order to avoid the tautology, a time element must be postulated to intervene between reciprocal cause and effect (Bandura, 1983; Phillips & Orton, 1983).

Homeostasis is a third principle of systems theory, one that is familiar throughout science. As in cell biology, the concept of homeostasis in family systems suggests that families exhibit a tendency to maintain a steady state. Changes occur, but the principle of homeostasis suggests that they will be resisted in order to maintain equilibrium. In fact, the focus on homeostasis is so dominant that a widely accepted view of change has yet to be recognized from within a family systems perspective (P. Minuchin, 1985).

The principle of homeostasis also suggests that a system is stressed by disequilibrium. An example of an unbalanced family system is one in which both parents maintain intensely positive relationships with their child but an intensely negative relationship with one another. In such a circumstance, the principle of homeostasis suggests that relationships will change in order to bring the system into balance. Possible solutions to the unbalance in the present example include the improvement of the parents' relationship, the distancing of one parent from both their spouse and the child, or the development of negative relationships between each parent and the child.

A fourth proposition from systems theory is that larger systems are composed of smaller subsystems, and these subsystems are separated by boundaries. Some subsystems are obvious and normative (e.g., the marital subsystem), but others are subtle and atypical (e.g., an alliance between a parent and a child against the other parent). Boundaries are the stated or unstated rules of behavior that serve to define a subsystem. The concept is akin to the social psychological concept of the boundaries that define interpersonal space. An example of an obvious and normative component of the boundary of the marital subsystem is the limited discussion of sexuality in the presence of the children.

Two Dimensions of Interpersonal Relationships

The systems concepts just outlined can be useful in describing the process of transactions in the family (or in virtually any other system). Their application in describing some processes linking marital and parenting relationships is illustrated throughout this chapter. Despite their value in describing processes, however, systems principles specify little about the content of what is processed in family interactions. What are the substantive dimensions of family relationships that are described by these systemic processes?

It is no surprise that this question has not been answered uniformly by psychologists. For a variety of reasons, however, this chapter focuses on the two central dimensions of interpersonal relationships that were made prominent by ego psychologist Harry Stack Sullivan (1968) and his followers (e.g., Leary, 1957). According to the Sullivanian view, one basic dimension of relationships reflects interpersonal power. Dominance anchors one end of this continuum, and submission is the opposite extreme. The second basic dimension focuses on the degree of emotional involvement in the relationship. One pole of this continuum is characterized by affiliation, and the opposite pole is characterized by hostility.

Some family systems theorists suggested that similar dimensions can be used to describe the core aspects of family relationships, as have some personality theorists in addition to Sullivan. Although the topic is a compelling one, this is not the appropriate forum for entering into the debate about whether interpersonal power and emotional involvement are the central or the only dimensions necessary to describe the major variations in relationships. It is worth noting in the present context, however, that these two basic dimensions of relationships are virtually identical to Diana Baumrind's (1971) highly regarded dimensions of parenting that have been used so effectively in summarizing and integrating the research literature on parenting (Maccoby & Martin, 1983). It also is worth noting that the dimensions of interpersonal power and emotional involvement bear a striking resemblance to the concepts of dominance and affiliation used commonly by ethologists as core constructs in explaining the social behavior of animals.

These observations hardly prove that Sullivan's views are either accurate or complete, but they do suggest that focusing on the relationship dimensions of interpersonal power and emotional involvement has proven valuable to researchers and theorists from outside of the Sullivanian realm. Thus, in this chapter systems views are used to characterize the "how" of the relation between marriage and parenting, and the dimensions of interpersonal influence and emotional closeness are used to organize the "what" of the topic.

Marriage and Parenting Across the Family Life Cycle

In addition to the more general theoretical issues regarding systems theory and the dimensions of interpersonal relationships, the relation between marriage and parenting must be understood within the context of the family's stage in its life cycle. Just as individuals proceed through normative transitions in development during childhood and throughout adult life, the family also has a developmental life course. Family psychologists and sociologists have pinpointed several key transitions in the life cycle of the family including the birth of the first child, the entry of children into public school, the transition to having adolescent children, the launching of the last child from the household, and the family in later life.

Each of these major developmental events requires the family system to reorganize and accommodate change. In terms of the theoretical concepts outlined earlier, the task at each developmental transition is for family members to renegotiate their existing boundaries in regard to relative interpersonal power and the degree of emotional closeness in their relationships. Although the most obvious family transitions occur in the relationships between parents and their children, systems theory predicts that the children's developmental transitions will necessitate renegotiation of the marital relationship as well.

This prediction is supported by one of the more interesting empirical findings in relation to marriage and parenting across the family life cycle. Some predictable changes in marital happiness correspond to changes in children's developmental status. Although the proportion of variance accounted for is not large, marital satisfaction has been found to follow a U-shaped function across the family life cycle. On average, marital satisfaction is higher early in the marriage, it declines when the first child is born, and it increases again later when the children become adolescents and begin to leave the home (Anderson, Russell, & Schumm, 1983).

THE TRANSITION TO PARENTHOOD

Perhaps the clearest evidence that children do affect the marital relationship comes from research on the transition to parenthood, a time when marital satisfaction has been found to decline on average. Increasingly sophisticated research has been conducted on this transition, which is both substantively important and theoretically informative.

Individual and Marital Strains

The challenges of the first newborn and shifts in roles necessitated by the infant affect parents' adjustment both as individuals and as partners. New parents commonly report mood changes characterized by fatigue, tension, and feelings of being overwhelmed (Feldman, 1987). Mothers and fathers report somewhat different concerns, however. Mothers typically focus on physical concerns relating to delivery and physical readjustment, whereas fathers more commonly focus on their financial worries. Both parents feel the strain of getting less sleep (Russell, 1974). The perceived strain is modest, but it has been found to persist even into the infant's sixth month. Increasing strain is predicted by low marital quality and instrumentality for women, and by stress and unplanned pregnancy for men (Feldman, 1987).

Cowan et al. (1985) also found that marital conflict increases from pregnancy to 18 months after birth. They found the declines in marital satisfaction to occur at different stages for men and women, however. Men's satisfaction changed little from pregnancy to 6 months postpartum, but declined more dramatically from 6 to 18 months. Women's satisfaction declined most sharply from pregnancy to 6 months postpartum, with the decline moderating from 6 to 18 months. Others have found linear declines for both partners' reports of satisfaction and love from pregnancy to 9 months postpartum, however, with the degree of the change being greater for wives (Belsky, Lang, & Rovine, 1985). Whatever its specific trajectory, a significant decline in marital satisfaction has been documented by most researchers. Still, it is important to note that the change is not very large (about 10 points on the Locke-Wallace or the Dyadic Adjustment Scale; Cowan & Cowan, 1988).

The type of role arrangement (e.g., traditional division of labor versus equal sharing of tasks), and especially the couple's satisfaction with their particular arrangement predict marital satisfaction and well-being. On average, life satisfaction and self-esteem are higher for mothers with less and fathers with more identification with the parenting role (Dickie, 1987). Jacoby (1969) pointed to the importance of expectations, and suggested that working-class families experience a smoother transition to parenthood. For working class parents, children may interfere less with expectations for leisure and with career aspirations, especially for mothers. Consistent with this speculation, gratification as a parent has been found to be negatively associated with education for men and women and with occupational prestige for men (Russell, 1974).

Both role arrangements and expectancies may explain why older parents are less likely to experience difficulties during the transition (Russell, 1974; Wright, Henggeler, & Craig, 1986). Older couples are less likely to have an unplanned pregnancy, are more likely to be financially stable, and are more likely to be emotionally prepared for parenting. They also have had more time to plan for parenting and to pursue other roles, such as work roles.

In spite of its negative effects on marital satisfaction, it is important to note that childbirth nevertheless serves as a protective factor against divorce. As discussed later, divorce rates for families with a preschool child are half of what they are for childless couples (Cherlin, 1977). This demographic finding again points to the influence of the child on the marriage.

Childbirth and the Redefinition of Marriage

In addition to global satisfaction, empirical evidence demonstrates that the process of becoming parents changes many facets of a couple's relationship. The birth of a child redefines the marriage. During the transition to parenthood, the goal of the marital relationship changes from its primary emotional and expressive emphasis to include many more instrumental functions (Belsky, Spanier, & Rovine, 1983; Belsky et al., 1985; Cowan et al., 1985). Expressions of affection diminish from the third trimester to 3 months postpartum, but remain relatively stable after that. Yet as couples see their relationship declining in its sense of romance, they note improvement in its sense of partnership (Belsky et al., 1983, 1985).

Belsky et al. (1985) offered one example of this line of research. These investigators explored changes for 67 White middle-class couples before and at 1, 3, and 9 months after the birth of their first child. They used questionnaires, joint parent interviews, and observational methods to assess the marital relationship.

Global satisfaction was found to decline linearly over time for both husbands and wives. Satisfaction with positive interactions also decreased, although husbands were consistently more satisfied than wives. There were no changes in negative interactions or conflict. Both partners spent less time maintaining their relationship, that is efforts at improving the relationship declined. Love decreased and ambivalence increased for both partners, but the degree of change was greater for wives. Finally, characterizations of the relationship as friendship and as a romance decreased, although the couples' ratings of partnership increased.

One aspect of the increased sense of partnership is that the couple's family roles become more specialized in order to deal with the formidable new tasks of parenting. Cowan et al. (1985) found that the partner/lover role became less important to new parents from 6 to 18 months after the birth of the first child. In turn, the worker role became more salient to new fathers and less salient to new mothers.

In general, the behavior of marital partners becomes more gender-typed following the birth of the first child. Even spouses who equally shared household tasks before pregnancy become more traditional in their division of labor after childbirth (Cowan et al., 1985; Dickie, 1987). Mothers spend more time with their babies than do fathers, and women perform a significantly larger portion of child-care tasks, even when neither parent expected this to be the case (Berman & Pedersen, 1987). Mothers' emotional expressiveness also increases during this time, both in relationships with their infants and with their own parents (Feldman & Nash, 1984).

The trend toward role specialization along traditional gender lines is neither universal nor necessarily optimal. Cowan and Cowan (1988) reported that those few couples who managed to negotiate a more equal sharing of housework and child care during the transition to parenthood were the most satisfied, both with the role arrangements and with the marriage. In fact, these investigators proposed that increased gender differentiation is the cause of the declining marital satisfaction. As their roles become more specialized, men and women become more different from each other than before. It may be that these differences create more opportunities for conflict over both the emotional and instrumental aspects of the marriage.

Together these findings are consistent with a change in the definition of the marital relationship from one that emphasizes emotional expression to one that serves many new instrumental functions. Evidence suggests that the decline in satisfaction is due more to a change in focus away from the marriage rather than an increase in conflict.

Individual Differences

Although it has been studied infrequently, the personality of the parents may be important in predicting psychological adaptation to parenthood. Fedele, Golding, Grossman, and Pollack (1988) found that indices of autonomy and interpersonal intimacy assessed through interview coding during pregnancy predicted adaptation up to a year postpartum. Mothers' interpersonal intimacy predicted emotional well-being at 2 months postpartum and protected against anxiety and depression at that time. Intimacy did not relate to women's adjustment at 1 year after childbirth, however. Capacity to be autonomous was somewhat related to adaptation at 2 months, but more strongly predicted increased confidence 1 year postpartum.

For fathers, measures of intimacy and autonomy did not predict early adjustment, but their effects were apparent at 1 year postpartum. Increased ratings of intimacy were associated with less anxiety and depression among fathers 1 year after childbirth, and increased autonomy also was related to lower levels of anxiety at this time (Fedele et al., 1988). Other findings indicate that men with high levels of social nonconformity experience more marital dissatisfaction during the transition to parenthood (Wright et al., 1986). These men may be more self-centered and less flexible during the transition.

Characteristics of the infant also affect individual and marital adjustment to childbirth. There is some evidence that fathers are more involved with the physical care of sons, and mothers are more involved with the physical care of daughters. Both play equally with children of each gender, however (Dickie, 1987). As further evidence of the effect of children on the marriage, mothers of fussy and difficult children have been found to experience lower marital adjustment (Wright et al., 1986). Likewise, parents, especially fathers, of temperamentally easy babies experience fewer negative changes (Sirignano & Lachman, 1985). Men may be less confident with the newborn, and may therefore be more attuned to the infant's behavior in their self-appraisals.

The Parenting Alliance. The quality of the parenting partnership may have important implications for parents' ability to successfully meet the demands of raising a child. Perhaps the most critical aspect of this partnership is what Cohen and Weissman (1984) term the *parenting alliance*, the capacity of a spouse to acknowledge, respect, and value the parenting roles and abilities of their partner. This component of the parents' relationship is independent from, although related to, the marital relationship, and serves to regulate self-esteem within the parental dyad. Cohen and Weissman (1984) argued that the role of a parent is one with great potential for self-esteem dysfunction because of its many demands. In addition to the enormous time demands parenting requires a great emotional investment. A parent must constantly relate to the child empathically, but the flow of empathy is unidirectional. The parenting alliance plays a sustaining role, fueling each parent's ability to provide the necessary emotional involvement. In this part of their relationship parents test their responses, perceptions, hopes, fantasies, and ideals relating to the child.

The parenting alliance construct, originating in the psychoanalytic literature, is largely based on clinical observations. Frank, Hole, Jacobson, Justkowski, and Huyck (1986), found that measures of the parenting alliance were correlated with marital intimacy, but only moderately, suggesting that the alliance has an independent contribution to parenting. Additionally, the parenting alliance was found to be related to parents' experiences of confidence and control over themselves and their children.

Further research is needed to elaborate on the interrelationships of the parenting alliance, marital intimacy, and parenting ability. There is evidence that a good marital relationship enables parents to better withstand the stress of parenting (Belsky, 1984), but investigations that identify more specifically what it is that parents provide for each other besides marital intimacy will be very useful, especially in understanding how some parents are able to continue working as effective parenting partners even after a divorce.

Summary

Research on the transition to parenthood provides sound evidence on one important link between marriage and parenting. In addition to its practical importance, this literature is of particular relevance because it highlights the reciprocal nature of the linkage. It is widely assumed that the marriage affects parenting. Research on the transition to parenthood documents that children clearly influence the marital relationship as well.

Perhaps because it is economical (Becker, 1981), increasing role specialization is a common outcome of the transition. The dynamics of this process of specialization can be conceptualized in terms of the systems concepts outlined earlier. New boundaries in the marital subsystem are negotiated as each parent forms a relationship with the newborn and copes with the necessary tasks of child care.

One normative change is the negotiation of a more distant boundary of emotional involvement between the couple as an intimate dyad. Although emotional intimacy decreases for the average couple, shared pride in parenting strengthens and redefines some aspects of the spouses' commitment to each other. Partners who are to become successful coparents begin to form a parenting alliance during this time. The parenting alliance has emotional as well as instrumental components, and it partially compensates for some of the costs of the transition to parenthood in terms of intimacy as lovers.

More dramatic than the increase in emotional distance is the shift in marital power dynamics during the transition to parenthood. One consequence of family role specialization during the transition to parenthood is decreased egalitarianism. Rather than sharing family tasks equally, women and men each gain and lose influence according to the roles they assume. Although the conclusion is in no way prescriptive, the normative shifts in the boundaries of power result in women assuming increased authority in parenting and family relationships, whereas men take on greater influence in the family's interaction with the outside world.

The new marital boundaries that redefine the couple's emotional intimacy and relative interpersonal power do not arrive with the newborn. They are negotiated and renegotiated before childbirth and throughout the first year of the infant's life. Both the process of change and the outcome of the negotiation can stress the marriage. The new rules for family relationships are not immutable, however. They are especially likely to be reworked during subsequent developmental transitions such as the birth of a second child or the entry of the youngest child into day care or elementary school. Nevertheless, the shift in marital and family roles during the transition to parenthood presages future marital role specialization.

MARITAL AND PARENTING ROLE SPECIALIZATION

The feminist movement helped to create a contemporary social ethos that men's and women's roles should be interchangeable inside the family as well as outside of it. Views about what men's and women's family roles should and should not be cloud interpretation of evidence about what they are, however. Research indicates that the marital and parenting role specialization that begins during the transition to parenthood is normative if not normal or ideal. In many respects, role specialization also is traditional. Even in dual-worker families (which also are normative), on average men assume greater responsibility in the workplace and women assume greater responsibility in the home. At a global level, this role specialization is yet another point of linkage between the marriage and parenting.

In general, women maintain greater responsibility than men do for promoting family relationships, especially in their expressive, nurturant roles as mothers (Lewis & Weinraub, 1976). Compared to fathers, mothers more often give their infants care, protection, comfort, and social stimulation (Lamb, 1977; Thompson & Walker, 1989). Mothers' play with their preschool children also differs from that of fathers. Mothers' style of play is more reserved, focusing on toys, verbal rather than physical stimulation, and lower levels of affective arousal (Belsky & Volling, 1987; Oliveri & Reiss, 1987). With older children, mothers are more involved with their daily lives than fathers are, and they offer the children more emotional support (Thompson & Walker, 1989). Mothers of adolescents also serve as *kinkeepers*. They actively influence and shape the relationships of all family members with extended kin (Oliveri & Reiss, 1987).

Fathers are more responsible than mothers for the instrumental role in the family, linking the child to society (Lewis & Weinraub, 1976). Although mothers focus on affective relationships, fathers are more concerned with children's education and values. Fathers do not spend as much time as mothers interacting with or caring for infants (Lewis & Weinraub, 1976). When they play with their children, fathers are more novel, unpredictable, exciting, and engaging. Their play is more physical and rough and tumble than that of mothers, and it elicits strong positive and negative affect in children (Belsky & Volling, 1987;

Oliveri & Reiss, 1987; Thompson & Walker, 1989). With older children, fathers tend to be more directive and instructive than mothers (Thompson & Walker, 1989). For example, they are more likely to give advice than emotional support to adolescents.

Yet another link between marriage and parenting is how role specialization influences marital satisfaction. Mothers who expected a more equal sharing of child-care and household responsibilities experience sharp declines in satisfaction during the transition to parenthood. They often experience their husbands' increased work involvement as pulling away from home at a time when their support is needed most (Thompson & Walker, 1989). Those with more traditional parenting role expectations are more satisfied with their marriages despite the specialization in roles, however.

Parenting in Dyads and Triads

Although reports about differing family responsibilities document the existence of parental role specialization, more direct evidence comes from research comparing mothering and fathering in the absence or presence of the other parent. The physical presence of the father alters patterns of mother–child interaction, and father–child exchanges also change when the mother is physically absent or present. These transitions in styles have been documented in an important and heuristically valuable study by Gjerde (1986).

Gjerde (1986) compared the mother–child and father–child interactions of 16 adolescent girls and 28 adolescent boys in the presence or absence of the other spouse. That is, each adolescent was observed interacting in three different family constellations: with the mother alone, with the father alone, and with both parents together. Trained judges independently rated each of the three interactions using a global Family Interaction Q-sort. Thus, mother–child and father–child interactions in dyads and in triads could be compared.

Differences in dyadic and triadic parent–child interactions were evident only for boys, a finding that is unlikely to result from a simple gender effect but instead from a gender by age interaction. When the father was present, mothers became more engaged, secure, affective, and consistent in relating to their adolescent sons in comparison to how they related when they were alone with the teenager. Although the quality of mother–son interaction improved when the father was present, the quality of father–son exchanges deteriorated in the mother's presence. When the mother was present, fathers were rated as being less involved, engaged, and egalitarian, and more critical and antagonistic in comparison to when fathers and sons interacted alone.

Triadic interaction also was found to exaggerate parenting role differentiation. In both their dyadic and triadic interactions, mothers were more affective, sharing of humor, and engaged than were fathers. However, mothers were found to be significantly more seductive than fathers only during dyadic interactions, but they were more relaxed, more protective, and less task-oriented than fathers only during the triadic interactions. When the father was absent, mothers appeared to be less secure in their traditional role with their adolescent sons. When he was present, they assumed this role with more ease. In contrast, fathers assumed a more active and engaged stance when alone with their sons, but apparently deferred the primary parenting role to their wives in their presence.

These findings clearly point to the importance of viewing parenting in the context of the entire family system. Not only do different individuals in the family reciprocally influence one another, but the relationships between any two individuals influence third parties to the relationship. In particular, these findings suggest that one important contribution that fathers make to parenting is providing support to mothers in their parenting role. But it would be wrong to therefore conclude that fathers are uninvolved in direct parenting. Fathers defer to mothers in regard to many parenting responsibilities when their wives are present, but men become more engaged in parenting when relating individually to their children.

In short, the physical presence of the spouse exaggerates (or strengthens) the boundaries of the parent–child subsystems. When their spouse is present, mothers become more and fathers become less affectively involved in parenting. As mothers' boundaries of nurturance of children become more clear in the presence of their husbands, so do fathers' boundaries of ultimate authority for discipline. This authority is part of the reason why mothers can be more emotionally engaged, and fathers less so when all three family members are together.

Because evidence clearly indicates that the marital relationship influences parenting, it becomes important to address the effects of a distressed marital relationship on parenting.

MARITAL DISTRESS AND PARENTING

Much research documents that marital distress is associated with a variety of difficulties in children's psychological functioning. In general, children have been found to have more psychological difficulties when conflict is more openly angry, occurs in front of the child, involves childrearing disagreements, is chronic, and remains unresolved (Emery, 1982; Grych & Fincham, 1990).

Marital conflict also has been linked with more problems in parenting. Much of this research focuses on the affective dimension of the parent–child dyad. Less close or more conflicted relationships have been found between parents and children when the marital relationship is strained (e.g., Brody, Pillegrini, & Sigel, 1986; Goldberg & Easterbrooks, 1984; Jouriles, Pfiffner, & O'Leary 1988; Peterson & Zill, 1986). Less research has been done on the relation between marital distress and discipline, but some evidence indicates that disruptions in this domain of parenting are associated with marital conflict as well (e.g., Johnson & Lobitz, 1974).

Theorizing from several perspectives predicts that the less adequate parenting that is associated with marital conflict accounts for the difficulties found among children whose parents are unhappy in their marriages. A handful of investigators examined this hypothesis by examining the direct versus the indirect influence of marital conflict on measures of children's psychological health. That is, researchers used regression or modeling analyses to compare the proportion of variance in child behavior accounted for directly by marital conflict versus the variance accounted for by the indirect influence of conflict through parenting style. In these studies, disruptions in parenting generally were found to account for a considerable proportion of the variance in troubled child behavior. This indirect effect also was found to lower the strength of the direct association between marital conflict and child behavior problems (e.g., Fauber, Forehand, Thomas, & Wierson, 1990; Hess & Camara, 1979; Tschann, Johnston, Kline, & Wallerstein, 1989).

This research supports the hypothesis that marital conflict first disrupts parenting, and problems in parenting in turn create difficulties for children. Alternative hypotheses also are tenable, however. Another possibility is that marital conflict directly alters children's behavior, and disturbed child behavior then disrupts parent–child relationships (Grych & Fincham, 1990). It also may be that difficult children sometimes are the source of both marital distress and troubled parent–child relationships. Moreover, a parent with an individual psychological disorder could be responsible both for marital conflict, parenting stress, and child behavior problems (a form of association that could be explained through genetic as well as environmental mechanisms).

It is likely that each of these various paths of effect has some influence on the reciprocal relationships within the family system. Marital and parenting relationships may be dominant influences because of the hierarchical structure of families, but the influence of children on their parents and on their parents' relationship cannot be overlooked. Moreover, an exclusive focus on dyadic influences can overlook rich systemic processes in the family. Marital distress may disturb mothering, and disturbed mothering may in turn cause problems for children, but such a linear, hypothetical path of dyadic causal influence fails to capture the dynamic processes of family interaction. Conflict in families is not dyadic.

Vuchinich, Emery, and Cassidy (1988) provided one example of how what sometimes appears to be dyadic conflicts between family members actually involve triadic family processes. These investigators videotaped 52 families eating dinner together, and studied the triadic processes involved in the 176 episodes of conflict that occurred naturalistically during the meals. They found that a third family member intervened in more than one third of the dyadic conflicts, and in more than half of the cases the intervention involved an alliance with one party against the other. Of particular relevance to the present topic is that boys were more likely than girls to intervene in parental disputes, although they were less likely to join into all other categories of family conflict. Children used distraction strategies most commonly when intervening in family conflicts. The most common strategy used by mothers was mediation, whereas fathers most commonly intervened in conflict by asserting their authority.

Eventual outcomes for children as assessed by various scales measuring child behavior problems may be predicted best by particular categories of family relationships, but this study illustrates some of the triadic dynamics of the processes involved in family conflict. Other research strategies also could be used to capture the richness of family interaction surrounding the linkage between distressed marriages and parenting problems. For example, consider what findings might emerge if partners in happy versus conflicted marriages were compared using the Gjerde (1986) paradigm discussed earlier. It is likely that the presence of the spouse has very different effects on parent–child interaction when the marriage is conflicted than when it is happy.

Researchers are only beginning to investigate these important triadic processes in families where the marriage is unhappy. Some research on marital distress and parenting has clearly documented that one aspect of parenting is both disrupted by marital conflict and linked with increased child behavior problems, however. This important aspect of parenting is inconsistent discipline (Block, Block, & Morrison, 1981; Stoneman, Brody, & Burke, 1989). In what remains the best documentation of this triadic linkage, Block et al. (1981) found that measures of parental disagreement about childrearing predict both subsequent divorce and future problems in children's behavior in school (externalizing problems among boys; internalizing difficulties among girls).

Although current research on the topic is limited, the aforementioned findings suggest that the marital distress is linked with a variety of difficulties in the family system. As marital boundaries become less stable they stress relationships throughout the family. The disruptions for the family system are seen most clearly among those families in which the marital bond is broken. Research indicates that divorce necessitates a renegotiation of the boundaries of all dyadic relationships in the family, and creates broader triadic dilemmas as well.

PARENTING IN SEPARATION AND DIVORCE

The study of separated and divorced families offers dramatic and socially relevant evidence on the influence of the marital relationship on parenting. Separation and divorce typically result in a drastic alteration in the quantity of contact between one parent and the children. The quality of both parent–child relationships often changes as well, especially during the first years of the family transition. The marital separation itself is not the only, or sometimes the most important, cause of disruption in parenting, however. The parents' continuing relationship with each other, especially the degree of conflict in their relationship, is one of the most powerful and consistent predictors of the psychological adjustment of children from divorced families (Emery, 1982, 1988).

Clearly, the most important link between marriage and parenting in divorce is the effect of the separation on children. Still, the relation is not unidirectional. We noted this by briefly examining data documenting the effect of children on divorce rates.

Children's Influence on Divorce Rates

Demographic data indicate that the presence of children may inhibit, increase, or have no apparent influence on the likelihood of divorce. Although not ubiquitous, the deterrent effect is most powerful.

Today's couples are not as likely to remain married for the children's sake, but even historical changes in this common principle document the influence of children on the marriage. Between 1950 and 1965 the proportion of divorces involving children rose from 44% to 60%, and approximately 60% of all divorces continue to involve children (Bane, 1979; Bumpass & Rindfuss, 1979). Despite the increase of the proportion of divorces involving children, evidence indicates that couples with children still are somewhat less likely to divorce than are childless couples (Waite, Haggstrom, & Kanouse, 1985).

The presence of children is not always a deterrent to divorce, however. Children's age is one important qualifying consideration. Divorce rates for families with a preschool child are about half of what they are for childless families (Waite et al., 1985). For families with school-age children, divorce rates are about equal to the rates for childless couples (Cherlin, 1977). The number of children in the family also affects the likelihood of divorce. Divorce rates are considerably lower for families with only one or two children, whereas families with three or more children have divorce rates that approach those of childless couples (Thornton, 1977). Finally, the presence of children can increase the likelihood of divorce in certain circumstances. Divorce rates are higher when a marriage is preceded by a premarital pregnancy or out-of-wedlock birth (O'Connell & Rogers, 1984), and when stepchildren are a part of a remarriage (White & Booth, 1985).

The effect of children on lowering divorce rates seems to contradict evidence indicating that children also lower marital satisfaction, as was discussed earlier. If children decrease the likelihood of divorce, how can they simultaneously increase marital distress? The answer is that although children decrease the benefits of marriage, they also increase the costs of divorce. Apparently, the increased costs outweigh the decreased benefits, at least while the children are young. This conclusion is consistent with one explanation of the relation be-tween the presence of children and marital distress. The average marital hap-piness of childless couples may be higher than that of couples with children, because children deter unhappily married couples from divorcing (Glenn & McLanahan, 1982).

The preceding global evidence provides further support for the reciprocal relation between the marital relationship and parenting. Children surely also affect the parental relationship in many more specific ways in divorce. Chil-dren can exacerbate parental conflict when they "play parents against each other," or children may strengthen the parenting alliance between divorced parents with shared pride in their successes. Perhaps the most important in-fluence of children on the parental relationship following separation and divorce is another global outcome, however. The presence of children necessitates that the parents maintain some form of a relationship with each other. Unlike other lovers, parents cannot cope with the grief that follows the end of their marital relationship by completely severing ties. Their common interest in the chil-dren binds them together even as they decide to end their marriage.

Shortly, we discuss some prominent issues in this continuing mother–child–father triangle following separation and divorce. First, we examine how the break-up of the marriage affects children's individual relationships with each of their parents.

Parenting in Separated and Divorced Families

There are many individual differences in parent–child relationships following divorce. Parenting differs widely between different divorced households. Nevertheless, it is possible to make some normative generalizations about parenting in divorce. Mothers and fathers typically have greater difficulty as-suming roles traditionally fulfilled by their opposite-gender partner. Mothers have more problems with discipline, whereas fathers have greater trouble main-taining affectional ties with their children. Custodial parents frequently are overwhelmed with the tasks of single parenting, whereas noncustodial parents often feel detached and powerless. Although it may seem stereotypical, it is a demographic reality that most custodial parents are mothers, and most non-custodial parents are fathers (Emery, 1988). The following discussion largely tracks this demographic fact.

Divorced Mothers With Custody.   Hetherington's well-known study is an excellent illustration of parenting following separation and divorce (Hethering-ton, 1989; Hetherington, Cox, & Cox, 1982). In this investigation, 36 boys and 36 girls from White middle-class families were assessed 2 months, 1 year, 2 years, and 6 years following their parents' separation, and compared over time with a matched group of children from two-parent families. All children in the study were enrolled in nursery school at the time of the first assessment, and families were evaluated on a number of interview, self-report, and observational measures.

As a group, divorced mothers were found to have more difficulties with parenting than married mothers. Although parenting problems diminished over time, differences were found as many as 6 years following the separation. In comparison to always-married women, divorced mothers were found to make fewer maturity demands, communicated less well, were less affectionate, more inconsistent, and less effective in controlling their children 2 months after the separation. Their relationships with their sons were particularly troubled. Boys received less positive feedback and more negative sanctions than did daughters.

Parenting problems actually increased during the first year following the separation. Two years after the separation, however, divorced mothers were more nurturant, consistent, and in better control of their children than they had been earlier (Hetherington et al., 1982). Changes in parenting practices were reflected in the children's behavior. Children's compliance to instructions first deteriorated then improved over time. Still, children from divorced families remained less compliant than children from two-parent families, even at the 2-year assessment.

At the 6-year point, divorced mothers were found to be as affectionate as married mothers. Still, they continued to be more negative and less effective in discipline with their sons. Consistent with the notion that they grow up faster (Weiss, 1979), children from divorced families were found to have more power in decision making, greater independence, and were monitored less closely by their mothers 6 years after the separation (Hetherington, 1989).

Other investigators also found that the parenting of divorced, custodial mothers is somewhat more negative, inconsistent, and less affectionate than that of married mothers (e.g., Hess & Camara, 1979; Wallerstein & Kelly, 1980). In all studies, however, the variability as well as the average differences are important to note. Consistent with our view that the divorce transition necessitates a renegotiation of the boundaries of warmth and discipline boundaries in parenting, problems at the opposite extremes are sometimes found. Demanding children, guilt, and the absence of a supportive partner can make divorced mothers more susceptible to giving in to children's coercive demands. Loneliness and depression can cause mothers to seek to fulfill their own needs for love through the children. Rather than becoming more punitive or emotionally distant, some custodial mothers become overly permissive or emotionally dependent on their children.

The concern with variability also is a reminder that most divorced mothers are as effective as their married counterparts once the parenting boundaries are renegotiated. Although the process of redefining the mother–child relationship is stressful, there is no one right amount of warmth or discipline to achieve. A diversity of affectional relationships and discipline practices are healthy

(Maccoby & Martin, 1983). As with married families, long-term difficulties are found at the extremes of parenting, not in the wide range in the middle.

Divorced Fathers With Custody. Although father-custody families have not been studied nearly as often or as well as mother-custody families, many of the same parenting concerns arise for custodial parents of either gender. Like custodial mothers, custodial fathers must renegotiate or reassert the boundaries of affection and discipline with their children. A general difference between mothers and fathers is that custodial parents typically have more difficulties establishing boundaries and assuming roles in those traditional areas of parenting and family role responsibilities that had been assumed by the opposite-gender partner. Although custodial mothers have more concerns with finances and with discipline, custodial fathers find it harder to complete household tasks and to offer their children time and affection (Luepnitz, 1982). As one example of this, custodial fathers use substitute child care more often than do custodial mothers (Santrock & Warshak, 1979).

An important point of comparison between parenting in father- and mother-custody families concerns the adjustment of the children. Some researchers have found that boys adapt better when they live with their fathers, whereas girls function better in the custody of their mothers (for a review, see Warshak, 1986). One study found that father-custody boys and mother-custody girls were more socially competent and more satisfied with their living arrangement than were children who were living with their opposite-gender parent (Santrock & Warshak, 1979). In another investigation, children living with their same-gender parent had fewer internalizing and externalizing problems according to parental report (Peterson & Zill, 1986). Finally, a third investigation found that children who lived with their opposite-gender parent were more aggressive and had lower self-esteem than those who lived with the same-gender parent (Camara & Resnick, 1987).

Although very little research has been conducted on within-family differences, these findings suggest the possibility that parenting in divorced families is more effective when parents and children are of the same gender. However, a plausible alternative hypothesis is that the findings are explained by nonrandom selection into mother or father custody (Emery, 1988). Fathers who have custody are known to differ from other divorced fathers—and from mothers with custody—in several respects. Fathers more often have custody of older children, particularly sons, an indication of normative views about the importance of fathering with teen-agers and with boys (Emery, 1988). Fathers with custody also have higher incomes and more education than noncustodial fathers (Chang & Deinard, 1982; Gersick, 1979), suggesting that men with higher socioeconomic status seek or win custody more often. Finally, custodial fathers more frequently have a former spouse who is psychologically impaired (Orthner, Brown, & Ferguson, 1976). The presence of difficulties in mothering seem to be more important to determining paternal custody than difficulties in fathering are in determining maternal custody.

The fact that selection into father custody is nonrandom raises important questions about the implications of research on the adjustment of children living with their same-gender parent. Fathers who have been particularly involved parents may be more likely to have custody of their sons. If so, boys in father custody may be better adjusted because they have always had and continue to have superior fathering. Similarly, fathers may get custody of their daughters primarily when there are serious problems with mothering. If so, girls who seem to be doing worse in father custody (or better in mother custody), may in fact have difficulties related to past or current problems in mothering. In short, nonrandom selection, not differences in relationships with the same-gender parent, may be the reason why researchers have found children who live with their same-gender parent to be better adjusted (Emery, 1988).

At present, the prudent conclusion is that there are few simple rules in predicting the outcome of parenting in mother- or father-custody families. What is clear is that all custodial parents go through a period of readjustment as they assume the difficult task of becoming a single parent. Parents of each gender have more difficulties assuming roles that are newer to them, but custodial parents of both genders apparently encounter similar difficulties in renegotiating their relationships with their children. The period of transition creates problems for both parents and children, but healthy readjustment, not pathology, is the rule once new parenting boundaries are established.

Noncustodial Parents.   Although custodial mothers and fathers face many similar challenges, the parenting of custodial parents (usually mothers) and noncustodial parents (usually fathers) differs dramatically. The most obvious distinction is the frequency of contact with children. In one survey of a nationally representative sample of 11- to 16-year-old children, over 50% had not seen their noncustodial fathers in the last year. Only about 15% saw them once a week or more (Furstenberg, Peterson, Nord, & Zill, 1983). Contact with noncustodial mothers was considerably greater. Of noncustodial mothers, 31% saw their children at least weekly, and only about 13% had not seen them in the last year (Furstenberg et al., 1983).

Frequency of contact may have been underestimated by cohort effects (the survey was conducted in 1981), the length of time since the divorce (some marriages had ended many years earlier), and the fact that visitation estimates were made by custodial parents. Still, the findings indicate that contact between noncustodial parents, particularly fathers, and their children is infrequent on the average. The amount of contact appears to be related to a variety of circumstances. Contact is less when more time has passed since the divorce, when fathers are less highly educated, when fathers live a greater distance from their children, and when one parent has remarried (Furstenberg et al., 1983).

Importantly, some suggested that the amount of contact cannot be predicted by the quality of predivorce parenting (Hetherington et al., 1982; Wallerstein & Kelly, 1980).

It is clear that noncustodial father–child contact is infrequent in many families, but less is known about the quality of noncustodial fathering and virtually no research has been conducted on noncustodial mothering. Not surprisingly, children report feeling less close to noncustodial than custodial fathers, but it is somewhat surprising that the same is not true for mothers. In the national survey cited earlier, 60% of children reported having a good relationship with their custodial mothers, whereas 57% reported a good relationship with their noncustodial mothers. For fathers, 69% reported a good relationship with their custodial fathers, whereas only 36% said their relationship with their noncustodial fathers was good (Peterson & Zill, 1986). Nevertheless, 50% of all children listed their noncustodial fathers as being members of their family, but only 5% of their mothers did so (Furstenberg & Nord, 1985). Although a much more distant affectional boundary between fathers and children is established following divorce, many children still view fathers as members of their family system.

Perhaps because noncustodial fathers are fearful about maintaining tenuous affectional ties with their children, they often abandon much of their role as disciplinarians. In general, noncustodial fathers have more lax rules and lower expectations for their children's conduct than do married fathers (Furstenberg & Nord, 1985). Shortly after the divorce, this may follow the frenzied pattern where "every day is Christmas" and attempts are made to meet the child's every wish (Hetherington, Cox, & Cox, 1976). Even as they reassert some boundaries of discipline over time, however, divorced fathers remain less restrictive than their married counterparts (Hetherington et al., 1982).

Although it has been a topic of considerable debate both in the psychological literature and among social policymakers, little research has addressed the link between the relationship with the noncustodial parent and children's social, psychological, or academic functioning. Moreover, available evidence does not indicate that frequency of contact is clearly related to children's adjustment (for a review, see Emery, 1988). It is clear that noncustodial parents, especially noncustodial fathers, renegotiate more distant and less clear parenting boundaries in relation to both affection and discipline, but the consequences of this process have not been adequately studied. Even if the effects on children's adjustment are not as clearcut as they are for custodial parents, we cannot ignore the tremendous symbolic importance that *both* biological parents hold in the eyes of their children. From the children's perspective, both parents remain members of their families.

Joint Custody Families.   The importance of both mothering and fathering to children from divorced families has given impetus to a tremendous growth in joint custody. Joint custody must be carefully defined, however. In joint legal custody, parental rights and responsibilities are shared, but the children typically spend considerably more time with one parent. In joint physical custody, not only is legal guardianship shared, but children also spend more equal amounts of time with each parent. By far the most common form of joint custody is joint legal custody, even in states like California where both forms of joint custody are encouraged by law. In one study of a large sample, 79% of California families had joint legal custody, whereas only 20% had joint physical custody (defined as at least four overnights with each parent during a 14-day period) (Albiston, Maccoby, & Mnookin, 1990).

Some differences in the coparenting between joint legal and sole legal custody families have been found, but they generally are not large in magnitude (Albiston et al., 1990; Emery 1988). In most cases, child-care arrangements in joint legal custody families are very similar to those found with mother custody. Some research does indicate greater cooperation among joint legal custody parents (e.g., Albiston et al., 1990), but again the effects are not dramatic. In general, quality of parent–child relationships, not the custody label, appear to be most important to children's adjustment. For example, in one study of 91 children with either maternal, paternal, or joint custody, no differences were found between groups on measures of children's behavior problems, self-esteem, or psychosomatic complaints. However, measures of family relationships, particularly the degree of parental conflict, were correlated with children's adjustment within each of the three custody groups (Luepnitz, 1982).

This last point is a reminder that even following divorce the original nuclear family remains a system. Consistent with the major thesis of this chapter, conflict or cooperation in the continuing relationship between parents may be the single most important contributor to parenting and child adjustment in divorced families.

Conflict Between Divorced Parents

As in married families, the mother–child–father triad is of great importance to parenting and child development in divorced families. As each parent renegotiates affectional and discipline boundaries with their children, they also must redefine the boundaries of love and power in their relationship. This is extremely difficult for most divorcing partners. Most divorces are not mutual. Typically, therefore, one partner maintains a desire for intimacy, whereas the other seeks emotional distance. For the partner who wants the marriage to continue the emotional choice often is to be either lovers or enemies. In contrast and in conflict, the partner who wanted the marriage to end may hope to be friends. This central boundary struggle frequently disrupts the parenting alliance, and places children in the middle of their parents' conflict. As parents struggle to redefine their relationship, the family system is unbalanced. Therefore, in addition to potential difficulties in their relationships with each parent, children often are confronted with loyalty dilemmas and inconsistent discipline as well.

Research indicates that interparental conflict is a strong and consistent predictor of children's adjustment to divorce (for reviews, see Emery, 1982, 1988). Divorce is typically preceded by lengthy periods of marital distress, hostilities often escalate at the time of separation and as a result of legal proceedings, and acrimony can continue long after the legal divorce. At each stage, increasing parental conflict predicts greater difficulties in children's adjustment.

Although some of the detrimental effects of parental conflict surely are indirect and result from disruptions in parenting (Fauber et al., 1990), an understanding of the dynamics of the divorced family system is essential to explaining the dyadic parent–child relationships. Theoretically, parental conflict can affect children in a number of direct and indirect ways. Aggression witnessed during angry parental battles may be imitated (Porter & O'Leary, 1980), and inconsistent discipline between parents can create behavioral problems at home and in school (Block et al., 1981).

A more systemic perspective begins to emerge from research indicating that exposure to conflict also is a stressor in its own right. Children as young as 18 months old are upset by angry exchanges between their parents, and by the age of 5 or 6, their distress is evident in attempts to intervene in the fighting (Cummings, Zahn-Waxler, & Radke-Yarrow, 1981, 1984). Intervening in parental conflict poses special problems for children, however, because of their relationships with each parent. Children may be pressed to form alliances with one parent or the other, and their most effective strategy may be to distract their parents from their disputes (Vuchinich et al., 1988). The immediate goal, perhaps for all family members, is to bring about a reduction in the threatening and aversive conflict. Thus, we have a three-stage systemic model in which parental conflict distresses children, this leads them to intervene directly or indirectly in the dispute, and their successful intervention attempts are maintained through negative reinforcement, namely the reduction in parental conflict (Emery, in press).

The degree of parental conflict and the manner in which children intervene in or withdraw from it therefore is extremely important to the divorced family system. Children can ally with one parent against the other, they can attempt to maintain an equal and balanced relationship with each parent, or they can unite their parents by serving as a scapegoat (S. Minuchin, 1974). Children can unite their parents through other maneuvers than their problematic behavior, however. Extremely prosocial behavior serves the same function of uniting the parents through a common focus on the child (Emery, in press). Other intervention strategies also are possible. Children may directly intervene in the conflict and attempt to mediate a resolution. Emotional or physical withdrawal is another way of relieving the distress that conflict creates (Emery, Hetherington, & DiLalla, 1984). At least a few children surely exploit the division between their parents, playing them off against one another. Finally, perhaps the wisest children are aware of the risks involved in their participation in parental conflict and maneuver to avoid getting trapped in it (Johnston, Campbell, & Mayes, 1985).

Children of different ages and genders likely employ unique interventions strategies, and they may form different alliances. In one study, 6- to 8-year-old divorced children were found to be more conflicted in their loyalties, whereas 9- to 12-year-olds tended to ally with one parent or the other (Johnston et al., 1985). Younger children also are probably less direct in their responses to conflict, whereas older children may actively try to mediate a resolution or withdraw from the family altogether. Children surely also attempt to influence their parents in ways consistent with gender-role behavior. Antisocial behavior is likely to be a more common scapegoating maneuver for boys, whereas for girls it may be more likely to unite their parents with a common focus on their extreme prosocial actions. Finally, when parental conflict persists there is likely to be a pull for same-gender alliances to be formed more strongly than is developmentally typical.

Even when children are not directly involved in parental conflict, the emotional distancing between the divorcing parents creates a loyalty dilemma for children. It is difficult to maintain a close relationship with two parents who do not maintain a strong parenting alliance. In one study, 55% of adolescents from two-parent families reported having a good relationship with both of their parents, whereas only 25% of those living with their divorced mothers and 36% of those living with their divorced fathers did so.

Of course, anger between former marriage partners must be expected during divorce, and the expression of that anger may help the former partners establish more distant emotional boundaries. At the same time, from the children's perspective the anger and conflict further disrupt the homeostasis of the family system. The task for parents is to isolate the anger they legitimately feel as hurt and rejected spouses, so that it minimally disrupts the alliance that is possible for them to maintain as parents (Emery, Shaw, & Jackson, 1987). Even when they are in conflict over other matters, cooperation in childrearing is linked with healthier adjustment among children (Camara & Resnick, 1987).

CONCLUDING COMMENT

The point that divorced parents serve their children by disentangling their former role as spouses from their continuing roles as parents once again illustrates the strong link between parenting and marital relationships. Marriage and parenting become intertwined when children are born, and the parents' relationship with each other continues in its importance to children even long after a marriage ends. Partners assume different roles as parents and as spouses, but the boundaries of these distinct roles are blurred in a happy marriage. In a troubled marriage the unclear boundaries invite conflict and create difficulties. In divorce, the boundaries between the parents' relationship with each other and their relationships with their children often must be explicitly defined in order to avoid continued family conflict.

The system of relationships in families involve complex linkages between marital, parenting, and other family roles, a complexity that can begin to be captured from a family systems perspective. Challenges for the future include further specifying the constructs of systems theory, finding better ways to operationalize the constructs, and testing predictions based on hypothesized networks of relationships. An even bigger challenge will be to integrate individual differences in personality and in family roles into the systems perspective. For now, we find systems theory to be an extremely useful heuristic for organizing the diverse literature on parenting and the marital relationship.

REFERENCES

Albiston, C. R., Maccoby, E. E., & Mnookin, R. R. (1990). Does joint legal custody matter? *Stanford Law and Policy Review, 2,* 167–179.

Anderson, S. A., Russell, C. S., & Schumm, W. R. (1983). Perceived marital quality and life-cycle categories: A further analysis. *Journal of Marriage and the Family, 45,* 127–139.

Bandura, A. (1983). Temporal dynamics and decomposition of reciprocal determinism: A reply to Phillips and Orton. *Psychological Review, 90,* 166–170.

Bane, M. J. (1979). Marital disruption and the lives of children. In G. Levinger & O. C. Moles (Eds.), *Divorce and separation* (pp. 276–286). New York: Basic.

Baumrind, D. (1971). Current patterns of parental authority. *Developmental Psychology Monograph, 4,* (1 pt. 2)

Becker, G. S. (1981). *A treatise on the family.* Cambridge, MA: Harvard.

Bell, R. Q. (1968). A reinterpretation of the direction of effects in studies of socialization. *Psychological Review, 75,* 81–95.

Belsky, J. (1984). The determinants of parenting: A process model. *Child Development, 55,* 83–96.

Belsky, J., Lang, M. E., & Rovine, M. (1985). Stability and change in marriage across the transition to parenthood: A second study. *Journal of Marriage and the Family, 47,* 855–865.

Belsky, J., & Volling, B. L. (1987). Mothering, fathering, and marital interaction in the family triad during infancy: Exploring family system's processes. In P. W. Berman & F. A. Pedersen (Eds.), *Men's transitions to parenthood: Longitudinal studies of early family experience* (pp. 37–63). Hillsdale, NJ: Lawrence Erlbaum Associates.

Belsky, J., Spanier, G. B., & Rovine, M. (1983). Stability and change in marriage across the transition to parenthood. *Journal of Marriage and the Family, 45,* 567–577.

Berman, P. W. & Pedersen, F. A. (1987). Research on men's transitions to parenthood: An integrative discussion. In P. W. Berman & F. A. Pedersen (Eds.), *Men's transitions to parenthood: Longitudinal studies of early family experiences* (pp. 217–242). Hillsdale, NJ: Lawrence Erlbaum Associates.

von Bertalanffy, L. (1968). *General systems theory.* New York: George Braziller.

Block, J. H., Block, J., & Morrison, A. (1981). Parental agreement–disagreement on child-rearing orientations and gender-related personality correlates in children. *Child Development, 52,* 965–974.

Brody, G. H., Pillegrini, A. D., & Sigel, I. E. (1986). Marital quality and mother–child and father–child interactions with school-age children. *Developmental Psychology, 22*, 291–296.

Bumpass, L., & Rindfuss, R. R., (1979). Children's experience of marital disruption. *American Journal of Sociology, 85*, 49–65.

Camara, K. A., & Resnick, G. (1987). Interparental conflict and cooperation: Factors moderating children's post-divorce adjustment. In E. M. Hetherington & J. D. Arasteh (Eds.), *Divorced, single-parent, and stepparent families* (pp. 169–196). Hillsdale, NJ: Lawrence Erlbaum Associates.

Chang, P., & Deinard, A. S. (1982). Single-father caretakers: Demographic characteristics and adjustment processes. *American Journal of Orthopsychiatry, 52*, 236–243.

Cherlin, A. J. (1977). The effect of children on marital dissolution. *Demography, 14*, 265–272.

Cohen, R. S., & Weissman, S. H. (1984). The parenting alliance. In R. S. Cohen, B. J. Cohler, S. H. Weissman (Eds), *Parenthood: A psychodynamic perspective* (pp. 33–49). New York: Guilford Press.

Cowan, C. P., Cowan, P. A., Heming, G., Garrett, E., Coysh, W. S., Curtis-Boles, H., & Boles, A. J. (1985). Transitions to parenthood: His, hers, and theirs, *Journal of Family Issues, 6*, 451–481.

Cowan, P. A., & Cowan, C. P. (1988). Changes in marriage during the transition to parenthood: Must we blame the baby? In G. Y. Michaels & W. A. Goldberg (Eds.), *The transition to parenthood: Current theory and research* (pp. 114–154). Cambridge: Cambridge University Press.

Cummings, E. M., Zahn-Waxler, C., & Radke-Yarrow, M., (1981). Young children's responses to expressions of anger and affection by others in the family. *Child Development, 52*, 1274–1282.

Cummings, E. M., Zahn-Waxler, C., & Radke-Yarrow, M., (1984). Developmental changes in children's reactions to anger in the home. *Journal of Child Psychology and Psychiatry, 25*, 63–74.

Dickie, J. R. (1987). Interrelationships within the mother–father–infant triad. In P. W. Berman & F. A. Pedersen (Eds.), *Men's transitions to parenthood: Longitudinal studies of early family experiences* (pp. 113–143). Hillsdale, NJ: Lawrence Erlbaum Associates.

Emery, R. E. (1982). Interparental conflict and the children of discord and divorce. *Psychological Bulletin, 92*, 310–330.

Emery, R. E. (1988). *Marriage, divorce, and children's adjustment*. Newbury Park, CA: Sage.

Emery, R. E. (in press). Family conflicts and their developmental implications: A conceptual analysis of meanings for the structure of relationships. In C. U. Shantz & W. W. Hartup (Eds.), *Conflict in child and adolescent development*. London: Cambridge University Press.

Emery, R. E., Hetherington, E. M., & DiLalla, L. F., (1984). Divorce, children, and social policy. In H. W. Stevenson & A. E. Siegel (Eds.), *Child development research and social policy* (pp. 189–266). Chicago: University of Chicago Press.

Emery, R. E., Joyce, S. A., & Fincham, F. D. (1987). The assessment of marital and child problems. In K. D. O'Leary (Ed.), *Assessment of marital discord* (pp. 223–262). Hillsdale, NJ: Lawrence Erlbaum Associates.

Emery, R. E., Shaw, D. S., & Jackson, J. A. (1987). A clinical description of a model for the comediation of child custody disputes. In J. Vincent (Ed.), *Advances in family intervention, assessment, and theory* (Vol. 4, pp. 309–333). Greenwich, CT: JAI.

Fauber, R., Forehand, R., Thomas, A. M., & Wierson, M. (1990). A mediational model of the impact of marital conflict on adolescent adjustment in intact and divorced families: The role of disrupted parenting. *Child Development, 61*, 1112–1123.

Fedele, N. M., Golding, E. R., Grossman, F. K., & Pollack, W. S. (1988). Psychological issues in adjustment to first parenthood. In G. Y. Michaels & W. A. Goldberg (Eds.), *The transition to parenthood: Current theory and research* (pp. 85–113). Cambridge: Cambridge University Press.

Feldman, S. S. (1987). Predicting strain in mothers and fathers of 6-month-old infants: A short-term longitudinal study. In P. W. Berman & F. A. Pedersen (Eds.), *Men's transitions to parenthood: Longitudinal studies of early family experiences* (pp. 13–35). Hillsdale, NJ: Lawrence Erlbaum Associates.

Feldman, S. S., & Nash, S. C. (1984). The transition from expectancy to parenthood: Impact of the firstborn child on men and women. *Sex Roles, 11*, 61–77.

Frank, S., Hole, C. B., Jacobson, S., Justkowski, R., & Huyck, M. (1986). Psychological predictors of parents' sense of confidence & control and self-versus child-focused gratifications. *Developmental Psychology, 22*, 348–355.

Furstenberg, F. F., & Nord, C. W. (1985). Parenting apart: Patterns of childrearing after marital disruption. *Journal of Marriage and the Family, 47*, 893–904.

Furstenberg, F. F., Peterson, J. L., Nord, C. W., & Zill, N., (1983). The life course of children of divorce: Marital disruption and parental contact. *American Sociological Review, 48*, 656–668.

Gersick, K. E. (1979). Fathers by choice: Divorced men who receive custody of their children. In G. Levinger & O. C. Moles (Eds.), *Divorce and separation* (pp. 307–323). New York: Basic Books.

Glen, N. D., & McLanahan, S. (1982). Children and marital happiness: A further specification of the relationship. *Journal of Marriage and the Family, 44*, 63–72.

Gjerde, P. F. (1986). The interpersonal structure of family interaction settings: Parent–adolescent relations in dyads and triads. *Developmental Psychology, 22*, 297–304.

Goldberg, W. A., & Easterbrooks, M. A. (1984). Role of marital quality in toddler development. *Developmental Psychology, 20*, 504–514.

Grych, J. H., & Fincham, F. D. (1990). Marital conflict and children's adjustment: A cognitive-contextual framework. *Psychological Bulletin, 101*, 267–290.

Hess, R. D., & Camara, K. A. (1979). Post-divorce relationships as mediating factors in the consequences of divorce for children. *Journal of Social Issues, 35*, 79–96.

Hetherington, E. M. (1989). Coping with family transitions: Winners, losers, and survivors. *Child Development, 60*, 1–14.

Hetherington, E. M., Cox, M., & Cox, R. (1976). Divorced fathers. *Family Coordinator, 25*, 417–428.

Hetherington, E. M., Cox, M., & Cox, R., (1982). Effects of divorce on parents and children. In M. Lamb (Ed.), *Nontraditional families* (pp. 233–288). Hillsdale, NJ: Lawrence Erlbaum Associates.

Jacoby, A. P. (1969). Transition to parenthood: A Reassessment. *Journal of Marriage and the Family, 31*, 720–727.

Johnson, S. M., & Lobitz, G. K. (1974). The personal and marital adjustment of parents as related to observed child deviance and parenting behaviors. *Journal of Abnormal Child Psychology, 2*, 193–207.

Johnston, J. R., Campbell, E. G., & Mayes, S. S. (1985). Latency children in post-separation and divorce disputes. *Journal of the American Academy of Child Psychiatry, 24*, 563–574.

Jouriles, E. N., Pfiffner, L. J., & O'Leary, S. G. (1988). Marital conflict, parenting, and toddler conduct problems. *Journal of Abnormal Child Psychology, 16*, 197–206.

Lamb, M. E. (1977). Father–infant and mother–infant interaction in the first year of life. *Child Development, 48*, 167–181.

Leary, T. (1957). *Interpersonal diagnosis of personality*. New York: Ronald Press.

Lewis, M., & Weinraub, M. (1976). The father's role in the child's social network. In M. Lamb (Ed.), *The role of the father in child development* (pp. 157–184). New York: Wiley.

Luepnitz, D. A. (1982). *Child custody: A study of families after divorce*. Lexington, MA: Lexington Books.

Maccoby, E. E., & Martin, J. A. (1983). Socialization in the context of the family: Parent–child interaction. In E. M. Hetherington (Ed.), *Handbook of child psychology* (4th ed., Vol. 4, pp. 1–102.) New York: Wiley.

Minuchin, P. (1985). Families and individual development: Provocations from the field of family therapy. *Child Development, 56*, 289–302.

Minuchin, S. (1974) *Families and family therapy*. Cambridge, MA: Harvard.

O'Connell, M., & Rogers, C. C., (1984). Out-of-wedlock births, premarital pregnancies and their effect on family formation and dissolution. *Family Planning Perspectives, 16*, 157–162.

Oliveri, M. E., & Reiss, D. (1987). Social networks of family members: Distinctive roles of mothers and fathers. *Sex Roles, 17*, 719–736.

Orthner, D., Brown, R., & Ferguson, D. (1976). Single-parent fatherhood: An emerging life style. *Family Coordinator, 25*, 429–437.

Peterson, J. L., & Zill, N. (1986). Marital disruption, parent–child relationships, and behavior problems in children. *Journal of Marriage and the Family, 48*, 295–307.

Phillips, D. C., & Orton, R. (1983). The new causal principle of cognitive learning theory: Perspectives on Bandura's "Reciprocal Determinism". *Psychological Review, 90*, 158–165.

Porter, B., & O'Leary, K. D. (1980). Types of marital discord and child behavior problems. *Journal of Abnormal Child Psychology, 8*, 287–295.

Russell, C. S. (1974). Transition to parenthood: Problems and gratifications. *Journal of Marriage and the Family, 36*, 294–301.

Santrock, J. W., & Warshak, R. A. (1979). Father custody and social development in boys and girls. *Journal of Social Issues, 35*, 112–135.

Sirignano, S. W., & Lachman, M. E. (1985). Personality change during the transition to parenthood: The role of perceived infant temperament. *Developmental Psychology, 21*, 558–567.

Stoneman, Z., Brody, G. H., & Burke, M. (1989). Marital quality, depression, and inconsistent parenting: Relationship with observed mother–child conflict. *American Journal of Orthopsychiatry, 59*, 105–117.

Sullivan, H. S. (1968). *The interpersonal theory of psychiatry*. New York: Norton

Thompson, L., & Walker, A. J. (1989). Gender in families: Women and men in marriage, work, and parenthood. *Journal of Marriage and the Family, 51*, 845–871.

Thornton, A. (1977). Children and marital stability. *Journal of Marriage and the Family, 39*, 531–540.

Tshann, J. M., Johnston, J. R., Kline, M., & Wallerstein, J. S. (1989). Family process and children's functioning during divorce. *Journal of Marriage and the Family, 51*, 431–444.

Vuchinich, S., Emery, R. E., & Cassidy, J. (1988). Family members as third parties in dyadic family conflict: Strategies, alliances, and outcomes. *Child Development, 59*, 1293–1302.

Waite, L. J., Haggstrom, G. W., & Kanouse, D. E. (1985). The consequences of parenthood for the marital stability of young adults. *American Sociological Review, 50*, 850–857.

Wallerstein, J. S., & Kelly, J. B. (1980). *Surviving the breakup: How children actually cope with divorce*. New York: Basic Books.

Warshak, R. A. (1986). Father-custody and child development: A review and analysis of psychological research. *Behavioral Sciences and the Law, 4*, 2–17.

Weiss, R. S. (1979). Growing up a little faster: The experience of growing up in a single-parent household. *Journal of Social Issues, 35*, 97–111.

White, L. K., & Booth, A. (1985). The quality and stability of remarriage: The role of stepchildren. *American Sociological Review, 50*, 689–698.

Wright, P. J., Henggeler, S. W., & Craig, L. (1986). Problems in Paradise?: A longitudinal examination of the transition to parenthood. *Journal of Applied Developmental Psychology, 7*, 277–291.

Chapter 6

Parenting and
Personal Social Networks

Moncrieff Cochran
Cornell University

In this chapter I examine the effects of parents' personal networks on their parenting attitudes and behavior. To limit myself to that single connection—between personal networks and parenting—would, however, run counter to the ecological perspective guiding this book, because personal networks are, in part, social lines of transmission, carrying the influences of the larger society into the life space of the individual and family. Thus, to a significant degree, a parent's network reflects his or her position in the social structure of a given society. For that reason, the impacts of that network on parenting attitudes and behavior must be understood as the impacts of that social structure, and his or her location in it.

In order to capture the ecology of parents' networks, and so do justice to ecological influences on parenting, I organized this chapter around a conceptual framework that includes articulation of the forces influencing the development of parents' networks as well as specification of those network dimensions affecting parenting attitudes and behavior. Using this framework I begin with a definition of the network of interest, and then review studies that illustrate the effects of culture, structural position (class, race, family structure), and neighborhood ecology on the network membership potential available to parents. Then I examine ways that personal initiatives by the parents themselves might also contribute to the form and content of their networks. Next there is consideration of evidence bearing on the processes by which network membership influences parenting, and the parenting outcomes that are affected. This is followed by the presentation of evidence suggesting that the size and composi-

149

tion of parents' networks can combine with other influences to affect the ways that children develop. Finally, I discuss some of the policy implications that flow from what we have learned about the societal factors affecting network development, and the effects of those networks on parents and children.

WHAT ARE PERSONAL SOCIAL NETWORKS?

Social networks are specific sets of linkages between defined sets of people (Mitchell, 1969). The type of social network of particular interest to the readers of this chapter is personal; that is, anchored to a specific person or family. In this case, our focus is on the personal networks of parents or children, or the whole family. These networks consist of those relatives, neighbors, coworkers, and other friends who are directly linked to a family member, and who may be linked to one another as well.

Some years ago, in an article linking child development with personal social networks, Brassard and I (Cochran & Brassard, 1979) defined the network of interest to us as consisting of "those people outside the household who engage in activities and exchanges of an affective and/or material nature with the members of the immediate family" (p. 601). In our original formulation we specifically excluded spouse and children from the parent's personal network, and siblings from the child's, as long as they lived together with the parent or child anchoring the network. More recently, Bryant (1985), examining sources of support in middle childhood, defined the network as including the family members in the child's household, and explicitly rejected our earlier definition.

From a conceptual standpoint the important distinction here is between the nuclear family and the personal network. Bott (1957), in her classic networks study *Family and Social Network*, emphasized the distinction in her attempt to show that the definition of roles in a marital relationship is a function in part of the structure of the personal networks that each person brings to the new family. In so doing she carefully distinguished membership in the nuclear family from membership in the networks of husband and wife. Study of nuclear families has a long tradition in sociology and anthropology, and the subdiscipline of family sociology has become well established since the 1950s. Family historians and others conceive of the family as an emotional entity resting on sentimental ties between husband and wife and parents and children, and as a social unit with economic significance (Haraven, 1984). Thus, the nuclear family is a concept that has meaning in the real world and significance for the development of the individual, separate from the impacts of other kin, associates, and friends.[1]

---

[1]I recognize that the distinction between nuclear and extended families may not be valid beyond societies in North America and Europe.

I am convinced that spousal and parent–child relations are qualitatively different from those relationships maintained by parents or children with people living outside the household. Brassard (1982) applied the in- versus outside the family distinction in the design of her own study of mother–child interaction and personal social networks, by comparing stress and support in one- and two-family families and measuring the contributions of the father separately from those of other kin and nonkin. She found that the effects of a supportive father on mother–child relations were quite different from the effects of a supportive network. Her research underscores the value of making a distinction between members of the nuclear family and the rest of the personal network. Others have also identified the independent effect of a supportive partner on the parenting behavior of the mother (Crockenberg, 1987; Quinton & Rutter, 1985).

When defining the social networks concept it is also important to distinguish it from social supports. Most of those using the social support concept refer to the work of Cobb (1976), who defined such support as information that leads an individual to believe that he or she is cared for and loved, valued, and a member of a network of mutual obligation. More recently, Crockenberg (1988) stated that social support refers to the emotional, instrumental, or informational help that other people provide to an individual. She went on to say that:

> With respect to families, emotional support refers to expressions of empathy and encouragement that convey to parents that they are understood and capable of working through difficulties in order to do a good job in that role. Instrumental support refers to concrete help that reduces the number of tasks or responsibilities a parent must perform, typically household and child care tasks. Informational support refers to advice or information concerning child care or parenting. (p. 141)

The personal social network has been defined earlier as a specific set of linkages among a defined set of persons. The content of those linkages ranges from information of various kinds (where to find work, how to rear your child, which day-care arrangement to choose) to emotional and material assistance and access to role models (Cochran & Brassard, 1979; Mitchell, 1969). Thus, the social support concept focuses primarily on the types of support provided (emotional, instrumental, informational) and the psychological state of the receiving individual (''cared for and loved, valued''), whereas with the personal network the emphasis is both on the characteristics of the set of linkages (structure) and on a broader range of types of exchanges between the anchoring individual and members of the network (content).

Researchers interested only in support tended to map the networks of their respondents with the use of probes that are oriented explicitly to support, like ''Please give me the names of all the people who provide you with emotional support.'' These particular defining characteristics lead to identification of a partial network, excluding all of those people in a person's life who are not thought of primarily in terms of support. Such other people are more likely to be included in response to an orienting question like ''Please give me the names of all the people who make a difference to you in one way or another.'' This more inclusive approach is the one we adopted in the Cornell studies described later in this chapter.

The emphasis by social support theorists and researchers on function (what is provided) much more than on role (the socially proscribed parameters of the relationship) helps to explain why they include partners as members of the social support network along with friends and relatives living outside the household. I and others interested in the broader social network concept are as interested in the limits imposed by society on personal relationships as we are in the content of those relationships. For this reason we assign spouses and partners living with the mother to the immediate family, and reserve network membership for those living outside the household.

Both the social network and the social support concepts are valuable. The distinction can be maintained, in part, by acknowledging that network relations are stressful as well as supportive, and that network members can influence parenting in ways that extend well beyond those included in the ''support'' concept.[2] In her study of low-income mothers with young children Belle (1982) was interested in the costs as well as the benefits of social ties, and concluded that ''one cannot receive support without also risking the costs of rejection, betrayal, burdensome dependence, and vicarious pain'' (p. 143). Wellman (1981) wrote an entire chapter on the application of network analysis to the study of support, in which he articulated the various ways that the concept of social support can oversimplify the nature of social networks.

> Its focus on a simple ''support/nonsupport'' dichotomy de-emphasizes the multifaceted, often contradictory nature of social ties. Its assumption that supportive ties form a separate system isolates them from a person's overall network of interpersonal ties. Its assumption that all of these supportive ties are connected to each other in one integrated system goes against empirical reality and creates the dubious expectation that solidary systems are invariably more desirable. Its assumption that there are no conflicts of interest between ''supporters'' invokes the false premise of a common good. (p. 173)

PERSONAL NETWORKS AND PARENTING: A MODEL

What forces and factors influence how personal networks develop? What determines their size and shape, and how they change over time? What is the

---

[2]Perhaps the most powerful articulation of network influences that are distinct from social support can be found in Granovetter's (1973) article ''The Strengths of Weak Ties.''

role of the individual parent in the network-building process? How do the resulting networks affect parenting attitudes and behaviors? A framework for addressing these questions is provided in Fig. 6.1, as a summarizing model. A
detailed presentation of the model and the empirical evidence on which the
framework is based are presented elsewhere (Cochran, Larner, Riley, Gunnarsson, & Henderson, 1990). The model incorporates the forces constraining
or shaping network development, the factors stimulating individual initiatives
at network building, the parent's network itself, and reference to the resultant
parenting processes and outcomes.

It is very important to project the dynamic qualities of the processes driving this model. Most of the potential for network change comes from the forces
and factors shown on the right side of the figure; shifts in developmental stage,
level of knowledge and skill, and personal identity all affect the amount and
direction of social initiatives taken by the parent. Initiatives themselves can
take two forms: (a) the selection of network members from the pool of individuals available to the parent, and (b) maintenance activities undertaken within
the existing network.

A "pool of eligibles" distinguishes between the people actually available
to the parent for inclusion in the network and those included as members. The
pool of eligibles consists of those people to whom the parent has access for potential inclusion in the network. Use of this concept permits definition of the constraints on the left side of the model as establishing the boundaries for the size
and content of the pool, while at the same time providing the individual parent with a role in building a network from that pool.

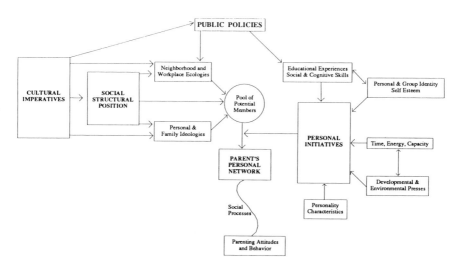

FIG. 6.1.   Development of the personal network: A model.

In selecting the term *constraints* to characterize the factors included on the left side of the model I have chosen the terminology of Fischer and other sociologists doing network research (Fischer, 1982; Wellman, 1979). This term connotes restraint on individual action. The emphasis here is on the ways in which parents may be restrained by societal forces beyond their control from establishing social relations that are crucial to their development as parents. At the same time, I also recognize that many of the constraints placed by societies on individual behavior are constructive. Limits placed on violence against children, for example, and on the right of parents to relinquish responsibility for financial support of their children are positive constraints.

It is also important to note the use of the word "initiatives," rather than Fischer's (1982) "choices," to characterize the behavioral contribution of the individual parent to the construction of his or her network. I prefer initiatives to choices because it conveys action without necessarily assuming that alternatives exist. That is, a parent can initiate the act of including or excluding a person available in the pool of eligibles without necessarily choosing among alternatives available in the pool.

Evidence presented later in this chapter indicates that a substantial number of parents experience severe constraints on free choice because of the structural forces arraying on the left-hand side of the figure. Fischer (1982) said early in *To Dwell Among Friends* that "In general, we each construct our own networks" (p. 4). The evidence presented in this chapter, taken as a whole, indicates: (a) that it is inappropriate to generalize across ecological niches, and (b) that the networks of poor and undereducated parents—who make up 20% to 25% of all parents in the United States—are largely constructed for them by their life circumstances. The model in Fig. 6.1 conveys the power struggle between cultural and social structural forces on the one hand and the individual on the other for control over the content of the personal social network. For any given adult the tilt in the power balance is determined by that person's location in the social structure of the society to which he or she belongs. Recent studies indicate, for instance, that in the United States an unemployed, poor, Black, single mother has far less control over who is included in her personal network than does a White, married, middle-income mother working outside the home (Cochran et al., 1990).

PERSONAL NETWORKS
AND LARGER SOCIAL SYSTEMS

Toward the end of his chapter, Wellman reminded the reader that personal networks operate within and must be influenced by the attributes of larger social systems. He referred in that regard to the social and spatial division of labor, the ways that bureaucracies are organized, and the social classes to which respondents belong. These more macrolevel constraints were included on the left side of the model shown in Fig. 6.1. In Fig. 6.2 they are shown in greater detail. I discuss only certain of these constraint factors, given the limited space available in a single chapter and my desire to illustrate other aspects of the overall model.

Social Class

Family income, the educational level of parents, and the status and complexity of the occupations parents engage in are thought of by sociologists as contributing to determination of the social class in which a family is located. The first sociologist to provide empirical evidence for the relationships between dimensions of social class and network ties was Fischer (1982) in his book *To Dwell Among Friends: Personal Networks in Town and City.* Fischer's team interviewed slightly more than 1,000 people in a 20 county area around San Francisco about their personal social networks. These people were all English-speaking, at least 18 years old, and permanent residents. Some were parents, others were not. They reflected rather well the diversity in educational, occupational, economic, gender and life-cycle characteristics of that part of California. It is these variations that are of particular importance to us, because Fischer was able to consider the extent to which various aspects of the personal networks described by the people in his study are associated with such social structural factors. Of these factors, Fischer found that educational level had the most consistent effect upon the personal networks. He stated:

> Other things being equal, the more educational credentials respondents had, the more socially active they were, the larger their networks, the more companionship they reported, the more intimate their relations, and the wider the geographic range of their ties. In general, education by itself meant broader, deeper, and richer networks. (p. 252)

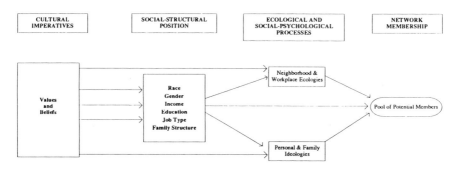

FIG. 6.2.   Constraint factors.

Fischer also found that household income made a sizeable difference in the networks reported, even with education held constant. People with more income included more nonkin in their networks, and were more likely to report adequate amounts of companionship and practical support than were the poor. In considering the meaning of these relationships between socioeconomic factors and network ties Fischer offered three, not necessarily contradictory, possibilities. Perhaps, he suggested, certain kinds of personalities result in both higher socioeconomic status (SES) and greater sociability. Another explanation, and the one he seemed to prefer, emphasizes the social skills and concrete resources that come with more education and income, and the ways that these skills and resources can be used to build and maintain network ties. The third explanation, which he thought of as operating "in a straightforward structural manner" (p. 252), is one in which schooling is viewed as providing the direct opportunity to meet and make friends with people of like mind.

Fischer's work also provided insight into the impacts of life-cycle stage and gender on personal networks. Married people named more relatives and neighbors than did those who were unmarried, whereas single people were more involved with nonkin. Children restricted the social involvement of their parents, and especially of their mothers. "Women with children at home had fewer friends and associates, engaged in fewer social activities, had less reliable social support, and had more localized networks than did otherwise similar women without children" (p. 253). From the gender perspective, women tended to be more involved with kinfolk and to report more intimate ties than did men.

Culture and Class

Some years ago Gunnarsson and I (Gunnarsson & Cochran, 1990) participated with colleagues in Wales and West Germany in a coordinated set of studies of mothers' social networks, which extended Fischer's general approach to a comparison of networks across cultures (Sweden, the United States, Wales, West Germany), social class (blue collar vs. white collar), and family structure (one- vs. two-parent families). The mothers in all four countries were Caucasian, and each had a 3-year-old child when first interviewed. During the course of a 90-minute social networks interview, parents in each country described ties with relatives and with nonkin in response to the question: "Please think of those parents who are important to you in one way or another." Kin and nonkin were further differentiated by role categories (neighbors, workmates, and other friends), and the set of functional ties joining each network member was determined from a list of nine possible interpersonal exchanges (child-care assistance, childrearing advice, help with illness, borrowing, financial assistance, emotional support, work-related advice, leisure-time involvement, and other social involvement). For each network member we also documented frequency of contact, geographic proximity, and the duration of the relationship.

Concentrating first on mothers in two-parent families, we found in all four countries that mothers in white-collar families reported larger networks than did women in blue-collar households. Interestingly, the magnitude of the difference proved to be about the same in every country except the United States, where the differences by occupational status were larger.

These comparisons also uncovered consistent network size differences by culture. The pattern was illustrated most dramatically by the contrast between Germany and the United States, in which the networks of young German mothers were about half the size of those reported by the mothers of young children in the United States. A closer examination of these size data distinguished two pairs of countries; German and Welsh mothers reported smaller total networks than mothers in either Sweden or the United States. The United States differed from all of the other countries in the amount of range in network size, however, which was twice as great as that of Sweden, and (in the blue-collar instance) more than three times that of Germany.

When we looked beyond network size for the functions performed by network members in every category of social support. This difference was most visible for social and recreational activities. The data suggest, as a hypothework members in every category of social support. This difference was most visible for social and recreational activities. The data suggests, as a hypothesis, that mothers in white-collar families have more leisure time at their disposal (especially in Sweden and the United States), and spend some of that extra time in social and recreational activities with network members.

The paired components introduced earlier, linking Germany and Wales on the one hand and Sweden and the United States on the other, were again useful. Although the most dramatic cultural contrasts were seen in the social and recreational activities just mentioned, even in the area of emotional support Swedish mothers reported 50%, and white-collar Americans almost 100%, more network members who they called upon for assistance than did mothers in Wales and Germany.

In considering both cultural and class-bound differences in these mothers' networks, we submit that the critical distinction involves both role and identity. Societies, and classes within societies, differ in terms of the roles women are permitted or encouraged to adopt (mother vs. worker, for instance), and the extent to which they can develop identities beyond those roles. From a developmental perspective, one can distinguish between development as a parent (parent role) and development as a person (personal identity). Network members can be thought of as contributing more or less to one or another of these developmental trajectories. It is reasonable to suggest, for instance, that kinfolk contribute heavily to definition and reinforcement of the parental role, whereas other friends are more likely to contribute to *development of self as person* or personal identity. The larger proportions of other friends engaged in social and recreational activities in the networks of white-collar women and those of U.S. and Swedish mothers suggests proportionately more involvement with personal development beyond the roles of wife and mother. This impression is reinforced by the data involving relatives and neighbors, which showed the German and Welsh mothers interacting more heavily around child-related and practical than social and recreational matters.

These changes in role and identity have been taking place at differing rates in West Germany, Wales, the United States, and Sweden. For instance, only 4% and 11% of the mothers with partners included in our Welsh and German samples were working full time outside the home, whereas in the United States and Sweden those numbers were 22% and 26%, respectively. In the Welsh sample, just 37% of the mothers were working at all outside the home when we interviewed them; in Sweden that number was a full 73%.

Our general understanding of class differences indicates that blue-collar expectations are somewhat more conservative than those of white-collar workers regarding the roles of men and women. This pattern is also reflected in our network data. Cutting across cultures is the picture of blue-collar networks as somewhat smaller, more kin-dominated, less geographically dispersed, and more child-related and practical in content than their white-collar counterparts. But the overall impression is that cultural expectations regarding the woman's place override those of class; that is, the network differences in our data are greater between pairs of countries than between occupational levels within country.

One-Parent Families

Gunnarsson and I were also interested in examining whether solo parenting is associated with patterns of social relationship that differ from those maintained by parents in two-parent families. This led to the oversampling of single parent families by the Swedish and U.S. teams in the Family Matters Project (Gunnarsson & Cochran, 1990). Forty-three Swedish mothers and 48 U.S. mothers were Caucasian single parents. This sample was somewhat more blue collar in occupational status than were their two-parent counterparts in the two countries, mirroring the overall differences between those two groups of women in the two societies. Analyses reported elsewhere also indicate that when they are in white-collar occupations, the single mothers in both countries are more likely than those in two-parent families to be working full time rather than part time (Cochran, Gunnarsson, Grabe, & Lewis, 1984).

Comparisons of these networks with those of mothers in two-parent families showed that they were smaller, regardless of culture or class. There is also a remarkably large difference in the U.S. sample between the average number of network members reported by white- and blue-collar single mothers (18 vs. 12). As mentioned earlier, this difference was also found in the U.S. two-parent sample. Differentiation by social class was not nearly as evident in the Swedish sample; in fact, there the tendency was for white-collar, single mothers to have somewhat smaller networks than their blue-collar counterparts.

One major factor accounting for the difference in total size of the networks was a smaller number of relatives in the networks of single mothers. In the U.S. sample there was an average difference of more than four relatives between mothers in two-parent families and single mothers, regardless of social class. In Sweden, where the networks of mothers in two-parent families were themselves smaller and less kin-centered than in the United States, there was still an average of two more relatives in the networks of the coupled women than in those of the single mothers.

In the "other friends" sector, single mothers in white-collar families included more membership than mothers in blue-collar families, both in Sweden and in the United States. The marked differences between the sizes of the total network reported by the U.S. white- and blue-collar single mothers was largely explained by this greater number of other friends. The average of eight nonkin friends in the networks of U.S. white-collar single mothers outranked all the other subgroups of women by a substantial margin, and was nearly twice as large as in the case of U.S. blue-collar single mothers. Several features of the circumstances surrounding single mothers in the United States help to explain this difference. It is important to understand that other friends are acquired rather than ascribed network members. Such acquisition requires access to people, interest and motivation to build and maintain such relationships, and the social and material resources with which to initiate and sustain the process. The white-collar single mothers in the U.S. sample were working outside the home to a much larger degree than were the blue-collar single mothers, and so had access to workmates. White-collar jobs are likely to provide more opportunities for socializing than is the case with jobs in the blue-collar sector. Training for such jobs usually involves educational situations where opportunities to meet people are present and social interaction and development of social skills encouraged. Finally, financial and material resources are likely to be more available to the white-collar single mothers in the sample; their jobs pay better.

It is interesting to note that in Sweden more than 70% of the neighbors included in the networks of single mothers were themselves mothers with young children, whereas in the United States the corresponding figures were only 48%–59%. This cultural difference was especially extreme for blue-collar single parents (86% vs. 48%). The difference may stem from the fact that in the United States such families are often forced by financial disadvantage to live in high-crime areas with substandard housing, where parents are suspicious of their neighbors and are afraid to allow their children to play outside, whereas in Sweden income redistribution has made it possible to ensure that all families can live in safe, relatively child friendly neighborhoods. Swedish single mothers tend to live in well-maintained public housing areas containing safe play areas designed especially for young children.

Another interesting finding involves the geographic location of network members in relation to the parents in our study. Swedish women in two-parent families lived further from their network ties than did mothers in any of the other three countries. This cultural difference was reinforced and extended by the data from Swedish single mothers, whose networks were still more dispersed geographically. Only about half the membership in the networks of the Swedish single mothers lived within 10 miles, compared with more than three quarters of U.S. membership. In fact, in the United States single mothers lived in closer proximity to network members than did their two-parent counterparts. In Sweden the reverse was true.

What prompts a mother, and especially a single mother, to live closer to or further from her relatives or friends? One reason might be economic necessity. We know that some single mothers in the U.S. sample were actually living with their parents because they could not afford to live elsewhere. Beyond housing there are other ways of relieving stress that require rather close proximity: child care, housework, transportation, and babysitting. Knowing of the greater need by single parents for these services, we were not surprised to find in the U.S. data that they were living closer to their network contacts than were mothers living with their spouses. Therefore, we were puzzled when the Swedish data produced the opposite pattern. Our hypothesis is that the sharp difference in proximity patterns is due to the much larger set of formal supports available to such mothers in Sweden—parental leave, housing allowance, child allowance, subsidized child-care arrangements—supports that may well reduce the need to live together with or right next to relatives or friends.

Differences by Race

Cross, a coinvestigator with the Family Matters Project referred to earlier, was interested in examining the personal networks of Black single and married mothers, and in comparing the size and functioning of those networks with the social ties reported by White ethnic and nonethnic mothers from similar socioeconomic circumstances living in the same city (Cross, 1990). When he compared the networks of Black, single mothers (n = 38) with those of their counterparts in two-parent families (n = 27), Cross found that overall the networks of the latter were more than 25% larger than those of the single women (19.1 members vs. 14.3 members), a pattern similar to that found by Gunnarsson and Cochran for White mothers. At the same time, the absolute number of kinfolk in these networks was virtually identical for all Black mothers, regardless of family structure. Thus, the larger networks of Black mothers in two-parent homes could be traced to the greater number of nonkin neighborhood and work-related contacts (workmates) in their networks.

Cross then compared the networks of the 65 African-American women with those of 50 ethnic and 40 nonethnic White mothers, again distinguishing women in one-parent from those in two-parent families. He found that the networks of the ethnic White mothers were larger than those of either nonethnic White or Black mothers, regardless of family structure. This difference in favor of ethnic White women was apparent both for kinfolk and for nonkin in their networks.

When he compared the networks of nonethnic White and Black mothers, Cross found very few differences in the kin sector, and numbers of nonkin neighbors and workmates were also similar. However, the White, nonethnic women reported many more ties with other friends, those nonkin who lived outside the neighborhood and were not workmates (White two-parent = 5.0; White one-parent = 6.6; Black two-parent = 2.9; Black one-parent = 3.4).

Cross also examined the cross-race membership in the networks of these women, testing the likelihood that at least one opposite race contact would appear at the functional level of the network. The results of this analysis showed that 21% of the Black mothers and 16% of the White parents in one-parent families had at least one opposite race friend. This modest disparity by race increased as family structure changed and socioeconomic level became higher; within the two-parent sample 41% of the Black women but only 11% of the Whites reported friends of the opposite race.

Cross postulated a relationship between the relative lack of Black people in the networks of White mothers and the smaller number of other friends reported by the Black women. On the one hand, he suggested that the exclusion of Blacks as potential friends would not have much of an effect on the overall size of White networks (reduce the pool of eligibles very much), because the large numbers of Whites in all sectors of everyday life provide numerous opportunities to meet and incorporate new White nonkin contacts. On the other hand, he pointed out, this is not the case for Black people living in the same community. In the northeastern city where this study was conducted only about 12% of the population was African-American. So the pool of potential same-race network members was much smaller for Black than for White mothers, meaning that any cross-race avoidance that might have occurred would have placed the Black women at a relative disadvantage.

The evidence that Cross has assembled strongly suggests that in the United States race continues to be a social divide. In his study, Cross asked what the consequences of such segregation might be for the development of children in these families, and answered the rhetorical question by pointing to identity studies showing that Black children develop a much more biracial orientation than White children, and so are better equipped to function in a truly multiracial society.

In this section of the chapter I have been presenting evidence that structural factors operating at the levels of culture, class, race, ethnicity, and family structure constrain the network-building opportunities of some parents more than of others. That is, the pool of network eligibles available to some parents is smaller than that available to others. Black parents, nonethnic White parents, parents with relatively little education, and parents living in cultures shaped by beliefs that lead to narrow definitions of the woman's role all have a smaller pool of potential network membership available to them than do their more socioeconomically and socially advantaged counterparts. Constraints accumulate for single parents, who often have less access to relatives, to further education, to jobs paying a decent salary, and to housing in neighborhoods that are supportive of neighboring activities.

THE NETWORK-BUILDING PROCESS

The underlying thesis of the previous section was that cultures are structured in ways that may limit the range of social relations available to some, and perhaps many, of their members. Equally important to acknowledge is the role played by the individual in challenging those limits. In his preface to *Network Analysis: Studies in Human Interaction*, Boissevain (Boissevain & Mitchell, 1973) referred to "the concept of man as an interacting social being capable of manipulating others as well as being manipulated by them" (p. viii). This concept of the human organism as a proactive participant in construction of the social environment implies a need to know how humans, and in this case parents, develop network-building skills, and whether different social, ethnic, and cultural groupings are more or less likely to promote such behavior by their members. Brassard and I devoted a section of our 1979 article to development in the child of such skills, and identified reciprocal exchange as the key cognitive process underlying network building developed during childhood. We also acknowledged the part that individual temperament and personality characteristics might play in affecting the propensity to initiate relationships, and pointed to the importance of studying children across developmental time for an understanding of network-building processes. More recently my colleagues and I (Cochran et al., 1990) carried this thinking further in relation to parents, as summarized in Fig. 6.3. Here the reader sees nine factors that we propose contribute to the propensity of the parent to engage actively in network building; that is, to recruit network membership from the pool of potential provided by the society of which she is a part. Much of this model is speculation, pure and simple, because the studies needed to examine these factors systematically have yet to be carried out. Again, space does not permit discussion of every possible element in the model, so I limit myself to some key illustrations.

Personal Identity and Education Experiences

McLanahan and her colleagues were the first researchers to link personal identity with personal social networks (McLanahan, Wedemeyer, & Adelberg, 1981). Working with data gathered through in-depth interviews with 45

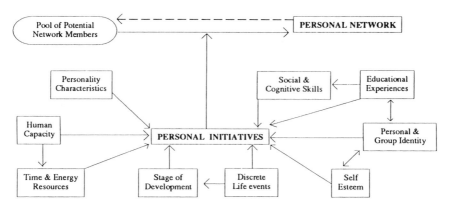

FIG. 6.3.   Personal factors affecting initiatives.

divorced mothers, they distinguished women who wished to maintain their existing identity after the divorce from those trying to create a different and less traditional identity for themselves. These researchers suggested that a close-knit network may be especially supportive to those interested in retaining their predivorce identity, and a loose-knit network can be helpful to those seeking change. In practice, involvement in a close-knit network typically meant that the mother had frequent contact with her own mother and other female relatives, who usually lived nearby. Women wishing to transition from one role orientation to another—for instance, from homemaker to working outside the home—seemed to be better served by more extended networks, which included significant numbers of nonkin, female friends.

The McLanahan et al. study alerted us to the fact that different kinds of network resources are useful to women with differing definitions of their own roles, and different future orientations. The differing identities of the women studied translated into greater or lesser expectations for change. Where role transition was sought, some kinds of social resources were more helpful than others. Implied by the findings, but not studied directly, is the notion that when the needed resources are not present in the network, women desiring change will seek them elsewhere, and attempt to recruit them into their networks.

Intrigued by the findings of McLanahan et al., Henderson and I decided to find out how single mothers' perceptions of their children as easy or difficult to raise might be affected by differences in their educational experiences (Cochran & Henderson, 1990). Of the 48 White, unmarried mothers in Family Matters families referred to earlier in the chapter, we identified 27 who were living with no other adults (either male partners or their own parents). Within this group of women more education was closely linked to paid employment. Seven of the nine least educated women in this group did not work outside the home, whereas five of the seven mothers with more than a high school education were employed. Our interest was in how these women's perceptions of their children were affected by having more or fewer kin and nonkin in their networks, paying particular attention to these network members as sources of child-related and emotional support, and as people who the mothers might have identified as ''making life difficult for them'' in one way or another.

Our findings indicated that perception of the child became more positive as a function of how many kinfolk the mother included in her primary network. That is, as the number of relatives the mother defined as ''especially important'' increased, her view of the child became more positive. But this positive relationship, although significant for all three of the subgroups defined by educational background, was strongest for the nine women with less than a high school education, followed by those with a high school diploma, and then those with more than 12 years of school. The picture that emerged was one of women with differing needs, expectations, and resources, for whom close involvement with kinfolk appeared to mean different things.

This distinction between women with more or less education and greater or lesser commitment to employment was dramatized by the network variable called ''difficult kin,'' those relatives identified as ''making things more difficult'' in one way or another. A larger number of such people was linked to more positive perceptions by the least educated mothers, and less positive perceptions by those with the most education. There was the impression, on the one hand, of women willing to accept the stress associated with close kinship relations in order to benefit from the support also provided, and on the other hand of women with stronger and more independent personal identities, who found certain kinds of relatives meddlesome and irritating.

This raises the question of what is meant when a network member is labeled ''difficult'' by a mother. It is important to emphasize, first, that this was not a contact who was listed in the network because of his or her difficult characteristics. Rather, mothers were told not to leave someone off the list because they were in some sense difficult. Once the list was completed the women were asked whether there was anyone included there who they found difficult in one way or another. So people who are identified as difficult also had other characteristics, some of which may have been very supportive.

Differences in educational achievement and employment history appear, then, to contribute to differing needs and expectations related to network relations. Like McLanahan et al., we were unable with our data to test the hypothesis that these differences in needs and expectations are manifested in different patterns of network-related social initiative. In Fig. 6.3 the arrows linking educational experiences with personal and group identity reflect my hypothesis that the most- and least-educated women in our sample of 27 women were operating with contrasting personal identities, and that their educational experiences contributed to development of those identities. It is also reasonable to predict that change in personal identity leads in turn to further education, and so I show the influence as reciprocal—flowing in both directions.

This reference to the possibility of reciprocal influence serves as a reminder that the relationships between personal identity and educational experiences, on the one hand, and the network, on the other, are by no means unidirectional. Alcalay (1983) summarized the differing functions of high and low density networks under different conditions in this way:

> Social networks can be both a source of direct help and a source of linkage to other resources. In crises a small, dense network with strong ties may be most valuable. At times of psychosocial transition, a low density network with weak ties . . . may be most useful. Under these circumstances social support networks provide a much needed sense of identity, a feeling of belonging, of being wanted and worthwhile. (p. 73)

Networks contribute to a sense of identity, just as changes in identity may contribute to modifications in network composition and function.

Stage of Development

There is growing evidence that both biological changes in the organism and changes in the expectations of significant others compel the developing person to periodically reassess the resource potential represented by members of the existing network. For instance, adult relatives seem to be especially salient for young children. In a study of the networks and school performance of first graders (Cochran & Riley, 1990), we found that the number of adult kinfolk (other than parents) engaging in task-oriented interactions with these 6-year-olds was a strong predictor of how well they were performing in school. Bryant (1985) focused on middle childhood, with a particular interest in possible relationships between sources of social support and socioemotional functioning during middle childhood. She found that there was a positive relationship between the support variables and socioemotional functioning for 10-year-olds but not for 7-year-olds. Bryant suggested, among several possible explanations, that a certain amount of parental distancing in middle childhood may nudge the 10-year-olds from the parental nest, thereby giving other supports more salience. Thus, it may not be that the amount of network resource changes from one developmental stage to the next, but that many of the same resources have different meaning, and are used differently, because the press for social relations is different at the succeeding stage.

In adolescence, nonkin come to the fore; analysis of Norwegian data indicates that it is the number of nonkin adults in the networks reported by 16-year-old boys that predicts their school performance (Cochran & Bø, 1989). Again, a reasonable explanation for the shift in importance from kin to nonkin adults involves developmental press. The extended family provides a secure base from which to develop new relations in the neighborhood and school, and at the same time permits the younger child to experience the behavior and expectations of adults different enough from the parents to require development of some new social skills and expansion of cognitive frames. In adolescence, when the transition into adulthood and work roles looms large, nonkin adults provide models for the future, challenge the teen-ager to accept increased responsibility for self, significant others, and the community, and provide information about where to obtain services, training, and paid work. Finally, for the young adults (parents) in our Family Matters samples both kin and nonkin were important, but for different purposes in different roles. Kinfolk had particular salience for perceptions and activities in the childrearing role, whereas nonrelatives were especially relevant to the work role, and for personal self-regard.

Discrete Life Events

It is important to distinguish developmental press from those presses caused by life events. Significant, time-limited life events like birth or death of a family member, marriage or divorce, or job acquisition, change, or loss, create social presses for the individual that are different from the demands stemming from developmental change. The causes of these events may be independent of the individual. However, they are not necessarily direct extensions of the environmental constraints discussed earlier (see Fig. 6.2). The interest here is in how such occurrences might stimulate networking initiatives by the individual. Two examples of such changes related to our Family Matters study were separation or divorce, and the opportunity presented by the Family Matters support program.

In the case of separation or divorce we did not examine networks before and then after the change, and so must rely on indirect evidence provided by comparing the networks of mothers living with and without husbands or male partners in the household. In our data the higher proportion of nonkin in single mothers' networks suggests the possibility that a shift into single status stimulates a search for friendship outside the kinship circle. The research by McLanahan and her associates discussed earlier underscored the importance of the divorcing woman's personal identity in determining the utility of existing network ties. Thus it is plausible to suggest, pending better evidence, that separation or divorce acts as a stimulus to network reorganization primarily in combination with an interest in establishing a new identity.

The Family Matters support program provided home visitors, parent support clusters, or a combination of these two types of support to 160 of the 225 families that participated in the longitudinal study. Thus, involvement in the support program over a 3-year period can be viewed as a discrete event in the lives of these families. Participation in this program stimulated network-building activity on a conditional basis, with the conditions in this case involving race and family structure. White single parents in the program added a significant number of nonkin to their networks over a 3-year period, when compared with a "no-program" control group, whereas with Black single parents the additions were both kin and nonkin. Married women showed no increases in the size of their networks as a function of the program, but assigned greater importance at follow-up than at baseline to people already in their networks.

Personality Characteristics

Researchers believe that personality traits like responsiveness, persistence, and introversion are temperamental; biologically wired into a child at birth, and affecting that person throughout life (Chess & Thomas, 1984; Hinde, Stevenson-Hinde, & Tamplin, 1985; Thomas & Chess, 1977). Whether or not this is the case, it is reasonable to propose that shy or introverted parents may be less likely to take advantage of social opportunities than are parents who are gregarious or extroverted. However, the research needed to test this proposal has not been carried out.

Other characteristics of a parent's personality develop through experiences during childhood and adolescence. The body of research in this domain focuses not on why some parents and not others engage in network building, but instead on an interest in why some parents are much more socially isolated than others. This interest stems from evidence linking this social isolation with child abuse and neglect. Crockenberg (1988), in summarizing these findings, introduced the possibility that "characteristics of the mothers account both for their low support and their abusive parenting" (p. 160). Polansky, Gaudin, Ammons, and Davis (1985) carried out a comparison of neglectful with nonneglectful mothers that supported this hypothesis. These researchers used a comparison group that was similar to the neglectful families not only in socioeconomic and family characteristics, but also regarding the geographic accessibility of relatives and proximity to where they grew up. One innovative feature of the study involving interviewing a neighbor of every neglectful and control family to determine perceptions of the friendliness and helpfulness of people in the neighborhood, whether there were people one could call on for help, and whether there were people who needed help in raising their children. Polansky et al. (1985) found, first, that neglectful mothers described their neighborhoods as less supportive and friendly than did parents in the control group or neighbors of the parents in either group. Thus, they described a different psychological reality, although there was no evidence from the neighbors of differences in the objective support potential (the size of what is referred to in Figs. 6.1–6.3 as the pool of potential network members). Second, there was evidence that neglectful parents were less helpful than control parents to others in the neighborhood; based both on their own reports and the reports of their neighbors. The researchers concluded from their data that "inadequacies of ability, and perhaps motivation, cut them off from helping networks dependent on mutuality. Related inadequacies lead to their being stigmatized and held at a distance socially" (p. 274).

Crittenden (1981, 1985a) conducted research that provides greater understanding of what the "inadequacies" referred to by Polansky et al. (1985) might consist of, and some indication of their origins. She drew on the work of attachment theorists to propose that adults have internalized working models of social relationships that are developed from experiences in early childhood, and then modified over time based on the social relations experienced during later childhood and adolescence. Crittenden documented that maltreating mothers have deviant patterns of interaction with their children, and inferred that these patterns result from working models of what a social relationship can and should be that are very different from those of mothers not maltreating their children. She showed that these deviant interaction patterns were leading, in turn, to more difficult and more passive child behaviors. The proposal is that the behavioral differences found in the children reflected the beginnings of working models for social interaction similar to those carried by their mothers.

Applying this conceptual orientation to network relations, Crittenden (1985b) proposed that "on the basis of her working model, a mother may influence her relationship with her network, just as she appears to do in her relationship with her child, through the processes of generalization and repetition of ingrained patterns of behavior" (p. 1301). This proposal receives support from her comparison of the networks and parent–professional relationships of adequate mothers with those of neglectful and abusive/neglectful mothers. She found that mothers in the adequate group had far more supportive and satisfying network relationships than the mothers in either of the other two groups. This was true despite the fact that the adequate and maltreating mothers were often living in the same neighborhoods. The adequate mothers were also more cooperative in the parent–professional relationship, and less defensive or withdrawn. Crittenden then examined the relationships of the network and parent–professional variables with the security of attachment between the mothers and their 1- to 4-year-old children. She found that a cooperative approach to the parent–professional relationship was substantially more powerful than network typology in predicting a secure attachment. Crittenden concluded that her data are "highly consistent with the notion that the mothers' approach to relationships of all kinds was reflected both in their relationships with their children and in their relationships with network members" (p. 1311). The terms she used to characterize the interaction styles of these women—

cooperative, defensive, withdrawn—can be thought of as learned personality characteristics. Crittenden argued that these characteristics reflect internalized working
models of relationships, and result in greater or lesser openness to and capacity for the establishment and maintenance of satisfying and supportive network
relations.

PERSONAL NETWORK INFLUENCES ON PARENTS

In the first section of this chapter I focused on the structural constraints defining the pool of network potential available to parents in differing ecological
niches. The second section was used to identify some of the factors that might
determine the propensity of parents to actively seek out relationships with people
in the pool of potential membership. Now I shift to the question of how networks with differing characteristics, once they are in place and functioning,
affect parenting attitudes and behavior (see "social processes," in Fig. 6.1).

Emotional and Instrumental Support

Studies of parents' social networks conducted during the 1980s indicate that
assistance with child care, unconditional emotional support, and advice about
how to maintain authoritative control over the child's behavior prove particularly helpful to young mothers, especially when the women are single, divorced,
or separated. Work by Belle (1982), cited earlier, provides important evidence
in this regard. Belle studied the costs and benefits of social ties identified as
important by 43 low-income mothers with young children. While working within the broader "social support and health outcomes" tradition of Cobb, with
particular interest in personal mastery and depression in adults, Belle was also
interested in the quality of interaction between the mothers and their children.
Belle found that it was not network size, proximity of membership, or frequency
of contact that was associated with emotional well-being, but rather the number of people reported as engaged specifically in providing child-care assistance
and "someone to turn to." This greater provision of concrete assistance and
support seemed to carry over positively to the quality of the interactions between these mothers and their children.

    Colletta (1981) considered the significance of social supports for maternal
functioning in several different studies. Working with 50 adolescent mothers,
both Caucasian and African-American, she found a link between emotional
support and maternal affection. Colletta noted that "with high levels of emotional support adolescent mothers reported being less aggressive and rejecting; less likely to nag, scold, ridicule or threaten their children" (p. 193).

    Longfellow and her colleagues (Longfellow, Zelkowitz, Saunders, & Belle,
1979) also considered social support in its relation to parent–child processes.

Working with data from the Belle study of low-income mothers cited earlier, Longfellow et al. found that availability of support in the area of child care (babysitting, discussions of childrearing problems) was positively related to the quality of mother–child interactions. Those women who reported access to child-care support were less dominating, emotionally warmer, and more sensitive to the needs of their children than were mothers who did not report this type of network support. The authors are careful to warn against overgeneralization, pointing out that their sample was limited to low-income mothers.

One strong message coming from several recent studies was alluded to earlier in the chapter; the importance of recognizing the stresses as well as the supports in network relations. In research referenced earlier, Brassard (1982) conducted a study of 20 single parents' personal social networks that included a comparison group made up of 20 married mothers, well matched with the divorced or separated women on occupation, educational level, family size, and religious background. One major advantage of the Brassard study, from our standpoint, was that it included assessment of mother–child interaction patterns, gathered through direct observation. All 40 families contained preschool children, divided equally by gender in each subgroup. Brassard found that network members contributed both support and stress to the lives of the mothers she interviewed, but that support outweighed stress in this sample of employed, lower middle-class, White women. The single mothers were experiencing more stress than were the women in two-parent homes, even when differences in working hours and income were controlled for, and criticisms were especially pronounced when the preschool child was a girl. Emotional support from adults in the network was especially important for these women.

Network support showed more associations with mother–child interactions in the one- than in the two-parent homes. In those families this support was related to increases in activities containing egalitarian power relationships, a more neutral stance toward children of both genders, and a more inhibiting style with sons. Brassard suggested that:

> the network supports and guides the single mother in making this role shift toward assuming primary, daily responsibility for being an authoritative leader with her child. . . She needs help in sorting out a reasonable, consistent style of home discipline that maintains a workable family equilibrium. The single mother looks to her network for this guidance. (pp. 152–153)

The Cochran and Henderson (1990) study of solo parents described earlier carries these support- and stress-related and parenting studies one step further by providing evidence indicating that the support and stress coming from network members may be perceived differently, and therefore translated into different perceptions of the child, depending on the aspirations the mother has for her own development.

Childrearing Advice and Other Informational Support

Riley (1990) broadened the discussion of networks and parenting to include men in the parenting role, by capitalizing on the fact that the Cornell Family Matters data set included information about the networks of fathers. The question he asked of these data was: In what ways would a father utilize his social ties in the service of his childrearing efforts? One important way is to use network members for discussion of parenting concerns and to gather childrearing advice. Who do the fathers go to for such advice? Do they favor advice from their own parents or siblings, or from other young parents? Are there fathers who report no one with whom they talk about childrearing? To answer these questions, Riley focused on the 70 married, non-Black, employed fathers from two-parent households who participated in the follow-up portion of the study. Most fathers in the sample reported that they discussed childrearing concerns with several of the people they knew well. The average network included 5.1 sources of childrearing advice. But there was great variation. Eleven of the 70 fathers reported 10 or more sources of advice, whereas 12 fathers (17%) reported no one.

Riley's next step was to relate aspects of the fathers' networks to those men's levels of involvement in the rearing of their 6-year-old children. Two areas of father involvement were examined: participation in routine child-care tasks and play interaction with the child. He was also careful to distinguish families by maternal employment status. Mothers employed outside the household for 10 hours or more each week were considered employed; all others were considered unemployed for the purposes of this study. By this definition, 37 of the 70 families had an employed mother. Analyses were carried out separately for families with and without an employed mother.

Riley found that in the two-earner families both nonkin allies and local female kin affected the child-care participation of the father. Nonkin allies are those highly elective and supportive network members who provided three or more of the following six kinds of support to the father: practical borrowing, financial assistance, work-related support, a person to talk with about marital issues, emotional support, and social activities. Local female kin consisted of the number of adult female relatives (including in-laws) in the father's network who lived in the same section of town. Of these two sources of network support, the nonkin allies variable was a much stronger predictor than was the number of local female kin. Riley noted that the two were related; fathers with fewer local kinfolk had more nonkin allies. He suggested the intriguing possibility that today some men are substituting multiply supportive nonkin bonds for the traditional extended family bonds sustained by other men.

In the case of the one-earner families the pattern was different: There was a powerful effect for what he called the "male network" variable, showing that as the percentage of men in the network increased, the father's share of parent–child play went down. The existence of local female relatives also decreased the father's play involvement. The local female kin seemed to reduce the demand for the father's assistance in childrearing, and the male peer group to maintain activities and attitudes in competition with the father's home role. Riley concluded by emphasizing that in two-parent households maternal employment status appears to represent a crucial ecological divide. It has the power to distinguish two types of U.S. families, each apparently responding to very different network influences. His findings indicate that fathers are often pushed into childrearing involvement, or away from it, by situational demands. The existence of a local female kin network appeared to relieve the pressure on the father to participate in childrearing (or it may have competed with him if he wanted more responsibility for his children). At the same time, there was evidence that fathers may to some extent select or construct the social environment that thereafter influences them. The male peer group and nonkin allies are highly amenable to active construction by the individual. This is especially true for the nonkin allies, because they represent social bonds encompassing diverse kinds of support content, often with an individual known through no regular role context.

Cotterell (1986), working in the rural towns of inland Australia, was interested in the influences on childrearing of the father's workplace, the mother's social network, and the community itself. With 96 married mothers he compared the personal networks of and the childrearing milieus provided by those with husbands regularly present with those whose partners' jobs routinely required periods of absence from home. Characteristics of the childrearing environment were measured with the Caldwell HOME inventory, and the quality of maternal expectations and beliefs was assessed with the Parent as a Teacher (PAAT) inventory. Analysis of the network data indicated that mothers with absentee husbands relied more heavily on their neighbors than those with husbands regularly at home. When the "quality of childrearing" variables were analyzed by father presence or absence and mother's amount of informational support from the network, the characteristics of the father's work exerted independent influence on only two of the variables, whereas the effects of support were statistically significant for six of the seven childrearing measures. In order to assess the separate and joint contributions of the three environmental dimensions, Cotterell entered them all with the childrearing variables in a regression equation. In his own words:

> Between 40% and 60% of the variance explained in the full model could be attributed to the factors of father absence, community characteristics, and mother's informational support. Of the three factors, the support factor had the greatest

prominence in terms of its power to add significantly to the variance in the measures of childrearing quality. (p. 369)

Cotterell is careful to point out the danger of assuming that these three environmental forces—general character of the community, father's work situation, and network support—operate independently and at the same level of influence. He suggested that "the chain of influence of father's work is connected to maternal behavior via the patterns of social relationships established by the mother" (p. 371). His evidence indicates that the wives of absentee husbands had smaller networks, and that these women had a more limited range of settings available for contacting network members.

Crockenberg (1988), in her review of the theories explaining how social support affects parental behavior, identified four processes by which benefits might be conveyed. First, support can reduce the sheer number of stressful events. The instrumental support described earlier probably operates largely in this manner. Babysitting, childrearing advice, and financial assistance simply provide relief from daily burdens that might otherwise accumulate to incapacitate the parent, or press her or him into inappropriate or even abusive behavior patterns.

It is possible that social support may not directly reduce the number of stressful events experienced by the parent, but may act as a buffer, preventing the parent from being as adversely affected by a stressful event, like divorce or job loss, and making it possible for parents to maintain satisfactory childrearing routines in the face of hard times. This second process is probably not an alternative to sheer reduction of stressful events, but rather operates in addition to it.

Crockenberg identified generation of active coping strategies as the third process by which social supports may have beneficial effects on parents. This process operates on the initiatives side of the model presented in Fig. 6.1; the mother's self-confidence is bolstered by praise from a supportive and more experienced network member, and her skills improve as a result of suggestions from this person. The result is willingness and ability to take positive initiatives, rather than passivity generated by inexperience and self-doubt.

The fourth process identified by Crockenberg involves the emotional support that emerged from several of the studies reviewed earlier as an important predictor of more constructive parenting behaviors. She tied emotional support to the idea of "working models of relationships" outlined previously in relation to maltreating parents (Crittenden, 1985b), pointing out that "ongoing emotional support or nurturance may affirm this sense [of herself or himself as a person deserving of care and capable of caring for someone else] and in doing so encourage the individual's inclination to be nurturant to others" (p. 146).

The Personal Networks of Mothers,
and Child-Related Outcomes

It is important to go beyond relationships between parents' networks and their childrearing attitudes and behaviors, to consider the question of whether the social resources available to parents actually have an impact on the development of their children. Space limitations permit the presentation of only three illustrative examples of the link to child development.

Crockenberg (1981) was interested in ways that social support might affect the nature of the emotional bond between mother and infant. Her sample was middle and working class in socioeconomic composition. She stated her primary findings rather unambiguously:

> The adequacy of the mother's social support is clearly and consistently associated with the security of the infant–mother attachment: low social support was associated with high resistance, high avoidance, and with anxious attachment. Moreover, that support had its strongest effects on the irritable babies and their mothers suggests that the availability of social support is particularly critical when the family is under particular stress. (p. 862)

The fact that the positive relationship between social support for the mother and the attachment behaviors of the child was obtained primarily in the case of irritable babies is important to note. An environmental demand, the irritable baby, appears to have created the conditions calling for mobilization of existing support.

Research by Tietjen (1985) produced findings that are especially interesting because they suggest a connection between the social networks of mothers and those of their children, and more specifically their daughters. Her sample consisted of 72 Swedish mothers and their 8- to 9-year-old children. Mothers and children were interviewed separately. Tietjen found similarities between the networks of mothers and their daughters that were not apparent for mothers and sons. For instance, the larger the percentage of neighbors in the married mother's network, the greater the likelihood that the daughter would play with several friends at the same time rather than with a single friend. Single mothers' involvement in instrumental exchange with network members was linked with daughters having more friends, especially at school. Tietjen proposed modeling, teaching, and the provision of opportunities for interaction as the processes that might account for such commonalities.

Homel, Burns, and Goodnow (1987) interviewed the fathers, mothers, and 9- to 11-year-old children in 305 Australian families. These families were drawn from areas in Sydney defined as high, medium, and low according to the number of social risk indicators contained in each area. Information about the family network was gathered from one or the other parent (alternating), yielding data about the frequency, location, and dependability of relations with neighbors, friends, and relatives and about affiliation with community organizations. Data collected from the children included information about their happiness, negative emotions, social skills, friendship networks, and school adjustment. The authors reported two primary clusters of findings. First, a number of child variables were related to the presence or absence or the number of dependable adult friends in the family network: happiness with the family, negative emotions, peer-related social skills, extensiveness and diversity of friendship networks, and school adjustment. Also important were local friendship networks and ties to community organizations. The family friends were nonkin, as distinguished from the kinfolk in the networks. One especially interesting detail in the larger array of findings pertains to the relationship between the friendship networks of family and child, and complements the results found by Tietjen mentioned earlier. Where the parents reported the presence of just one dependable friend, the child was likely to report friendship with one or two children or membership in a small clique. Children whose parents reported a number of dependable friends tended themselves to describe peer contact with a number of equally liked friends.

CONCLUSION

In this chapter I considered parenting and social networks in ecological context. Evidence that personal networks influence the attitudes and behaviors of parents is accumulating slowly. Kinfolk certainly are important as primary supporters, and to reinforce traditional parenting values and childrearing practices. Nonrelatives also appear to play important roles as supplementary (and even in some cases primary) supports and as sources of new information for parents. There is growing evidence, coming from Sweden and the United States, that nonkin can, within supportive environmental circumstances, function like kin in their support of friends who are parents.

There are also a few studies indicating that the support and assistance provided to parents by their network membership translates into more constructive childrearing practices, and positive outcomes in the child. Much more fine-grained, process-oriented studies are needed before we will be able to trace exactly how this support translates into parenting activities that produce more competent children.

If certain kinds of networks are more beneficial than others for parents, then it behooves us to better understand network development, because in those developmental processes lie the keys to identifying ways that local communities and the larger society can structure themselves to facilitate the functioning of families in their childrearing roles. The policy implications of the constraints identified on the left-hand side of Fig. 6.1 deserve serious consideration. Policies that increase the availability of postsecondary education would appear to deserve highest priority, because those parents who acquired such schooling were much richer in network resources than those who had not. College scholarships, student loans, and programs providing incentives to adolescents and young adults for continuation of schooling through high school and beyond would seem to be an especially good investment to society from this standpoint.

Policies that stimulate job creation and continuation would also deserve high priority from a "networks in context" perspective. The workplace has been seen in our studies to be an important context for network building, and the economic returns associated with working provide the resources needed to sustain network relations. Just as importantly, the absence of job security for much of today's semiskilled or unskilled and nonunionized work force reduces the capacity of the workplace to support the development of social relationships among coworkers. Economic instability also contributes to residential mobility as families leave the state to seek better fortune in another part of the country. The protection of job security and assurances of fair treatment for employees during hard times would support the social as well as the economic well-being of working families.

I would be remiss, however, if in closing I left the impression that enhancement of network development can come only through removal of societal constraints. Several of the factors contributing to parental initiative in developing their network relations are accessible to public policies and programs. Educational opportunity has already been mentioned. Home visiting and parent support groups, if carried out in an empowering way, enhance parental self-esteem, and thereby increase network-building potential. Any family support program that provides parents with respite, and more time to devote to family life, increases the capacity of parents to engage in the social activities that develop and maintain network ties.

At the same time, the most important policy lesson to be learned from the Family Matters studies of networks and parenting is that it is not nearly enough simply to provide opportunities for social interaction, and the message that social ties are important, if parents are to be supported on behalf of their own development and that of their children. Public policies must give first priority to freeing parents, and those who will become parents, from the constraints of inequality and oppression, by ensuring the provision of adequate and sufficient education, employment, and housing conditions. Our findings suggest that freedom to grow, through schooling, work, and leisure activities, will lead in turn to the social network connections that form the basis for healthy, productive communities.

REFERENCES

Alcalay, R. (1983). Health and social support networks: A case for improving interpersonal communication. *Social Networks, 4*, 71–88.

Belle, D. (1982). Social ties and social support. In D. Belle (Ed.), *Lives in stress: Women and depression* (pp. 168–181). Beverly Hills, CA: Sage.

Boissevain, J., & Mitchell, J. C. (1973). *Network analysis: Studies in human interaction.* The Hague: Mounton.

Bott, E. (1957). *Family and social networks.* London: Havistock.

Brassard, J. (1982). *Beyond family structure: Mother–child interaction and personal social networks.* Unpublished doctoral dissertation, Cornell University, Ithaca, NY.

Bryant, B. (1985). The neighborhood walk: Sources of support in middle childhood. *Monographs of the Society for Research in Child Development, 50* (3, Serial No. 210).

Chess, S., & Thomas, A. (1984). *Origins and evolution of behavior disorders.* New York: Bruner/Mazel.

Cobb, S. (1976). Social support as a moderator of life stress. *Psychosomatic Medicine, 39,* 300–314.

Cochran, M., & Bø, I. (1989). The social networks, family involvement, and pro- and anti-social behavior of adolescent males in Norway. *Journal of Youth and Adolescence, 18*(4), 377–398.

Cochran, M., & Brassard, J. (1979). Child development and personal social networks. *Child Development, 50,* 609–615.

Cochran, M., Gunnarsson, L., Grabe, S., & Lewis, J. (1984). *The social support networks of mothers with young children: A cross-national comparison* (Research Bulletin No. 25, Department of Educational Research). Gothenburg, Sweden: University of Gothenburg.

Cochran, M., & Henderson, C. (1990). Network influences upon perception of the child: Solo parenting and social support. In M. Cochran, M. Larner, D. Riley, L. Gunnarsson, & C. Henderson, Jr. (Eds.), *Extension families: The social networks of parents and their children* (pp. 119–130). London/New York: Cambridge University Press.

Cochran, M., Larner, M., Riley, D., Gunnarsson, L., & Henderson, C., Jr. (Eds.). (1990). *Extending families: The social networks of parents and their children.* London/New York: Cambridge University Press.

Cochran, M., & Riley, D. (1990). The social networks of six-year-olds: Context, content, and consequence. In M. Cochran, M. Larner, D. Riley, L. Gunnarsson, & C. Henderson, Jr. (Eds.), *Extending families: The social networks of parents and their children* (pp. 154–178). London/New York: Cambridge University Press.

Colletta, N. (1981). Social support and the risk of maternal rejection by adolescent mothers. *Journal of Psychology, 109,* 191–197.

Cotterell, J. (1986). Work and community influences on the quality of childrearing. *Child Development, 57,* 362–374.

Crittenden, P. (1981). Abusing, neglecting, problematic, and adequate dyads: Differentiating by patterns of interaction. *Merrill-Palmer Quarterly, 27,* 1–18.

Crittenden, P. (1985a). Maltreated infants: Vulnerability and resistance. *Journal of Child Psychology and Psychiatry, 26,* 85–96.

Crittenden, P. (1985b). Social networks, quality of child rearing, and child development. *Child Development, 56,* 1299–1313.

Crockenberg, S. (1981). Infant irritability, mother responsiveness, and social support influences on the security of infant–mother attachment. *Child Development, 52,* 857–865.

Crockenberg, S. (1987). Support for adolescent mothers during the postnatal period: Theory and research. In C. F. Z. Boukydis (Ed.), *Research on support for parents and infants in the postnatal period* (pp. 216–238). Norwood, NJ: Ablex.

Crockenberg, S. (1988). Social support and parenting. In H. Fitzgerald, B. Lester, & M. Yogman (Eds.), *Theory and research in behavioral pediatrics* (Vol. 4, pp. 67–92). New York/London: Plenum.

Cross, W. (1990). Race and ethnicity: Effects on social networks. In M. Cochran, M. Larner, D. Riley, L. Gunnarsson, & C. Henderson, Jr. (Eds.), *Extending families: The social networks of parents and their children* (pp. 67–85). London/New York: Cambridge University Press.

Fischer, C. (1982). *To dwell among friends: Personal networks in town and city.* Chicago: University of Chicago Press.

Granovetter, (1973). The strength of weak ties. *American Journal of Sociology, 78,* 1360–1380.

Gunnarsson, L., & Cochran, M. (1990). The social networks of single parents: Sweden and the United States. In M. Cochran, M. Larner, D. Riley, L. Gunnarsson, & C. Henderson, Jr. (Eds.), *Extending families: The social networks of parents and their children* (pp. 105–118). London/New York: Cambridge University Press.

Haraven, T. (1984). Themes in the historical development of the family. In R. D. Parke (Ed.), *Review of Child Development Research* (Vol. 7, pp. 137–178). Chicago: University of Chicago Press.

Hinde, R., Stevenson-Hinde, J., & Tamplin, A. (1985). Characteristics of 3- to 4-year-olds assessed at home and their interactions in preschool. *Developmental Psychology, 21,* 130–140.

Homel, R., Burns, A., & Goodnow, J. (1987). Parental social networks and child development. *Journal of Social and Personal Relationships, 4,* 159–177.

Longfellow, C., Zelkowitz, P., Saunders, E., & Belle, D. (1979, March). *The role of support in moderating the effects of stress and depression.* Paper presented at the biennial meeting of the society for Research on Child Development, San Francisco, CA.

McLanahan, S., Wedemeyer, N., & Adelberg, T. (1981). Network structure, social support, and psychological well-being in the single-parent family. *Journal of Marriage and the Family, August* (601–612).

Mitchell, J. C. (1969). *Social networks in urban situations.* Manchester, England: Manchester University Press.

Polansky, N., Gaudin, J., Ammons, P., & Davis, K. (1985). The psychological ecology of the neglectful mother. *Child Abuse & Neglect, 9,* 265–275.

Quinton, D., & Rutter, M. (1985). Parenting behavior of mothers raised "in care." In R. Nicol (Ed.), *Longitudinal studies in child psychology and psychiatry* (pp. 326–341). Chichester, England: Wiley.

Riley, D. (1990). Network influences on father involvement in childrearing. In M. Cochran, M. Larner, D. Riley, L. Gunnarsson, & C. Henderson, Jr. (Eds.), *Extending families: The social networks of parents and their children* (pp. 131–154). London/New York: Cambridge University Press.

Thomas, A., & Chess, S. (1977). *Temperament and development.* New York: Brunner/Mazel.

Tietjen, A. (1985). Relationships between the social networks of Swedish mothers and their children. *International Journal of Behavioral Development, 8,* 195–216.

Wellman, B. (1979). The community question: The intimate networks of East Yorkers. *American Journal of Sociology, 84,* 129–131.

Wellman, B. (1981). Applying network analysis to the study of support. In B. H. Gottlieb (Ed.), *Social networks and social support* (pp. 171–200). Beverly Hills, CA: Sage.

Chapter 7

The Long Arm of the Job: Influences of Parental Work on Childrearing

Ann C. Crouter
Susan M. McHale
The Pennsylvania State University

In *Middletown*, the classic monograph about U.S. culture, Lynd and Lynd (1929) coined the phrase "the long arm of the job" to describe the considerable influence that fathers' employment situations had on the family.[1] As the Lynds explained, the temporal rhythms of work life and the specter of unemployment helped to shape many aspects of family life in Middletown, including parents' childrearing activities. More than 60 years later, the influence of work on family life is no less important, but the interrelationship between these important social institutions is all the more complex because mothers have entered the labor force in such large numbers (Hayghe, 1986). In many families today, there are two long arms of the job, one reaching back to the father's world of work and the other to the mother's work setting. This dual-earner lifestyle poses certain opportunities and constraints for contemporary parents that are the focus of this chapter.

Researchers from a variety of disciplines examined work–family relations. Their findings are sometimes difficult to integrate because some researchers look at the work–family interface through the lens of the workplace and others examine these interconnections through the lens of the family (Kline & Cowan, 1989). When researchers examine the work–parenting interface through the lens of the workplace, parents' jobs are seen as settings with certain charac-

---

[1]The phrase "long arm of the job" has been borrowed by other scholars over the years. Willard Waller used it as a chapter title in his book *The Family: A Dynamic Interpretation* (1938), as did Mirra Komarovsky in *Blue Collar Marriage* (1962). We could not resist joining the tradition.

teristics and features. Work may be conceptualized broadly, as the means by which adults in a culture provide for their families or narrowly, as a source of daily fluctuation in parents' psychological well-being. When seen through the lens of the workplace, the question for researchers becomes: How does parents' involvement in certain work ecologies (as defined by their roles, activities, and relationships) influence the ways in which they rear their children?

When the researcher's lens focuses on families, characteristics of parents' jobs are often peripheral or even ignored. Instead the emphasis is on how families that differ in terms of mothers' and fathers' roles in the paid labor force function as settings for childrearing. An ecological approach involves an examination of those familial processes that are similar and different across families with different connections to paid employment.

In this chapter, we describe research that examines the work–parenting interface through both lenses, examining the strengths, limitations, and unexplored territory in each. We begin by examining characteristics of parents' jobs that may affect their patterns of childrearing and then turn to a consideration of how living in a dual-earner family may influence women's and men's activities as parents.

THROUGH THE LENS OF THE WORKPLACE: CHARACTERISTICS OF WORK THAT INFLUENCE CHILDREARING

When the impact of parental work on parenting is viewed through the lens of the workplace, there are three levels of analysis to consider. At the broadest, most general level, work is adults' means of subsistence and, as such, is a central determinant of their "world view" (Kanter, 1977). Work informs parents' conceptualizations of how their environment operates and the qualities required to be successful in that environment (Ogbu, 1981). These ideas in turn shape parents' values about the characteristics that are important to inculcate in their young.

At an intermediate level, the characteristics of parents' jobs and the organizations in which they are employed pose opportunities and constraints for parenting. For example, some jobs encourage the acquisition of skills that are applicable not only at work but at home. Other work settings provide informal support to working parents via helpful co-workers and supervisors or access to formal workplace benefits and programs that enable parents to carry out their parenting role more effectively.

Finally, the work–parenting system can be examined at a very proximal, immediate level, a view of work–family dynamics that focuses on daily work experiences. Although most jobs have certain stable characteristics, such as a schedule, an assortment of supportive or unsupportive co-workers, and the activities that make up the nature of the work itself, there are also daily fluctuations in work demands, unexpected events, and interpersonal interactions that shape the emotional state of the employed person (Bolger, DeLongis, Kessler, & Wethington, 1989). "How was your day?" may be the most common question in the post-work reunion of family members. The answer to that question is usually based on the unusual occurrences of that particular day, often with reference to how those events made the employed parent feel. Here, work is seen as an influence on parents' emotional states, moods that in turn may be brought home to influence the tenor and content of parent–child interactions.

Work and the Acquisition of Parenting Values

Anthropologist John Ogbu (1981) argued that adults acquire ideas about what it takes to be successful in their culture by observing prevailing subsistence patterns, that is by observing work roles in the culture that are associated with success. In a hunting-and-gathering culture, for example, adults identify the characteristics of successful hunters (e.g., individualism, risk-taking, and independence), as those traits that they value and wish to inculcate in their children (Barry, Child, & Bacon, 1959). Ogbu explained that adults form "native theories of childrearing" that correspond to these values and, in turn, develop childrearing techniques designed to foster these desirable qualities in children.

Miller and Swanson (1958) posed a similar hypothesis in their study of entrepreneurial versus bureaucratic work settings. The qualities associated with success in an independent business, they imagined, would be quite different from those associated with success in a complex, hierarchical organization. Indeed, these researchers found that women whose husbands were employed in entrepreneurial settings emphasized achievement and striving in their children, whereas their counterparts whose spouses worked in bureaucracies emphasized interpersonal skills and getting along with others in their reports of their childrearing values and practices.

The idea of work as a source of parenting values finds additional support in Kohn's classic monograph, *Class and Conformity* (1969). Kohn argued that men, by virtue of their occupational position in the stratification system, come to see the world differently and that the characteristics associated with success in their occupational niche influence the qualities they value and want for their children and, consequently, the characteristics they will support or discourage in the context of daily childrearing activities. In a survey of more than 3,000 employed men, Kohn provided evidence that men in middle-class occupations tended to value independence and initiative in their offspring, whereas their working-class counterparts emphasized obedience and conformity.

The mechanisms through which parents translate abstract childrearing values into daily childrearing activities are murky in Kohn's research. He found that middle-class fathers were more likely to report using reasoning and withdrawal of love as discipline techniques than were working-class fathers. Middle-class fathers also reported taking their child's intentions into account when determining disciplinary action; misbehavior perceived as accidental would receive less severe punishment than misbehavior seen as intentional. Working-class fathers, on the other hand, reported using more physical punishment and indicated that they punished on the basis of the consequences of their child's behavior rather than the child's intentions. In brief, compliance seemed to be the primary goal of working-class fathers, although an internalized standard could be seen as the goal for middle-class fathers. Nonetheless, a clear correspondence between values and childrearing strategy is missing in Kohn's research. Additional limitations of these data were that they were focused only on fathers and were based on fathers' self-reported practices in hypothetical situations. It is difficult to ascertain what their behavior would be in real life.

Luster, Rhoades, and Haas (1989) extended Kohn's line of reasoning in a sample of 65 mother–infant dyads. These researchers not only replicated the finding that social class is related to parents' values of conformity and self-direction in their children, but also identified a set of specific parental beliefs that mediated the relation between parental values and parenting behavior. Global parenting values were related to specific attitudes about spoiling the baby, giving babies freedom to explore the home environment, discipline, and the importance of verbal stimulation. These specific beliefs in turn were related to mothers' supportive and constraining behaviors toward their babies, as reported by the mothers themselves and as rated by interviewers.

The dual-earner arrangement, so prevalent today, raises the issue that mothers and fathers, by virtue of their occupational positions, may identify different qualities as important and come to favor different childrearing practices. A mismatch in childrearing values and strategies may be unusual, given patterns of assortative mating in this culture (i.e., men and women who marry tend to have similar levels of education and thus would probably gravitate to jobs at similar levels in the occupational hierarchy). On the other hand, due to the prevalence of occupational segregation even within occupations, men and women tend to hold quite different jobs (Baron & Bielby, 1985). Consequently, husbands and wives in some families may acquire significantly different world views and come to favor contrasting approaches to childrearing. Such differences in opinion have been identified as a correlate of marital dissatisfaction; inconsistent parenting, which may arise from differing childrearing philosophies, has also been linked to adjustment difficulties in children whose parents are experiencing marital discord (Emery, 1988; McHale, Freitag, Crouter, & Bartko, 1991).

Workplace Opportunities and Constraints for Parenting

By virtue of the job that a parent holds and the nature of the specific workplace in which that job is carried out, mothers and fathers are exposed to certain opportunities and constraints vis-à-vis their parenting role. In his review of the "determinants of parenting," Belsky (1984) conceptualized the influence of work on parenting in terms of stress and support. Although stress and support are certainly important, a full consideration of the place of work in parents' lives requires thinking about dimensions of work experiences that are perhaps neither stressful nor supportive but serve to encourage parents to structure childrearing in qualitatively different ways.

Skill Development.   Work has long been recognized as an important setting for adult socialization and development (Mortimer & Simmons, 1978). Little research has focused, however, on whether and how the skills and orientations attained at work make their mark on employed adults' behaviors in other settings, such as the family. For example, qualitative research suggests that the skills employees acquire in a workplace that subscribes to participative management are the very qualities conducive to effective childrearing. Crouter (1984) conducted interviews with workers in a manufacturing plant renowned for the extent to which its employees were involved in managing their own work activities. Organized into small work teams, machinists and assembly workers participated in hiring fellow team members, monitoring work performance, ordering inventory, handling machine breakdowns, monitoring quality and safety, and interacting with external vendors and customers. Teams held frequent meetings where members were expected to voice their points of view constructively, listen to one another, problem solve, and make collective decisions. At various times, workers would leave the team area to participate in training exercises designed to improve team communication and decision making. In semistructured interviews, workers noted that they found themselves using the democratic approach to teamwork emphasized at work in their parenting. One employee described holding team meetings at home, adding, "After all, a family is kind of like a team" (Crouter, 1984, p. 82). A divorced mother made this analogy: "I say things to my daughter that I know are a result of the way things are at work. I ask her, 'What do you think about that?' or 'How would you handle this problem?' I tend to deal with her the way we deal with people at work. The logic is the same" (Crouter, 1984, pp. 81–82).

These anecdotes suggest a democratic or authoritative parenting style, an approach to childrearing that is characterized by "a high degree of warmth or acceptance, a high degree of psychological autonomy or democracy, and a high degree of behavioral control" (Steinberg, Elmen, & Mounts, 1989, p. 1425). There is ample evidence in the literature that young children develop such positive qualities as self-reliance, independence, and initiative when their parents utilize an authoritative childrearing style, as opposed to an authoritarian or permissive approach to parenting (see review by Maccoby & Martin, 1983). Scholars debated about which features of authoritative parenting are most responsible for positive outcomes in children: warmth, control, or their combination (Maccoby & Martin, 1983). If, as seems plausible, participative management in the workplace instills skills in employees that generalize to their childrearing activities at home, it would be important to know which specific skills acquired in the workplace (e.g., communication, perspective taking, group decision making, management) are most directly linked to effective parenting. Moreover, the effects of participative work are probably not uniform across all types of workers. Future research should attempt to identify the characteristics of workers who are most likely to experience the participative work milieu as a *developmentally instigative* context (Bronfenbrenner, 1989), as well as the characteristics of those employees who are most likely to generalize skills acquired at work to their interactions with their children.

Work-Based Relationships

Although work consumes a large portion of adults' time and is doubtless a setting in which many relationships are formed, little systematic research has been conducted on personal relationships at work. This lacuna is particularly unfortunate in regard to employed parents of young children for whom work may be one of the few opportunities for peer interaction. Informal friendships among co-workers may be an important setting in which parents seek advice and are exposed to norms about childrearing.

Greenberger, Goldberg, Hamill, O'Neil, and Payne (1989) surveyed more than 300 parents of preschool children about informal and formal sources of support in their work environments and the relationship between those workplace supports and parents' job-related attitudes (e.g., organizational commitment) and personal well-being (i.e., role strain and health). In the area of informal support, parents completed separate measures of the extent to which their co-workers and supervisor were supportive (e.g., made their work life easier, were easy to talk to, were willing to listen) and the extent to which the supervisor was willing to accommodate to the parents' home responsibilities (e.g., tolerating schedule changes and home-related work interruptions). Multiple regression analyses, controlling for demographic characteristics and other sources of workplace support, revealed that co-worker support was a significant correlate of role strain for married fathers and single mothers, but not married mothers; the greater the perceived co-worker support, the less role strain was reported. In this study, supervisor support and flexibility were not associated with parents' reports of role strain. Moreover, none of these informal supports was associated with parents' health problems. What is important, for our purposes, is that having supportive co-workers was related to reduced role strain for some parents, indicating that this aspect of the work environment merits further investigation.

For example, in future research it will be important to examine whether co-worker support buffers parents' role strain such that actual parenting behavior is enhanced. In addition, longitudinal research is needed to rule out alternative hypotheses. For example, a selection effect may be operating such that socially competent individuals are those who are best able both to forge relationships at work and to manage work and family roles with minimal strain. The role of the supervisor also deserves closer scrutiny. Although supervisor support did not emerge as a correlate of role strain in Greenberger et al.'s study, Repetti (1987) found that supervisor support mitigated depression in female bank tellers who experienced stressful work conditions. There is considerable evidence that parental depression is negatively associated with effective, nurturant parenting (Belsky, 1984). Thus, to the extent that experiences or relationships at work enhance employees' mental health, parents may be better able to focus on their children's needs and to provide both emotional warmth and developmentally appropriate limits for children's behavior, key components of authoritative parenting.

Workplace Policies.　　In addition to the informal support provided by some supervisors and co-workers, work settings vary in terms of the extent to which they formally acknowledge or support employees' roles and responsibilities in the family (Kamerman & Kahn, 1987). Workplace policies such as flexible time (flextime) scheduling, rules about the use of sick time and personal leave time, maternity or parental leave, and provisions for the care of employees' dependents presumably relieve the strain that results from balancing work and family roles, a support that may ultimately enhance parenting. The logic of such a causal chain is intuitively appealing. The empirical evidence for it, however, is very scant (Friedman, 1990).

Bohen and Viveros-Long (1981) examined the effects of flextime scheduling (giving employees a choice, within a range of options, as to when they begin and end their work day) on employees' work–family role strain and division of family work. Surveying two federal agencies, one with flextime and one without, Bohen and Viveros-Long found few differences between employees in the two contrasting settings. Single people and married people without children appeared to experience reduced strain in the flextime setting, but the group in which the research team was most interested—employed parents, especially mothers—had equal levels of strain and similarly inequitable patterns of dividing up housework and child care in the two work settings. Indeed, when Bohen and Viveros-Long conducted follow-up discussion groups to explore why these null findings emerged, employed parents noted that the relatively conservative form of flextime offered by the agency in the study was insufficient. Thus, family-responsive benefits should be of sufficient magnitude to make a difference in the daily lives of working parents. Moreover, as long as workplace supports for parents are rare and piecemeal, effects will be uneven because only one parent in a family may be affected; flexible scheduling at work, for example, may have much more impact if both parents have the option to be creative about their work hours.

Other evidence that formal workplace policies or supportive programs actually make a difference in terms of employees' parenting practices is scarce. Some evaluations of family-responsive benefits and practices have been conducted, but usually with an eye to work-related outcomes rather than parenting (see, e.g., Miller, 1984). In the study described previously, however, Greenberger et al. (1989), asked their respondents to report the extent to which they utilized family-responsive benefits that were available from their employer. These investigators found that mothers used formal benefits (e.g., flexible scheduling, parental leave policies, assistance with child care) more than fathers did and that, for single mothers, use of formal benefits was related to reduced role strain, even controlling for other sources of support at work. As we emphasized with regard to informal co-worker support, it will be important to explore whether single mothers are able to be more effective parents if they have access to workplace benefits that are responsive to family roles.

Work as an Influence on Parents' Moods at Home

A third level at which to examine the connections between parental work and parents' childbearing behavior at home focuses on the work day as an influence on parents' psychological states. This perspective recognizes that individuals experience considerable day-to-day variability in work demands, interpersonal dynamics at work, and work accomplishments that may influence their mood at the end of the work day. A handful of researchers recently have begun to examine the extent to which work-induced moods influence employees' behavior off the job (e.g., Bolger et al., 1989; Crouter, Perry-Jenkins, Huston, & Crawford, 1989; Repetti, 1989a, 1989b).

Such studies are challenging to conduct because they require careful measurement of psychological states, repeatedly assessed over a period of days or weeks, and, ideally, attention to the temporal sequencing of mood and subsequent behavior. Researchers identified several promising strategies in their initial attempts to explore this level of analysis.

Bolger et al. (1989) asked 166 married couples to complete a short questionnaire diary each day for 42 consecutive weeks. The diary included two indicators of work stress: work overload (''a lot of work'') and arguments with supervisors, co-workers, or work subordinates, as well as similar measures of overload and arguments at home (completed separately with regard to spouse and children). Using correlational techniques that examined the extent to which the work-related stresses were related to behavior at home, Bolger et al. found an increased probability of arguments with spouse after a day in which the husband had had an argument at work. Wives, however, did not have more arguments with their husbands on days when they had experienced arguments at work. With regard to arguments with children, no effects were found for either mothers or fathers; arguments at work did not increase the likelihood of subsequent arguments at home with children.

The research design that Bolger and his colleagues employed could be extended to other indices of parenting such as the quality and quantity of parent–child interaction or the extent to which parents effectively monitor and supervise their children at the end of the day, topics we consider in the next section of the chapter. Parents who have had demanding work days or arguments on the job may not argue with their children when they return home from work, but such stresses may manifest themselves in other ways. For example, parents may be too preoccupied to communicate effectively about the child's own experiences that day, too tired to effectively mediate children's sibling disputes, or too self-absorbed to detect that their child is troubled about something.

Repetti (1989b) examined the connections between work-induced stress and parents' behavior at home using a somewhat different strategy. She focused on air traffic controllers, an occupation that is notoriously stressful, to take advantage of daily records on work conditions and demands maintained by the Federal Aviation Authority. Twenty-seven air traffic controllers, all parents, completed daily reports on work stress and parent–child interactions on 3 consecutive days. Repetti found that parents tended to be more socially withdrawn and less emotionally expressive on days when work had been stressful. Work stress appeared to dampen both positive and negative emotions. In a separate analysis, Repetti focused on the 15 air traffic controllers who were fathers of children between the ages of 4 and 10. Although findings generally paralleled those for the whole sample, Repetti also found that when the father's work group collectively perceived the social environment at work to be unfriendly and negative, fathers reported less positive and more negative affect in their descriptions of their interactions with their children. Although appropriately cautious about overgeneralizing from the small-scale study, Repetti emphasized the need for researchers to examine the consequences of both day-to-day variability in effects of work-induced psychological states on the family, as well as the consequences of chronic or long-term work stress.

Recent research by Wells (1988) illustrates that the utility of examining fluctuations in psychological state extends beyond studies of stress. She focused on variations in the self-esteem of mothers across various contexts of daily life. For 2 weeks, 49 middle-class employed mothers completed brief questionnaires about their psychological well-being four or five times a day in response to signals randomly emitted from a pager that they carried. She found that mothers' state of self-esteem was significantly higher when they were in the presence of adults than when they were with children. In addition, the more time women devoted to their paid work outside the home, the lower their self-esteem. Thus, women had the lowest scores on self-esteem when they worked full time and when they were in the presence of children.

A number of studies suggested that mothers' self-esteem, measured in a more global way than Wells operationalized it, is related to parenting. Patterson (1980), for example, identified low maternal self-esteem as a correlate of ineffective, coercive parent–child interaction. Small (1988), in a questionnaire study of 139 parent–child dyads, found that mothers with higher self-esteem were more likely to provide their adolescent children with greater decision-making freedom, to communicate more often in a friendly way with their children, and to view their children as independent. In addition, mothers with higher self-esteem tended to have children who were more satisfied with the level of autonomy they were given in decision making. Wells' research is important because it suggests that a self-evaluative process is at work at a very immediate, proximal level. Her data revealed, for example, that mothers' evaluations of the extent to which they were living up to the expectations of others were related more strongly to mothers' self-esteem when in the presence of children than when in the presence of adults. Wells speculated that mothers' estimates of how well they are balancing work and family roles may affect their evaluations of themselves and, as these other data suggest, the way they relate to their children.

A promising direction for future research is to examine the extent to which work conditions influence the self-esteem of employed mothers and fathers in various contexts. For example, do employed mothers feel better about themselves when in the presence of children if their work environment is responsive to the needs of employed parents? How does the self-esteem of fathers vary as a function of context? Do parents who acquire interpersonal skills at work manifest different patterns of self-esteem by context than parents for whom work is incompatible with parenting? These questions require that researchers interested in approaching the work–parenting relationship through the *lens* of the workplace adopt strategies that enable them to examine the issue at multiple levels of analysis.

THROUGH THE LENS OF THE FAMILY: PARENTING IN DUAL-EARNER FAMILIES

The second way researchers examined the opportunities and constraints that working outside the home imposes on parents pays little attention to the nature of the work parents perform or to the setting in which that work is done. This approach focuses instead on the fact that one or both parents are working outside the home. And, given that the two paycheck family has become the norm in U.S. society, much of this research examined the question of whether a dual-earner lifestyle affects parental activities and, in turn, children's well-being and development.

Until recently, investigations focusing on the family component of the work–family interface have been limited to the study of the dual-earner family as a *social address*. As Bronfenbrenner and Crouter (1983) noted, such efforts are limited in that comparisons of families from different social addresses provide no information about the processes underlying group differences that are detected. For this reason, although we discuss the development of children who reside at the dual-earner address with implicit or explicit comparisons to those from single earner families, our goal here is to begin to identify the dynamics of parenting in dual-earner families that may exert an impact on children's development and well-being.

An additional limitation of extant studies of dual-earner families is that the focus of this research has tended to be on maternal employment; fathers' work and parenting activities have been largely ignored. Mothers' entry into the labor force likely has ramifications throughout the family system, but extant studies are generally limited to a focus on the mother's work hours and attitudes toward her job and family experiences. When differences between children in dual- and single-earner families are found they tend to be attributed to maternal employment because we know almost nothing about fathers' work and parenting activities in these contrasting family ecologies. Thus, in reviewing what is known about parenting in dual-earner families, we place special emphasis on studies that provide information about both mothers' and fathers' activities.

Dual-earner parents likely have in common a number of childrearing challenges including: (a) finding time to share activities with their children, (b) monitoring children's activities when parents are absent, and (c) maintaining close and satisfying relationships with children. These issues become challenges for parents to the extent that work involvement saps the time and energy fathers and mothers otherwise might devote to these activities. We consider each of these potential alterations in the lives of dual-earner families in the following pages.

Parent–Child Activities

A number of studies revealed that parents' temporal involvement in work affects their availability for activities with children. In fact, the time crunch appears at the top of the list of problems experienced by dual-earner couples (Bohen & Viveros-Long, 1981; Moen, 1982). This issue becomes important given evidence that parental involvement in child-oriented activities has important implications for children's development and well-being (Maccoby & Martin, 1983).

The optimal balance between involvement with parents and autonomous activities by children is likely to vary, however, depending on children's personal characteristics. For example, during the school-age and adolescent years, children may become increasingly involved in activities outside the home. Provided relationships with parents are warm and supportive, such increasing autonomy in youngsters' daily activities actually may be indicative of greater maturity (Grotevant & Cooper, 1986).

Although images of the time crunch imply that lower levels of parental involvement may be characteristic of dual-earner families, evidence from studies of families with children ranging in age from infancy through the early adolescent years reveals a complex picture of how parents' involvement in work and their time spent in parenting are linked. Specifically, the evidence suggests that a dual-earner lifestyle may have different implications for mothers' and fathers' involvement with sons and daughters at different stages of development.

Assessing paternal involvement, large-scale diary studies indicate few differences between dual- and single-earner fathers' time with their children (e.g., Pleck, 1983; Robinson, 1977). Pleck suggested, however, that such data may mask the fact that dual-earner fathers are more involved in child care than single-earner fathers when children are very young. Evidence for this notion comes from our own research in families of first-born children in the first 2 years of life. Based on nine nightly telephone interviews in which fathers and mothers reported on their day's activities, we found that dual-earner fathers engaged in significantly more activities with their children than did single-earner fathers (Crouter, Perry-Jenkins, Huston, & McHale, 1987). Closer examination of fathers' activities revealed that the major differences between these groups of fathers was in dyadic child-care activities (i.e., activities that took place without the mother present). Dual-earner fathers were more than twice as likely to be involved in such activities as single-earner men but did not differ from single-earner men when it came to the extent of their involvement in leisure activities or caregiving that included both their wives and their children.

The picture for mothers' involvement with infants and young children as a function of their employment is similarly complicated. A central issue is how researchers have conceptualized and measured the construct of parental involvement. In the study of parents with infants cited earlier, mother–child activities were measured via daily telephone calls. Analyses revealed that the more hours per week women worked the less frequent were their caregiving and play activities with their children (McHale & Huston, 1984). In contrast, Pederson and Zaslow and their colleagues adopted a strategy of observing infants at home in the evening when both parents were present (Pederson, Cain, Zaslow, & Anderson, 1982; Zaslow, Pederson, Suwalsky, Rabinovitch, & Cain, 1985). Recording frequencies of specific behaviors, these investigators discovered that, after spending the day at work, employed mothers actually displayed higher rates of certain forms of interaction (e.g., verbalizations) than did homemaker mothers. This was particularly true for mothers when infants were younger and when mothers had recently returned to work. What may have been an attempt to compensate for the time mothers and babies spent apart during the day in turn had ramifications for fathers' involvement with their infants. Observations indicated that dual-earner fathers showed lower rates of some behaviors than did fathers in single-earner families. The investigators concluded that "the working mother's special need to interact with the infant inhibited or 'crowded out' the father" (Pederson et al., 1982, p. 218). On first consideration, these data may give rise to concerns about the father–child relationship in dual-earner families. However, the evidence cited earlier showing that dual-earner fathers' *modal activities with infants are dyadic* (i.e., mothers are not present) suggests that although mothers may crowd fathers out of *triadic* interactions, dual-earner fathers still have more opportunity to interact with their infants than do fathers from single-earner families.

Returning to the issue of employed mothers' compensating for time spent away from their young children, we find evidence of this phenomenon from other sources. For example, based on a large-scale time-use study, Hill and Stafford (1980) suggested that mothers of infants and preschoolers, particularly mothers with higher levels of education, may compensate for their lack of time during the work day by spending more time with their children during nonwork hours. Employed mothers seem to be able to do this by engaging in less personal leisure and getting less sleep than homemaker mothers. In addition, a recent study suggests that children actively collaborate in this effort to maximize their time with their parents (Manlove & Feagans, 1990). This analysis of children's daily activities indicated that infants and toddlers in day care spent almost as much time at the center napping (2.8 hours per day) as they spent awake (3.6 hours). By staying awake later in the evening, they were able to spend about three quarters of their waking hours with either their mothers or their fathers. Although this study was somewhat small in scale (n = 41 families) and thus requires replication, the results highlight the importance of moving beyond a focus on the dual-earner address or even a simple assessment of parents' work hours to obtain a more complete picture of the daily lives of parents and children in dual-earner families.

Most research on parental involvement focuses on young children; we know less about how dual and single-earner parents differ in their involvement with school-age children and adolescents. Some evidence suggests, however, that discrepancies between employed and nonemployed women in time spent with children decrease with the age of the child, as youngsters presumably become more involved in activities outside the family (Hill & Stafford, 1980). In fact, our research on school-aged children has revealed seasonal differences in the extent of mother–child involvement by employed and homemaker mothers. The research indicates that homemaker mothers are more frequently involved in activities with their children only during the summer months when school is not in session (Crouter & McHale, in press).

The picture for fathers, however, is somewhat more complicated. Analyzing children's and fathers' reports of their daily joint activities across 7 days, we found that both dual- and single-earners fathers spent approximately 60 minutes per week in dyadic activities with their children as compared with an average of 90 minutes for mothers (Crouter & Crowley, 1990; Stocker & McHale, 1992). When we examined paternal involvement for sons and daughters separately, however, a different pattern of results emerged: Whereas dual-earner fathers spent equal amounts of time with sons and daughters (60 minutes per week), single-earner fathers spent an average of 90 minutes a week with their sons but only 30 minutes per week with their daughters (Crouter & Crowley, 1990). Studies that revealed advantages of dual-earner family life for girls (e.g., in self-esteem or autonomy) and potential disadvantages for some boys (i.e., school achievement; see Hoffman, 1989, for a review) generally attribute such findings to alterations in the mother–child relationship brought about by maternal employment. Our findings on paternal involvement underscore the notion that maternal employment alters the roles, relationships and activities of all family members in ways that may exert an impact on children's well-being and development.

We found only one study that focused explicitly on adolescents' time with their parents in dual- and single-earner families, and the results of this research stand in sharp contrast to the general pattern of results showing few overall differences between dual- and single earner parents of older children. Studying 10th graders, Montemayor (1984) found that homemaker mothers spent significantly more time (particularly with daughters) than did full-time employed mothers, with part-time employed mothers falling between these two groups. Comparison of paternal involvement revealed a similar pattern of findings, although effects were more pronounced for sons.

The inconsistency between these findings and those from other research may stem in part from differences in data collection methodology and the age and social backgrounds of the subjects (over half were from Mormon families who are likely to be considerably more traditional in gender-role ideology). Additionally, however, data on these adolescents' activities were collected on only 3 days. Using a procedure in which we collected information on daily activities over a 7-day period, we were able to compare fathers' involvement in activities with preadolescents on weekdays versus weekend days. Our results reveal that highly involved and uninvolved fathers differ only in their time spent with children on *weekend* days (McHale, Crouter, & Bartko, in press). Such findings suggest that investigations which include a limited "slice" of time or which focus only on one setting in which family members interact may provide an inaccurate picture of parents' and children's experiences in dual-earner families.

Parental Supervision and Monitoring

In addition to direct involvement in activities with other children, parents also must keep track of their children's activities, whereabouts and companions when parents and children are not together. Although much less is known about this dimension of parental involvement, work by Patterson and his colleagues on the antisocial behavior of boys focuses on the importance of parental monitoring of youths' activities (e.g., Patterson & Stouthamer-Loeber, 1984). Their findings revealed that mothers' knowledge of their sons' activities accounted for more variance in preadolescent and adolescent boys' problem behavior than did other dimensions of parents' behavior, such as discipline style. Along these lines, Steinberg (1986) found that latchkey children and preadolescents who "hang out" after school are more susceptible to peer pressure to engage in antisocial activity than are those whose activities are supervised, even if indirectly, by adults. These findings are important in light of other data showing no differences between children who are on their own after school (usually because parents are employed) versus those who are directly supervised by adults (e.g., Galambos & Garbarino, 1983; Rodman, Pratto, & Nelson, 1985). A simple comparison of whether or not children are directly supervised by adults is less informative than a more detailed analysis of how children spend their time when not directly supervised by parents and how much parents know about the activities children undertake in their absence.

Some writers suggested that adequate levels of parental monitoring may be more difficult to maintain in dual-earner families. In fact, a finding from some studies that middle-class sons of employed mothers may perform somewhat less well in school (e.g., Banducci, 1967; Gold & Andres, 1978; Reese & Palmer, 1970) has been attributed by some writers to the possibly lower levels of parental monitoring these boys may receive (e.g., Bronfenbrenner & Crouter, 1982).

The only empirical data addressing this issue, however, revealed no differences between dual- and single-earner parents of school-age children in this regard (Crouter, MacDermid, McHale, & Perry-Jenkins, 1990). In this study, parental monitoring was measured by telephoning children in the evening and interviewing them about their experiences during the day (e.g., successes or problems in school, homework, chores, fights with friends). The index of monitoring was the discrepancy between children's reports of their experiences and their parents' independent reports of what they knew about those same events. Although mothers were generally more informed about their youngsters' activities than were fathers, we detected no differences in the level of parental monitoring experienced by fourth- and fifth-grade boys and girls from dual- versus single-earner families. Nonetheless, parental monitoring had different implications for children with different personal characteristics and children from different family contexts. Specifically, results revealed that boys who were less well monitored received lower grades in school than other children although this effect was not apparent in girls who also received less parental monitoring. Furthermore, the conduct of less well-monitored boys from dual-earner families was rated more negatively both by parents and the boys themselves. In discussing these results, Crouter et al. (1990) point to boys' vulnerability and the potentially more stressful dual-earner lifestyle as "person" and "context" factors that may mediate the effects of the process of parental monitoring.

Parents' Emotional Involvement

Maintaining warm and supportive relationships is a third dimension of parental involvement that may represent a challenge for some dual-earner families. Of the three dimensions of involvement we identified, parents' emotional involvement received the most scrutiny. Findings from a number of studies are in agreement that feelings of closeness and warmth are associated with positive outcomes for children (Maccoby & Martin, 1983). Although less research has focused on parent–child relationships in adolescence, investigators emphasized the importance of maintaining emotional closeness with parents even as youth become more autonomous and independent (Grotevant & Cooper, 1986).

There is little evidence, however, that directly links parents' work involvement (either time spent on the job or emotional absorption in work) to parents' closeness and warmth with children. In one longitudinal study of professional men, Heath (1977) noted that the work absorption required of demanding jobs made men feel guilty because they were unavailable to their children and irritable when at home, but no direct measures of the father–child relationship or potential consequences to children were assessed. Reviewing survey evidence on mothers' work involvement, Berndt (1983) noted that working mothers regard their lives as more stressful than homemaker mothers. Conflicts between work and family demands, in turn, may make mothers more irritable and tired when they are at home, a consequence that may have implications for mothers' emotional availability to children. On the other hand, women who derive a sense of competence from their jobs may generalize these positive feelings to their roles as parents. Such a view is consistent with results of several reports indicating that a mother's satisfaction with her role, be it homemaker or employee, is more consistently related to children's well-being than is the fact of her being employed or not (e.g., Lerner & Galambos, 1986).

Studies of the emotional tone of parent–child relationships in dual-earner families during infancy generally have focused on the security of infants' attachments to their mothers and, rarely, to their fathers. A detailed review of this research is beyond the scope of this chapter; the reader is directed to recent reviews by Belsky (in press) and Clarke-Stewart (1989) for critical analyses of this literature. Such reviews reveal that most studies find no differences between the kind of attachment infants exhibit toward their mothers as a function of maternal employment. A handful of studies, however, found higher proportions of insecure mother–infant attachments among babies with full-time working mothers as compared to families in which mothers work part time or not at all. Given the press for greater paternal involvement in dual-earner families, it is unfortunate that we know little about how parents' employment patterns are linked to the emotional tone of father–infant relationships: Findings from three published studies provide an inconsistent picture of father–infant attachment in sons and daughters from dual-earner versus single-earner families (Belsky, 1988; Belsky & Rovine, 1988; Chase-Lansdale & Owen, 1987; Owen, Easterbrooks, Chase-Lansdale, & Goldberg, 1984).

Part of the problem with this literature is that the theoretical framework from which the attachment construct is derived is acontextual. From this perspective the mother–infant bond is seen as the source of children's emotional development and prototype for future relations; more distal factors that may affect the emotional tone of the mother–infant relationship have been largely ignored. Choosing from the complex array of factors impinging on the developing child only one element of this causal web, (i.e., the mother–child relationship) is an overly simplistic strategy for the ecologically minded researcher. Research that examines mother–infant attachment simply as a function of maternal employment suffers from the limitations we mentioned earlier: The processes underlying differences in outcome can only be imagined and the role of the father is generally ignored. Furthermore, we can not assume that parent–child relationship processes will have similar consequences for children with different characteristics or from different contexts. For example, research on the correlates of mother–infant attachment shows that whereas secure toddlers from single-earner families exhibit more dependency behavior, those from dual-earner families show less (Weinraub, Jaeger, & Hoffman, 1988). Further, in the Belsky and Rovine (1988) study, whereas 50% of boys whose mothers were employed full time ($\geq$ 35 hours per week) were insecurely attached to their fathers, 50% of girls whose mothers were full-time homemakers were classified as insecure (i.e., avoidant or resistent). These results again alert us to move beyond what may be thought of as developmental universals, to consider how characteristics of contexts and characteristics of persons may mediate the effects of particular parenting processes.

One important context in which parent–child relationships develop is the marriage relationship. The connections between marriage and parenting have received a great deal of scrutiny by investigators who are interested in explaining individual differences in parenting style as well as differences in children's well-being and development (Belsky, 1984; Emery, 1988). Investigations documenting significant associations between marital harmony and the emotional tone of parent–child relationships (e.g., Easterbrooks & Emde, 1988) underscore the importance of moving beyond a focus on maternal employment and the mother–child relationship if we are to fully understand the implications of a dual-earner lifestyle for parents' emotional involvement with their children.

Data focusing specifically on families with two earners, for example, reveal that the likelihood of insecure mother–infant attachment is greater in families with more problematic marital relationships (Belsky, in press). Additionally, some research suggests that negotiating the still relatively novel, more egalitarian roles of a dual-earner lifestyle may be associated with more conflict in marriage. Studying a sample of young parents with infants, for example, Crouter et al. (1987) found that, although husbands' reports of love for their wives were positively and significantly associated with wives' work hours, the more child care these men performed, the higher levels of marital conflict and the lower levels of love for their wives they reported. Clearly, some elements of an egalitarian role structure are easier to adjust to than others!

Using data from our sample of dual and single-earner families of grade school children, we studied marital conflict in terms of sex-typing in marital roles. In one study, we examined the implications of incongruity between a parent's sex role attitudes and the couple's division of labor in the home (i.e., housework and child-oriented activities; McHale & Crouter, in press). We were particularly interested in men and women who were more involved in family work than their sex role attitudes would suggest they "ought" to be: (a) men with traditional attitudes but more egalitarian family roles; and (b) women with nontraditional attitudes but traditional family roles. Our analyses revealed not only that individuals in these "risk" groups were less satisfied with their marriages than other men and women, but within-couple analyses suggested that they also were less satisfied than their own spouses. Additional analyses revealed that job-related resources, including income and job prestige, were linked to spouses' risk status. For women, greater discrepancies between their own and their husband's work-related resources characterized the group with attitude/role incongruence. For men, absolute measures of work-related resources, particularly job prestige, were linked to risk-group status, with lower status men more likely to experience attitude/role incongruence. Like others, we have discussed these findings in terms of marital power. Important directions for future research are to examine the marital difficulties that may arise as a function of alterations in the roles and relationships of spouses in dual-earner families and to explore the connections between these and both spouses' activities as parents and their children's development and well-being.

In addition to indirect effects via the marriage relationship, the alterations in family roles that characterize dual-earner families can also have direct implications for the emotional tone of children's relationships with parents. In our research on school-age children in dual- and single-earner families, for example, we examined children's involvement in "masculine" and "feminine" household tasks that they reported during seven nightly interviews (McHale, Bartko, Crouter, & Perry-Jenkins, 1990). Following from the results of Mac-Dermid, Huston, and McHale's (1990) research, we were particularly interested in the implications of an incompatibility between children's family roles and their parents' attitudes about gender-appropriate activities. Results revealed that the connection between boys' feminine task involvement and their reports of paternal warmth were mediated by their fathers' gender role attitudes and their parents' work status. In dual-earner families, when sons of less traditional fathers performed fewer feminine tasks, the boys reported lower levels of warmth in their relationships with mothers and fathers (as well as scoring more poorly on other measures of adjustment). In contrast, in single-earner families, when sons of *more traditional* fathers performed *more feminine tasks*, the sons reported lower levels of parental warmth (and poorer adjustment). Incongruity between girls' family roles and their parents' gender role attitudes was not linked to girls' perceptions of their parents' warmth and acceptance.

An important feature of these results was the finding that incongruities between children's gender roles and their parents' gender-role attitudes were more frequent in dual-earner than in single-earner families. This pattern is consistent with results of our earlier work on parents showing that incongruity between psychological orientations and actual role behavior is more apparent in dual-earner than in single-earner families.

In short, a dual-earner lifestyle imposes changes in the experiences of all family members, changes for which some individuals may not be psychologically prepared. As sociologist Davis Kingsley (1984) noted: ''A century may seem a long time, but it is a short time to alter the basic structure of an institution. The new egalitarian system of sex roles still lacks normative guidelines. Each couple has to work out its own arrangement which means in practice a great deal of experimentation and failure'' (p. 413). The dual-earner family is a family in transition with all the risks and opportunities that situation implies. To fully appreciate the dynamics of this evolving family structure, we must look beyond the social address and into families' lives to explore the altered roles, relationships, and activities of all family members.

CONCLUSIONS

We attempted to show that scholars interested in the interrelationship of work and parenting have taken quite different approaches depending on whether their focus is that of work, and the roles, activities, and relationships associated with employment, or family and the dynamics associated with that context. Work influences childrearing via its effects on parents' views of the world, the opportunities and constraints jobs pose for parent who need to balance multiple roles, and the daily stresses and exhilarations of the work day that influence parents' emotional states as they leave work to resume their parenting role. All three levels are important, and the next challenge is to design research that bridges these levels of analysis. A second general approach researchers have taken to examining work and family life has been to focus primarily on family processes, such as parent–child activities, monitoring, and parent–child closeness, with an eye to how family processes interact with characteristics of children and family contexts (e.g., dual-earner vs. single-earner). There is some evidence that processes differ across single- and dual-earner family contexts. Less often studied, but of great importance, is the issue of how family contexts and child characteristics interact with family processes to influence children's development.

Whether the lens for examining the impact of work on parenting is that of the workplace or the family, exciting research is being conducted in both domains. One important challenge for future investigators, however, is to combine these two perspectives. To what extent, for example, are optimal levels of parental involvement facilitated by family-responsive policies and practices in parents' workplaces? How does chronic work stress influence the extent and quality of parent–child activities? Such questions require that researchers design studies to focus not only on parents' childrearing activities within families but on the effects of particular job characteristics on such activities. In addition, for dual-earner families, this means paying attention to both ''long arms of the job,'' a formidable but important challenge.

We are at a time in our history when the dual-earner family has become the norm, but, because this is a relatively new development, parents lack models and guidelines about how to structure household and childrearing responsibilities. This time of transition and uncertainty represents an opportunity for investigators interested in work, parenting, and child development: we can take advantage of such ''experiments of nature'' (Bronfenbrenner, 1979) to gain both practical and theoretical insights into the nature of human development.

ACKNOWLEDGMENTS

Some of the data reported in this chapter are from the Penn State Family Relationships Project. The authors serve as co-directors of the project which has been funded by NICHD (R01-HD21050). We gratefully acknowledge the assistance of all project families and staff, as well as Elliot Robins who first alerted us to the origins of the phrase alluded to in the title of the chapter.

REFERENCES

Banducci, R. (1967). The effects of mother's employment on the achievement, aspirations, and expectations of the child. *Personnel and Guidance Journal, 46,* 263–267.
Baron, J. N., & Bielby, W. T. (1985). Organizational barriers to gender equality: Sex segregation of jobs and occupations. In A. S. Rossi (Ed.), *Gender and the life course* (pp. 233–251). New York: Aldine.

Barry, H., Child, I. L., & Bacon, M. K. (1959). Relation of childtraining to subsistence economy. *American Anthropologist, 61*, 51–63.

Belsky, J. (1984). The determinants of parenting: A process model. *Child Development, 55*(1), 83–96.

Belsky, J. (1988). The "effects" of infant day care reconsidered. *Early Childhood Research Quarterly, 3*, 235–272.

Belsky, J. (in press). Developmental risks associated with infant day care: Attachment insecurity, noncompliance, and aggression? In S. Chehrazi (Ed.), *Balancing working and parenting: Psychological and developmental implications of day care.* New York: American Psychiatric Press, Inc.

Belsky, J., & Rovine, M. (1988). Nonmaternal care in the first year of life and the security of infant–parent attachment. *Child Development, 59*, 157–167.

Berndt, T. J. (1983). Peer relationships in children of working parents: A theoretical analysis and some conclusions. In C. Hayes & S. Kamerman (Eds.), *Children of working parents: Experience and outcomes* (pp. 13–43). Washington, DC: National Academy of Sciences.

Bohen, H., & Viveros-Long, A. M. (1981). *Balancing jobs and family life: Do flexible working schedules help?* Philadelphia: Temple University Press.

Bolger, N., DeLongis, A., Kessler, R. C., & Wethington, E. (1989). The contagion of stress across multiple roles. *Journal of Marriage and the Family, 51*, 175–183.

Bronfenbrenner, U. (1979). *The ecology of human development: Experiments by nature and design.* Cambridge, MA: Harvard University Press.

Bronfenbrenner, U. (1989, April). *The developing ecology of human development: Paradigm lost or paradigm regained?* Paper presented at the biennial meeting of the Society for Research in Child Development, Kansas City, MO.

Bronfenbrenner, U., & Crouter, A. C. (1982). Work and family through time and space. In S. Kamerman & C. Hayes (Eds.), *Families that work: Children in a changing world* (pp. 39–83). Washington, DC: National Academy Press.

Bronfenbrenner, U., & Crouter, A. C. (1983). The evolution of environmental models in developmental research. In P. Mussen (Ed.), *The handbook of child psychology* (Vol. 1, pp. 358–414). New York: Wiley.

Chase-Lansdale, P. L., & Owen, M. T. (1987). Maternal employment in a family context: Effects on infant–mother and infant–father attachments. *Child Development, 58*, 1505–1512.

Clarke-Stewart, K. A. (1989). Infant day care: Maligned or malignant. *American Psychologist, 44*, 266–273.

Crouter, A. C. (1984). Participative work as an influence on human development. *Journal of Applied Developmental Psychology, 5*, 71–90.

Crouter, A. C., & Crowley, M. S. (1990). School-age children's time alone with fathers in single- and dual-earner families: Implications for the father–child relationship. *Journal of Early Adolescence, 10*, 296–312.

Crouter, A. C., MacDermid, S. M., McHale, S. M., & Perry-Jenkins, M. (1990). Parental monitoring and perceptions of children's school performance and conduct in dual- and single-earner families. *Developmental Psychology, 26*, 649–657.

Crouter, A. C., & McHale, S. M. (in press). Temporal rhythms in family life: Seasonal variation in the relation between parental work and family processes. *Developmental Psychology.*

Crouter, A. C., Perry-Jenkins, M., Huston, T. L., & Crawford, D. (1989). The influence of work-induced psychological states on behavior at home. *Basic and Applied Social Psychology, 10*, 273–292.

Crouter, A. C., Perry-Jenkins, M., Huston, T. L., & McHale, S. (1987). Processes underlying father involvement in dual-earner and single-earner families. *Developmental Psychology, 23*, 431–440.

Easterbrooks, M. A., & Emde, R. N. (1988). Marital and parent–child relationships: The roles of affect in the family system. In R. Hinde & J. Stevenson-Hinde (Eds.), *Relationships within families: Mutual influences* (pp. 83–103). Oxford: Clarendon Press.

Emery, R. E. (1988). *Marriage, divorce, and children's adjustment.* Beverly Hills: Sage.

Friedman, D. E. (1990). Corporate responses to family needs. In D. G. Unger & M. B. Sussman (Eds.), *Families in community settings: Interdisciplinary perspectives* (pp. 77–98). New York: Haworth.

Galambos, N., & Garbarino, J. (1983, July–August). Identifying the missing links in the study of latchkey children. *Children Today*, 2–4, 40–41.

Gold, D., & Andres, D. (1978). Developmental comparisons between 10-year-old children with employed and nonemployed mothers. *Child Development, 49*, 75–84.

Greenberger, E., Goldberg, W. A., Hamill, S., O'Neil, R., & Payne, C. K. (1989). Contributions of a supportive work environment to parents' well-being and orientation to work. *American Journal of Community Psychology, 17*, 755–783.

Grotevant, H. D., & Cooper, C. R. (1986). Individuation in family relationships. *Human Development, 29*, 82–100.

Hayghe, H. (1986, February). Rise in mothers' labor force activity includes those with infants. *Monthly Labor Review*, pp. 43–45.

Heath, D. B. (1977). Some possible effects of occupation on the maturing of professional men. *Journal of Vocational Behavior, 11*, 263–281.

Hill, C. R., & Stafford, F. P. (1980). Parental care of children: Time diary estimates of quantity, predictability, and variety. *Journal of Human Resources, 15*, 219–239.

Hoffman, L. W. (1989). Effects of maternal employment in the two-parent family. *American Psychologist, 44*(2), 283–292.

Kamerman, S. B., & Kahn, A. J. (1987). *The responsive workplace: Employers and a changing labor force.* New York: Columbia University Press.

Kanter, R. M. (1977). *Work and family in the United States: A critical review and agenda for research and policy.* New York: Russell Sage Foundation.

Kingsley, D. K. (1984). Wives and work: The sex-role revolution and its consequences. *Population and Development Review, 10*, 397–417.

Kline, M., & Cowan, P. A. (1989). Rethinking the connections among "work" and "family" and "well-being." *Journal of Social Behavior and Personality, 3*, 61–90.

Kohn, M. L. (1969). *Class and conformity: A study in values.* Homewood, IL: Dorsey Press.

Komarovsky, M. (1962). *Blue collar marriage.* New York: Random House.

Lerner, J. V., & Galambos, N. L. (1986). Child development and family change: The influences of maternal employment on infants and toddlers. In L. P. Lipsitt & C. Rovee-Collier (Eds.), *Advances in infancy research* (Vol. IV, pp. 39–86). Norwood, NJ: Ablex.

Luster, T., Rhoades, K., & Haas, B. (1989). Relation between parenting values and parenting behavior. *Journal of Marriage and the Family, 51*, 139–147.

Lynd, R. S., & Lynd, H. M. (1929). *Middletown: A study in modern American culture.* New York: Harcourt, Brace, & World.

Maccoby, E., & Martin, J. (1983). Socialization in the context of the family: Parent–child interaction. In P. H. Mussen (Ed.), *Handbook of child psychology* (Vol. IV, pp. 1–101). New York: Wiley.

MacDermid, S. M., Huston, T. L., & McHale, S. M. (1990). Changes in marriage associated with the transition to parenthood: Individual differences as a function of sex role attitudes and change in the division of labor. *Journal of Marriage and the Family, 52,* 475–486.

Manlove, E. E., & Feagans, L. V. (1990, March). *Links between infant day care and family environment: Care arrangements and the role of the father.* Paper presented at the biennial meeting of the Southeastern Conference on Human Development, Richmond, VA.

McHale, S. M., Bartko, W. T., Crouter, A. C., & Perry-Jenkins, M. (1990). Children's housework and psychosocial functioning: The mediating effects of parents' sex role behaviors and attitudes. *Child Development, 61*, 1413–1426.

McHale, S. M., & Crouter, A. C. (in press). You can't always get what you want: Incongruence between sex role attitudes and family work roles and its implications for marriage. *Journal of Marriage and the Family.*

McHale, S. M., Crouter, A. C., & Bartko, W. T. (in press). Traditional and egalitarian patterns of parental involvement: Antecedents, consequences, and temporal rhythms. In D. Featherman, R. Lerner, & M. Perlmutter (Eds.), *Lifespan development and behavior* (Vol. 11). Hillsdale, NJ: Lawrence Erlbaum Associates.

McHale, S. M., Freitag, M., Crouter, A. C., & Bartko, W. T. (1991). Connections between dimensions of marital quality and school-aged children's adjustment. *Journal of Applied Developmental Psychology, 12*, 1–18.

McHale, S. M., & Huston, T. L. (1984). Men and women as parents: Sex role orientations, employment, and parental roles with infants. *Child Development, 55*, 1349–1361.

Miller, D. D., & Swanson, G. E. (1958). *The changing American parent: A study in the Detroit area.* New York: Wiley.

Miller, T. I. (1984). The effects of employer-sponsored child care on employee absenteeism, turnover, productivity, recruitment or job satisfaction: What is claimed and what is known. *Personnel Psychology, 37*, 277–289.

Moen, P. (1982). The two-provider family: Problems and potentials. In M. E. Lamb (Ed.), *Nontraditional families: Parenting and child development* (pp. 13–44). Hillsdale, NJ: Lawrence Erlbaum Associates.

Montemayor, R. (1984). Maternal employment and adolescents' relations with parents siblings and peers. *Journal of Youth and Adolescence, 13*, 543–557.

Ogbu, J. U. (1981). Origins of human competence: A cultural-ecological perspective. *Child Development, 52*(2), 413–429.

Owen, M. T., Easterbrooks, M. A., Chase-Lansdale, L., & Goldberg, W. A. (1984). The relation between maternal employment status and the stability of attachments to mother and to father. *Child Development, 55*, 1894–1901.

Patterson, G. R. (1980). Mothers: The unacknowledged victims. *Monographs of the Society for Research in Child Development, 45*(5, Serial No. 186).

Patterson, G. R., & Stouthamer-Loeber, M. (1984). The correlation of family management practices and delinquency. *Child Development, 55*, 1299–1302.

Pedersen, F., Cain, R., Zaslow, M., & Anderson, B. (1982). Variation in infant experience associated with alternative family roles. In L. M. Laosa & I. E. Sigel (Eds.), *Families as learning environments for children* (pp. 203–221). New York: Plenum.

Pleck, J. (1983). Husbands' paid work and family roles: Current research issues: In H. Lopata & J. H. Pleck (Eds.), *Research in the interweave of social roles: Vol. 3. Families and jobs* (pp. 251–333). Greenwich, CT: JAI Press.

Repetti, R. (1987). Individual and common components of the social environment at work and psychological well-being. *Journal of Personality and Social Psychology, 52*, 710–720.

Repetti, R. (1989a). Effects of daily workload on subsequent behavior during marital interaction: The roles of social withdrawal and spouse support. *Journal of Personality and Social Psychology, 57*, 651–659.

Repetti, R. (1989b, April). *Daily job stress and father–child interaction.* Paper presented at the biennial meeting of the Society for Research in Child Development, Kansas City, MO.

Reese, A. N., & Palmer, F. H. (1970). Factors related to change in mental test performance. *Developmental Psychology Monograph, 3.*

Robinson, J. (1977). *How Americans use time: A social-psychological analysis.* New York: Praeger.

Rodman, H., Pratto, D., & Nelson, R. (1985). Child-care arrangements and children's functioning: A comparison of self-care and adult-care children. *Developmental Psychology, 21*, 413–418.

Small, S. A. (1988). Parental self-esteem and its relationship to childrearing practices, parent-adolescent interaction, and adolescent behavior. *Journal of Marriage and the Family, 50*, 1063–1072.

Steinberg, L. (1986). Latchkey children and susceptibility to peer pressure: An ecological analysis. *Developmental Psychology, 22*, 433–439.

Steinberg, L., Elmen, J. D., & Mounts, N. S. (1989). Authoritative parenting, psychosocial maturity, and academic success among adolescents. *Child Development, 60*(6), 1424–1436.

Stocker, C., & McHale, S. M. (1992). The nature and family correlates of preadolescents' perceptions of their sibling relationships. *Journal of Social and Personal Relationships*, *9*, 179–195.

Waller, W. W. (1938). *The family: A dynamic interpretation*. New York: Cordon.

Weinraub, M., Jaeger, E., & Hoffman, L. W. (1988). Predicting infant outcomes in families with employed and nonemployed mothers. *Early Childhood Research Quarterly*, *3*, 361–378.

Wells, A. J. (1988). Variations in mothers' self-esteem in daily life. *Journal of Personality and Social Psychology*, *55*(4), 661–668.

Zaslow, M., Pedersen, F., Suwalsky, J., Rabinovitch, B., & Cain, R. L. (1985, April). *Fathering during the infancy period: The implications of the mother's employment role.* Paper presented at the biennial meeting of the Society for Research in Child Development, Toronto, Canada.

Chapter 8

Neighborhood and Community Influences on Parenting

James Garbarino
Kathleen Kostelny
Erikson Institute for Advanced Study in Child Development, Chicago

In this chapter, we argue that all poverty is not alike in its impact on families. Some conditions of poverty are worse than others, and these conditions exist within the United States today. Using a systems approach (Bronfenbrenner, 1979, 1986; Garbarino et al., 1992), we examine the ways in which conditions within impoverished communities—many of which are external to the family unit—shape the lives of families within those communities.

The chapter is divided into three major sections. First, we consider the impact living in an impoverished community has on parenting. To understand the complex ways in which conditions of poverty affect families, we present our two-fold concept of risk, which considers high absolute rates of risk factors relative to national norms and high actual incidence of risk factors relative to predicted rates based on local socioeconomic and demographic factors. We provide evidence that illustrates the utility of using this analysis of risk factors for understanding the impact of local conditions of poverty on parenting. Second, we discuss the challenge of life in high-risk communities for parents and for institutions within those communities. What strategies do parents use to protect their children from the negative forces within those communities? What factors within high-risk communities can attenuate the stress on families? Finally, we conclude by examining current conditions in the United States that have created or could potentially create high-risk communities for child-rearing.

PARENTING AND THE CONCENTRATION
OF POVERTY

In the United States, the increasing concentration of high-risk families in a geographically concentrated *underclass* is exerting dramatic influences on the needs and the competence of many parents (Lemann, 1986; Wilson, 1987). In Cleveland, for example, the proportion of poor people living in neighborhoods in which at least 40% of the population is poor has risen dramatically since the 1970s: 21% in 1970; 49% in 1988 (Coulton & Pandey, 1992).

This increasing concentration of poor families is relevant to parenting because it represents a decline in the proportionate availability of individuals who are "free from drain" (Collins & Pancoast, 1976) and a proportionate increase on a neighborhood level of "needy" parents. What is more, whereas in the 1970s, 37 out of 100 people who were poor moved out of poverty within a year, by the 1980s that figure was only 23 out of 100 (Bane & Ellwood, 1989).

Looking over the 10-year period from 1969 to 1979 (basically good times for the nation as a whole), roughly 25% of families slipped below the poverty line at least once, whereas about 3% (mainly African-American, one-parent households headed by women) remained below that level continuously (Duncan, Coe, & Hill, 1981). Since 1979, economic polarization has worsened. The lowest 20% of the income distribution lost 10% of its income whereas the upper 20% increased its income by 16%. Child poverty grew by more than 25% during the same period. The social concern of the 1980s focused attention on the underclass, the chronically poor, clustered as they increasingly are in homogeneous neighborhoods and communities.

Although chronic impoverishment poses a serious threat to child welfare, so does acute, episodic impoverishment—the much more common variety in our system. Many projections lead to the expectation that poverty will persist for one in four young children, particularly in single-parent households, unless there is some dramatic change in demography, policy, and/or the structure of the economy (Garbarino, 1992). These projections reflect the fact that the experience of single parenthood—a major correlate if not a direct cause of poverty—is expected to continue as a feature of life for one in two children at some point in their first 18 years of life. It also reflects the expectation that outbreaks of unemployment will continue, above and beyond the chronic unemployment and underemployment characterizing the inner-city underclass.

There is considerable debate about the exact processes that translate unemployment into a threat to parenting, but there is consensus that acute economic deprivation represents a challenge to the coping resources of individuals, families, and communities (Fisher & Cunningham, 1982). The connection between unemployment and developmental crisis is mainly indirect, but it is real nonetheless. Unemployment tends to diminish resources and precipitate problems in mental health and welfare through effects on parents. Male identity and parental status have traditionally been tied to occupational position. Unemployment diminishes that identity and gives rise to ambiguity or even outright conflict in the family.

This psychic threat is compounded by the fact that employment is the principal source of basic health and welfare services. Unemployment thus precipitates crises in both the psychic and the fiscal economy of the family. Both increase the likelihood of risky conditions for children and decrease the likelihood that such risky conditions will be observed and attended to effectively. This is particularly important for workers in financially marginal employment, where reserves are minimal or nonexistent—"one paycheck away from disaster" as they are often described.

One source of concern is the growing recognition that there has been a steady increase in the politically tolerable level of normal unemployment—from 4% in the 1960s to 7% in the 1980s. It may go higher, and already is in fact higher due to methods of public accounting that do not include those too discouraged to seek work, and others who are not fully employed. As recessions occur, they produce double digit levels of unemployment (i.e., 10% or more), with localized hotspots in excess of 20%. These deteriorating economic conditions, characterized by increases in the number of parents falling below the poverty level, are a major force driving the human ecology of parenthood. And, they increasingly produce neighborhoods with highly concentrated pockets of poverty as socioeconomic and geographic polarization proceed.

These neighborhoods with pockets of marked vulnerability show child abuse and infant mortality rates many times the average found in unafflicted communities. In Chicago, for example, the rate of child abuse in the poorest neighborhoods of the city is four times what it is in more affluent areas, and for infant mortality the rate is higher by a factor of five (Gabarino et al., 1992).

In this section, we discuss research on infant mortality and child maltreatment. Our focus in both instances is on understanding why communities with similar socioeconomic and demographic profiles may differ with respect to the actual risk experienced by families within those communities.

A Case Study: Community Influences on Infant Mortality

In the United States, death in the first year of life brings development to an abrupt halt for more than 40,000 children annually. Aside from merely recording deaths, infant mortality rates are useful indicators of the quality of prenatal and perinatal care for infants, and may be seen as indirect indices of potential developmental disabilities, a community's infant health, and the level of child abuse and neglect in a community (Gabarino et al., 1992). In short, infant mortality is one of several social indicators of the conditions of life for families, and as such is an important measure of the conditions of parenthood.

Although primary risk factors, such as low birthweight, and secondary risk factors, such as young maternal age, affect an infant's chance of survival, tertiary risk factors, such as access to health services, reflect community level influences. Mortality due to low birthweight reflects preexisting biological conditions of the mother, inadequate prenatal medical care, adverse physiological changes, and social deprivation. All are linked to the quality of the mother's social environment, which in turn plays a crucial role in determining infant mortality. Similarly, infant mortality is associated with teen-age pregnancies. Teen mothers experience higher levels of socioeconomic stress, such as incomplete education and reduced levels of economic well being, which are critical risk factors for infant mortality.

Two Meanings of Risk.   Although the infant mortality rate in the United States in 1986 was estimated at 10.4 per 1,000 live births, a wide variation is found across communities. Among Chicago's 77 communities, infant mortality rates vary dramatically—in 1985, they ranged from 0 to 79.0, with an overall rate of 16.5 (11.3 for White infants and 22.4 for Black infants). Some of the variance in local infant mortality rates can be explained by the variance in local rates of risk factors. In some Chicago communities, low birthweight rates were as high as 19% in 1985 (compared to 6.8% nationally), and some community areas had rates that exceeded 40% for births to teen-age mothers (compared to 12.8% nationally). These disturbing figures point to the need for an analysis designed to illuminate the origins and correlates of communities as high-risk environments for infants.

Obviously, risk is more than simply the sum of infant mortality rates. Our previous research has generated a model that incorporates two meanings of risk (Garbarino, 1987; Garbarino & Crouter, 1978a; Garbarino & Kostelny, 1992; Garbarino & Sherman, 1980). In identifying high- and low-risk areas for child maltreatment, the model looked not only at absolute rates based on actual incidence in a given population, but also at rates that were higher or lower than would be expected in the context of what is known about a community's socioeconomic and demographic constitution.

For example, two communities might have the same actual child maltreatment rate. One community however, might be labeled *high risk* because its rate exceeded what it should be given its socioeconomic and demographic characteristics. In contrast, the other would be labeled *low risk* because its rate was lower than what would be expected, given its socioeconomic and demographic profile.

Building on this model, our analysis examined the socioeconomic and demographic factors of communities, the stability of communities as social environments for childbearing, and community level factors as possible explanations for different patterns of infant mortality. Actual infant mortality rates were tabulated for Chicago's 77 community areas for each year during the period

1980 to 1985 and assigned to one of three categories for each year: low actual risk (infant mortality rates at or below the national average); average actual risk (rates that ranged from above the national average up to and including the average for Chicago); and high actual risk (rates that were above the average for Chicago). Not surprisingly, we found a strong correlation between economically impoverished communities and high rates of infant mortality.

Predicted infant mortality rates for each community were also computed using a multiple regression analysis with nine socioeconomic and demographic variables. Communities were then assigned to low, average, or high predicted risk categories (see Table 8.1).

Trends for infant mortality rates throughout this 6-year period were analyzed for stability. For communities with infant mortality rates not explained by socioeconomic and demographic factors, rates of low birthweight and births to teen mothers were examined.

For example, two adjacent communities, Avalon Park and Burnside, have similar socioeconomic and demographic variables (e.g., 88%–96% African-American, 32%–40% female-headed homes, 10%–15% below poverty level) and fall into the high actual risk category (i.e., rates above the Chicago average). However, Avalon Park has infant mortality rates placing it in the lower than predicted risk category, whereas Burnside is in the higher than predicted risk group. Thus, although both communities have some of the highest infant mortality rates in the city, Avalon Park's rate should be higher, and Burnside's should be lower. Both deviations from the predicted range may be attributed to the pattern of rates of births to teenage mothers, with lower than predicted rates in Avalon Park and higher than predicted rates in Burnside.

Four of the 77 communities were not explained either by socioeconomic and demographic variables or the additional factors of low birthweight and births to teens. In these neighborhoods, idiosyncratic community factors were examined. Two of these communities, Belmont Cragin and Chicago Lawn, were in the lower than predicted risk category, and two communities, West Elsdon and Grand Boulevard, were in the higher than predicted risk category.

Our results found that Belmont Cragin's low infant mortality rates were correlated with a high participation rate in the community's prenatal class,

TABLE 8.1
Risk Categories for Infant Mortality

	Low Risk	Average	High Risk
1980	< 12.6	12.6–20.7	> 20.7
1981	< 11.9	11.9–18.0	> 18.9
1982	< 11.5	11.5–18.6	> 18.6
1983	< 11.2	11.2–17.6	> 17.6
1984	< 10.7	10.7–16.4	> 16.4
1985	< 10.6	10.6–16.5	> 16.5

with over 90% of the mothers delivering at the community hospital attending classes.

Although the two communities of Chicago Lawn and West Elsdon are geographically contingent and show similar socioeconomic and demographic characteristics they exhibit very different profiles in terms of infant mortality, births to teen-agers, and low birthweight infants.

Chicago Lawn had lower than expected infant mortality rates, and like Belmont Cragin, the utilization of parenting education and support programs by new mothers was a community level factor. West Elsdon had infant mortality rates that were higher than expected despite lower than predicted rates of births to teens and low birthweight infants. In this community, the only hospital in the area closed in 1975 and was never replaced, one presumed effect of which is a lack of prenatal care and parent educational programs. This, in contrast with the situation in Belmont Cragin and Chicago Lawn, strongly suggests that we are observing the effect of negative institutional policy and practice at work in the social environment for childbearing.

The other high-risk community with higher than predicted infant mortality rates, Grand Boulevard, was the only community in this study that had both one of the city's highest actual rates (ranging from 21.5 to 32.8 over this 6-year period) as well as rates that were even higher than would be predicted for such an impoverished community. In Grand Boulevard, 51.4% of the population live below the poverty level, 24.2% are unemployed, and 71.1% of families are headed by a single female.

The unexplained infant mortality may be attributed to a social environment that has deteriorated even further than the already sad socioeconomic and demographic data indicate. Informal observations and discussions with expert informants tend to support this view. Overall, our study of community influences on infant mortality serves to illustrate the nature of the ecological conspiracy that afflicts many parents—most notably high-risk parents living in high-risk environments.

In short, specific conditions (e.g., community prenatal classes) within some impoverished communities strengthen and support parents so that the actual risk of infant mortality is reduced. But, in contrast, conditions within other poor communities (e.g., hospital closings) exacerbate the problems faced by parents and increase the risk for children.

Case Study: Child Maltreatment as a Community Problem

A second illustration of our belief that specific local conditions can influence the consequences of poverty on childrearing comes from the child abuse literature. In addition to the well-established connection between poverty and infant mortality, researchers have identified a link between economic deprivation and child maltreatment. Child maltreatment is one of the crucial indicators of parenting and family functioning (Garbarino & Crouter, 1978a; Garbarino & Sherman, 1980; NCCAN, 1981; Pelton, 1978; Steinberg, Catalano, & Dooley, 1981).

Briefly, these studies report a correlation between low income and the risk for child maltreatment on both the individual and community level. Thus, the rate of child abuse and neglect computed as part of the federally financed National Incidence Study, which dealt with many of the issues of class-biased reporting, ranges from 27.3 per 1,000 children among families with 1979 incomes of under $7,000, to 14.6 per 1,000 for families in the $15,000 to $24,999 range, and 2.7 per 1,000 for families with annual incomes in excess of $25,000 (NCCAN, 1981). Our own studies of the links between social and economic impoverishment and child maltreatment provide an appropriate conclusion to our analysis of the ecology of parenting.

Child maltreatment takes place in a social as well as psychological and cultural context. Prevention, treatment, and research should incorporate this contextual orientation (Garbarino et al., 1980). This means examining high-risk communities as well as high-risk families as the context for child maltreatment (Garbarino & Gilliam, 1980).

Our previous research has sought to explore and validate the concept of social impoverishment as a characteristic of high-risk family environments, and as a factor in evaluating support and prevention programs aimed at child maltreatment. The starting point was identifying the environmental correlates of child maltreatment that provided an empirical basis for screening neighborhoods to identify high- and low-risk areas (Garbarino, 1976; Garbarino & Crouter, 1978b).

As noted earlier in our infant mortality study, two meanings of high risk exist—the first meaning refers to areas with a high absolute rate of child maltreatment and the second definition means that an area has a higher rate of child maltreatment than would be predicted knowing its socioeconomic character.

In Fig. 8.1, Areas A and B have high actual observed rates of child maltreatment (36 per 1,000 and 34 per 1,000, respectively). Areas C and D have lower actual rates (16 per 1,000 and 13 per 1,000). However, Areas A and C have higher actual observed rates than would be predicted (10 per 1,000 predicted for A; 7 per 1,000 for C), and Areas B and D have lower actual observed than predicted rates (55 per 1,000 for B and 54 per 1,000 for D). In this sense, A and C are both high risk and B and D are both low risk. Areas E and F evidence a close approximation between predicted and actual rates. As we see here, this classification system can provide the basis for identifying contrasting social environments.

What do low- and high-risk social environments look like? Addressing this question involves examining a pair of real neighborhoods with the same predicted but different observed rates of child maltreatment (i.e., one high risk and

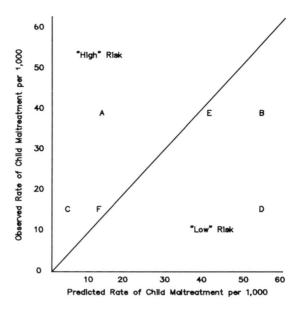

FIG. 8.1.   Two meanings of "risk" in assessing community areas.

the other low risk for child maltreatment). This permits a test of the hypothesis that two such neighborhoods present contrasting environments for child-rearing.

In an earlier study we confirmed this hypothesis: Relative to the low-risk area, and even though it was socioeconomically equivalent, the high-risk neighborhood was found to represent a socially impoverished human ecology (Garbarino & Sherman, 1980). It had less positive neighboring and more stressful day-to-day interactions for families. Our recent study of four Chicago communities illuminates this further (Garbarino & Kostelny, 1992). Two predominantly African-American communities with similar socioeconomic and demographic characteristics, and two communities with substantial Hispanic populations, also socioeconomically and demographically similar, were selected. Common prevention and family support programs operated across these communities.

Our initial analysis sought to replicate the earlier research documenting the role of socioeconomic and demographic factors in differentiating among neighborhoods. The results approximate the earlier studies (e.g., Garbarino & Crouter, 1978a). Much of the variation among community rates of child maltreatment is linked to variations in socioeconomic and demographic characteristics (with the multiple correlation being .89, thus accounting for 79% of the variation). Figure 8.2 presents these results by plotting actual and predicted rates of child maltreatment. North is Area 3, South is 4, West is 2, and East is 1.

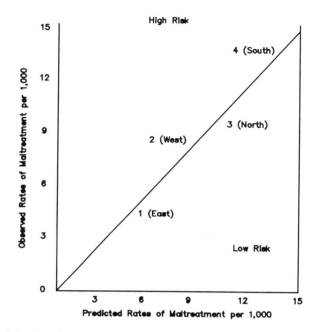

FIG. 8.2. Actual and predicted rates of maltreatment for four community areas.

We charted child maltreatment rates for the four community areas for the years 1980, 1983, and 1986, to observe trends over time. As Fig. 8.3 indicates, there is wide variation of child maltreatment rates in these four areas. In East and West, child maltreatment rates have been consistently below the city average during these 4 years. In contrast, in North and South, rates of child maltreatment have been consistently above the city average.

As a result of our initial statistical analyses, we undertook a small set of interviews to illuminate the important but elusive variable of community climate in the area North. To shed some light on this factor, we interviewed community leaders in North as a higher than predicted abuse rate community and West as a lower than predicted abuse community. We used a 12-item questionnaire based on prior research (Garbarino & Sherman, 1980).

Our hypothesis was that in the high abuse community we expected social service agencies would mirror the high social isolation of the families in the community, and conversely, that the low abuse community would have a strong, informal support network among the social service agencies. The results of the 14 interviews with community leaders supported this hypothesis. This is evident in a question-by-question analysis of the interviews.

The results of this small piece of the study suggest that there is a clear difference in the climate of these two communities. The strength of this difference

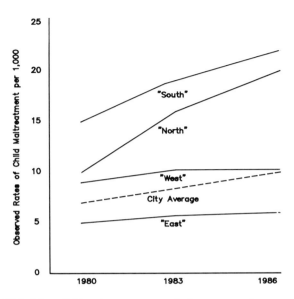

FIG. 8.3.   Child maltreatment rates in four community areas.

is perhaps best illustrated as follows: Jobs were mentioned as being of primary importance in both communities. However they were talked about very differently. In North, three respondents reported that it was important to remember that North had an 18% unemployment rate; in contrast, five of the West respondents described West as a community of the working poor. The consequences of these differences in employment are profound.

The general tone of the North visits was depressed; people had a hard time thinking of anything good to say about the situation. The physical spaces of the programs themselves seemed dark and depressed, and to a casual visitor the criminal activity was easily spotted. In West, people were eager to talk about their community. Although they listed serious problems, most of them felt that their community was a poor but decent place to live. "Poor but not hopeless" was the way one respondent described it. West subjects also reported drug and crime problems, but they were not apparent to the casual visitor.

In North, the subjects knew less about what other community services and agencies were available, and demonstrated little evidence of a network or support system, either formal or informal. In West, there are more services available, agencies know more about what is available and there are very strong formal and informal social support networks. The subjects in West also reported strong political leadership from the local state senator. The North subjects did not report positive feelings about their political leaders.

At least in terms of this study, it seems fair to say that the social service agencies in a community mirror the problems facing the community. In North, the leaders interviewed described a situation in which their agencies mirrored the isolation and depression of their community. In West, the agencies mirrored the strong informal support network that exists between families in their community. They seemed hopeful because many of their families were hopeful.

These interviews provide further indication of the serious difficulties facing North as a social system. The extremity of the negative features of the environment—poverty, violence, poor housing—seem to be matched by negative community climate—lack of community identity, and fragmented formal support system networks. Even clients of the leading agency identified in the social service provider interviews exhibit a general lack of community identification.

The final piece of evidence available to us in our analysis concerns child deaths due to maltreatment. Such child deaths are a particularly telling indicator of the bottom line in a community. There were 19 child maltreatment deaths reported for the four community areas we studied during the 1984–1987 period. Eight of these deaths occurred in North, a rate of 1 death for each 2,541 children. For West, the rate was 1 death for each 5,571 children. The fact that deaths due to child maltreatment were twice as likely in North seems consistent with the overall findings of our statistical analyses and interviews. This is an environment in which there is truly an ecological conspiracy against children (Garbarino et al., 1992).

The U.S. Advisory Board on Child Abuse and Neglect has concluded that our nation faces a child maltreatment emergency. Rates of child maltreatment continue to increase in many areas, and public agencies are pushed beyond their capacity to respond. The link between poverty and child maltreatment continues as a powerful feature of the problem. In the current socioeconomic climate in which poverty for families has been increasing, it is little wonder that the problem of child maltreatment is worsening in urban areas of concentrated poverty such as are included in our study.

Conditions of Poverty and Risk

In summary, both the research on infant mortality rates and the research on child maltreatment indicate that local community factors can work to attenuate or to increase the negative effects of poverty on families. Comparing communities with similar predicted rates of risk factors, but different actual rates can provide useful insights for the development of intervention strategies in high-risk neighborhoods.

LIVING IN HIGH-RISK COMMUNITIES

Given that high-risk communities exist in the United States today and are not likely to disappear in the near future, what do we know about the processes that parents and institutions within those communities employ to ameliorate the stressful situations for families? In this section, we examine the roles that parents take to protect their children from the negative aspects of high-risk communities. We discuss one developmental consequence of living in high-risk communities for children. Finally, we consider institutions within the communities and processes that occur at a community-level that can ameliorate some of the negative consequences of living in high-risk communities.

The Challenge to Parents:
Mediating Environmental Influences

One important feature of the ecology of parenting lies in the role of parents as mediators and buffers of stress for children. To a large degree, the impact of living in stressful neighborhoods and communities derives from the impact of that stress on parents, most notably on mothers. Children in the care of their parents or familiar parent substitutes can cope with stressful life circumstances if parents can maintain day-to-day care routines and project high morale.

This theme of parents as mediators of stress emerges from a recent study of safety issues for children in two Chicago communities to explore how mothers and their preschool children cope with danger (Dubrow & Garbarino, 1989). A structured interview was conducted with 20 mothers: 10 who live in a high-rise public housing development and 10 residents of a nearby community. Mothers were asked to name the most serious dangers faced by their children and to explore their feelings about their ability to control these dangers. Mothers were also asked to describe the awareness and knowledge their children had of these dangers, whether they believed their children were concerned about the dangers, and how these dangers affected their children's future.

Both samples were drawn from preschool programs in two community-based Head Start and day-care programs. Center coordinators selected mothers who had at least one child age 3 to 5 enrolled at the center, and who lived in the target community. Head Start eligibility based on federal income guidelines ensures approximate socioeconomic comparability.

In the public housing sample, all 10 mothers named shooting as the most serious danger for their children—all the children in this sample had experienced first-hand encounters with shooting by age 5.

In contrast to the housing development mothers, the nonhousing development mothers reported a perception of danger in keeping with U.S. parents generally—revealing concerns with kidnapping, drugs, and auto accidents. Despite their low-income status, the nonpublic housing mothers lived in a world more like mainstream United States than the isolated housing development parents.

The mothers living in public housing believed that their children were aware of the dangers, and described their children's behaviors demonstrating this belief. Although these mothers had ways of coping with the environment, they generally were not aware that they had developed these strategies. Mothers often employed the wise strategy that Anna Freud believed protected children from long-lasting harm in World War II: They stayed physically close to their children. It seems a natural bit of coping strategy for families under extreme stress (Garbarino, Kostelny, & Dubrow, 1991).

Neighborhoods and communities differ significantly (and dramatically) in the degree to which they challenge parents and children to cope with environmental violence. For example, in a survey dealing with another Chicago inner-city community, it was documented that by age 17, 30% of the children had witnessed a homicide (Bell, 1991). In Chicago the homicide rate for the first half of 1990 for the city as a whole was 29.6 per 100,000 at a time when the overall national rate was 9.7. Furthermore, the number of children under 10 who were killed in Chicago increased by 70% from 1988 to 1989. And, some communities have much more than their share of child victims. In a study of child homicide in Cook County, Cristoffel found that all child homicides occurred in only 22% of the county's census tracts. The homicide rate alone does not fully present the magnitude of the violence problem when viewed from an historical perspective, however. The homicide rate in Chicago in 1974 equaled the 1990 rate. The problem is worse now, however, because the current death rate is taking place in the context of dramatically improved medical trauma technology: Many of the victims of violence who died in 1974 would now live. Supporting evidence for the deteriorating condition is found in the fact that the rate of serious assaults in 1974 was 400 per 100,000, whereas in 1989 it was 1,254 per 100,000 (Fountain & Recktenwald, 1990).

Poor, inner-city, minority neighborhoods were the sites for most of these murders and serious assaults. Neighborhood variation in violent crime means that some children and their parents face environmental violence as a fact of day-to-day life, whereas for others it is a frightening, but generally remote, "news story."

Parental Adaptation to Violent Neighborhoods.   Children will continue to cope with difficult environments and maintain reservoirs of resilience as long as parents are not pushed beyond their "stress absorption capacity." Once that point is exceeded, however, the development of young children deteriorates rapidly and markedly. Reservoirs of resilience become depleted, infant mortality rates soar, day-to-day care breaks down, and rates of exploitation and victimization increase. Moral development itself may be compromised.

Parents forced to cope with chronic danger in their community may adapt in ways that are dysfunctional. The psychopathological dimensions of such adaptation are now widely recognized—most notably Post Traumatic Stress Disorder (PTSD). The social dimensions are equally worthy of attention, however. Parents may cope with danger by adopting a world view or persona that may

be dysfunctional in any normal situations in which they are expected to participate. Some adaptations to chronic danger, such as emotional withdrawal, may
be socially adaptive in the short run, but become a danger to the next generation, when their children become parents. This phenomenon has been observed
in studies of families of Holocaust survivors (Danieli, 1985) and in the parenting patterns of parents who were abused as children (Egeland & Farber, 1984;
Gelles & Lancaster, 1987).

Even in the absence of this intergenerational process, parental adaptations
to dangerous environments may produce childrearing strategies that impede
normal development, as in the case of a mother who does not allow her child
to play on the floor because there is poison on the floor to kill the rats that
infest the apartment, but who, in doing so, may deprive the child of important
opportunities for exploratory play. Likewise, the parent who prohibits the child
from playing outside for fear of shooting incidents may be denying the child
a chance to engage in social and athletic play, as an undesirable side effect
of protecting the child from assault.

Similarly, the fear felt by parents of children in high crime environments
may be manifest as a very restrictive and punitive style of discipline (including
physical assault) in an effort to protect the child from falling under the influence
of negative forces, such as gangs, in the neighborhood. Unfortunately, this
approach is likely to have the result of heightening aggression on the child's
part, with one consequence being a difficulty in succeeding in contexts that
provide alternatives to the gang culture, and endorsing an acceptance of violence as the modus operandi for social control, which in turn rationalizes the
gang's use of violence as the dominant tactic for social influence. Holding the
child back from negative forces through punitive restrictiveness is generally
much less successful as a strategy than expressing confidence in the child's capacities and promoting positive alternatives to the negative subculture feared
by the parent (Scheinfeld, 1983).

In all these examples, the parental adaptation is well intentioned and may
appear to be practically sensible, but its side effects may be detrimental in the
long run. The onus here is on the social forces that create and sustain danger
in the family's environment, thus forcing the parent to choose between the lesser
of two evils.

Developmental Consequences of High-Risk Neighborhoods

One of the consequences of living in a violent community is that the parent's
role in enhancing moral development is undermined. Advanced moral reasoning
seems to reflect the degree to which children are supported in engaging in issue-
focused discussions and social interactions. These interactions invoke the child's
emergent cognitive capacities and stimulate perspective taking and intellectual encounters with values and principles. Developmentalists have come to recog-

nize that it is the dynamic relationship between the child's competence and a guiding teacher that leads to forward movement, and is particularly important in the case of moral development. The key here is a process of *optimal discrepancy*, in which the child's moral teachers lead the child toward higher order thinking by presenting positions that are one stage above the child's characteristic mode of responding to social events as moral issues.

When all this happens in the context of a nurturant affective system—a warm family, for example—the result is ever-advancing moral development, the development of a principled ethic of caring (Gilligan, 1982). What is more, even if the parents create a rigid, noninteractive authoritarian family context, and thus block moral development, the larger community may compensate: ". . . the child of authoritarian parents may function in a larger, more democratic society whose varied patterns provide the requisite experiences for conceptualizing an egalitarian model of distributive justice" (Fields, 1987, p. 5).

However, this becomes problematic when we consider that only a minority of adults ever achieve the highest levels of moral reasoning in the Kohlberg system, or ego development in Loevinger's scheme. Thus, the issue of stimulating moral development beyond the lower levels becomes in large measure a social issue: Do adults in the community outside the family demonstrate the higher order moral reasoning necessary to move children from the lower to the higher stage (i.e., "rational/beneficial/utilitarian" and "principled")?

Situations of chronic danger can stimulate the process of moral development if they are matched by an interactive climate created by adults (and endorsed—or at least not stifled—by the larger culture through its political, educational, and religious institutions) and if the child is free of debilitating psychopathology. Families can provide the emotional context for the necessary processing to make positive moral sense of danger, and even trauma itself.

Communities must usually carry things to the next step (i.e., stimulating higher order moral development). They do this by presenting a democratic milieu (e.g., in schools). If school teachers and other adult representatives of the community are disinclined to model higher order moral reasoning or are intimidated if they try to do so, then the process of moral truncation that is natural to situations of violent conflict will proceed unimpeded. This appears to have happened in Northern Ireland, for example, as both Protestant and Catholic teachers learned that if they tried to engage their students in dialogue that could promote higher order moral reasoning they would be silenced by extremist elements (Conroy, 1987). The result is likely to be the "truncated" moral reasoning observed by Fields (1987), particularly among boys, who are more vulnerable to this consequence of living at risk as they are to most other risks (Werner, 1988). Community institutions are critical resources in this process.

The Challenge to Communities:
Attenuating the Debilitation of Poverty

Convergent findings from several studies of life course responses to stressful early experience suggest a series of ameliorating factors that lead to prosocial and healthy adaptability (Lösel, & Bliesener, 1990):

1. actively trying to cope with stress (rather than just reacting)
2. cognitive competence (at least an average level of intelligence)
3. experiences of self-efficacy and a corresponding self-confidence and positive self-esteem
4. temperamental characteristics that favor active coping attempts and positive relationships with others (e.g., activity, goal orientation, sociability) rather than passive withdrawal
5. a stable emotional relationship with at least one parent or other reference person
6. an open, supportive educational climate and parental model of behavior that encourages constructive coping with problems
7. social support from persons outside the family.

Several of these factors involve community and neighborhood factors, both directly and as mediators of parenting. Community factors influence whether or not parents adopt an "activist" ideology that provides philosophical, moral, spiritual, and political support for the kind of active coping that helps children develop and express resilience.

Community influences affect cognitive competence. They also affect the degree of support and guidance given to parents to become effective partners in the child's cognitive development.

What is more, communities can provide activities that offer experiences of self-efficacy for parents and for children. The Missouri Parents as Teachers program is such an effort. It seeks to involve and validate parents in active and developmentally enhancing relationships with their children from the first weeks of life. This both reduces the risk of developmental impairment to the child and bolsters resources for resilience.

For parenting to be successful in such high-risk ecological niches, parents must overcome powerful negative forces that include the depressive effects of living in chronic stress. Chicago's Center for Successful Child Development ("The Beethoven Project") is an effort to prevent developmental delays among an entire birth cohort in a public housing project (i.e., all the children born in 1 year who live in the same kindergarten catchment area).

The program provides home health visitors, early developmental screening, prenatal health care, parent education, job training for parents, infant day care, child abuse prevention programming, Head Start participation, and other transforming and supportive services (Barclay-McLaughlin, 1987). When such efforts are conducted in the context of thoughtful evaluation research they can serve as the kind of transforming experiments that advance an ecologically valid science of parenting (Bronfenbrenner, 1979).

Community influences are important also in providing the open, supportive educational climate that is itself a source of resilience for children. Communities can do much to set the tone and the context of individual parenting decisions. For example, the growing campaign to end corporal punishment (i.e., physical assault as discipline) in U.S. schools is driven by the belief that this will help shape the context for disciplinary practices in the home.

Finally, the informal nature of the community and neighborhood are, in a sense, defined by the social support from persons outside the family, which has been documented as an important facet of resilience for children.

Maintaining a Minimum Standard of Care. The challenge to high-risk communities is to create—both through formal support services and through informal neighborhood networking—an environment that helps to maintain the integrity of the family. Maintaining the minimum standard of care for young children in a society depends on how well that society is doing in sustaining the basic infrastructure of family life. There are three critical elements of this infrastructure: parent–child attachment, parental self-esteem and identity, and stability of routine caregiving arrangements (cf. Bronfenbrenner, 1986).

When we look at infant mortality rates, at rates of abandonment and exploitation of young children, and at the overall level of stress-related behavioral and developmental problems in children, we begin to see a common picture in communities around the world. If parents, particularly mothers in most cases, can sustain a strong attachment to their children, can maintain a positive sense of self, and can have access to rudimentary shelter, food, and medical care, then children will manage, although it may be at great cost to the psychic and physical welfare of those parents. Thus, in villages in the Sudan in which children were cared for by their mothers who themselves had access to food, fuel, water, and basic medicines, children appeared normal. This was true even in the midst of drought, true even as most fathers were absent for long periods from their villages to seek work in the cities. From a child's point of view, there was semblance of normality in day-to-day life, even in the midst of national crisis.

Environments that maintain a stable infrastructure under stress have a different impact from situations of acute disaster, in which there is a dramatic and overwhelming destruction of the infrastructure of daily life. Kai Erikson's study (1976) of an Appalachian community devastated by flood found young children who were confronted with vivid and concrete evidence of their vulnerability. Their homes were destroyed and their parents were demoralized and apparently socially powerless: "The major problem, for adults and children alike, is that the fears haunting them are prompted not only by the memory of past terrors but by a wholly realistic assessment of present dangers" (p. 238). When parents are emotionally and or spiritually incapacitated children rightly fear for their future.

The quality of life for young children—and their reservoirs of resilience— thus becomes a *social indicator* of the balance of social supports for parents and parental capacity to buffer social stress in the lives of children (Garbarino et al., 1992). This hypothesis emerges from a wide range of research and clinical observation. For example, in studies of World War II victims, researchers found that the level of emotional upset displayed by adults in a child's life, not the war situation itself, was the most important factor in predicting the child's response (Janis, 1951). That is, the impact of the war on children was a function of the "meaning" that parents assigned to the war for themselves and for their children.

Some observers argue that strong ideologies—strong, communally held beliefs or world views—can enhance adults' abilities to function under extreme stress. In his observations of life in Nazi concentration camps, Bettelheim (1943) noted that those who bore up best were those with intense ideological commitments (most notably the ultra-religious and the communists), commitments that offered meaning impervious to day-to-day brutalization.

Punamaki (1987) saw exactly this process at work in the case of Palestinians under Israeli occupation and in refugee camps, where every feature of day-to-day stress and physical deprivation is met with a process of ideological response that mobilizes social and psychological resources:

> . . . the psychological processes of healing the traumatic experiences drew strength from political and ideological commitment. Nationalist motivation was present at all stages of the stress process: The meaning and harmfulness of an event as well as sufficiency of one's own resources to cope with stressors were approached in the wider social and political context of a victimized and struggling nation. (pp. 82–83)

Punamaki's report goes beyond simple formulations of the "buffering model":

> Classical pronouncements that the mother functions as a buffer between traumas of war and the child's well-being assumes new dimensions when it is realized that it leads to an additional stress on the mother. The trend to concentrate on the mother's significance as the main determinate of their children's well-being, distorts our understanding of the psychological processes which are characteristic of a population exposed to political violence . . . the women's success in retaining their psychological integrity is related to their political and ideological commitment to the national struggle. (p. 83)

Such ideological issues exist for parents in U.S. neighborhoods and communities and tend to coalesce around shared economic situations.

To summarize, we argued that the negative physical and psychological consequences of living in high-risk neighborhoods are great for both parents and children. However, there are strategies that individual families, as well as communities, can utilize to cope with these problems and to minimize the negative developmental consequences to the children who are growing up in these high-risk areas.

CONCLUSION: HIGH-RISK COMMUNITIES IN THE UNITED STATES

Having argued that features within local communities can dramatically affect family life, we conclude with a discussion of why consideration of the effects of high-risk communities on parenting should be an urgent priority in the United States in the 1990s.

In reviewing the state of the nation during the 1970s, several blue-ribbon panels charged with the task of assessing risk to families deriving from the social environment identified economic deprivation as the principal villain (see, e.g., the National Academy of Sciences 1976, the Carnegie Corporation, Keniston, 1977). In the 1980s, these reports seem mild as the relative economic position of parents—particularly parents of young children—has deteriorated. Reversing the traditional pattern for the United States, in which poverty has been concentrated among the elderly, economic deprivation is now most common among families with young children. In 1985, for example, approximately 25% of U.S. children under the age of three were living in poverty, as compared with 13% of the general population, including the elderly (U.S. Census, 1980). For African-Americans and Hispanic Americans, the rates are even higher.

The kind of economic crisis of which the U.S. system is capable—a crisis described as probable by some economic forecasters—could mean an epidemic of threats to child welfare (Garbarino, 1992; Garbarino & Associates, 1992). This happened during the 1980s in unemployment hot spots around the country as child maltreatment rates followed climbing unemployment rates (and has not abated as the economic recovery evident in data averaged across the society obscures the fact that some communities and many neighborhoods were left behind).

In Oregon, for example, where a depressed lumber industry prompted double digit unemployment rates, officials reported a 46% increase in child maltreatment for 1981 (Birch, 1982). The resulting upsurge in the need for child welfare and other human services typically coincides with a diminished capacity of formal services to respond during troubled economic times. As an economic crisis unfolds, for example, it simultaneously increases the demand for state-supported services across the spectrum from health care to food stamps, and typically decreases the tax revenues available to finance such services.

A further disturbing trend is the finding that the economic recovery of the mid-1980s, with unemployment dipping below 7% in 1987, did not (and in all likelihood will not) reach the growing underclass, where unemployment, poverty, and demographic adversity are becoming ever more entrenched and chronic (Wilson, 1987).

Although most industrialized societies support parents by entitling all families to maternal and infant health care and basic child support subsidies, ours does not (Kahn & Kammerman, 1975; Kammerman & Kahn, 1976; Miller, 1987). Although the federal budget includes a substantial commitment to entitlement programs, five-sixths goes to programs that disproportionately assist affluent adults, whereas relatively little goes to families in the service of child welfare-related objectives (Fallows, 1982).

As noted by Bronfenbrenner (1986), this may explain why correlations between measures of income or socioeconomic status and basic child outcomes are often higher in the United States than in other modern societies. That is, low income is a better predictor of deficits in the United States than in other countries because our social policies tend to exaggerate rather than minimize the impact of family income on access to preventive and rehabilitative services.

The phenomenology of poverty is dominated by the experience of deprivation, and exacerbated by widespread promulgation of highly monetarized affluence as the standard. Low paying jobs can come to be interpreted as an affront in such a context; the accoutrements of affluence a right. None of this contributes to the well-being of young children—all of it sustains rage and despair among parents. Add to this the geographic concentration of economically marginal families as communities become more homogeneous (e.g., through clustering public housing), and the developmental effects on parenting—and thus on children—are profoundly disturbing.

Children become the incidental and deliberate targets of concentrated and often unmitigated rage and despair, in the form of neglect and abuse. Children cost too much when their caregivers cannot generate enough income to meet popular expectations for participating in the monetarized economy of day-to-day life.

In a nation where everything costs money and continues to cost more, most families need two incomes to keep up, although because of divorce and single-parenthood more and more families have only one potential wage earner. This was not the case at the outset of the economic depression of the 1930s, when most families with children contained two adults, and wives represented a largely untapped resource that could be and was mobilized to generate cash-income in response to the unemployment and income loss experienced by male workers (Elder, 1974). Now, this resource has already been tapped to meet basic family expenses, and therefore does not represent a reserve in the sense that it did in the 1930s.

Currently, employed wives earn on average about 60% of what their husbands do per hour, and in all contribute 26% of total family income (U.S. Department of Labor, 1981). Furthermore, children are increasingly an economic burden, directly because of what it costs to raise them and indirectly because of what they "cost" in lost parental income (i.e., time away from the job that over a childhood comes to tens of thousands if not hundreds of thousands of dollars).

The politics of risk and opportunity for parents in the 1990s portend a long series of battles pitting the basic well-being of some children and their families against the affluence of others. The politics of choosing between those two thrusts will intensify as they become more clearly mutually competitive. The internal situation in the United States will thus mirror the global choices to be made between more luxuries for the "haves" versus more necessities for the "have nots." According to the Bureau of Labor Statistics, in 1982 for a family of four to live at a high level required about $38,000, and to live at a lower (struggling) level required about $15,000.

Should the goal of policy be to bring as many families up to $15,000 as possible or to enhance the prospects of those who have reached the $38,000 level? The former goal is much more germane to early intervention and the prevention of developmental risks; the latter may be more in keeping with the spirit of the time.

Economic issues play a very large role in the dynamics of early risk. Family structure and activities interact with the parents' participation in the workforce. Culture provides a context for this. To the degree to which the community's day-to-day life is monetarized, families will be drawn or driven into the cash economy. If the institutional structure of the community (local government, philanthropic institutions, etc.) remains aloof from this process, those who cannot generate sufficient cash income to participate in basic activities will become even poorer. Impoverished microsystems will begin to form systematic patterns of deprivation—family, school, and social networks will reinforce developmental delay and deviant socialization.

We see this played out in the human ecology of infant mortality and child maltreatment, particularly in socially impoverished urban areas where the entire human ecology seems to operate in a concerted attack upon the foundations for successful child development. In this sense, the underclass represents a kind of ecological conspiracy against children.

The greatest risks come when families lack the financial resources to purchase support services in the market place and are cut off from the informal helping relationships. It is when monetarized and nonmonetarized economy are both impoverished, however, that child maltreatment and infant mortality flourish, and the challenges to early intervention are greatest (Garbarino et al., 1980).

This is seen most clearly in the urban underclass that has become the focal point for emergency intervention. Marginal or submarginal economic resources interact with diminished psychosocial resources born of violence, academic failure, exploitation, despair, fear, and deteriorated community infrastructure. In such environments most women experience their first pregnancy while still an unmarried teen-ager, living with very little prospect of economic self-sufficiency or two-parent family status. Many of these pregnancies result from sexual exploitations by much older men (Ounce of Prevention Fund, 1987).

These are the environments in which prenatal care is inadequate, intervals between births are often too small, beliefs about child care too often dysfunctional, access to and utilization of well baby care inadequate, early intervention for child disabilities insufficient, and thus in which child mortality and morbidity are rampant.

Parents both shape their social surroundings and are shaped by them. This interactive process can enhance or undermine family functioning (Garbarino, 1977; Martin, 1976). More systematic efforts to study and serve families in context can enrich research and intervention, both preventive and rehabilitative. For many practical purposes, this means examining high-risk neighborhoods as well as high-risk families (see Garbarino & Sherman, 1980; Sattin & Miller, 1971).

In the Middle Ages, half the children died by age 5. Now, child death is relatively rare; the nature of parenting has changed. As standards and expectations for the care and life prospects of children have improved in the last century, developmental risk has become a focal point for research and policy. Thus, parental focus has shifted from sheer quantitative concern with child survival to a qualitative concern with development. This is a major accomplishment.

This chapter has explored the sources of supports and stresses for parents that derive from the character of neighborhood and community influences. The challenge is both intellectual and "spiritual." The intellectual challenge is to insist upon analytic models that are ecologically valid—that is, that incorporate (or at least address) the full range of influences upon parents and thus children, from the organismic to the macrosocial.

This strains our intellectual resources to their limits, and sometimes beyond. The spiritual challenge is to refuse to despair when faced with the ecological conspiracies that envelop parents and children in high-risk social environments, in neighborhoods and communities in which parental synergy is negative rather than positive.

REFERENCES

Barclay-McLaughlin, G. (1987). The Center for Successful Child Development, The Ounce of Prevention Fund, Chicago, IL.

Bane, M. J., & Ellwood, D. (1989). One fifth of the nation's children: Why are they poor? *Science*, *245*, 1047–1053.

Bell, C. (1991). Traumatic stress and children in danger. *Journal of Health Care for the Poor and Underserved*, *2*, 175–188.

Bettelheim, B. (1943). Individual and mass behavior in extreme situations. *Journal of Abnormal and Social Psychology*, *38*, 417–452.

Bronfenbrenner, U. (1979). *The ecology of human development: Experiments by nature and design*. Cambridge: Harvard University Press.

Bronfenbrenner, U. (1986). Ecology of the family as a context for human development research perspectives. *Developmental Psychology*, *22*, 6, 723–742.

Birch, T. (1982, May 25). *Memo on child abuse and neglect*. Washington, DC: National Child Abuse Coalition.

Collins, A., & Pancoast, D. (1976). *Natural helping networks*. Washington, DC: National Association of Social Workers.

Conroy, J. (1987). *Belfast diary*. Boston: Beacon Press.

Coulton, C., & Pandey, S. (1992). Geographic concentrations of poverty and risks to children in urban neighborhoods. *American Behavioral Scientist*, *35*, 238–257.

Danieli, Y. (1985). The treatment and prevention of long-term effects and intergenerational transmission of victimization: A lesson from holocaust survivors and their children. In C. R. Figley (Ed.), *Trauma and its wake*. New York: Bruner/Mazel.

Dubrow, N., & Garbarino, J. (1989). *Living in the war zone: mothers and children in public housing developments. Child Welfare*, *68*(1).

Duncan, G., Coe, R., & Hill, M. (1981). *The dynamics of poverty*. Ann Arbor, MI: University of Michigan.

Egeland, B., & Farber, E. (1984). Infant–mother attachment: Factors related to its development and changes over time. *Child Development*, *55*, 753–771.

Elder, G. H. (1974). *Children of the great depression*. Chicago: University of Chicago Press.

Erikson, K. (1976). *Everything in its path: Destruction of community in the Buffalo Creek flood*. New York: Simon & Schuster.

Fallows, J. (1982). Entitlements. *The Atlantic Monthly*, *250*, 51ff.

Fields, R. (1987, October). *Terrorized into terrorist: Sequelae of PTSD in young victims*. Paper presented at the meeting of the Society for Traumatic Stress Studies, New York.

Fisher, K., & Cunningham, S. (1983). The dilemma: Problem grows, support shrinks. *APA Monitor*, *14*, 2.

Fountain, J., & Recktenwald, W. (1990, September 24). One youth's death sums up '90 summer. *Chicago Tribune*, p. 1.

Garbarino, J. (1976). A preliminary study of some ecological correlates of child abuse: the impact of socioeconomic stress on mothers. *Child Development*, *47*, 178–185.

Garbarino, J. (1977). The human ecology of child maltreatment: A conceptual model for research. *Journal of Marriage and the Family*, *39*, 721–736.

Garbarino, J. (1992). *Toward a sustainable society*. Chicago: The Noble Press.

Garbarino, J., Abramowitz, R., Benn, J., Gaboury, M., Galambos, N., Garbarino, A., Kostelny, K., Long, F., & Planz, M. (1992). *Children and families in the social environment* (2nd ed.). New York: Aldine.

Garbarino, J., & Crouter, A. (1978a). Defining the community context of parent–child relations. *Child Development*, *49*, 604–616.

Garbarino, J., & Crouter, A. (1978b). A note on assessing the construct validity of child maltreatment report data. *American Journal of Public Health*, *68*, 598–599.

Garbarino, J., & Gilliam, G. (1980). *Understanding abusive families*. Lexington, MA: Lexington Books.

Garbarino, J., & Kostelny, K. (1992). Child maltreatment as a community problem. *Child Abuse and Neglect*, *16*(4), 455–464.

Garbarino, J., Kostelny, K., & Dubrow, N. (1991). *No place to be a child: Growing up in a war zone.* New York: Lexington Books.

Garbarino, J., & Sherman, D. (1980). High risk neighborhoods and high risk families: The human ecology of child maltreatment. *Child Development, 51,* 188–198.

Garbarino, J., Stocking, S. H., Collins, A., Gottlieb, B., Olds, D., Pancoast, D., Sherman, D., Tietjen, A., & Warren, D. (Eds.). (1980). *Protecting children from abuse and neglect.* San Francisco: Jossey-Bass.

Gelles, R., & Lancaster, J. (1987). *Child abuse and neglect: Biosocial dimension.* New York: Aldine De Gruyter.

Gilligan, C. (1982). *In a different voice.* Cambridge, MA: Harvard University Press.

Janis, I. (1951). *Air war and emotional stress.* New York: McGraw-Hill.

Kahn, A., & Kamerman, S. (1975). *Not for the poor alone: European social services.* Philadelphia: Temple University Press.

Kamerman, S., & Kahn, A. (1976). *Social services in the United States: policies and programs.* Philadelphia: Temple University Press.

Keniston, K. (1977). *All our children.* New York: Harcourt, Brace, Jovanovich.

Lemann, N. (1986). The origins of the underclass. *Atlantic, 257,* 31–61.

Lösel, F., & Bliesener, T. (1990). Resilience in adolescence: A study on the generalizability of protective factors. In K. Hurrelmann & F. Lösel (Eds.), *Health hazards in adolescence* (pp. 299–320). New York: Walter de Gruyter.

Miller, A. (1987). *Maternal health and infant survival.* Washington, DC: National Center for Clinical Infant Programs.

Martin, H. (Ed.). (1976). *The abused child: A multidisciplinary approach to developmental issues and treatment.* Cambridge, MA: Ballinger.

National Academy of Sciences. (1976). *Towards a national policy for children and families.* Washington, DC: U.S. Government Printing Office.

National Center on Child Abuse and Neglect. (1981). *The National Incidence Study of child abuse and neglect: Report of findings.* Washington, DC: National Center on Child Abuse and Neglect.

Pelton, L. (1978). The myth of classlessness in child abuse cases. *American Journal of Orthopsychiatry, 48,* 569–579.

Punamaki, R. (1987). Psychological stress responses of Palestinian mothers and their children in conditions of military occupation and political violence. *Quarterly Newsletter of the Laboratory of Comparative Human Cognition, 9*(2), 76–84.

Sattin, D., & Miller, J. (1971). The ecology of child abuse. *American Journal of Orthopsychiatry, 41,* 413–425.

Scheinfeld, D. (1983). Family relationships and school achievement among boys of lower-income urban Black families. *American Journal of Orthopsychiatry, 53*(1), 127–143.

Steinberg, L., Catalano, R., & Dooley, D. (1981). Economic antecedents of child abuse and neglect. *Child Development, 52,* 975–985.

United States Bureau of the Census. (1980). *Money, income and poverty studies of families and persons in the United States* (Current population reports, series P-60, No. 127). Washington, DC: Author.

United States Department of Labor. (1981, March 25). *New income levels defining poverty* (pp. 81–156). Washington, DC: Author.

Werner, E. (1988). Individual differences, universal needs: A 30-year study of resilient high risk infants. *Zero to three, 8*(4), 1–5.

Wilson, W. (1987). *The truly disadvantaged: The inner city, the underclass, and public policy.* Chicago: The University of Chicago Press.

Chapter 9

Multiple Influences on Parenting: Ecological and Life-Course Perspectives

Tom Luster
Michigan State University

Lynn Okagaki
Purdue University

The various chapters in this volume provide support for the view that parenting behavior is multiply determined. Characteristics of the parent, of the child, and of the context in which the parent–child relationship is evolving contribute to differences among parents in their approaches to childrearing. Consequently, it stands to reason that our understanding of parenting behavior will be enhanced if we consider the combined influence of several factors rather than thinking about each factor singly. In addition, it is evident that there are many linkages among the various influences on parenting discussed in this volume. For example, characteristics of the parents, such as personality characteristics, influence contextual factors such as social networks and marital relationships. Likewise, contextual factors, such as the workplace, influence characteristics of the parent (e.g., psychological well-being, values). Therefore, to understand parental behavior at the present time, it is also important to consider the relation between characteristics of the parent and characteristics of the context over time.

The purpose of this chapter is to review illustrative studies that demonstrated the value of examining several potential influences in the same study. We discuss five ways in which studies examining multiple influences at one point in time, or over time, contributed to our understanding of parental behavior. The most obvious reason for examining several potential influences in the same study is that the effects of the various influences on parenting may be additive or cumulative (see Fig. 9.1A). Collecting information on several possible influences

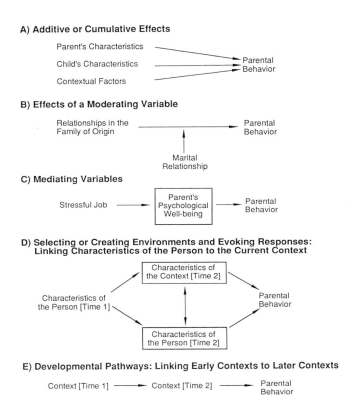

FIG. 9.1.   Multiple influences on parental behavior.

in one study is likely to allow the investigator to make a better prediction about which parents are at risk for providing relatively unsupportive care than if he or she considered only one factor at a time. For example, knowing that a parent has an explosive temper, that a child is temperamentally difficult, and that the family is experiencing an economic crisis would lead us to believe that the child is at risk for receiving poor parenting; knowing only one of these three facts would make any prediction more tenuous.

Second, the effect of a given factor on parenting may be contingent on a third factor. In other words, the third variable may act as a moderating variable (Fig. 9.1B). For example, the effects of poor rearing experiences in the family of origin on parenting behavior are likely to depend on the quality of the relationships the person has in subsequent years, particularly in the marital relationship.

A third contribution from studies that have looked at several potential influences is that, in some cases, one factor may mediate the relation between two other variables (Fig. 9.1C). For example, if a parent is in a highly stressful job, the job may take a toll on the parent's psychological well-being, which may in turn affect how he or she relates to his or her children. Such studies often contribute important information about the process by which the larger context influences characteristics of the parent and ultimately family dynamics.

Fourth, studies that look at several variables over time can help us understand how characteristics of a person at one point in time can influence the context in which parenting occurs at a later point in time. Put another way, when thinking about multiple influences on parenting, it is not only important to think about the combined effect of several contemporaneous influences, but also about how characteristics of the person and the context influenced each other over time. Personal characteristics are related to the environments people select, the life-course options they experience, and the way in which other people respond to them. So to some extent, people create the context in which they will act as parents. If a person is ill-tempered and has difficulty relating to others in positive ways, these characteristics may eventually affect his or her career trajectory, social network composition and choice of spouse. These contextual factors, in turn, influence his or her characteristics and behavior as a parent (Fig. 9.1D).

Finally, longitudinal studies show how characteristics of a context at Time 1 can make subsequent events more or less likely to occur. People who live in disadvantaged circumstances in childhood typically have greater obstacles to overcome than more advantaged peers, and consequently are at greater risk for raising their own children in disadvantaged circumstances (Fig. 9.1E). For example, a poor school milieu may contribute to low educational attainment which in turn limits occupational mobility. In this case, the context experienced at Time 1 (quality of the school) has implications for the context in which parenting occurs at Time 2 (financial resources of the family, job satisfaction of the parent). Thus, to understand parenting, we need to consider the life course of the parent, and the way in which the life course of the parent is related to the parent's characteristics and the current circumstances in which the parent–child relationship is developing.

This chapter is divided into five sections corresponding to the five ways in which multivariate studies contributed to our understanding of parenting behavior as just described and shown in Fig. 9.1. The review is not intended to be comprehensive, but instead focuses on the studies that we believe were most illuminating.

We begin by considering the value of simultaneously attending to characteristics of the parent, the child, and the context in explaining parenting behavior. The examples we use are from the literature on child abuse, infant–mother attachment, and quality of the home environment.

The Cumulative Effect of Parent, Child,
and Contextual Influences on Parenting Behavior

In an influential paper, Belsky (1984) argued that parenting behavior is multiply determined and that the factors that influence parental behavior could be
grouped into three broad categories: (a) parental personality and psychological well-being, (b) contextual sources of stress and support, and (c) child characteristics. Belsky's conceptual model of the determinants of parenting was
influenced by the literature on the etiology of child abuse (Belsky, 1980). With
respect to parental characteristics, researchers had shown that parents who
maltreated their children were more likely than other parents to have long stand-
ing personality problems that often stemmed from poor childrearing experiences
in the family of origin. The effects of contextual influences were also evident
in several studies of child abuse; abusive parents were more likely than other
parents to experience high levels of stress (e.g., poverty or marital difficulties),
and to have inadequate support systems. Finally, children who were mistreat-
ed were more likely than their peers to be unhealthy, handicapped, or difficult
in some fashion. That is, characteristics of the child were shown to make a
particular child a more likely target of abuse.

One study of child abuse that nicely illustrates the way in which the ecologies
of abusive families differ from the ecologies of nonabusive families is the prospective study of neonatal intensive care unit infants conducted by Hunter and her
colleagues (Hunter & Kilstrom, 1979; Hunter, Kilstrom, Kraybill, & Loda,
1978). This study involved 255 newborns, who were considered to be at risk
for maltreatment because of prematurity and/or low birth weight, and their
families. Hunter and her colleagues believed that these high-risk infants would
be more at risk for abuse or neglect if the parents were contending with additional stressors (e.g., poverty) or were vulnerable because of their personal
characteristics. To test this hypothesis, the researchers collected extensive information on the families of these infants during the neonatal period, and then
followed the infants for 1 year to see which of them experienced maltreatment.

Parents who eventually maltreated their infants were more likely than other
parents to have experienced abuse at the hands of their parents and to have
dysfunctional personality characteristics. Maltreating parents also tended to
be living in more stressful circumstances. Abusive parents were significantly
more likely to be experiencing marital and financial difficulties, and to have
several closely spaced children in the family. In addition, they were more likely to be described as socially isolated. Infants who were eventually maltreated
were lighter than other infants at birth, were more likely to be born with con-
genital defects, and spent more time in the hospital at the time of their births.
Although causal relations cannot be determined from this study, the results
are consistent with the contention that parenting is multiply determined and
that the effects of these multiple factors may be cumulative.

The value of the ecological perspective for understanding parent–child relationships is also evident in the literature on infant–mother attachment. Ainsworth and her colleagues showed that infants are likely to form secure attachments with their mothers if the mothers are sensitive and responsive to the needs and cues of the infants (Ainsworth, Blehar, Waters, & Wall, 1978). Other researchers also showed that secure attachments are fostered by parents who are nurturant and respond appropriately to the individual qualities of the child (Belsky & Isabella, 1988).

Although parental behavior appears to be the proximal cause of a secure or insecure relationship with the infant, a variety of studies called attention to a number of more distal factors that may influence the quality of the relationship that develops between the mother and her infant. Among the factors that have been linked to the quality of the relationship between an infant and the mother are the developmental history and personality of the mother (Ricks, 1985). Contextual factors that have been found to be predictive of attachment classifications are the level of social support available to the mother (Crockenberg, 1981), the level of stress experienced by the mother (Vaughn, Egeland, Waters, & Sroufe, 1979), and marital quality (Goldberg & Easterbrooks, 1984). Evidence regarding the extent to which infant characteristics contribute to the quality of the attachment relationship is less clear cut. Some studies reported an association between temperament and attachment, whereas others have found no relation (for a summary, see Belsky & Isabella, 1988). The extent to which temperament is related to security of attachment may depend on other factors such as level of support available to the mother (Crockenberg, 1981).

Collectively, these studies suggest that the quality of the relationship between the mother and an infant is influenced by several factors. However, most studies of the antecedents of attachment focused on only a small number of potential influences. An exception is a study by Belsky and Isabella (1988). Drawing on the theoretical framework described earlier (Belsky, 1984), they examined the influence of maternal characteristics (developmental history, personality), child characteristics (temperament), and contextual influences (marital quality, social networks, neighborhood characteristics) on the quality of the infant–mother relationship.

First, the data were analyzed to look at each potential influence on the attachment relationship separately, and then the cumulative effect of several factors was examined. Although several of the variables assessed did not distinguish between families with secure and anxious infants (e.g., developmental history, observational measures of temperament, social networks), other factors did distinguish between the groups. Mothers with infants rated as secure had more favorable scores on a personality factor labeled *interpersonal affection* than mothers with insecure babies. Mothers with avoidant babies had less favorable scores than mothers of secure or resistant babies on a measure of ego strength.

Marital quality was also related to security of attachment. Infants who were eventually rated as insecure were more likely than other infants to have mothers who reported a substantial decline in the quality of the marital relationship over the baby's first year of life. In addition, mothers of insecure babies were more likely than other mothers to report living in relatively unsupportive neighborhoods.

Although observer ratings of temperament did not distinguish between anxious and secure babies, mother's perceptions of temperament were related to strange situation classifications. Mothers of anxious babies were more likely than other mothers to report that their infants became more unpredictable and unadaptable over the course of the first year.

In the next set of analyses, Belsky and Isabella examined the combined effect of maternal personality, marital quality, and perceptions of infant temperament on the quality of the infant–mother relationship. For these analyses, the sample was divided at the median for each of the predictor variables (e.g., personality), and a family was given a plus (+) for the variable if they had a favorable score and a minus (–) if they had an unfavorable score for each of the indicators. Thus a family could receive a score of 3 (+ + +) if the mother scored well on the personality composite, had a relatively harmonious marriage, and if the infant was seen as being predictable and adaptable over the first year of life. In contrast, a score of 0 was obtained if the family scored below the median on all three indicators (– – –). Intermediate scores of 1 or 2 were given for families who scored above the median on one or two of the indices respectively.

The probability of having a baby classified as securely attached in the strange situation was then determined for families scoring from 0 to 3 on the index. Of the infants from families with a score of 3 on the index, 92% were securely attached compared to 17% of the infants from families with a score of 0. Thirty-eight percent of the infants from families with a score above the median on only one of the three predictors were rated as securely attached; 83% of the infants from families with favorable scores on two of the three indicators were rated as securely attached. These findings again point to the value of considering characteristics of the parent, the child and the context in our efforts to understand parent–infant relationships. The chances of a secure relationship increased markedly when the family had favorable scores on at least two out of the three factors included in Belsky and Isabella's analyses.

The last study to be reviewed in this section is a study that examined factors related to the quality of the home environment mothers provided for their infants. Utilizing data from the National Longitudinal Survey of Youth (NLSY), Hannan and Luster (1991) focused on 602 families with 1 year-olds. The quality of home environment that was provided for each of the infants was assessed with a shortened version of Caldwell and Bradley's (1984) Home Observation for Measurement of the Environment (HOME). Multiple regression analyses were used to identify factors related to the quality of the home environment in this sample. Six factors emerged from these analyses as contributing uniquely to the quality of the home environment. Two of these variables were maternal characteristics (level of intelligence and age at first birth), three were contextual factors (presence of spouse or partner, number of children, and family income), and the last variable was difficult infant temperament.

On the basis of these analyses, a family risk index was developed. The predictor variables were converted to dichotomous variables (low risk vs. high risk), and a family's score on the risk index was the total number of risk factors out of six possible factors that were applicable to that family. Each of the following was considered to be a risk factor: (a) the mother's intelligence test score was in the bottom third of the distribution for this sample, (b) the mother was a teen-ager at the time of the first birth, (c) there was no spouse or partner in the home, (d) the mother had three or more children, (e) the level of family income was below the median for this sample, and (f) the child's difficult temperament score was above the mean.

The dependent variable, the quality of the home environment, was also converted to a dichotomous variable (the lowest 35% of the scores vs. the upper 65%). Crosstabulations were done to determine the probability of a family being in the lower home environment group for each level of risk. The findings are presented in Fig. 9.2.

There was a positive relation between scores on the risk index and the probability of providing a relatively unsupportive environment. Eighty-eight percent of the families with all six risk factors were in the low home environment group compared to 11% of the families with a score of 0 on the family risk index. Consistent with the findings on child abuse and attachment, the results from this study suggest that most parents can cope adequately when exposed

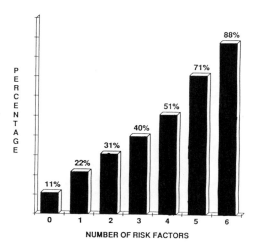

FIG. 9.2. The probability of having a low HOME-SF score at each level of risk.

to modest levels of adversity, but fewer can provide high quality care when they must deal with several disadvantages simultaneously. Menaghan and Parcel (1991), who also used data from the NLSY, reported similar findings for working mothers with 3- to 6-year-old children. Once again, we found that the effects of the parent, child, and contextual risk factors are cumulative.

The child abuse research by Hunter and her colleagues, the infant attachment research by Belsky and Isabella, and the quality of the home environment research by Hannan and Luster provide evidence regarding the value of examining multiple factors within one study. Each of these studies indicates that risk factors can have a cumulative effect. Our ability to identify which parent–child relationships are at risk is greatly enhanced when we consider the broader contextual picture, rather than focusing on a limited aspect of that family portrait.

Moderating Variables

As noted earlier, some studies that looked at multiple influences on parental behavior demonstrated that the extent to which a given factor influences parental behavior may depend on a third factor. An excellent example of such a moderating effect is found in the study of ex-institutional women by Quinton and Rutter (1988). Most of the ex-institutional women had been removed from their homes in early childhood because of the low quality of care they were receiving from their parents, and they subsequently spent a substantial proportion of their formative years in a residential institution for children. Given the combination of poor childrearing experiences in the family and institutional care, Quinton and Rutter expected that these women would be at risk for providing poor care for their own children when they reached adulthood. Consistent with this expectation, the ex-institutional women were much more likely than a comparison group of women, who were reared exclusively by their biological parents, to provide unsupportive care for their children. Thus, in many cases, poor childrearing experiences in one generation were repeated in the following generation.

However, about one third of the ex-institutional women provided very good care for their children. A comparison of ex-institutional women who were providing high quality care with those who were not showed that good parenting tended to be found among mothers who had supportive spouses. In fact, ex-institutional women who had supportive spouses were as likely to provide high quality child care for their children as the mothers in the comparison group. Unfortunately, the ex-institutional women, who often married shortly after leaving the residential setting, were less likely to be in supportive relationships than the comparison group mothers.

As Vondra and Belsky (this volume) pointed out, the extent to which poor childrearing experiences in childhood are reenacted in the next generation is likely to depend on the relationship history of the person outside the family of origin. In other words, there is a fairly strong link between poor childrearing experiences in the family of origin and poor parenting if the parent has not had the opportunity to develop positive relationships with others that would offset the effects of the poor developmental history. Positive relationships with others, on the other hand, can reduce the effect of poor relationships in the family of origin on parenting (Crockenberg, 1987; Egeland, Jacobvitz & Sroufe, 1988; Hunter & Kilstrom, 1979). Thus, the quality of subsequent relationships acts as a moderating variable, affecting the likelihood of poor experiences in the family of origin being repeated in the next generation.

A second example of the influence of a moderating variable comes from the work of Elder and his colleagues, who examined the effects of the Great Depression on family functioning (Elder, Liker, & Cross, 1984; Elder, Nguyen, & Caspi, 1985). In a series of studies, Elder established that income loss during the Great Depression increased the risk of family dysfunction primarily through its effects on paternal behavior. Fathers who experienced a sharp drop in income became more arbitrary, punitive, and rejecting in their interactions with their children (Elder et al., 1984, 1985). However, the effect of economic loss on paternal behavior was not uniform across families.

For daughters, the extent to which family hardship resulted in poor parenting by fathers depended on the physical attractiveness of the girls. Fathers who experienced economic loss were found to be less emotionally supportive and more demanding and exploitive if their daughters fell below the median on a measure of physical attractiveness. More attractive daughters were spared this treatment. In contrast, physical characteristics of sons were unrelated to how the effects of the Great Depression were manifested in the behavior of the father (Elder et al., 1985). Thus, the physical attractiveness of daughters acted as a moderating variable. An accurate portrayal of the effect of economic loss on the behavior of fathers toward their daughters could only be made by taking into consideration the physical attractiveness of the daughter.

The final examples of moderating variables are provided by Crockenberg and her colleagues (Crockenberg, 1981; Crockenberg & McCluskey, 1986). Crockenberg assessed the relationship between infant irritability (assessed during the newborn period) and maternal sensitivity in the Ainsworth Strange Situation when the infants were 12 months old. Crockenberg and McCluskey found that mothers with irritable babies provided less supportive care over the first year of life if they believed that responsive behavior would reinforce the demanding characteristics of their infants. Thus, in this case, maternal beliefs functioned as a moderating variable, influencing the extent to which neonatal irritability was predictive of maternal sensitivity.

Crockenberg and McCluskey (1986) also examined the effect of social support on maternal sensitivity. Mothers who were well supported were rated as being more sensitive to their infants but the effects of social support were strongest for mothers with irritable babies. Presumably the support of network members was most essential if the mother was contending with an irritable child. The findings from this study are consistent with those from an earlier report from this project. Crockenberg (1981) found that social support was particularly important for the formation of a secure relationship between the mother and the infant if the infant was irritable. Thus, these studies indicate that both maternal attitudes and social support can function as moderating variables by influencing the relation between infant irritability and maternal sensitivity.

In the first section, we saw that characteristics of the parent, of the child, and of the context can directly influence the quality of care parents provide for their children in an additive fashion (i.e., a main effect for each variable). In this section we saw that characteristics of the parent (maternal attitudes), of the child (physical attractiveness), and of the context (social support) can also act as moderating variables influencing the extent to which another factor is related to parenting behavior (i.e., an interaction between two of the predictor variables).

Mediating Variables:
Linking the Larger Context to Parenting

Bronfenbrenner's (1979) book, *The Ecology of Human Development*, called attention to the fact that forces external to the family often affect family functioning and ultimately the development of children. Some of the most interesting research that has been conducted since the early 1980s explored how the larger context influences characteristics of the parents which, in turn, influence parental behavior. In this section, we review a few of these studies.

Several studies have shown that economic hardship can lead to punitive behavior on the part of parents (Lempers, Clark-Lempers, & Simons, 1989; Pelton, 1978; Steinberg, Catalano, & Dooley, 1981). One of the most illuminating studies of the process by which a macroeconomic event, an economic downturn, can influence family functioning is provided by Elder and his colleagues, who studied the effects of the Great Depression. Elder, Caspi, and Downey (1986) showed that income loss increased rates of instability among fathers. Instability on the part of fathers led to problem relationships within the family. Unstable fathers tended to have more marital difficulties and were more likely than relatively stable fathers to respond to their children in a punitive fashion. Thus, income loss had an effect on paternal behavior but the effect was largely indirect, via the father's personality.

For mothers, income loss was not associated with increased instability. However, it was associated with increased marital tension, which in turn was related to punitive parenting on the part of the mother. Thus, for mothers, marital harmony mediated the relation between income loss and punitive parenting.

Crouter and McHale (this volume) summarize various ways in which the workplace influences the parent. As they noted, one factor that may mediate the relation between characteristics of the workplace and parental behavior is parental values (Kohn, 1977). Parents' ideas about the characteristics needed by their children in order to be successful can be shaped on the job. If parents are in traditional blue-collar jobs where advancement depends on following orders, parents are likely to value obedience and conformity on the part of their children. If on the other hand the parents are in white-collar jobs in which they have considerable autonomy and responsibility, they are likely to value self-direction on the part of their children (e.g., thinking for oneself). In other words, the parents try to pass on the lessons they have derived from their experience. As one would expect, parental values are reflected in the way in which parents care for their children (Conger, McCarty, Yang, Lahey, & Kropp, 1984; Luster, Rhoades, & Haas, 1989).

At a more macrolevel, culture shapes parents' views about the appropriate goals of socialization, and provides strategies for achieving those goals. The physical settings occupied by diverse cultural groups and the adaptive strategies adopted by members of each group to survive in these settings lead to quite distinct approaches to childrearing in various cultures. Thus, culture influences parents' childrearing goals and beliefs about appropriate practices which, in turn, influence the way in which parents carry out their childrearing responsibilities.

LeVine (1980) provided a good example of this by contrasting the practices of parents in tropical Africa with those of middle-class United States. Agrarian groups in tropical Africa had to contend with high rates of infant mortality. Thus, one of the goals of childrearing is to maximize the number of children who survive so that the children can eventually contribute to the subsistence economy and attend to the needs of their parents in old age. Lavish attention is provided for the infants to help ensure that they survive beyond infancy, but infants are also encouraged to be relatively passive so that mothers can be productive in the fields while carrying the infants. After infancy, the goal of childrearing is obedience, which is not uncommon in agricultural societies (Barry, Child, & Bacon, 1959). Obedient children are seen as responsible agricultural workers, and likely candidates to support their parents in their twilight years. After the child is weaned, the mother is likely to have another infant who becomes the focal point of her attention (to aid survival), and the care of older children falls largely to the oldest children or other family members. LeVine noted that parents "are normatively expected to invest most of their time in work and in interaction with other adults; they are not expected to devote much interactive attention to each postinfancy child, and no one will criticize them for not doing so as long as the child is supervised by someone who is older than himself" (p. 20).

In contrast to the parents of tropical Africa, middle-class Americans have relatively low infant mortality rates, no child labor, and institutional arrangements for the care of the elderly. Children typically are not needed for the contribution they make to the family economy. Nevertheless, U.S. parents expend great effort to provide their children with the skills and advantages that they believe are needed for eventual socioeconomic success. Parents in the United States try to instill in their children such character traits as independence and self-confidence, and parents act on the premise that a great deal of parental investment is needed to achieve these outcomes. They provide much praise and attention for each child over several years in hopes of shaping the desired characteristics. Having relatively few children makes sense if a considerable amount of the parent's time and resources are invested in each child over an extended period of time.

As LeVine pointed out, parents in each culture, tropical Africa and U.S. suburbia, are responding to their children by using strategies that have been generated in their respective cultures. The formulas for childrearing in each culture worked reasonably well for each group, and parents in each culture acquire these culturally derived notions about appropriate child care as part of their socialization for parenthood.

In this section, we saw several examples of how characteristics of the parents (e.g., values, beliefs, psychological well-being) mediate between the characteristics of the larger context and the experiences of children. These studies provide support for Bronfenbrenner's (1979) contention that in order to understand the child's development, attention must be paid to forces at the macrosystem and exosystem levels. The studies reviewed in this section are exemplary in that they have not only shown that parents at different social addresses behave differently, but additionally, they have explored the process by which the larger context influences parental behavior. To do this, both proximal (e.g., values) and distal (e.g., characteristics of the workplace) influences on parenting must be considered in the same study.

Studies Linking Person to Context

In the previous section, it was evident that contextual factors can influence the characteristics that parents bring to the parenting situation. Although to some extent environments are imposed on people, people also have some role in selecting or creating their environments. In addition, characteristics of the person influence how others respond to them (Scarr & McCartney, 1983). In this section we consider studies that show how characteristics of the person at Time 1 are related to the context in which parenting occurs at Time 2. The studies reviewed in the first three sections of this chapter examined ways in which multivariate studies contributed to our understanding of why parents do what they do with their children. The studies reviewed in this section and the subsequent section are concerned to a greater extent with the question:

How does a life-course perspective contribute to our understanding of the context in which the parent–child relationship develops? Consideration of the interaction between person and context over time will add substantially to our understanding of parenting behavior.

Caspi, Elder, and Bem (1987, 1988) showed that personality characteristics in childhood were related to adult characteristics and contexts. In the first study, they examined the life-course patterns of explosive children, that is children who were ill-tempered and prone to expressing anger by displaying temper tantrums. Among the males, they found that ill-tempered boys were often ill-tempered men 20 years later. In addition to finding continuity in these dispositions, Caspi and his colleagues noted that ill-tempered boys completed fewer years of education than their even-tempered peers. Education, in turn, affected the occupational attainment of these men, with ill-tempered men achieving lower occupational status and having more erratic careers (e.g., changing jobs often, getting fired). In other words, by the time these ill-tempered males became parents they were more likely than their even tempered peers to be living in disadvantaged circumstances.

The researchers proposed that this study provides a good example of *cumulative continuity*. Cumulative continuity occurs when maladaptive behaviors channel people into environments that perpetuate their behavioral tendencies. In this case, ill-tempered characteristics tended to channel the boys into low status jobs, largely because the ill-tempered characteristics had contributed to low educational achievement. The low status jobs were often a source of frustration for these men and the frustration on the job tended to provoke ill-tempered behavior on the part of the men.

The characteristics of these men also affected the emotional climate in the home. Men with a childhood history of temper tantrums were twice as likely as their even-tempered peers to be divorced by age 40 (46% vs. 22%), and thus often had less contact with their children than their even-tempered peers. In addition, an erratic work career was linked to poor parenting on the part of fathers in this study.

Caspi and his colleagues argued that the continuity seen in ill-tempered behavior from childhood to adulthood can also be explained by *interactional continuity*. Interactional continuity occurs when a person develops a style of relating to others that evokes reciprocal, maintaining responses from other people. Ill-tempered children, who have developed a style of relating to others that is combative and coercive, carry these patterns into adulthood and consequently evoke coercive responses from spouses and employers that help to maintain the ill-tempered style of these men. Interactional continuity is used to explain the link between temper tantrums in childhood and marital conflict and erratic work lives in adulthood.

Ill-tempered characteristics also had implications for the girls in this study. Ill-tempered girls were more likely than even-tempered girls to eventually marry men who achieved lower occupational status. Ill-tempered girls were also twice as likely as even-tempered girls to be divorced women at midlife (26% vs. 12%). If the marriage had not dissolved, men who married women who had been ill-tempered children reported less satisfaction with their marriages and more conflicts than men who married women who had been more even-tempered. Finally, women who had a childhood history of temper tantrums were perceived by both their husbands and their children as being ill-tempered parents. The difficulty that these women had relating positively to their husbands and their children could be explained by interactional continuity. Thus, for both boys and girls, ill-tempered personality characteristics were predictive of the context in which parenting occurred. Ill-tempered children were more likely than their even tempered peers to end up in households at the lower end of the social status hierarchy, and were more likely to be divorced or involved in conflicted marriages.

In the second study, Caspi and his colleagues explored the effects of childhood shyness on the life-course patterns of men and women. The effects of shyness were less dramatic than the effects for ill-tempered behavior but nevertheless had implications for family life. For men, shyness primarily affected the timing of role transitions. Men with a childhood history of shyness married later than other men and, on average, became fathers 4 years later than those who were less shy. They also entered a stable career line at a later age; later entry into a career was in turn related to lower occupational achievement and stability. Shyness had no direct effect on marital quality; however, if shyness resulted in entering a career late, the probability of divorce was increased.

Shyness was not related to the timing of marriage and childbearing among females. As the authors noted, these women were reaching the age of majority in the 1940s, and men were likely to take the most active role in courtship at that time. Thus, the lack of relationship between shyness and family formation for females is not surprising.

Once married however, shy women spent fewer years in the labor force and were more likely than other women to be full-time homemakers. Unlike ill-tempered women, shy women were more likely to be married to high status men. This may be due, at least in part, to the fact that the shy women ran the household and cared for the children full time. This allowed more time for their husbands to pursue career goals. Although data on parenting are not presented in this study, it is clear that shyness had implications for the circumstances in which the parent–child relationship developed.

The links between characteristics of the person and of the parenting context are further illustrated by a series of studies on neglectful mothers by Polansky and his colleagues (Polansky, Chalmers, Buttenwieser, & Williams, 1981; Polansky, Gaudin, Ammons, & Davis, 1985). Polansky et al. (1981) compared neglectful mothers with nonneglectful mothers who were similar in terms of social class. The neglectful mothers were described as having dysfunctional personality characteristics. As compared to nonneglectful mothers, these women were more likely to be impulsive, dependent, and apathetic. As we see here, these personality characteristics not only had implications for how these women interacted with their children, but also for the parenting context. These personality characteristics were associated with the way the women interacted with other adults.

Neglectful mothers were more likely than comparison mothers to have very limited support networks, and to be uninvolved in organizations such as church groups. The lack of involvement with others was a longstanding problem for many of these women. Retrospective reports revealed that these women were often nonparticipators in their high school years. The lack of contact with others presumably reflected the personality problems alluded to earlier. Polansky concluded that these negative personality characteristics were often the result of rejecting or abusive treatment in childhood.

Neglectful mothers were also more likely than comparison mothers to lack a male partner. If a neglectful mother had a male partner, she was more likely than comparison mothers to have a male partner with similar limitations. Polansky argued that the lack of a supportive context for these neglectful mothers was due, in part, to the mothers' characteristics—that is, their aversive personality characteristics and lack of skill in developing and maintaining relationships. Additionally, the poor relationship histories of these women, may have led many of them to doubt the value of developing close relationships with others. Thus, mothers who could have benefitted the most from supportive relationships with others often had difficulty enlisting such support.

In a subsequent study, Polansky and his associates (1985) compared the level of support and perceptions of neighborhoods that neglectful and nonneglectful mothers had. Neglectful mothers perceived their neighborhoods as being less supportive than other mothers. They also reported having less instrumental and emotional support available to them from network members. Overall, neglectful mothers were more isolated and more likely to report feelings of loneliness than comparison mothers.

Polansky and associates then interviewed the neighbors of neglectful mothers to see if they also perceived their neighborhoods as being relatively unsupportive places to live. The neighbors tended to have more positive views of their neighborhoods than the neglectful mothers; the neighbors' perceptions of their neighborhoods were comparable to the perceptions of neighborhood that nonneglectful mothers had.

Further analyses, however, revealed that the neglectful mothers' views on characteristics of their neighborhoods were not unwarranted. They often lacked support from neighbors because their neighbors shunned them. Their neighbors often did not approve of the way in which they interacted with their children, and thereby did not want their own children to associate with the children of neglectful mothers. The neighbors also believed that their neglectful neighbors could not be relied on to reciprocate favors, and therefore neighbors were hesitant to engage in exchanges with the neglectful mothers. Thus, although they shared the same neighborhoods, the neglectful mothers experienced the neighborhoods in very different ways from their neighbors. In the words of the authors:

> In short, we seem to have an unfortunate spiral of causation in which neglectful women, a majority of whom are rearing their broods alone anyway, are apt to be isolated within their own neighborhoods. No wonder they report great loneliness. Theirs is not a particularly friendly world, and they are less likely to have psychological access to the warmth and caring that does exist. (Polansky et al., 1985, p. 274)

Throughout this section, we have seen that characteristics of parents have implications for the context in which the parent–child relationship develops. In the studies by Caspi and his colleagues, we saw evidence that personality characteristics in childhood are predictive of parents' educational attainment, occupational prestige, marital quality, and the timing of family formation. In the Polansky study we saw that parents can evoke responses from others in their environments. Because of their characteristics, neglectful mothers tended to be relatively isolated and uninvolved in helping relationships. Thus, characteristics of the person not only influence parenting directly, but also indirectly, via the context in which parenting occurs.

Developmental Pathways: Linking One Context to the Next Context

In the preceding section we saw that people play some role in shaping the contexts in which parenting occurs, and that they evoke responses from those around them. However, it would be inappropriate to conclude that most parents who live in disadvantaged circumstances simply created or selected their circumstances. Disadvantaged circumstances in adulthood may largely represent a continuation of disadvantaged circumstances in childhood (Rutter, 1989).

Disadvantaged circumstances in childhood can limit one's options and opportunities, just as advantaged circumstances often lead to opportunities not available to everyone. Thus, circumstances in childhood may make some subsequent events more or less likely to occur (Bowlby, 1988; Rutter, 1989). Efforts to understand these developmental pathways are useful for thinking about the context in which parenting occurs.

One study documenting such a chain of events is the study referred to earlier on ex-institutional women by Quinton and Rutter (1988). The ex-institutional women had been cared for by inadequate parents in most cases, which led to placement in the institution. Thus, the girls often went from one undesirable circumstance to another. The options upon leaving the institution in adolescence were also not good. Some girls returned to the same discordant families from which they had been removed. Others essentially had no family to return to and sought to make it on their own. Many of the girls, particularly those who returned to discordant homes, married hastily either to escape their situation or to legitimate a pregnancy (Rutter, 1987). These marriages were often to unsupportive men who had problems of their own; thus the risks of either divorce or ongoing marital conflict were substantial for these women. Consequently, the ex-institutional women were likely to raise their children with few financial resources, without a supportive male partner and with little support from the family of origin.

Although the sequence of events just described was typical of the experiences of many of these women, others experienced a more positive chain of events. Girls in the institution were sent to various schools in the community in order to avoid having the girls stigmatized by their schoolmates. This meant that the girls had quite diverse experiences at school. The girls who had positive experiences in school, broadly defined, tended to have more positive developmental trajectories. Girls with positive experiences in school were less likely to marry hastily and tended to know their prospective spouses for at least 6 months before cohabiting. Quinton and Rutter proposed that these girls were more planful because positive experiences in school had convinced them that they had some control over events in their lives.

The women who spent more time getting to know their male partners were less likely to marry a deviant spouse, and were more likely to have a supportive relationship with their spouse. A supportive relationship with the spouse contributed to positive psychosocial adjustment on the part of the mother and good parenting (Rutter, 1989).

The Quinton and Rutter study demonstrates that disadvantaged circumstances at Time 1 elevate the probability that the person will experience similar circumstances at Time 2. Although it would be an overstatement to say the women had no control over their destinies, their options were often quite different from the options of women reared in more favorable conditions.

Harris, Brown, and Bifulco (1987) reported a similar chain of events in their study of women who had lost their mothers to death in childhood. The loss of a mother increased the risk that the child would receive inadequate care during the formative years, which increased the risk of a premarital pregnancy in the teen years or while the women were in their early 20s. Unplanned pregnancies were associated with lack of male support or relationships with deviant males, and with a low position in the social structure. Harris and associates argued that this series of events often culminated in psychiatric disorder (i.e., depression) on the part of the women who had lost their mothers in childhood. The authors likened the process of going from one disadvantaged circumstance to another to a conveyor belt. In their words, "It was as if loss of mother placed a person on a conveyor belt of increasing environmental deprivation and adversity off which relatively few could be expected to jump to better psychological health" (p. 166). The link between loss of a mother in childhood and depression in adulthood was not direct, and depression was not likely to occur if this chain of events was broken. Unfortunately, many of the girls had difficulty redirecting the course of events.

As Rutter (1989) pointed out, studies like those by Harris and colleagues and Quinton and Rutter help us to understand why disadvantaged circumstances in childhood often lead to similar adversity in adulthood. These studies show that the processes by which disadvantaged circumstances lead to further disadvantage are often more complex than the theories that have been generated to explain cycles of disadvantage. These studies also provide clues about how cycles of disadvantage are broken. A downward developmental trajectory in early childhood can be diverted by positive experiences in school (Berrueta-Clement, Schweinhart, Barnett, Epstein, & Weikart, 1984; Quinton & Rutter, 1988) or other settings (Elder, 1986), or by the development of supportive relationships in later childhood (Hodges & Tizard, 1989; Koluchova, 1976) or adulthood (Quinton & Rutter, 1988). Overall, the longitudinal studies reviewed in the past two sections of this chapter call attention to the need to consider the interaction between person and context over time if we are to understand the context in which parenting occurs and the characteristics the person brings to the parenting situation.

Conclusion

How do we explain differences among parents in their approaches to childrearing? Why do some parents fail to meet the needs of their children? Because of recent research in this area, we are now in a much better position to address these questions than we were in years past.

To summarize, we saw that parental behavior is influenced to a large extent by what the parent brings to the situation. In this chapter, and in the chapters by Vondra and Belsky, by Luster and Mittelstaedt, and by Okagaki and Divecha, we saw that characteristics of the parent, such as personality characteristics, skills (e.g., interpersonal and problem-solving skills), level of maturity, values and childrearing beliefs, contribute to individual differences in parenting behavior.

In order to understand what the parent brings to the situation, it is necessary to consider the history of the person prior to parenthood. Over the course of their lives, parents develop styles of interacting with others, ways of coping with demanding circumstances, and approaches to problem solving that eventually affect their performance in the parenting role (Caspi et al., 1987; Rutter, 1989; Vondra & Belsky, this volume). They also construct working models of relationships that can affect how they develop relationships with partners, children, and network members (Crittenden, 1985). The parent's relationship history also influences the personality characteristics that the parent brings to his or her adult roles (Sroufe & Fleeson, 1986; Vondra & Belsky, this volume). To understand who the parent is today, we have to look at who the parent was, where the parent was, and what the parent was doing in the years prior to parenthood.

Throughout this volume, we have also seen that characteristics of the context, both the immediate context and the larger context, influence the characteristics and behavior of the parent. Characteristics of the immediate context, such as the quality of the marital relationship, can influence the parent's psychological well-being and his or her behavior toward the children (Emery, this volume). Members of the parent's network can provide emotional support for the parent and they can contribute information that is useful in carrying out the responsibilities of parenting. On the other hand, network members can undermine effective parenting by being sources of stress for the parent, or by providing questionable childrearing advice to the parent (Cochran, this volume). Characteristics of the larger context, such as the health of the economy and the quality of the neighborhood, influence the level of stress experienced by the parent and consequently how the parent relates to his or her child (Garbarino & Kostelney, this volume; McLoyd, 1990).

The ecological niche that a parent occupies also provides the information he or she uses in making judgments about the characteristics a child needs in order to be successful, and the strategies that can be used to help children acquire needed competencies (Crouter & McHale, this volume; LeVine, 1980; Ogbu, 1981). In a society like the United States where parents occupy quite diverse niches, parents tend to have very different views on the childrearing practices that are needed to produce desirable characteristics in children (Luster et al., 1989). The parent's niche also influences the types of concerns that the parent has for his or her children (Dubrow & Garbarino, 1988). Do parents have to worry about their children getting caught in a drug related cross-fire, or are their concerns the more typical concerns of suburbia (e.g., a child running into a busy street)?

In this chapter we argued that characteristics of the parent and of the context are, at least partially, intertwined. To some extent, parents select and shape their environments. They also evoke responses from family members and others around them. Characteristics of the parents are related to who and when they marry (Caspi et al., 1987, 1988), and they are related to the development of social networks (Cochran, this volume; Polansky et al., 1985). Parental characteristics also affect occupational choices and career trajectories (Caspi et al., 1987, 1988). Thus, just as contextual factors can affect parents' psychological well-being and their behaviors, parents can influence their environments.

Finally we saw that characteristics of the child must be considered if we are to understand the evolution of the parent–child relationship. Children may elicit positive behaviors from their parents, or they may possess characteristics that the parents find aversive thus leading to difficulties in the relationship. As Lerner pointed out in her chapter, much depends on the fit between the characteristics of the parents and characteristics of the child. Characteristics of the child, such as physical attractiveness and temperament, may be particularly influential when the parent is trying to cope with adverse circumstances (Elder, et al., 1985; Rutter, Quinton, & Yule, 1977; Werner & Smith, 1982).

Although much has been learned about influences on parenting, particularly since the early 1980s, many questions require further study. For example, to what extent does one's experience as a parent influence parental beliefs and subsequently parental behavior? Under what circumstances are we likely to have a poor fit between characteristics of the child and characteristics of the parent? In other words, when we are considering the fit between the parent and the child, which characteristics of each person are most important to consider? To what extent are differences in parenting behavior between adolescent and older mothers due to differences in age, and to what extent do other factors that distinguish between the groups account for the differences?

In addition, some potentially important influences—for example, the parent's level of intelligence and family size—received insufficient attention. There is growing evidence that maternal intelligence is related to maternal behavior (Longstreth et al., 1981; Scarr, 1985), but not much has been done to illuminate the process by which intelligence influences parental behavior. Is the effect largely direct (parent's problem-solving ability, interest in intellectual activities) or indirect (via level of education obtained and occupational status)? To what extent is the parent's intelligence related to his or her beliefs about child care? Similarly, there is considerable evidence that a large family size has deleterious effects on the competencies of children after confounding factors are controlled, and some suggested that this is due to the fact that the parent's resources have to be divided among many children in a large family (Blake, 1989; Dubow & Luster, 1990; Furstenberg, Brooks-Gunn, & Morgan, 1987; Rutter, 1978; Werner & Smith, 1982). However, few studies examined how family size actually affects parental behavior.

In this chapter, we emphasized that much can be gained by examining multiple contemporaneous influences on parenting, and by considering the interaction between person and environment over time. Studies of the life course that have done both, such as those of Elder and his colleagues (Elder et al., 1984, 1986), contributed much to our understanding of parental behavior. Unfortunately there are relatively few data sets available thus far like the Berkeley/Oakland archive utilized by Elder. As additional longitudinal studies reach maturity, research on human development over the life course is likely to contribute much to our understanding of individual differences in adult behaviors such as parenting (Robins & Rutter, 1990).

The methods used by behavioral geneticists may also contribute much to our understanding of parenting in the years ahead. Pioneering works in this area by Plomin and his colleagues (Plomin, 1990; Plomin, DeFries, & Fulker, 1988) demonstrated the value of applying twin and adoption research designs to the study of parenting. For example, Plomin and his colleagues (1988) found that ratings of the HOME environment were more highly correlated for nonadoptive siblings than for adoptive siblings (rs = .50 and .32 respectively). As Plomin (1990) noted, this "suggests that the parental behavior, as assessed by the HOME, in part reflects genetic differences among children" (p. 134).

Finally, although we consider the effects of different factors on parenting behavior, we ought to also consider what we mean by parenting behaviors. To date, not much of a distinction has been made among the many behaviors that fall under the rubric of "parenting." The factors that effect some aspects of parenting (e.g., being sensitive) may differ from those that effect other aspects of parenting (e.g., providing a cognitively stimulating environment). Besides looking at multiple influences within one study, future studies ought to consider the relative effects of these multiple influences on a variety of parenting behaviors.

Although much remains to be learned, the advances that have been made since the early 1980s provide a good foundation on which to build, and reasons to be hopeful about what will eventually be understood. What we would hope is that as we learn more about parenting and the development of parent–child relationships, we will be better able to provide parents with the supports they need to achieve their parenting goals.

REFERENCES

Ainsworth, M. D. S., Blehar, M. C., Waters, E., & Wall, S. (1978). *Patterns of attachment: A psychological study of the strange situation.* Hillsdale, NJ: Lawrence Erlbaum Associates.

Barry, H., Child, I., & Bacon, M. (1959). Relation of child training to subsistence economy. *American Anthropologist, 61,* 51–63.

Belsky, J. (1980). Child maltreatment: An ecological integration. *American Psychologist, 35*(4), 320–335.

Belsky, J. (1984). The determinants of parenting: A process model. *Child Development, 55,* 83–96.

Belsky, J., & Isabella, R. (1988). Maternal, infant, and social-contextual determinants of attachment security. In J. Belsky & T. Nezworski (Eds.), *Clinical implications of attachment* (pp. 41–94). Hillsdale, NJ: Lawrence Erlbaum Associates.

Berrueta-Clement, J. R., Schweinhart, L. J., Barnett, W. S., Epstein, A. S., & Weikart, D. P. (1984). *Changed lives: The effects of the Perry Preschool Program on youths through age 19.* Ypsilanti, MI: The High/Scope Press.

Blake, J. (1989). Number of siblings and educational attainment. *Science, 245,* 32–36.

Bowlby, J. (1988). *A secure base: Parent-child attachment and healthy human development.* New York: Basic Books.

Bronfenbrenner, U. (1979). *The ecology of human development.* Cambridge: Harvard University Press.

Caldwell, B. M., & Bradley, R. (1984). *Home Observation for Measurement of the Environment.* Little Rock: University of Arkansas at Little Rock.

Caspi, A., Elder, G. H., & Bem, D. J. (1987). Moving against the world: Life-course patterns of explosive children. *Developmental Psychology, 23,* 308–313.

Caspi, A., Elder, G. H., & Bem, D. J. (1988). Moving away from the world: Life-course patterns of shy children. *Developmental Psychology, 24,* 824–831.

Conger, R. D., McCarty, J. A., Yang, R. K., Lahey, B. B., & Kropp, J. P. (1984). Perception of child, childrearing values, and emotional distress as mediating links between environmental stressors and observed maternal behavior. *Child Development, 55,* 2234–2247.

Crittenden, P. (1985). Social networks, quality of childrearing, and child development. *Child Development, 56,* 1299–1313.

Crockenberg, S. (1981). Infant irritability, mother responsiveness, and social support influences on the security of infant–mother attachment. *Child Development, 52,* 857–865.

Crockenberg, S. (1987). Predictors and correlates of anger toward and punitive control of toddlers by adolescent mothers. *Child Development, 58,* 964–975.

Crockenberg, S., & McCluskey, K. (1986). Change in maternal behavior during the baby's first year of life. *Child Development, 57,* 746–753.

Dubow, E. F., & Luster, T. (1990). Adjustment of children born to teenage mothers: The contribution of risk and protective factors. *Journal of Marriage and the Family, 52,* 393–404.

Dubrow, N., & Garbarino, J. (1988). *Living in the war zone: Mothers and young children in public housing developments.* Chicago: Erikson Institute.

Egeland, B., Jacobvitz, D., & Sroufe, L. A. (1988). Breaking the cycle of abuse. *Child Development, 59,* 1080–1088.

Elder, G. H. (1986). Military times and turning points in men's lives. *Developmental Psychology, 22*(2), 233–245.

Elder, G. H., Caspi, A., & Downey, G. (1986). Problem behavior and family relationships: Life course and intergenerational themes. In A. Sorensen, F. Weinert, & L. Sherrod (Eds.), *Human development and the life course: Multidisciplinary perspectives* (pp. 293–340). Hillsdale, NJ: Lawrence Erlbaum Associates.

Elder, G. H., Liker, J. D., & Cross, C. (1984). Parent–child behavior in the Great Depression: Life course and intergenerational influences. In P. B. Baltes & O. G. Brim (Eds.), *Life-span development and behavior* (Vol. 6, pp. 109–158). Hillsdale, NJ: Lawrence Erlbaum Associates.

Elder, G. H., Nguyen, T. V., & Caspi, A. (1985). Linking family hardship to children's lives. *Child Development, 56,* 361–375.

Furstenberg, F., Brooks-Gunn, J., & Morgan, S. P. (1987). *Adolescent mothers in later life.* Cambridge, UK: Cambridge University Press.

Goldberg, W. A., & Easterbrooks, M. A. (1984). The role of marital quality in toddler development. *Developmental Psychology, 20,* 504–514.

Hannan, K., & Luster, T. (1991). Influence of parent, child, and contextual factors on the quality of the home environment. *Infant Mental Health Journal, 12*(1), 17–30.

Harris, T., Brown, G. W., & Bifulco, A. (1987). Loss of parent in childhood and adult psychiatric disorder: The role of social position and premarital pregnancy. *Psychological Medicine, 17,* 163–183.

Hodges, J., & Tizard, B. (1989). IQ and behavioural adjustment of exinstitutional adolescents. *Journal of Child Psychology and Psychiatry, 30,* 53–75.

Hunter, R. S., & Kilstrom, N. (1979). Breaking the cycle in abusive families. *American Journal of Psychiatry, 136*(10), 1320–1322.

Hunter, R. S., Kilstrom, N., Kraybill, E. N., & Loda, F. (1978). Antecedents of child abuse and neglect in premature infants: A prospective study in a newborn intensive care unit. *Pediatrics, 61,* 629–635.

Kohn, M. L. (1977). *Class and conformity: A study of values* (2nd ed.). Chicago: University of Chicago Press.

Koluchova, J. (1976). The further development of twins after severe and prolonged deprivation: A second report. *Journal of Child Psychology and Psychiatry*, *17*, 181–188.

Lempers, J. D., Clark-Lempers, D., & Simons, R. L. (1989). Economic hardship, parenting, and distress in adolescence. *Child Development*, *60*, 25–39.

LeVine, R. A. (1980). A cross-cultural perspective on parenting. In M. Fantini & R. Cardenas (Eds.), *Parenting in a multicultural society* (pp. 17–26). New York: Longman.

Longstreth, L. E., Davis, B., Carter, L., Flint, D., Owen, J., Rickert, M., & Taylor, E. (1981). Separation of home intellectual environment and maternal IQ as determinants of child IQ. *Developmental Psychology*, *17*(5), 532–541.

Luster, T., Rhoades, K., & Haas, B. (1989). The relation between parental values and parenting behavior: A test of the Kohn hypothesis. *Journal of Marriage and the Family*, *51*, 139–147.

McLoyd, V. C. (1990). The impact of economic hardship on Black families and children: Psychological distress, parenting, and socioemotional development. *Child Development*, *61*, 311–346.

Menaghan, E. G., & Parcel, T. L. (1991). Determining children's home environments: The impact of maternal characteristics and current occupational and family conditions. *Journal of Marriage and the Family*, *53*, 417–431.

Ogbu, J. (1981). Origins of human competence: A cultural-ecological perspective. *Child Development*, *52*, 413–429.

Pelton, L. (1978). Child abuse and neglect: The myth of classlessness. *American Journal of Orthopsychiatry*, *48*, 608–617.

Plomin, R. (1990). *Nature and nurture: An introduction to human behavioral genetics*. Pacific Grove, CA: Brooks/Cole.

Plomin, R., DeFries, J. C., & Fulker, D. W. (1988). *Nature and nurture during infancy and early childhood*. New York: Cambridge University Press.

Polansky, N. A., Chalmers, M. A., Buttenwieser, E., & Williams, D. P. (1981). *Damaged Parents*. Chicago: University of Chicago Press.

Polansky, N. A., Gaudin, J. M., Ammons, P. W., & Davis, K. B. (1985). The psychological ecology of the neglectful mother. *Child Abuse and Neglect*, *9*, 265–275.

Quinton, D., & Rutter, M. (1988). *Parenting breakdown: The making and breaking of intergenerational bonds*. Aldershot, UK: Avebury.

Ricks, M. (1985). The social transmission of parental behavior: Attachment across generations. In I. Bretherton & E. Waters (Eds.), *Growing points in attachment theory and research. Monographs for the Society for Research in Child Development*, *50* (Nos. 1–2, Serial No. 209).

Robins, L., & Rutter, M. (1990). *Straight and devious pathways from childhood to adulthood*. Cambridge, UK: Cambridge University Press.

Rutter, M. (1978). Family, area, and school influences in the genesis of conduct disorders. In L. A. Hersov, M. Berger & D. Shaffer (Eds.), *Aggression and antisocial behavior in childhood and adolescence*. Oxford: Pergamon Press.

Rutter, M. (1987). Psychosocial resilience and protective mechanisms. *American Journal of Orthopsychiatry*, *57*(3), 316–331.

Rutter, M. (1989). Pathways from childhood to adult life. *Journal of Child Psychology and Psychiatry*, *30*(1), 23–51.

Rutter, M., Quinton, D., & Yule, B. (1977). *Family pathology and disorder in children*. London: Wiley.

Scarr, S. (1985). Constructing psychology: Making facts and fables for our times. *American Psychologist*, *40*(5), 499–512.

Scarr, S., & McCartney, K. (1983). How people make their own environments: A theory of genotype-environment effects. *Child Development*, *54*, 424–435.

Sroufe, L. A., & Fleeson, J. (1986). Attachment and the construction of relationships. In W. Hartup & Z. Rubin (Eds.), *Relationships and development* (pp. 51–71). Hillsdale, NJ: Lawrence Erlbaum Associates.

Steinberg, L. D., Catalano, R., & Dooley, D. (1981). Economic antecedents of child abuse and neglect. *Child Development, 52,* 975–985.

Vaughn, B., Egeland, B., Waters, E., & Sroufe, L. A. (1979). Individual differences in infant–mother attachment at twelve and eighteen months: Stability and change in families under stress. *Child Development, 50,* 971–975.

Werner, E. E., & Smith, R. S. (1982). *Vulnerable but invincible.* New York: McGraw-Hill.

Author Index

Subject Index

A

Abuse of child. *See Child maltreatment*

Abuse of spouse, 14–15

Academic achievement, *see also Education;
School*
  beliefs about parenting behavior and,
    60–61
  of child and effects of parental beliefs, 53

Adaptation, 107–108, 110–111
  of parents to violent neighborhoods,
    215–216

Adolescent mother, 49, 56, 69–95, *see also
Teen-agers*
  age of, 82–84
  characteristics of child of, 85–86
  childrearing attitudes, beliefs, and
    knowledge of, 84–85
  comparisons of to older mothers, 73–81
    child maltreatment, 78–80
    limitations on studies involving, 80–81
    mother-child interaction, 75–77
    quality of home environment, 73–75
    secure vs. anxious attachment, 77–78
  consequences of parenthood for, 70–71
  contextual influences on
    number of children, 89
    residential status and division of child-
      care responsibilities, 87–88
    social support, 86–87

    sociocultural background, 89–91
    socioeconomic status, 89
  and the cost of adolescent parenthood for
    society, 72–73
  differing from their peers, 70–71
  four outcomes of parenthood for, 73–80
  limitations of within-group studies, 91–92
  and number of kin vs. nonkin in personal
    social networks, 165–166
  outcomes of children of, 71–72
  personality and psychological well-being
    of, 81–82
  as primary vs. secondary caregiver, 88
  program and policy implications concern-
    ing, 92–95

Adult
  attachment patterns and developmental
    history, 13–14
  childhood experiences of the continuity in
    adulthood, 22–25
  depression and developmental history, 11–13
  and early loss of mother in childhood, 20,
    243–244
  and poor parenting experiences in childhood,
    12–13
  relationships of, 16

Adult Attachment Interview, 15

Affordances, 105

Africa
  and strategies for childrearing, 237–238

263